TWO CENTURIES OF
RAILWAY
SIGNALLING

TWO CENTURIES OF
RAILWAY SIGNALLING

Geoffrey Kichenside & Alan Williams

Oxford Publishing Co.

A catalogue record for this book is available from the British Library.

ISBN 0 86093 541 8

Library of Congress catalog card no. 97-77756

Oxford Publishing Co. is an imprint of Haynes Publishing, Sparkford, Nr Yeovil, Somerset BA22 7JJ.

Tel. 01963 440635 Fax: 01963 440001
Int. tel: +44 1963 440635 Fax: +44 1963 440001

E-mail: sales@haynes-manuals.co.uk
Web site: http://www.haynes.com

Haynes North America, Inc., 861 Lawrence Drive, Newbury Park, California 91320 USA.

Designed and typeset by G&M, Raunds, Northamptonshire.
Printed in Hong Kong.

CONTENTS

DEDICATION

THIS BOOK IS dedicated to signal engineers and suppliers for making the equipment, to the signalmen, especially the older generation who went by the rules and regulations rather than with automation, who worked with it, and the drivers, again the older generation, leaning out of the cab of a steam locomotive on a misty night looking for that speck of red or green light high up on a tall signal post and who had to interpret it.

Equally, we acknowledge the support and encouragement of our respective partners, Paula and Sue, whose forbearance while this book has been in preparation has amazed even us, coming on top of our equally busy working lives.

RIGHT *Interior of a typical country signalbox in the mechanical signalling era which has lasted for more than 130 years. This one, at Smallbrook Junction on the Isle of Wight, was probably the busiest controlling single lines in the whole of the British Isles. In one direction it controlled double track to Ryde St Johns Road and in the other two separate single lines towards Cowes and Ventnor. At its peak on summer Saturdays it passed six trains in each direction every hour as part of the busy holiday traffic. The lever frame was unusual with the locking within the casing, and was known as a knee frame (partly we suspect from the bruises acquired banging the knees on the case in leaning forward to the levers). Notice the key token instruments at each end of the lever frame and the block instruments on the block shelf, also the oil lamp hanging from the roof. Like many rural signal boxes toilet facilities were primitive. (Geoffrey Kichenside)*

LEFT *Primitive levers controlling the signals at Bricklayers Arms Junction on the Brighton line at its meeting point with the London & Croydon, 1843.* (Illustrated London News)

BELOW *About 130 years later and control of the signalling in the Bricklayers Arms area is from the entrance–exit panel in the new London Bridge signalbox completed in the mid-1970s. The track diagram at the back carrying the track circuit, train describer, and signal indications shows the South Eastern lines from Charing Cross and Cannon Street at the left hand end towards Lewisham and Hither Green on the right.* (British Railways, Southern Region)

INTRODUCTION

RAILWAYS IN PUBLIC service carrying passengers and goods have existed for over 170 years, and for longer than that in mining and industrial uses. From the start it was obvious that a guided way lacked the freedom for vehicles to steer around obstacles and each other, so some form of operating system and discipline was needed if vehicles with wheels constrained by rails were not to come into conflict with others on the same track. Thus was born from primitive beginnings the need for railway signalling.

This survey looks at railway signals and signalling methods right from those early days to the present time. This is largely from the operating viewpoint, covering what the signals and equipment do and the message they impart rather than how they do it, although we take a look behind the scenes in the past and more recently. We also open the doors to see what is inside some equipment cabinets and where a description of how it works is inseparable from what it does. After all, mention of interlocking is meaningless without some idea of how it is achieved, and a description of the automatic warning system certainly needs a closer look at its components even if a full circuit diagram is not necessary for understanding the basic principles. But the fine detail of signal engineering in all its forms is a separate subject. It is interesting to reflect, though, that the work of the signal engineer and supplier from those early days down to the present time has embraced the skills of craftsmen working in wood, cast iron, steel, non ferrous metals, electrical equipment, pioneer electronics, and today, computers. Indeed, a computer programmer is now as much a signal engineer as was his counterpart a century and a half ago forging the iron rod to link the handle to operate a wooden-arm semaphore signal.

Was it just a coincidence that the powers of electromagnetism were beginning to be understood with the invention of the electric telegraph in the mid-1830s? The development of electrical communication in all its forms has gone hand in hand with the progress of railway signalling right to the present. It is perhaps difficult to understand today why early railway

managements did not rush to embrace the developing technology which provided much more positive signalling with trains separated by a space interval rather than time interval. This needed nothing more than a sand timer or clock but at greater risk to trains and for all its imperfections lasted for over 50 years. But perhaps it was the same attitudes of railway management and the same financial constraints then as it is today when we might ask why the railways in Britain have not been equipped with automatic train protection (ATP) which would virtually eliminate drivers' errors. The technology is available now and has been in use for some years in other countries. After all, modern signalling equipment has made safety errors by signalmen almost a thing of the past, so why not the same automation for drivers?

In each of the chapters right through this book it will be obvious that the steps in the progress of signalling as new developments in methods or equipment are described, it is hard to divorce signalling from safety, for the primary function of railway signalling is to ensure the safe operation of trains. Each development played its part in adding to safety levels, sometimes not obviously or directly but perhaps in reliability and so avoiding failures calling for emergency procedures which bypass the regular signalling and its inbuilt safety equipment.

While the book concentrates primarily on British signalling, the opening of the Channel Tunnel has brought true international train services to Britain with vast opportunities for onward rail journeys to other parts of Europe and we have therefore included a glimpse of how other countries signal their railways. In any case, with closer economic ties between the countries of the European Union, signalling supply and installation is now very much an international operation, not merely in Europe but worldwide. Look out of a train window in parts of Australia or the Far East and you will see signals which could be straight out of the mould of the latest in Britain. In the Indian subcontinent, parts of Africa, or South America you can still be transported through a time warp into a past era which has almost disappeared in Britain with stately semaphore signals, and equipment bearing the names of signal engineering manufacturers almost forming a role of honour covering all the years of railway history. There is nothing quite so evocative of our railway past as a tall semaphore signal silhouetted against the last rays of the setting sun with its arms lowered for a train to steam off into the night. This book is about that era, what went before, and what has happened since.

Geoffrey Kichenside,
Newton Abbot, Devon.

Alan Williams,
East Horsley, Surrey

ACKNOWLEDGEMENTS
AND REFERENCES

I N A WORK of this nature, covering the whole of the century and a half of what might be termed the main line railway era, and almost two whole centuries by taking the story right back to the mine railways and the initial puffs of Trevithick's first self-propelled locomotive of 1803, clearly we have looked at a mass of material from a wide variety of sources. Our main problem has been what to leave out.

Although this book has really got under way with potential material being gathered together and put into some sort of order during the last 10 years, with fingers being put to (originally) typewriter keys and then word processors since 1992, it has its origins (but perhaps not then with the precise focus as a book), 40 or even 50 years ago. Both of us have been interested in signalling from an early age, perhaps because we were brought up within sight and sound of important main lines, one the West Coast route out of Euston and the other the South Western line from Waterloo. Certainly, the trains interested us but so too did the signals. One of your authors, at a very tender age, learnt basic signalling sitting on Grandfather's knee (he was a Southern Railway guard) with demonstrations given by Dinky Toy signals. Later, as a very junior clerk on a real railway, he was instructed by his stationmaster as part of his indoctrination into signalling and safe working, to spend some of his own time learning about signalling in a major junction signalbox.

But whatever the influences, we have both had an interest in signalling from our respective schooldays, and they are further back than we would care to remember. Files of signalling notes, cuttings, photographs, accident reports and the like have been amassed over the last half-century and have provided a valuable source to trigger more detailed research into many aspects of railway signalling. We have been fortunate to have seen in visits to installations, in our capacities as technical journalists, what had been the traditional methods of signalling with mechanical equipment and the block telegraph, the new power signalling schemes from the 1950s up to the latest in automation with IECCs and the Channel Tunnel.

During that period, the various BR Regional Press Offices and the headquarters Press Office, also London Transport, were freely issuing descriptions of new signalling schemes with photographs. They were always responsive to queries on technical details, even looking back to historical matters and providing long hidden photographs from the archives. To the Press Officers and their staff over many years we must offer our thanks for their assistance and for arranging the many visits we have made to old and new signalling installations. And we must not forget such more recent newcomers to the railway network as Tyne & Wear Metro and Docklands Light Railway and the many signalling suppliers from private industry who have helped, even though now it may have been a long forgotten question, and the firm concerned may no longer have an independent existence.

The hundred years of *The Railway Magazine*, its sister journal *Railway Gazette*, the much younger *Modern Railways* and its predecessor *Trains Illustrated*, and *Railway World* have all provided a rich store of background signalling material and comment. The *Illustrated London News* covered railway signalling in some depth in the early 1840s and was involved in publicising the electric telegraph by staging a game of chess over a railway telegraph line. Any book on railway signalling would not get far without reference to the technical papers, publications and newsletters of the Institution of Railway Signal Engineers, not just for the essential detail covering the nuts and bolts, electrics, electronics, and processors involved in railway signalling which provided the foundations, but particularly the thinking behind developments, the trends, the politics and the countless discussions on ways forward. We made use of the Public Record Office and the National Railway Museum library and in particular its collection of railway accident reports going back to the earliest, published a century and a half ago. They proved to be a mine of information, not only on the circumstances of an accident, but the signalling practice of the time, the working conditions, and the recommendations for the future. It took many years but here was signalling development unfolding in those Victorian and later reports. To all these organisations and the journals where appropriate, and the Railway Inspectorate, we acknowledge our indebtedness. Although we have used official sources this is in no way an 'official' book and the interpretation and comments are ours alone.

We also consulted many other secondary sources, especially the many histories of individual railways, back to the last century, far too numerous to mention, some in vain for there was not a mention of signalling, others with but a few sentences. But the Great Western was more expansively covered in E. T. MacDermot's history, and the various highly illustrated books published in the last two decades devoted to the fine detail of signals and equipment of specific railways, notably the Great Western, LMS, LNWR and SR, left few nuts and bolts undiscovered. *Modern Railway Signalling* by Tweedie and Lascelles, published in the 1920s, the classic title on railway signalling of that era, was encyclopaedic in its coverage of equipment, the detail of its construction and how it worked, and we could not fail to have seen the writings and commentaries on signalling matters by the late O. S.

Nock. Naturally, we have looked back at our own articles and other work related to signalling which we have penned in the last three decades to see what is still relevant and whether our interpretation is still right. We have also been fortunate to have in our collections rule books and other regulations from official sources of the past, not just from this country but from several European countries, North America, Australia and New Zealand, all of which have been consulted. There are many more items far too numerous to mention which have resulted in the odd comment or sentence in our text. To all the sources we have used, whether named or not, we express our thanks.

The photographs have come from many sources over the last five decades and have been acknowledged where there is a name to acknowledge, but some prints are completely bare and if we have inadvertently failed to mention a source through lack of information then we apologise in advance. Finally, we must acknowledge the assistance of Alan Prior who prepared the black and white and colour diagrams while working in Turkey, with a few problems in getting queries to and from by fax, and for organising a personal courier to get the artwork safely from the Middle East to Devon.

Chapter 1

EVOLVING
A SYSTEM

WHEN RICHARD TREVITHICK took the first very tentative step in 1803 towards the creation of what was to become a new transport system, he could hardly have envisaged that it would be the means of thrusting the world out of an era which had lasted for thousands of years in which movement on land had been governed solely by the speed and capacity of a horse, in to one where people and goods could be moved en masse at speeds never before even dreamed about. The two technologies which he combined and which had been taken up by others, the power of steam, and the guided way – the rail way – were not new. Guidance of sorts with ruts in roadways was known in Roman times, and more positive guidance with wooden ways had been developed in mines and for mineral workings from the 15th century in parts of Europe, and with iron components, first as a protection for the wooden rails in the mid-18th century and then as iron rails in their own right, from about 1800.

The use of steam in an industrial application for drawing water from mines had been evolved by several pioneers in the early 18th century, probably seen at its best by the pumping engine designs of Thomas Newcomen. James Watt and then Trevithick took it a stage further by using steam as a direct propulsive force. These ingredients came together from 1810 for the development, first of the steam-worked colliery railways for moving coal from pit to port and then, in 1825 the Stockton & Darlington Railway which carried passengers as well, although still using some horse power. This was followed by the all-steam Liverpool & Manchester Railway in 1830. But one important factor in the creation of the newly emerging steam railways, which was to play a vital part in safe operation, was missing, or at least was limited, and that was communication. This word will be found time and time again in these pages with a variety of meanings, whether visual, as between lineside messages and train drivers, audible between signalmen, or electronic between computers. It is a term which, in whatever form it takes, is at the heart of railway signalling and in its simplest concept means nothing more than telling a train either through its driver or automated equipment whether the line ahead is clear for it to move and how fast it can go.

As soon as wooden guideways were introduced to allow man or horse-propelled trucks to have an easier passage through mine workings, and developed into wooden railways on the ground for horse drawn wagons of coal to get to rivers for unloading into barges or ships, a discipline was created in which the wagons had to proceed in order. They could not steer round each other. If just a single line of way was provided there had to be control so that wagons in one direction did not come up against wagons returning empty in the other. As the industrial revolution progressed in the 18th century so mining and quarrying expanded and colliery and mineral railways were built in ever increasing numbers to take coal, iron ore and minerals to rivers as, until then, water transport had been the only practical means of bulk movement of goods from one part of the country to another.

The wooden rails gradually gave way to iron, wagon wheels were given flanges and the principles of the railway we know today developed slowly. The introduction of the steam locomotive to colliery lines in the second decade of the 19th century took the railway a stage further. But in so doing it added to the operating discipline needed to avoid collisions.

The horse-worked colliery railways of the previous century were fairly straightforward in operation. One horse, one wagon, and one man to control it. On the level or uphill the horse pulled the wagon. Downhill, the horse was uncoupled, walked round behind the wagon and attached behind to act as a brake supplemented by the wooden brake block pressed on by the man holding down a lever. But there were many horses and wagons. Speeds were low and horses and wagons ran on sight. Ideally colliery lines were built to allow loaded wagons to run downhill to the waterways and the horses would pull the empties back uphill without too much problem. Gradients had to be reasonable but a few lines had sections as steep as 1 in 10. Clearly, care was needed when going down with a loaded wagon and, if the wagon brakes were less than effective, wagons could easily run away taking horse and often man with them since there was little time to unhitch the horse at the back. Collisions then were inevitable with horses and wagons ahead, sometimes extending to a multiple pile-up.

Generally the colliery wagons were worked one at a time and only on a few level routes would one horse work two or three wagons. Where mine output was heavy then separate main lines for the loaded trips heading for the waterways, and what were often called bye ways for the returning empty trips were provided, establishing directional operation over a double-track route. Sometimes only passing places or sidings were provided off the single track main line and the empties had to shunt out of the way of loaded wagons coming in the opposite direction. But the whole operation was conducted at low speeds and the only communication was by sight as one wagon driver saw another approaching, or that the wagon ahead had slowed down or stopped. Indeed the only communication possible in 1800 was sight within the range of the human eye whether by direct vision or seeing a visual signal, or by sound within the limits of human hearing. Visual signals had not even been thought of however, although there is evidence of sound signals in mines where it is recorded that men in charge of wagons struck rails or posts by a set number of beats to warn of the approach of wagons.

The steam colliery railways did not expand coal transport overnight but they enabled heavier loads to be pulled at higher speeds, higher in the sense that a steam locomotive could travel at 5 to 10mph against the 2 to 3mph of a horse but pulling perhaps 90 tons against 2 tons. Certainly the steam railway needed much more operating discipline because the very inadequate brakes meant that a train could not stop quickly on sight of another train close in front. Most of the colliery lines were short, within the range of one to ten miles, and with only few trains in action at any one time, perhaps with only one locomotive in steam. Some lines could not be worked throughout by steam locomotives because of the topography. The Hetton Colliery Railway, set out by George Stephenson and opened in 1822, was eight miles long but had two independent lengths of line, $1^1/_2$ and $2^1/_2$ miles in length respectively, worked by travelling steam locomotives. These lines were separated by balanced inclined planes where loaded wagons going down attached to a rope hauled up returning empties. The locomotive-worked sections were thus short and needed no formal signalling other than organisation which effectively meant a timetable of sorts with written or verbal instruction.

Just three years later the Stockton & Darlington Railway opened in September 1825. This railway was different, for its Act of Parliament allowed the carriage of passengers as well as goods, its prime traffic being the conveyance of coal from the Auckland collieries to the navigable part of the River Tees at Stockton. But although the Act allowed the carriage of passengers by steam traction, in its first years passengers were transported in single road-style coaches adapted to run on rails and hauled by horses. Moreover, passenger operations were franchised out to local operators who ran coaches on rails much as they would have done on roads and they had to be licensed similarly. These trains were run in between the coal trains hauled by steam locomotives and goods wagons hauled by horses. It was a right mix of traffic and one which needed tight operational control.

Apart from a semblance of a timetable, and then only individual times published by the respective coach operators, regulations prescribed which trains or coaches took precedence over others. The S&D line, laid out for locomotive working, was single throughout but with what were called sidings at intervals as frequently as four in a mile. In practice the sidings were passing loops. Locomotive-hauled trains took precedence over others but if two locomotive-hauled trains were seen to be coming towards each other the empty one had to give way to the loaded train. If they met at a passing loop there was no problem, but if they did not see each other at a distance and drew to a stop between passing places the empty train had to back until it reached the previous passing loop to give way. Loaded horse-drawn wagons took the next priority, even passenger coaches having to get out of their way. But if a horse-drawn passenger coach was coming up behind a horse-drawn wagon or steam-hauled train in the same direction, the regulations gave the passenger coach a right to overtake the slower train or wagon at the next passing place. A passenger coach was expected to wait at a passing loop if the driver saw another coach coming towards him but whatever the regulations might have said the drivers were independent characters and not always receptive to rules. It has been recorded that on one occasion when two coaches met between loops neither would give way and their respective drivers were determined to stick it out. Eventually one of the drivers with the help of his passengers lifted his coach off the track and his horse stepped to one side to allow the other coach to continue after which the first coach was restored to the track. Honour was satisfied. By 1833 the S&D took over the working of all traffic by locomotives, by which time its main line had been doubled and squabbles over who had right of way were a thing of the past.

Although lineside signals had not been considered at this time on the S&D the company was, nevertheless, considering the use of signals in the broadest sense for traffic control. In 1832 it planned to erect telegraph signals which at that time would have doubtless been large semaphore telegraph structures similar to naval relay stations. This would have allowed some form of communication between the colliery area and the ports so that if, for example, bad weather at sea prevented ships from docking or leaving, and wagons congested the staiths and were unable to drop their coal, the men at the ports, which now included Middlesbrough, could advise the men at the collieries not to despatch any more loaded wagons. If they did the trains would have to be parked in some of the passing loops thus obstructing other traffic. Another important consequence would have been that empty wagons would not have been able to return to the collieries to provide an ascending load on the balanced inclines, without which they could not operate. The plan was for three telegraph stations, at Middlesbrough, Great Stainton, and Eldon, but opposition by the local landowner, Lord Eldon, to having the visual intrusion of these great structures on his estate put an end to the idea. Had they been constructed they would have been the first method of long distance communication with a direct application to railway operation.

Yet the S&D and the other developing railways of the time sometimes had signalling for working inclines. In one pattern a gong at one end was worked by a direct pull on a rope from the other. In another a disc was fixed to a post at one end visible from the other end and by rotating the disc the operator could indicate to the man at the far end that he was ready, while in a third two poles, one at the bottom and one at the top, both hinged were linked by wire in such a way that when the pole at the bottom was pulled down level with the ground it raised the pole at the top to let the man in charge of the winding gear know that the wagons at the bottom end were ready. The systems were neither fool-proof nor fail safe.

While the S&D had no signals and the enginemen and coach drivers were masters of their own circumstances in respect of safe running, in daylight with low speeds and in clear visibility there was usually little problem. At night it was different and often some form of signalling had to be used, however primitive, particularly with the steam locomotives to give warning of approach. The simplest was for the fireman of a steam locomotive to take out a shovelful of burning cinders from the fire and throw it into the air. A burning brazier suspended from the last vehicle was used as a tail signal. From an early date on the S&D a square board with the word 'signal' painted on it was placed at the approaches to level crossings to remind drivers to slow down and ring their bells. At night lamps were placed at the signal boards, not to illuminate them but if aimed towards a passenger train the light indicated that passengers were waiting to get on and the train should stop. If no light was displayed then there were no passengers and trains need not stop unless passengers wanted to get off. A candle in the window of a station house served the same purpose.

First steps to creating a system

The opening of the Liverpool & Manchester Railway in September 1830 marked the first real step towards a general steam-worked goods and passenger railway system not related to coal extraction and export. It was the first railway to be built exclusively for locomotive haulage right from the start. With higher speeds than the colliery railways – passenger trains taking little more than two hours for the 31 miles – and the relatively frequent service with around ten passenger trains scheduled on weekdays in each direction mixing with between 15 and 20 goods trains, on a double-track main line, it was essential for an awareness of safety to be instilled in operating staff who had no assistance from any formal signalling methods. How could they? They were venturing into the unknown with a steam passenger railway. There was still no means of distant communication other than by the naval semaphore telegraph and there was then little thought of adapting that to railway use.

Right at the start the directors did not even know how many passengers they would carry or how much

The early 'signalmen' were policemen, looking after general security around the railway and giving signals to drivers by hand or flag as here at the entrance to a tunnel. (Illustrated London News)

goods would be sent by train. During the first years speed limits were used as part of the safety culture, partly for the need for caution in case the trackbed settled and caused track problems, but also as a measure to try to ensure that one train did not run into another. Passenger trains were not to run at more than 20mph and less than that when going over level crossings with public roads, running on embankments, and at places where trains regularly stopped or took on water. Goods trains often could not reach the maximum speed because of the loads, but braking was much more of a problem than reaching a reasonable speed.

However, some form of control there had to be and at stations the L&M used the services of policemen on the company's staff whose duties included general security. For the first few years from the opening of the L&M a basic form of signalling by hand or by flags became established but not necessarily linked to safety procedures. The attitude of a policeman as a train approached was intended to be a signal in itself to a driver. A policeman standing to attention with an arm outstretched indicated that the line ahead was clear, but if he stood at ease making no positive hand signal then it meant that all was not well and the train was to slow down and continue with caution. Flag signals were used to indicate whether passengers were waiting to board the next train. If they were, a red flag was hauled up to the top of a pole. Hand lamps were used at night and any light waved violently meant danger. Tail lamps were carried on the back of the last vehicle of a train aimed at any following train and these at first showed one of two colours, red when on the move and blue if stopped at a station. Within a few years a red flag at the top of a pole at a station meant danger of any sort and that trains should stop regardless of its meaning

Even though by the early 1840s colours were beginning to be standardised to denote danger, caution, or clear, flag signals sometimes had different meanings depending on how they were displayed. With the policeman standing more or less to attention and not showing a flag the line was clear. A green flag raised meant 'proceed with caution under time interval rules' and a green flag shown diagonally down meant 'caution there is a track defect'. These were signals on the London & Birmingham Railway. (Illustrated London News)

that passengers were waiting to be picked up. But in severe weather flags could be blown off the post or torn, and by 1834 the railway had adopted flag boards which were wooden boards hanging from one side of a post and painted red to represent a flag. They were turned to be face on to a train to indicate danger and away from the train edge on for clear. Soon after, the boards were attached centrally across the post. The boards were mounted at the top of cast iron posts, rather like a lamp post, and indeed a lamp housing was carried above the board rotating with it to show a red light with the board face on and white when edge on.

Although red was the generally accepted colour meaning danger – stop, it was by no means universal and was used at one or two places for clear. At Brockley Whins south east of Newcastle at the junction of the Stanhope & Tyne Railway and the Brandling Junction Railway in the mid-1830s, each line was equipped with three posts at intervals towards the meeting point. At the first post on the Brandling Junction line a white flag was hung out. On the Stanhope & Tyne line a red flag was displayed on the first post. The instruction to enginemen was that at the first post on passing the flag they were to sound the engine whistle, at the second the train was to slow down and if no flag was shown at the crossing the train was to stop at the third post. But if the line was clear and the train could proceed a white flag was displayed at the crossing for a train on the Brandling Junction line or a red flag for a train on the S&T line, a case where red indicated clear. Another example where red was used for clear was on London's first railway, the London & Greenwich opened in 1836, at Corbett's Lane Junction where the London & Croydon Railway, opened 2½ years later in June 1839, diverged. A rotating disc painted red was used face on to trains when the junction was set to the Croydon line and edge on to be invisible when the points were set to and from Greenwich. It was worked from what was the first railway signalbox known as the lighthouse, which was an elevated structure equipped with lamp reflectors so that at night lights could be beamed towards the trains, white when the line was set for the Greenwich route and red when set for the Croydon line.

By the late 1830s railway expansion had started to take off and in 1837 the first stage of the London & Birmingham Railway was opened from Euston to Boxmoor, and a year later the first sections of the Great Western Railway from Paddington to Maidenhead, and the London & Southampton Railway, all intended right from the start as long distance trunk routes.

After experience on the Liverpool & Manchester Railway and with the impending link from the L&M to the Grand Junction Railway to Birmingham and on through to London it was inevitable that much of what had been tried on the L&M should be adapted for use on the linking lines to London. Yet what had been tried

In the absence of flags, signals were given by hand. One arm stretched out horizontally meant 'line clear', one arm raised meant 'caution', both arms raised meant 'danger, stop'. These same clear and danger hand signals were also used in Spain and in the USA. In Britain the clear and caution hand signals exchanged meanings in the mid-1930s. (Illustrated London News)

on both the L&M and the S&D by no means offered anything like standard indications or even common use of colours for flags or lamps. Running on sight was still a feature and even though a policeman giving a hand, flag or lamp signal to a driver that the line was clear it only meant that he could not see a train in the way. What was further along the line was in the great unknown.

From the opening of the first trunk lines hand, lamp, or flag signals were adopted. Hand signals at least had some common meaning and with the exchange in meaning of two of the hand signals, the hand positions survive to this day. Both arms raised above the head indicated danger, stop, one arm raised above the head meant caution, and one arm held forward level with the shoulder meant line clear. The hand positions of the last two exchanged meanings in 1936. As an aside, in today's signalling in which fail safe is emblazoned across the hearts of all signal engineers, it has always puzzled your authors as to why *two* arms raised meant danger since, if the railway employee be he (or she) signalman, guard, engineman in running towards an oncoming train speeding into danger should slip and fall, injuring an arm to an extent that it could not be raised, only one good arm being left to give the hand danger signal, what interpretation would the oncoming driver make of it?

In the first years of the new trunk lines traffic was not all that dense since it took time to build up. Passenger trains at least were expected to run to a timetable. With only eight passenger trains scheduled to leave Paddington each day at the start it was unlikely that one would catch up with another, unless there was a prolonged breakdown and even then there would be time to send a man back along the line to give a danger signal if the following train approached. Goods traffic was also developing however and often did not run to a schedule. There was often extra traffic when special trains were run without published times, being fitted between the scheduled trains in the best way possible. With the contrast in speed between the slow moving goods trains and the fast light express passenger trains, or the few passenger trains that called at intermediate

stations, it was soon becoming clear that some form of control was needed to prevent collisions.

Time interval operation

Without the means for one station to communicate with the next, except by messages passed on the trains themselves, or by a messenger on horseback, there was no certain way for station staff to know whether trains were running as booked, or whether extras were on the line, or if they had broken down. But gradually a system developed in which timetables and printed or written instructions were used as the basis of what today would appear to be a very primitive set of safety precautions and carried into practice by the time separation of trains, the time interval system. It was that very absence of a practical means of communication that brought the time interval system into being although even as these early railways were being built, the first moves towards electrical communication were being tried out. Had those experiments come a decade earlier so that a proven communications system could have been available to the railway pioneers, time interval would never have been needed. As it was, it became a widespread and fairly standard method of operation on railways in Britain from the 1830s and was not finally displaced until 60 years later with many accidents resulting from its use.

The basis of time interval operation was that once a train had passed or departed from a station if a following train approached within the first few minutes the policeman would show a danger signal to stop the approaching train and warn its driver that there was another train close in front. If instead the second train approached after those first few minutes had elapsed then the policeman would show a caution signal to the driver without the need for it to stop. The driver had to understand that he could continue on but at reduced speed since the first train was not all that far ahead. The exact times varied a little but generally the danger signal was displayed to a second train if it arrived within five minutes of the first. After five minutes had elapsed then the caution signal was shown for another five minutes. After that, ten minutes in all, a clear signal could be shown to a second train although the caution signal only meant that the train ahead had passed the station between five and ten minutes before. If the clear signal was displayed to a second train it denoted that the first train had been at least ten minutes ahead when it left the station. Whether it was still ahead by that same time interval depended entirely on how the first train was running. If the engine was steaming well and there was no technical fault then it probably was running ahead by the same interval. But if it was not steaming well it might be running more slowly so that the second train might easily catch it up. If there was a technical fault or total breakdown it could have stopped. In that case hopefully, one of the guards would run back showing a light, flag or hand signal to stop the following train in good time to avoid a collision. The engines of the late 1830s often had no more than a hand brake on the tender, and on some of the coaches, or in the brake vans of goods trains, and could not stop quickly. Sometimes the only means of stopping a locomotive was by reversing it.

The first signals

Flag or hand signals alone given by the policemen were not without problems. What if a train approached when the policeman was not in position to give a signal? They had other duties around the station and to a certain extent had been established for railway work after the style of the then newly formed Metropolitan Police in London. Railway security was in their domain and they might have been called away to deal with an unruly passenger or general station work. Hand signals could not be seen clearly by a driver at a distance and flag signals could not be distinguished easily unless hoisted to the top of a pole, and even then its colour might not be identified until the train was close. A fixed signal, fixed in the sense that it was a permanent structure, gave a much better chance of informing a driver on whether he could continue or stop, and could be left in position while the policeman had gone away. Already the Liverpool & Manchester Railway had started with its flag boards and rotating boards from about 1838. The London & Birmingham and the other trunk lines soon realised that there was a need for fixed signals and rotating boards worked from a handle at the bottom of the post began to be used more widely. Face on to a train they indicated danger and turned at 90 degrees to be edge on they indicated clear. Shapes varied, some were rectangular, some were circular discs, and the Stockton & Darlington had some in the shape of a triangle. Some of the signals were intended to show whether the line was clear under time interval operation, others were points indicators showing which way points were set. Sometimes separate signals were provided for the tracks in opposite directions on double lines, and at others just one signal applied both ways so that if a train was making a call at a station or had just left, the signal board would be in the danger position for both directions. If a train then approached on the other line its driver would see the danger signal and would either stop or be called on to proceed by hand signal.

The London & Birmingham Railway gradually installed disc signals but usually there was just one signal or pair of signals near the centre of the station. At junctions the signals were often near the hand levers for the points or were connected to them. This meant that a train approaching a danger signal might have to stop well short of the signal clear of the points or before reaching the platform because another train was

A rotating crossbar signal similar to those of the 1840s but this one survived in a coal yard for shunting until the 1950s. In fact, a few signals of this pattern were installed in yards long after they had been displaced by semaphores on main lines, to control crossings between two tracks, showing clear one way and stop for the other (BR, LMR)

Another form of rotating board used in the pioneering days but this one was situated in Londonderry on the Londonderry & Lough Swilly Railway which originally opened in the 1860s.

worthy of that description although it was attached to a post. It was installed at Reading from the opening of the line in March 1840 and consisted of a red disc attached to wires passing through pulleys at the top of the post. There is some ambiguity in contemporary records of the exact form of the disc, for some descriptions refer to it as a ball, and others as a ball disc. It seems unlikely that it would have been a plain disc since being merely suspended from a wire through the pulley at the top of the mast it could swing and turn in the wind. A ball would remain visible as a ball even if turning. The instruction to drivers has gone down in history as a classic:

'If the ball can be seen the line is right for the train to go in. If the ball is not visible the train must not pass it.'

Remarkably for this period the signal was fail safe, more by chance than planning. If it was not there it was to be treated as a danger signal. Ball discs were used at one or two other places on the GWR for a year or two. But whether these signals were actual balls or discs, certainly ball signals hauled up or down a post were known and used in one or two places and appeared in North America leading to the term 'highball' indicating a clear line. The ball signal was undoubtedly derived from naval signalling with a ball, or two interlaced discs at right angles appearing as a ball, hauled to the top of a mast as a daytime land or sea signal. Could Isambard Kingdom Brunel's father Sir Marc Brunel, as he later became, with personal naval experience have suggested the idea to his son?

A rotating diamond board was also used at Shrawardine on the reconstructed Shropshire & Montgomeryshire Railway from its reopening in 1911, probably a relic of the original 1860s Potteries & North Wales Railway. Face on at danger it instructed trains to stop to pick up passengers. (L&GRP)

actually alongside the platform or might be shunting, blocking the main line. The location of the signal was thus not necessarily the place at which a train had to stop.

On the Great Western, point indicating targets first appeared in 1839 at Maidenhead when on the opening of the line on to Twyford two trains went through Maidenhead on the main line without stopping and were not switched into what was called the siding. Attached to the lever operating the switches were two targets. If both were visible the points were set for the siding but if they merged so that a driver could see only one the points were set straight ahead. Soon after, the GWR devised discs attached to the points lever or capstan at facing points, painted green with a white target, sometimes with a red ring, face on when set straight ahead and edge on when set for the branch.

The first 'fixed' signal on the GWR was hardly

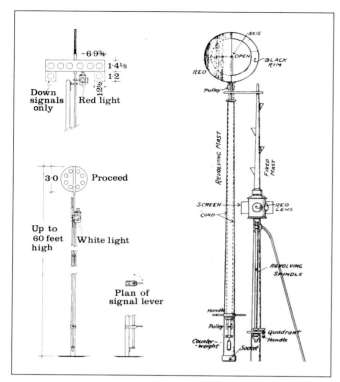

Fig. 1. LEFT *Great Western disc and crossbar signal.* RIGHT *Martin disc of the London & South Western Railway. (Alan Prior; National Railway Museum)*

In Britain the disc signal was gradually spreading in the 1840s, but not with any consistency of style or meaning. On the London & Birmingham the disc face

Martin disc signals and GWR disc and crossbar signal at Eastleigh in the 1880s after replacement by semaphores. (National Railway Museum).

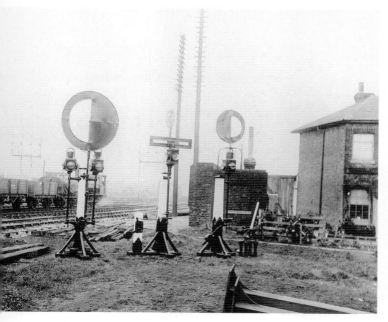

on meant danger and edge on (and thus virtually invisible) meant clear. By February 1841 the Great Western was well ahead with a new pattern signal which, unlike those elsewhere, gave positive danger and clear indications. This was Brunel's notable disc and crossbar pattern. Like other disc types the signal rotated through 90 degrees to give the appropriate indication. At the top of the mast were two signals, a red painted disc and at a right angle to it a red painted horizontal bar. To lessen wind resistance the disc had holes in its face and the bar had slots. With the bar face on to a train it meant danger, stop. With the disc face on the signal denoted proceed, line clear. So already a disc face on to a train had different meanings on different railways, clear on the Great Western and danger on some of the others.

The London & South Western had a different approach since a disc was used face on to represent all manner of meanings. It was developed by one Albinus Martin. Just one disc served trains in both directions at double line stations but without the problems of earlier single disc signals effectively stopping trains in both directions. The Martin discs were about 4ft in diameter and in one half was a half-moon shaped cut out. The whole disc rotated in the vertical plane from a central pivot controlled by rope round the pulley vee round the outer edge of the disc. This meant that the disc could be turned to show the cut-out in different positions. With the cut out in the bottom half the signal was at danger in both directions. With the cut out in the left half the left hand track was clear but the right hand (for traffic coming the other way) was obstructed. If a driver approached the signal with the cut out in the right hand half then he had to stop, for this signal meant that the track in the opposite direction was clear. But the post on which the disc and its rope assembly and operating handle were mounted itself rotated about a vertical axis thus allowing the disc to be turned at a right angle and parallel to the tracks, and thus invisible to trains in both directions, the clear both ways position.

Enter the semaphore

Strictly, the word semaphore, from the Greek, means to bear a sign, and could literally be applied to any form of signal but almost from the dawn of railways came to mean a signal giving different messages by the position of an arm. The origin of sending visual messages from structures with wooden arms protruding and pivoted from a frame by combinations of arms at varying angles, dates back to the French revolution in the 1790s. It was adapted two decades later in Britain to provide a chain of visual telegraph stations with semaphores built on hilltops within sight of each other to transmit messages from authority in London to such strategic places as naval bases at Portsmouth and Plymouth. The semaphores had two arms working in one of seven positions, inclined down at 45 deg to the

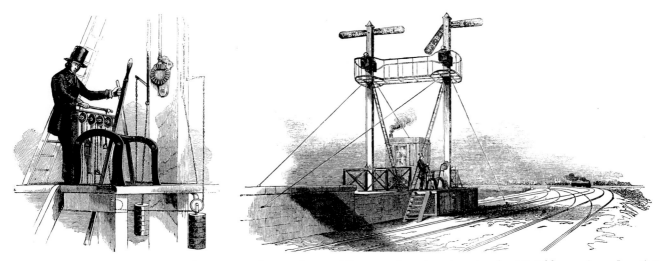

left, horizontal to the left, inclined up at 45 deg to the left, vertically above the post, and similarly through the three other positions to the right. Each position of either a single arm or in combination with the second arm denoted a letter or figure. Although in existence almost a decade before the opening of the Stockton & Darlington Railway, its potential for railway use was not appreciated at once other than as a possible means of communication between Middlesbrough staiths and Eldon to control coal traffic in 1832 as already described.

Late in 1841 the first semaphore signal for the direct control of trains was erected on the London & Croydon Railway at New Cross. Devised by Charles Gregory, engineer of the Croydon Railway, it had just a single arm working within a vertical slot in the wooden post and pivoted inside. The arm was designed to work in three positions, horizontal, meaning danger – stop, inclined down at 45 deg meaning caution, slow down, and vertical, invisible inside the slot meaning clear, proceed. This prototype had an independent rotating lantern worked from a separate lever on the post to give the night time lamp signals, red for danger, green

The semaphore junction signals at Bricklayers Arms Junction installed in 1843. (Illustrated London News)

for caution and white for clear. There was no rush to adopt the semaphore signal even though it was capable of giving the three indications associated with time interval working, danger, caution, and clear, which the rotating disc signals could not do except by supplementary signals for the caution indication.

Primitive semaphore signal not unlike the auxiliary signals of the 1850s onwards but this one was used on the narrow gauge Penrhyn Quarry Railway in North Wales until the 1950s. (Kenneth Field)

Fig. 2. *The stirrup locking between the signal levers at Bricklayers Arms, 1843. (National Railway Museum)*

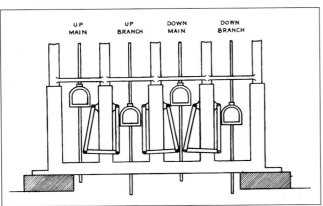

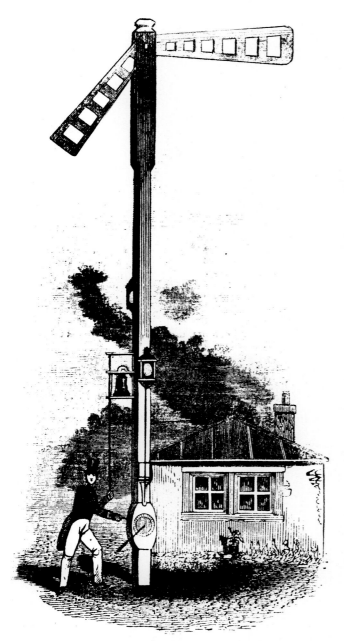

Back to back three-position semaphore of the early 1840s then gradually being installed on principal routes. Note the cut outs in the arms to lessen wind resistance. Although not perpetuated in Britain, cut outs were used until recent years on French and some German style semaphores. (Illustrated London News)

Semaphore signals were next installed at Bricklayers Arms Junction in 1843 at the meeting point of the branch of the Brighton railway to its new Bricklayers Arms terminus with the London & Croydon Railway to provide a more formal signalling arrangement than the Corbetts Lane signals half a mile or so towards London Bridge. The Bricklayers Arms Junction signals had an element of interlocking in that the four levers which worked the four signal arms were grouped together in a frame and linked by stirrups which prevented the signals for opposing movements from being cleared together. There was no connection to the points and thus no means of preventing signals and points from disagreeing.

Regulation of railways

The first moves towards government regulation of railway safety were already beginning to appear, for in 1840 a railway inspections procedure had been devised under railway inspectors working within the Board of Trade, the origins of today's Railway Inspectorate. The inspectors were qualified engineers with a military background. One of the first inspectors was Sir Frederick Smith and as part of his comments on the opening of the Brighton railway in 1841 he referred to the junction at Corbetts Lane. Around 150 to 200 trains passed through the junction every day controlled solely by a switchman and a signalman with flags, or lamps at night. The safety record had been excellent. The selection of good men was thought to be the best safeguard for safety rather than the introduction of new mechanical devices. So the lack of interlocking between signals and points at Bricklayers Arms in 1843 was not of vital concern at least at that time. The railway inspectorate was soon to change its ideas as accident statistics began to be compiled. In the last five months of 1840 there were 28 train accidents involving 22 fatalities on all lines then open in Britain and Ireland. Two years later with more mileage added there were only ten accidents in the whole year and just one passenger killed. But it was clear the accident potential was there as speeds increased and trains ran more frequently. Certainly a system had evolved but in the 1840s it was by no means standardised and needed much more refinement. There was also just the dawn of a new form of communication, the electric telegraph which was to play such an important part in railway signalling in subsequent years.

Chapter 2

FIRST STEPS TO COMMUNICATION

BY THE TIME that the first of the trunk railways were under construction in the mid-1830s a new form of long distance communication was under trial which did not rely on direct visual signals. This was the electro-magnetic telegraph devised by W. F. Cooke and Professor C. Wheatstone. It employed battery power using zinc plates in a solution of sulphuric acid and was operated by the magnetic force of an electric current passing through a coil of wire which attracted a small piece of iron attached to a pivoting needle. When a switch, which may have been no more than two pieces of metal in close contact in the circuit, was closed to complete a circuit from battery through wires to the coils and back, the needle could be made to deflect. With two coils, one on each side of the needle, and a switch suitable to reverse the direction of current the needle could be made to swing either way from the centre. When no current flowed, the needle was biased to an upright position. Cooke and Wheatstone's earliest instruments had five needles arranged in a line across the face. A diamond grid of lines led from each of the needles down and up to ten points of intersection each one representing a letter of the alphabet although with only 20 indications available, not all letters could be used and there was no space for C, J, Q, U, X, and Z, so they had to be represented phonetically. By deflecting any two needles and looking along the lines towards which they pointed, the letter at the intersection was the one to be read. Messages had to be spelled out letter by letter, although certain letters on their own indicated a message such as 'understood' or 'repeat'.

Telegraph trials

Right from the start the London & Birmingham Railway had planned to work trains from Euston to Camden up and down the 1 in 70 incline by rope haulage. It was therefore necessary for the operator of the winding engine at the top of the climb at Camden, a mile from the start, to know when trains were ready to depart so that he could apply steam to the engine to start hauling the train. In June 1837, a month before the opening of the first stage of the L&B line as far as

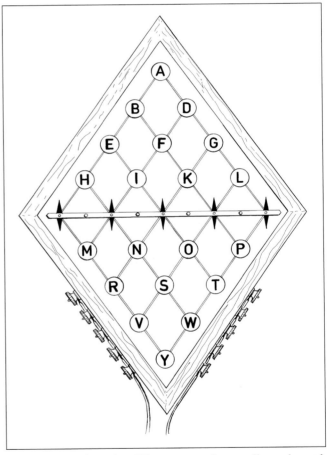

Fig. 3. *Cooke & Wheatstone five-needle telegraph instrument. Deflection of any two needles would point to specific letters on the grid but its disadvantage lay in the equivalent number of line wires.*

Boxmoor on 20 July, Cooke and Wheatstone successfully demonstrated their telegraph system between Euston and Camden. Robert Stephenson, the line's engineer, was much in favour of adopting the telegraph along the whole line, but the L&B board could not be persuaded. Undaunted, Cooke and Wheatstone took their equipment a little further west and demonstrated it to the GWR in a trial between Paddington and West Drayton. Installation of the telegraph instruments and wires, five being needed, insulated and carried inside an iron pipe above the ground, was started just as the line opened and was not completed until mid-1839. The 13-mile length was more than a direct line could manage and intermediate telegraph instruments were put in at Hanwell where messages had to be re-transmitted. It was the first application of the electric telegraph to a railway but its use to help in signalling trains was still not appreciated. Certainly there were operating benefits as on occasions of engine failure the telegraph could be used to advise Paddington of the problem, instructions could be sent to overcome it, and it could also be used to get staff to warn trains of an out of course event if they had not passed the crucial telegraph station. It was also used for sending general messages about the business of the railway and for public messages, for the new installation was one of the talking points in contemporary London.

The system did not last however and within a year or so the insulation had deteriorated to an extent that the equipment would not function. Yet in 1842 the parties were willing to have another try with Cooke responsible for renewing the system, and running it, taking the charges from it but handing it over to the GWR after 14 years. This time though the design had changed to a twin needle pattern needing only two wires which were carried in the open on cast iron poles. It was commissioned a year later and it was its non railway use which gained the system massive publicity when it transmitted the news of the birth of Queen Victoria's

Fig. 4. *Cooke & Wheatstone instrument which indicated specific letters by prescribed numbers of deflections to left or right. This type of instrument was used on the Croydon Atmospheric Railway.*

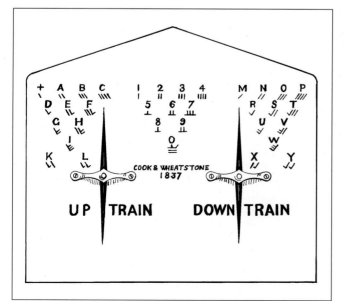

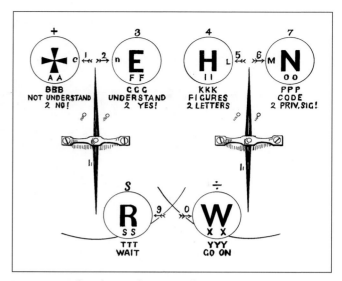

Fig. 5. *Another form of two-needle instrument, but needing both needles to denote a letter or figure.*

Operation of the needle telegraph on the Croydon Atmospheric Railway. One needle was used for up trains and one for down. (Illustrated London News)

was telegraphed ahead to Paddington and the police were able to identify and follow him until enough evidence was available to arrest him. He was later convicted and hanged. Because of the limitations on the available alphabet his description as a Quaker had to be transmitted as 'Kwaker' but the receiving telegraph clerk knew what was meant.

As for the London & Birmingham it lost the race to have the first telegraph and instead the Camden incline was controlled by what was called a pneumatic tube. This was rather like blowing a whistle in a speaking tube, in which signals at one end were induced by pumping air into the other. It was not all that effective but survived until the winding engines were taken out of use in 1845 when sufficiently powerful locomotives had become available to work trains right in and out of Euston.

But still the Great Western seemed to be out of luck and again the telegraph fell into disrepair and by the end of the 1840s the GWR had decided that the telegraph was not worth the bother. It was a different story elsewhere as other railways realised that the telegraph was worth pursuing. Even then the telegraph was not used exclusively for railway business. On 10 April 1845 a game of chess was conducted over the London & South Western Railway telegraph between players at Nine Elms and Portsmouth, hardly a lawful railway use but the game had been suggested by the staff of the *Illustrated London News* as a means of showing the versatility and ability of the electric telegraph for

Operating the two-needle telegraph. (Illustrated London News)

second son in 1844, and just into 1845, when it was the means of arresting a murderer. The description of a man seen leaving the crime at Slough and boarding a train

On 10 April 1845 the Illustrated London News *organised a game of chess played over the London & South Western Railway two-needle telegraph between London and Portsmouth, which took nine hours to reach a conclusion. This was hardly in the realms of railway signalling but it helped to publicise the wonders of the electric telegraph.* (Illustrated London News)

varying forms of communication. There is no doubt that by then the expanding railway network was beginning to realise the value of the telegraph as an aid but still not as an essential part of railway operation.

Signal variety

During the 1840s lineside signals continued to be given by a variety of methods – hand, flag, lamp, and fixed signals of varying patterns as rotating discs or bars, and semaphores were gradually being adopted by different railways. As time interval operation was becoming the standard method of separating trains, on double lines at least, which called for a period when the danger signal was exhibited to a following train arriving within usually five minutes of the one ahead, and then a further period when caution was displayed for another few minutes, it followed that when fixed signals were erected they ought to be capable of showing three indications, danger, caution, and clear. The rotating disc or bar signals could do nothing more than show danger or clear and a supplementary signal had to be given for caution. On some lines this was

ABOVE LEFT *GWR disc and crossbar signal in the clear position.*

ABOVE RIGHT *GWR disc and crossbar signal at danger with a fantail caution board also in the danger position.* (Illustrated London News)

The Great Western Railway disc and crossbar type of signal. Normally these signals were mounted at the top of tall masts but this one, at West London Junction where the West London Railway from Willesden to Clapham Junction crossed the Great Western main line at a flat crossing, was low down and since the tracks were almost at a right angle the one disc and crossbar signal would show danger to one line and clear to the other. (Illustrated London News)

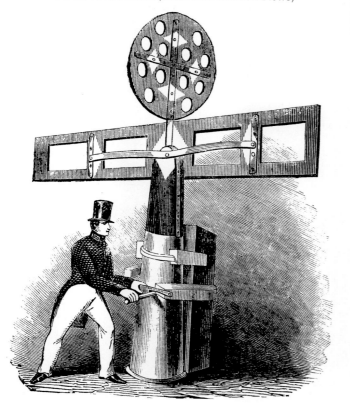

done by turning the disc to the clear position after the five minute danger period with the policeman ready to show a caution signal by hand or flag. It was almost like the combined stop and distant semaphore signals on the same post today, with the stop signal at clear saying proceed the line is clear and the distant at caution saying, 'yes continue but you will need to slow down'. In the 1840s the actual meaning was not quite like that for the signal was saying 'continue but have caution since the train ahead was only between five and ten minutes ahead of you when it passed here'.

On the Great Western, disc and crossbar signals were installed on the new sections opened to Bristol, and beyond on the Bristol & Exeter and South Devon railways to Plymouth. To give the caution indication the GWR adopted another type of signal using flags or curtains carried in a quadrant shaped frame, which acquired the name of fantails. The quarter circle frame was mounted upwards on a mast and divided into two sections, the left with a green curtain suspended on rings from the top curve of the frame and a red curtain in the right half. Ropes attached to the rings could be pulled to draw the curtain in one half across the frame to be fully displayed while the curtain in the other was at the same time drawn tightly together leaving an open space in the frame. In this way either the red curtain could be shown or the green. When the disc and crossbar was turned to danger with the bar displayed the fantail was also drawn to show red. After the prescribed time had elapsed and caution could be shown, the disc and crossbar was turned to show the disc for clear and the green curtain was displayed. As soon as the clear indication could be shown both curtains were drawn up tightly to show virtually no display. Night time indications were given by lamps mounted on separate posts. At first the lamp housings were fitted with slots into which coloured glasses were placed in front of the plain glass of the lamp as needed to show the red danger signal or green caution indication.

In designing the fantail signals Brunel had reckoned without the wind which occasionally ripped the curtains from the frames. Within a year of their introduction in 1841 a new form of caution signal had been devised, a rectangular rotating board but distinguished by a fishtail end on one side and a pointed end on the other. It too displayed danger or caution as a positive signal. At danger the board pointed right towards the track and the side facing oncoming trains was painted red. For caution the board was rotated through 180 degrees to point to the left, away from the track and the side shown to approaching trains was green. These signals were mounted on separate masts just in front of and lower than the disc and crossbar signals with which they applied. After ten minutes, or other time after the passage of the previous train when the clear indication could be shown to a following train, the disc and crossbar signal remained with the disc displayed or clear but the caution board, or fantail since they inherited the nickname from the flag signals which preceded them, were turned through another 90 degrees to be edge on and thus displaying no indication. It was ironic that here was a rotating signal capable of giving three indications, the clear position by default in not being seen and which would have been quite happily accepted by other railways, but the Great Western was adamant in giving a positive clear signal by the display of the disc face on.

The Great Western also took great pains to ensure that its signals could be seen clearly from a distance by mounting the disc and crossbar at the top of masts as high as 60ft in places. Initially the entire mast rotated but because of wind damage, which on occasions blew down the whole assembly, the masts were made permanent fixtures with guy wires to support them while the disc and cross bar were carried on separate spindles bracketed to the mast in bearings. Lamp housings were also attached to the spindles so that they rotated with the boards above them. The different colour glasses were carried on the respective sides but, although needing only a red glass for danger since the natural light of the lamp flame served for clear, in fact a green glass acted as a small back light at danger, although not seen by an approaching train except in the opposite direction. Lamps relating to fantail signals did of course display a green light at night.

In a report to the inspector general of railways in the late 1840s, then acting under the Railway Commissioners rather than the Board of Trade, the Great Western reckoned that at night some of its signal lamps which used Argand burners and reflectors behind the lamp could be seen four to five miles away on straight lines. But in daytime at a distance, drivers could not always distinguish which signal was which, particularly where stations had down and up signals. Some of the wayside stations had only one signal applying to both directions which as already described could be somewhat restrictive if two trains approached together from opposite directions. Later a second signal was added so that each line had its own signal. To distinguish down and up signals at danger a short vertical bar was added at both ends of the main bar, extending downwards on down line signals, the up line signals remaining as they were. At level crossings equipped with a signal only one was necessary since, if the gates were across the track, then trains on both lines needed to be stopped. In this case the bar was also given a vertical extension at the ends, but this time it extended evenly up and down as a sideways T piece.

Junctions soon called for special treatment and here GWR signals applying to and from branch tracks had a double disc with a smaller one mounted above the main disc, and two crossbars one above the other. For down line signals the lower bar had the vertical end extensions. Both bars and discs rotated together since it was not a case of having an upper signal for one line and a lower signal for the other. The main line had its own single disc and crossbar signal on its own mast alongside that for the branch. At night the branch signals had double lamps as well, one above the other so that the driver of a train approaching a facing junction clear for a branch to the right would see a single red light on the left and two vertical white lights to the right. It might have been more disconcerting for drivers clear on the main line to see one white light to the left and two red on the right. The same double disc and crossbar signals were used for trains coming off a branch track to join a main line. While a single disc and crossbar placed a little way back on the branch would not have led to confusion with main line signals it must be remembered that at junctions in these early years the signals were usually placed near the junction points to be handy to the switchman or policeman even though their controls were not grouped together or related in any way. Thus a branch train coming towards the main line at a junction with the branch signal at danger was expected to stop some way short before the train reached the points or the signal, which might in any case have been beyond the points.

The disc and crossbar was regarded by authority as an excellent signal because of its positive indications. But it had limitations on a sharp curve as at Windsor where, on the approach to the station, a driver would first see the disc displayed but on getting nearer to the signal after the line had turned through about 90 degrees the bar would then be seen so the signal was at danger. If the signal was at clear the converse applied. To overcome this problem Brunel devised a shape rather like a thin drum, a sheet of metal curved round

Fig. 6. In the pioneering days of railways many inventions were patented, among them a proposal in the early 1840s for a railway signal given by white lights only by day or night which by use of different combinations of lights would match the coded headlights of an approaching train. Thus if the driver of a train carrying three vertical lights saw a signal with three vertical lights he would know that the signal was intended for his train. It was not pursued. (Illustrated London News)

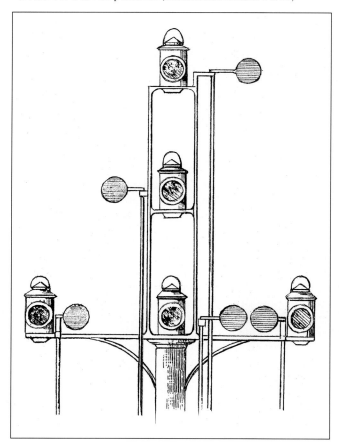

in a circle and presenting what appeared to be a flat face from whichever direction it was viewed. The drum was mounted on a horizontal pivot so that when swung up to a vertical position a disc signal was displayed instead. At danger it showed as a bar when first sighted right up until a train drew up in front of it. At clear the drum first showed as a vertical bar which while not a regular Great Western signal was understood by drivers to mean that it was clear, and as the train came near to the signal the disc would come into view.

The disc form of signal, as we have already seen, appeared on other lines. It was used widely on what had been the London & Birmingham Railway, merged in 1846 with the Grand Junction, Manchester & Birmingham and the Liverpool & Manchester to form the London & North Western Railway. Like the Great Western, drivers sometimes found it difficult to distinguish between up and down signals at a distance. But in this case the problem was different. The disc face on was a danger signal and if one signal was clear, that is edge on and invisible, drivers could not see whether it was the one which applied to them or the signal for the opposite direction. A cross bar was added below the disc but in the same plane as the disc. In no sense was this the Great Western disc and crossbar, for the crossbar and the disc were displayed together and neither was visible when turned to clear. The crossbar was added simply to distinguish up and down signals. The bar on down line signals had the same downward vertical extension at the ends as on the Great Western signals but up line signals had an upward extension at the ends. Thus if a driver of a down train saw the disc and crossbar with the crossbar ends turned up and no other signal he knew that it was the up line signal which was at danger. Some railways using disc or rotating board signals certainly did not share the Great Western philosophy of making signals easy to see from a distance. Often they were low down at about train height and on curves might not be seen until a train was close so that drivers had to slow down until they could see the signal.

There was no confusion with semaphore signals since the arms protruded from the left of the post and a signal seen with the arm to the right of the post was for the opposite direction. Even the double arm signals pivoted within a common post were quite distinct with the arms to left and right. Semaphore signals were gradually being adopted more widely, being installed on the Brighton line and the South Eastern by the end of the 1840s. As new lines were built from then on semaphores gradually become the predominant form but discs remained well into the 1860s on several lines before being replaced by semaphores. On Great Western broad gauge routes it was well after that.

Operating procedures in the 1840s
Yet even with these early beginnings towards a more

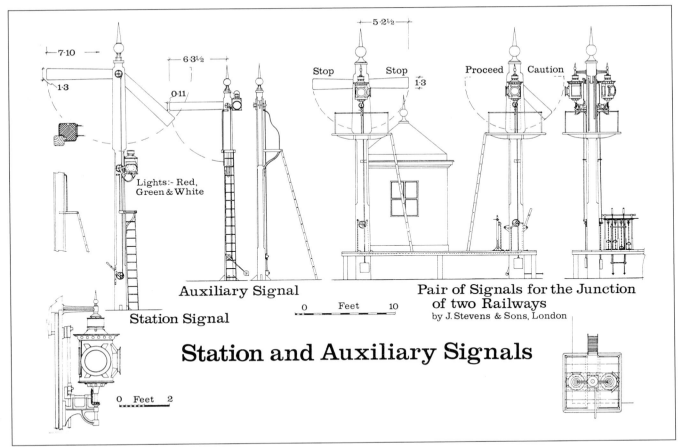

— 7·10 —

1·3

Lights:- Red,
Green & White

— 6·3½ —

0·11

← 5·2½ →

Stop   Stop

1·3

Proceed   Caution

Auxiliary Signal

0   Feet   10

Station Signal

**Pair of Signals for the Junction
of two Railways**
by J. Stevens & Sons, London

Station and Auxiliary Signals

0   Feet   2

Fig. 7. Detailed drawings of early semaphore signals. On the left is a back to back station signal, then a single auxiliary signal and on the right a set of junction signals. At converging junctions if the time interval rules allowed clearance of the principal signal whether or not a train was approaching, and a train approached on the secondary route the policemen were instructed to set the signal on the principal route to danger and to ensure that no train was approaching on that route before clearing the signal for the secondary line.

standardised form of signalling, railway operation in these middle years of the last century was still very much, and often literally, a hit and miss affair. The time interval system was the basic operating method on double lines but the exact time intervals varied although it is hard to see that a couple of minutes difference in the intervals would have much effect on a safe run or an obstruction standing in the way. On one or two lines only a caution signal was shown for ten minutes rather than a danger period. Generally the interval was five minutes danger followed by five minutes at caution. The Great Western at first adopted a very short interval of three minutes for danger and three minutes for caution but, soon after, the caution period was extended to seven minutes. A decade later, by which time there was a busy mix of passenger and goods trains all on the same tracks, the intervals were again altered to five minutes danger and five minutes caution behind a passenger train, and eight minutes danger and seven minutes caution behind a goods train. With the higher speeds of trains as more powerful engines were introduced, passenger trains reaching 50 or even 60mph, particularly on the broad gauge, the margin of safety with the shorter intervals if a train ahead stopped out of course between stations was being cut to the bone. Brakes were primitive and even Brunel, perhaps unwisely, had told a House of

Commons Select Committee in 1841 that they were 'tolerably useless' often with nothing more than a tender brake and perhaps hand brakes on one or two guard's coaches, so that stopping quickly was out of the question. From 60mph it would take a mile or more to stop even a lightly loaded passenger train. If a train broke down or ran short of steam it would take more than ten minutes for a guard or fireman to get back much more than $\frac{1}{2}$ mile if a following train was right on the ten minute interval to give warning with flags or lamps or a hand signal. But there was an added audible protection, for detonators placed on the rail top exploding to give a loud bang as they were crushed by wheels could alert a driver to danger. They were an invention by E. A. Cowper in 1841 and were quickly taken up on the GWR and soon by other railways. To protect a failed train one had to be put down at a quarter mile behind the obstruction, one at half a mile and two at threequarters of a mile, but by the 1850s the higher speeds demanded a longer warning and the GWR at least required the initial warning to be at one mile. Whether under time interval operation the man going to carry out protection could get to the full mile before another train approached was a matter of luck.

Other safeguards in the working of the time interval were also used, particularly the timetable itself or in standing instructions which forbade the sending of a low speed train forward at less than a given interval in front of a faster passenger or mail train. On the LNWR special goods trains were not allowed to be sent on less than 45 minutes ahead of a scheduled express. Advice about a following special train was often denoted by special tail lamps on the back of the preceding train. While instructions and intervals were one thing, what actually happened out on the line might have been something different as successful and safe operation depended entirely on the quality of the men on the locomotives and at stations. Today we take education for granted but in the 1840s and 1850s, as the railway building boom took off there was a vast call for staff to drive trains, to work at stations as porters, clerks, shunters and policemen and on all the other jobs that make up a railway. Many of the men employed on the railway came from the country, brought up in an agricultural environment with little education and certainly with not a shred of knowledge of running a railway. Even the managers and superintendents were

Detonators were among the early inventions in the 1840s in which small explosive charges in a flat metal container clipped to the rail head were set off by wheels passing over them, with the explosion heard by the driver above the noise of the engine. They were so successful that they survive in use to this day. (Illustrated London News)

learning the hard way by experience, while often staff could not read or write or tell the time by a conventional clock. Sand timers were sometimes used to show the passage of time to operate the time interval. Training of sorts was given, but often only briefly.

Instructions ignored

Some idea of operating methods of the time can be gleaned from accident reports as, for example, an inquiry into a collision at Harrow on the LNWR on 6 July 1850. Soon after 9pm the policeman at Harrow saw a train approaching from the London direction but realised it was a special of empty cattle wagons drawn by two engines instead of the 8.45pm mail train from Euston due at that very time. He turned on his signal to show a red light instead of the white light for the expected mail train and ran towards the engines calling to the leading driver that the train would have to shunt into the siding beyond the station to get out of the way of the mail train. The policeman ran on with his hand lamp but had only got about 500 yards beyond the back of the cattle train when he saw the mail train coming round the curve from Kenton. He waved his lamp towards the oncoming train and saw that steam was shut off but the mail train could not stop before running into the back of the cattle train, and several passengers were hurt. The cattle train was having to draw right past the station clear of the points and then reverse into the siding. It was a long train with 70 wagons on and unfortunately, as the engines of the cattle train moved forward after being told to shunt they must have snatched the train and a coupling drawbar was pulled out thus dividing the train. The back part was left where it was, but how did the empty cattle train come to be running so close in front of the mail? At Camden yard just outside Euston earlier that day there was heavy cattle traffic and the clerk was worried about the large numbers of wagons making it difficult to shunt. The empty special should have left after the 9pm mail from Euston had gone by and which would have had the special tail signals showing that a special was following. The driver of the empty cattle wagon train was told to move his train out of the way by the clerk, by implication meaning to go and wait on the departure track for the order to start. Instead the drivers of the cattle train took it as an instruction to go, so they did aided by the policeman at the entrance to Primrose Hill Tunnel who let them out on to the down line in contravention of the instruction not to allow cattle specials to run in front of mail trains less than 45 minutes behind.

Time interval dangers

Not all signals were placed at clear after the time interval had elapsed following the passing of the previous train. On the Great Western, signals, certainly at principal stations, were kept at danger until passenger trains at least were due. The time interval instructions regarding the display of caution or clear signals were applied if a second train approached within the time interval limits, but if no train approached, the signals would have been kept at danger until the next was due or whistled on approach. Clear signals did not always mean the line was clear. At Shrivenham, on the Paddington–Bristol main line, on the afternoon of 10 May 1848, the 12 midday express from Exeter to Paddington was running late because of delays on the South Devon Railway atmospheric system. More time was lost at Bristol and the 4-2-2 engine was slipping through Box Tunnel so that on leaving Swindon it was 21 minutes late. Without any means of communication none of this was known at Shrivenham. So at the scheduled passing time there of 3.3pm the Shrivenham policeman turned the up line disc and crossbar signal to clear. Then he had to deal with a down train due to call at 3.17pm but which in fact arrived at 3.10pm. The down line signal was 50 yards from the up so the policeman had to go across the down line to work the down disc and crossbar. While he was dealing with this the down train left at 3.17pm and two porters went over to the up siding which converged with the up line just short of the up platform. Just inside the siding was a wagon turntable leading to two short spurs away from the main line and also a connection across the up line to the down line.

There was not enough space to stand a wagon between the turntable and the trailing points with the up line although the porters wanted to move a wagon out of one of the spurs and on to the turntable. They were then going to put the wagon behind a cattle truck and horsebox which were already further along the siding. This meant pushing the cattle truck and horsebox by hand over the turntable towards the up line points which they did without regard to the signal for the up express. With the two wagons fouling the main line the up express approached at nearly 60mph, its driver having seen the clear disc at over a mile away. The policeman did not see what was going on in the siding and supplemented the disc with his arm outstretched to indicate clear. The driver did not see the wagons in his path until he was about 150 yards from them. There was no chance of stopping and the huge 4-2-2 smashed the wagons into a pile of debris at the platform end. The locomotive was little damaged but the coupling broke between the tender and leading coach and several carriage bodies were wrecked, killing four passengers. The written instructions to porters merely told them their duties and did not say how they were to be carried out. The clerk in charge who should have explained verbally what they should do or not do did not really understand how the signals worked himself. The inspecting officer seemed to be more critical of the late running of the express but did recommended that the two running signals should be closer and with thought for the level crossing which

was also worked by the policeman. The main suggestion was that one person should have charge of the main line and its signals and that nobody else should obstruct the main lines without permission. It was also recognised that the turntable should be moved to allow wagons to stand on each side without fouling the main line and that a self acting stop should be placed on the siding so that wagons could not get on to the main line except by proper authority. It was the beginning of calls for signalling controls to be concentrated in one position under the supervision of one responsible person.

Later that year, on 17 August, the York and Birmingham to Euston mail train ran into the Peterborough to Euston mail train stopped by a locomotive failure near Roade on the LNWR. The policeman at Blisworth had cautioned the York mail because of the Peterborough mail running ahead while the policeman at Roade had shown the York mail a white light having guessed the time since the Peterborough mail had passed. Although the Peterborough mail had passed Roade it had then stopped and the accident occurred. What emerged was the fact that both drivers of the double-headed York and Birmingham mail had only been on the footplate for two weeks, they did not have any firing experience, did not know the line, and knew nothing of how the locomotives worked. Both were under instruction by non-drivers. The inspecting officer strongly recommended that the timetable should be adhered to and that policemen and signalmen should look at the clocks. There were also comments about the abilities of drivers.

The newly developing inspectorate of railways under its inspector general was set up initially in 1840 within the Trade Department of the government but for five years, from 1846 to 1851, was hived off under a Commissioner of Railways before returning to the Board of Trade where it remained until 1919. Its Royal Engineer officers appointed as railway inspectors at first had no formal safety standards within which the new railways had to work. They were trained in what was considered to be good engineering practice but railways were a whole new concept. Recommendations following investigation of accidents or after inspections of new work were often based on what seemed to be good practice on other lines, and on what worked well and safely from experience already gained elsewhere.

The inspecting officers soon appreciated the advantages of the electric telegraph and were beginning to recommend its adoption following time interval accidents but they did not have the power to enforce such measures. Even for general control measures the telegraph was beginning to be an important aid. Without the telegraph even simple alterations to train services or emergency working could be thrown into disarray. Back in August 1836 a train from Newcastle to Carlisle had become a total failure on the down line with a broken axle. On the following day it had been arranged for a Newcastle to Carlisle down train to travel on the up line from Wetheral in the wrong direction to get round the failure. To ensure that the up line was clear a message was sent by horseman for an up train from Carlisle to shunt to the down line at Milton to wait for the down train to arrive. But the down train had not been told to leave Wetheral since the driver was waiting for the up train to come from Carlisle. Both trains were thus waiting for each other neither knowing what the other was doing. The electric telegraph was still in a very early stage and was not then available but had it been the problem would not have arisen.

The telegraph and the block system

By 1845 several railways were going ahead with the installation of the telegraph for general messages after the early trials on the GWR, curiously at that time mostly in the south. The LSWR, SER and part of the London & Brighton line had been equipped and within another two or three years it had spread to the north on the York & North Midland, York & Newcastle and the Newcastle & Berwick railways. Much of what became the East Coast main line was thus covered, always provided that competent staff were available to work it. By this time the instruments were becoming simpler and by the early 1850s Tyer's single-needle telegraph had been devised using only one line wire and an earth return and thus less costly than the multi needle instruments with several line wires. Moreover it could be a form in which the needle was held deflected pointing one way or the other towards a written message denoting the state of the line and whether it was clear or obstructed. By the end of the 1840s there were quite a number of variations in telegraph instruments.

Even on lines not generally equipped with the telegraph system, the potential danger in long tunnels if one train stopped inside on the time interval system led to an early form of block working in conjunction with the telegraph. The first to be worked in this way on the GWR was Box Tunnel from 1847. The telegraph instruments had something like a clock face with a single needle rotating to point at numbers or letters and driven by a clockwork mechanism released step by step round the face by electric impulses from the instrument at the far end. There was also a bell for calling attention but the procedure for sending and acknowledging messages was fairly complicated. It was though a form of absolute block in which not more than one train was allowed in the tunnel at one time and a second train had to be stopped unless the one ahead was clear of the tunnel. An additional feature was the provision of what in effect was a distant signal for up trains at Box station where a red and green board, presumably a fantail, was placed alongside the disc and crossbar for the station. The fantail actually repeated the position of the disc and crossbar at the mouth of Box Tunnel although the wording of the instructions of the time is a little ambiguous on whether the fantail showed caution at Box station when the tunnel disc was displayed, and danger when the tunnel crossbar was on. It was a start. Once again GWR experience with the telegraph was less than encouraging for a year later the telegraph was out of order and three years later the wires were reported without insulation and lying in water for part of the way. Maintenance clearly was not a top priority. It was repaired again however and the telegraph was installed at other tunnels on the system.

The telegraph, even on the one or two lines using it in the 1850s to operate a form of absolute block, was often regarded as an add-on to time interval and some railways felt that it instilled a sense of false security into drivers who might not take as much notice of signals as they should since they had been told from the telegraph station that the line was clear. Not all companies which installed the telegraph as an aid to train signalling saw it as a means of working an absolute block system but considered it more of a help in working the time interval system. Absolute block as we know it today means not more than one train in a block section on one line at one time. A block section today can mean the section of line between two successive colour-light signals capable of showing a stop aspect, or in mechanical signalling effectively the distance between the most advanced stop signal of one signalbox to the first stop signal of the next signalbox ahead. Forget for the moment the fine detail of overlaps and clearing points which will be discussed in later chapters. In the 1850s a block section as such had not been defined but broadly the time interval system operated from station to station or station to junction and junction to station. It was logical when the telegraph was installed as a general means of communication to provide instruments in station offices but perhaps only at principal stations with one telegraph circuit serving several stations. Messages were addressed to specific stations by code letters transmitted before the message itself. In the case of the telegraph for train signalling it had to be installed from station to station, or in the case of a junction remote from a station then at that junction as well. In the early 1850s the grouping of signal and points levers into a single frame had hardly been thought of let alone putting them under cover into a building for the specific purpose of train signalling. So where the telegraph was used for train signalling the instruments were at first usually in the station office where the policeman would be able to operate them and then go outside to get the pointsmen to change the points if necessary while he would clear the signals.

Auxiliary signals

Accidents on lines equipped with the telegraph did nothing to convince unbelievers that the telegraph was really a good thing. Moreover, what part of the line was covered by the telegraph and how far did it or previous practices go in overriding signals? We have already seen that the GWR had added a caution or fantail signal at Box station to repeat Box Tunnel disc and crossbar signal indications in 1847. At the same time, within the following few years, there appeared on many lines what were called auxiliary signals usually placed a few hundred yards on the approach side of a station, partly used to repeat the information given on the station signals and partly to give added protection to trains standing or shunting in the station. But how they were used varied greatly from place to place. On the LNWR they were first used towards the end of the 1840s. The board was painted green as a caution signal and when face on to a train was intended to mean that a driver could expect to find the station signal at danger and should be ready to stop. If the station signal was clear then no signal was displayed at the auxiliary. Some were even painted yellow rather than green for a short period. A few years later the auxiliary signals were altered to show a danger indication as well. If the main signal was at danger for an approaching train but the line was clear to the station signal then the auxiliary would show caution. If a train or part of a train was already standing at the station on the approach side of the main station signal then the auxiliary was to show danger. It was thus being used for two different purposes, today corresponding both to distant signals at caution because the home signal is at danger, and as an outer home signal at danger because of a train occupying the station ahead. The Great Western added auxiliary signals at a few places from the early 1850s but in the form of disc and crossbar signals meaning stop or proceed. Trains were expected to stop if they could at the auxiliary and then draw slowly forward to the main station signal. Auxiliaries were only required in a few places on the GWR because of the good sighting of most station signals.

The problems of telegraph aided signalling and how far the line was deemed to be clear were highlighted in a collision on the South Eastern Railway at Lewisham Old Station on the North Kent line on the evening of Sunday 28 June 1857 when one heavily loaded train ran into the back of another, killing 12 people and injuring 62. The South Eastern was very advanced for its day in having the telegraph available for its whole line by then. Much of the system was equipped with a general purpose 'correspondence' telegraph supplemented by a bell or 'alarum' to alert the signalmen, as the policemen were now beginning to be called, that a train message was about to be transmitted. The North Kent and Greenwich lines were equipped with the new Tyer's single-needle telegraph instrument and bells and gongs. Bells were used for sending audible signals in one direction and gongs in the other so that the signalmen would not confuse which adjacent signalbox was calling. The telegraph instrument needles pointed to one of two messages – all clear up, or stop all up – for up trains and similar messages with the appropriate wording for down trains. Each station office had four indicators, one each for the up and down lines to the next station in one direction and in the other. The signalman controlled the needles in the instruments for trains coming towards him, repeated on the instrument at the station to the rear. The signals themselves were still controlled from levers on the post or for the auxiliary signals by wire from a lever at the station. At Lewisham the main station signal (a semaphore arm), from Blackheath was just before the entry to Lewisham platform and no more than 281 yards further back was what was described as a distant signal which showed a red light for danger and white for clear. The lamp was of the rotating pattern.

It had been a busy day in the Kentish countryside that Sunday and the 9.15pm from Strood was well loaded and was being followed by the 9.30pm also from Strood. The first train was not booked to call at Lewisham but the line ahead towards New Cross was not clear. As this train left Blackheath the driver could not see the good white light of the Lewisham distant signal normally visible clearly as it was gas lit. As the train approached the distant signal it was showing red so the driver slowed down passing the red signal and stopped at the station signal just short of the platform. There were many people waiting on the platform and the stationmaster called on the signalman to go and ask the guard if there was room for any more passengers but the train was full. A porter was then called to look after the signals and telegraph. Meanwhile the following train had called at Blackheath. The guard asked the stationmaster if it was alright to go, he in turn asked the porter in charge of the telegraph who replied 'all right up' and the driver was given the white handsignal to start. As the train was about 1/4 mile from the distant signal the guards saw a red light and applied their handbrakes from about 20mph and then they saw a second red light. The driver said he thought he saw the distant signal showing white but when he got near it was more red than white. The train ran past the distant signal at danger and the second red light was the tail lamp of the standing 9.15 train. The 9.30 hit it at about 10mph. Most of the casualties occurred in a heavily loaded uncovered carriage whose buffers were about 6in lower than the adjoining brake van which over-rode it.

The absolute block system had been introduced earlier that year but on the basis that the section between stations was deemed to be clear unless a train was actually in the section. As a train entered the section the signalman sent the bell code to the next box ahead for the type of train, 2 beats – up North Kent train – and the signalman at the box ahead would acknowledge and move the telegraph needle from all clear up to stop all up. There was some dispute among the Blackheath staff on whether the signalman had received all clear up after the 9.15 train but when the 9.30 train arrived, without looking at the telegraph needle they thought it was clear.

Whatever the situation displayed on the block telegraph instruments the first train was at a stand between the distant and station signals at Lewisham, the distant signal should have shown red, but might have been partly turned to show an imprecise red, and neither train stopped at the distant signal. The inspecting officer, Lt Col Yolland, could find no reference in the SER's rule book of 1851, which was still in force, to distant signals because they had not then existed. However, a red light was a red light and meant stop and on no account pass it. There was a lack of discipline in which drivers were regularly passing distant signals at danger. The question then arose as to whether the telegraph indication of all clear up applied right to the next station and if the line was clear in nine cases out of ten, and on the tenth time the distant signal was at danger with a train standing between it and the station signal then drivers might be over confident. Several factors needed to be sorted out by the management but generally Lt Col Yolland thought the telegraph signalling of trains had worked well even if not supported by an adequate code of signals in this case. The report makes fascinating reading since the SER's General Manager fired back against the criticisms only to have Lt Col Yolland come back amplifying some of the detail of his comments.

Single line signalling in the early years

Although the first flush of railway building in the 1840s was for important routes expected eventually to carry heavy traffic and thus built with double tracks, by the late 1850s single line routes had appeared both as dead end feeder branches to main line junctions and as long single line cross country routes with a few stations laid out with passing loops. Clearly the potential for head-on collisions with trains running in opposite directions on the same track was a very real threat. This was recognised by the railway management of the time and special working instructions were adopted, varying according to the type of line. The shorter single ended branches without intermediate crossing places could be simply protected by instructions for operation by a single locomotive which merely shuttled backwards and forwards, establishing the one-engine-in-steam principle which survives today under one-train-operation rules.

This form of working could also be applied to longer routes with passing loops but it was very restrictive. To add flexibility the pilot engine system was used on some routes in which a designated locomotive for the specific section of single line had to be attached in front of all trains passing through. There was only one pilot engine for each section so the system was safe but it

meant that it had to shuttle alternately in each direction. This was the system used through the three-mile single-track Standedge Tunnel across the Pennines opened in 1849. The telegraph was also installed so that the staff at each end of the tunnel could advise each other on train movement. As a further precaution a wooden 'stick' or staff was made with the name Standedge Tunnel painted on it as a token which was also carried on the pilot locomotive. Soon it was realised that the wooden staff was an authority on its own without the need for a pilot locomotive. There was only one staff and no train was allowed to enter the tunnel without the staff. This too was inflexible where trains needed to follow in the same direction. The working was modified to allow engine drivers to be shown the staff and then to proceed into the tunnel, the staff actually being carried on a following train. This was where the telegraph came into its own for advice to be sent when trains entered and left the tunnel.

On the GWR one or two longer single lines were built in the 1850s, one off the South Wales route from Grange Court through Ross on Wye to Hereford, and the other from Westbury to Weymouth. Both were equipped with the telegraph and operated on the telegraph and written train order system. Trains worked to the timetable with scheduled crossings at passing places unless in the event of late running they had to be altered in which case the drivers concerned were given a written order authorising the altered working. It was a system which did not last for much longer than the mid-Victorian years in Britain but survives to this day on a few lines elsewhere in the world.

Another written form of authority was devised for single lines in the late 1850s, working in conjunction with the wooden staff and known as staff and ticket. The single staff as employed at Standedge or elsewhere had the drawback that drivers merely shown the staff and instructed to proceed actually carried no form of authority. The ticket was evolved to give them that authority. The tickets were pre-printed with the name of the stations between which they applied and the train details were written in. The tickets were kept in a locked box unlocked by a key on the staff so that provided the rules were obeyed and the driver was actually shown the staff when being given a ticket the system was basically safe. The signalman was required to take not more than one ticket out of the box at a time and to withdraw the staff had to re-lock the box. This prevented tickets being taken out when the staff was not present. Where trains were due to follow one another all but the last in a group were shown the staff and given a ticket, and the final train actually carried the staff through the section. Thus by the 1860s single lines had much more basic protection than double lines and generally the systems worked well although they were not foolproof, particularly if there were errors in telegraph messages on lines worked on the telegraph and train order system, as we shall see.

Chapter 3

DEVELOPING TECHNOLOGY IN MID-VICTORIAN YEARS

AS TRACK LAYOUTS gradually became more complicated, particularly at the larger stations, it was beginning to be realised that a more formal method of changing the position of points switches and turning signals to danger or clear was needed. At the smaller wayside stations one policeman could undoubtedly look after a station signal for each direction and the switches for a crossover between the main lines and the points into sidings. Each item was worked from its own lever at the site, the term lever here meaning any means of operation such as a lever pulled, pushed or turned, a handle, or a capstan turned to wind wire to operate a more distant signal. Signals were normally worked by handles near the bottom of the post but the auxiliary signals two or three hundred yards or more away might be worked by a lever at the station through single wires with a balance weight or double wires pulling in opposite directions for danger or caution and clear. Points were often worked from weighted levers alongside the switches (the actual switch rails or blades). Where there were several points in a layout the policeman would often spend much of his time racing from one to another and would certainly not be short of exercise.

At the larger stations additional men known as pointsmen or switchmen were employed to assist the policeman in changing points but they had to have good communication between them which, as we have seen, was limited. Often in this situation it would have been no more than hand or audible signals or calling from one to another. While this form of operation was destined to survive in Britain until the end of the 1880s when the last vestiges of such basic methods were swept away by parliamentary legislation, it survives in a few places abroad. In Switzerland, even as late as the 1960s, one of your authors was watching the working at a major narrow gauge junction with numerous tracks and realised that a switch pressed on the track diagram in the station office merely turned on a light in a hut out in the yard approach to tell the pointsman to change the points by hand lever for the specified route. When he had done so he pressed a switch in his hut which put on a light in the station office to say that he had changed the points. Then the stationmaster cleared the signal. The procedure was identical to that in Britain 100 years earlier but then there were no electric light indications.

Clearly the grouping of signal and points levers either near each other or in a common operating lever frame had advantages since it avoided the need for pointsmen to walk or run round the layout to reach the individual levers of points or in some cases signals. Signals were less of a problem as there was usually no more than one main signal applying to an approaching train, often sited at or near the station itself, supplemented by an auxiliary signal perhaps three or four hundred yards out from the station and worked from a lever near the main signal with wire connection. At converging junctions the signals applying to the main and branch lines could be located near each other, perhaps well beyond the converging points and drivers should have known that if the signal applying to them was at danger they would need to stop their train short of the points and clear of other lines. Indeed some of the early rule books were quite precise on the need to stop before obstructing other lines. Yet this very imprecise location of where to stop left drivers considerable latitude in bringing their trains to a halt. This ambiguity was also seen in rules applying to the use of the auxiliary signals whether as a warning signal of conditions ahead or as an outer-stop signal. On a number of lines drivers were required to stop at an outer auxiliary signal seen to be at danger but were permitted to pass it and continue towards the main signal if they could see that the line was clear, effectively making it a permissive signal, rather like the French *disque rouge* (red disc) which survives in a few locations today.

Lever frames
The grouping of levers working related signals and points together in a common lever frame did not help to mark precise stopping points since the policeman and his pointsmen still might have had only one main

signal to control. Also, other points linking sidings with main running lines were often still worked from hand levers at the points themselves. Bringing levers together in a frame, sometimes on a raised staging, provided the opportunity to link the working of the levers to ensure that conflicting indications could not be given, in other words interlocking. Gregory, in installing his semaphore signals at Bricklayers Arms Junction in 1843, had brought the levers together and arranged them to work with attachments to the stirrups so that conflicting levers could not be changed together. Atkinson, the engineer of the Manchester, Sheffield & Lincolnshire Railway, had devised a point rod detector between signal wire and points at Retford in 1852, another form of interlocking designed to prevent signals giving conflicting indications to the lie of the points. The following year another engineer, C. F. Whitworth, patented his version of a signal wire/point slide detector in the signal wire run so that the signal would only move to clear if the points were set for the relevant direction. This system was later employed in the 1860s on many routes as 'wire locking' but in no sense was it proper interlocking between levers. It survives today as an essential part of the safety equipment in mechanically signalled areas in conjunction with lever interlocking.

Interlocking

The installation of a lever frame with a limited form of co-working in which the points lever also worked the

Ideas on achieving interlocking between signal and points levers were many and varied. This curious looking framework was patented by Ransomes & Rapier. The sliding lock bars were moved by hand to lock some levers and release others. (National Railway Museum)

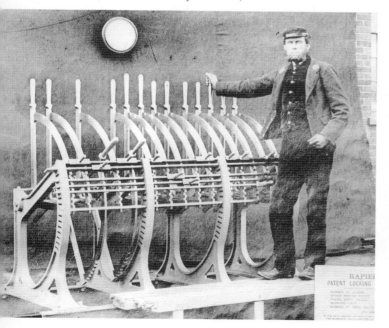

relevant signals at Bricklayers Arms Junction in 1856 devised by John Saxby, was a start towards what became lever interlocking. However, it was the installation four years later of a fully interlocked lever frame controlling points and the related junction signals at Kentish Town Junction, between the Hampstead Junction line and the North London Railway (today's Camden Road), ready for the opening of the NLR's line via Kentish Town and Hampstead Heath to Willesden High level, which laid the foundations for the signalbox of the future. One of the early entrants to the signal engineering business, Stevens & Sons, had originally provided a stirrup/lever frame to operate the new Kentish Town Junction which was ready for opening in October 1859, but the inspecting officer, Col W. Yolland, refused to sanction the arrangement since by deliberate action it was possible to clear conflicting signals. Austin Chambers, an employee of the North London Railway with an interest in signalling, devised equipment to add on which prevented a lever from being pulled until other levers on which it was dependent had completed their movement or were already in the correct position. It was sufficient to convince Col Yolland that here was a new safety development and he authorised the new junction to open on 2 January 1860. Three days later Chambers patented his interlocking arrangement, the first to be recognised since then as true interlocking.

The signalling pioneers

John Saxby was to become prominent in the signal engineering business from then on and took out a number of patents for various equipment forming interlocking lever frames and other safety devices. With John Farmer as partner he founded what became the signal engineering firm of Saxby & Farmer in the early 1860s. Both men had been employed by the London, Brighton & South Coast Railway during the 1850s, the former as a foreman carpenter in the Locomotive and Carriage Department and the latter as a traffic manager. Clearly they could see a future for more formal signalling methods and equipment. Saxby had already taken out a patent in 1856 to cover his method of simultaneously working signals and points, applied by him at Bricklayers Arms Junction in 1856. By the early 1860s Saxby and Farmer felt that their future lay wholly in providing signalling equipment rather than continuing their employment with the LBSCR. They were among a number of names who came to prominence with inventions and developments in the signal engineering field in following years which led to the establishment of notable firms in the provision of signalling equipment at home and overseas for the rest of the century. We have already noted Edward Tyer who at 22 took out patents for electrical signalling devices on locomotives, and developed the single-needle telegraph instrument which was at the heart of block signalling. He went on to found the firm that bore his name which became synonymous with equipment for double and single line block instrument and token systems. In future chapters we shall meet others, C. E. Spagnoletti, telegraph superintendent of the GWR, William Sykes, an employee of the London, Chatham & Dover Railway and Charles Walker, telegraph superintendent of the South Eastern Railway to name but a few of the men who advanced the cause of railway safety with their inventions and developments.

Although standards for equipment had hardly been thought of in 1860, by the end of the century the general shape and size of semaphore signals, for example, had developed within fairly common parameters, but detail differences in the exact size and proportion of signal arms, the shape of the spectacles through which the night time light indications were shown and the style of posts or masts often identified the products of the individual firms. Not all railways used equipment from the independent signal engineering industry and had their own signal engineering workshops. Notable in this respect was the Great Western Railway whose Reading signal workshops provided that company with most of its signalling equipment, and continued to do so until the 1980s, long after the Great Western had ceased to exist in 1948 to form the Western Region of British Railways.

The signalbox makes its appearance

Just into the 1860s Saxby & Farmer built two signalboxes with interlocked frames at the approaches to London Bridge on the South Eastern line. They were impressive structures built on legs spanning the tracks

The early 1860s signalboxes by Saxby & Farmer spanning the tracks approaching London Bridge. The signals were carried on masts above the signalboxes and did not necessarily represent the actual places at which trains had to stop if the signals were at danger. (Illustrated London News)

The interior of one of the 1860s signalboxes on the approach to London Bridge. Already much of the equipment can be recognised and was little different from that in mechanical signalboxes which survive today. The lever frame is obvious, at the far end are the Walker pattern block instruments and bells, the solid fuel stove only needs a kettle and a teapot and the booking lad is working the telegraph with the register books to his right to record the times at which trains were signalled in and out of the block sections. (Illustrated London News)

and with signal posts elevated above the signalboxes, each carrying an array of semaphore arms for both directions. Because of the complexities of the layout the front faces of the semaphore arms had initial letters of the tracks to which they applied D – Dover, G – Greenwich, NK – North Kent and the routes to which they led beyond. But with the concentration of arms above the signalbox again it meant that the signals did not necessarily mark the exact stopping point particularly for the converging routes. Although the semaphore signals themselves were of the developing standard three-position type they were worked as two-position signals, showing only danger with the arm horizontal and a red light at night, and caution with the arm inclined down at 45 degrees and showing a green light at night. It was felt that caution should be exercised by drivers when passing through junction points and therefore signals should show no more than caution as a reminder. Indeed at many other running junctions in mid-Victorian times semaphore arms were limited to displaying no more than danger or caution

The 'hole in the wall' signalbox installed by Saxby & Farmer in 1861 at London Victoria for the Brighton company's side of the station. (National Railway Museum)

Saxby & Farmer produced signalling schemes for a number of principal stations in the 1860s including Charing Cross. Note the black stripe on the front face of the signals as well as the back. (National Railway Museum)

indications and even at GWR running junctions certain disc and crossbar signals were altered to show green caution lights at night. Even today with modern fail safe signalling controls many colour-light junction signals show danger or no more than caution as trains approach as a reminder to drivers of speed restrictions through points, so the practice is hardly new.

Inside, these signalboxes approaching London Bridge had many of the features which became a hallmark of mechanical signalboxes from then on. The lever frame would certainly be familiar today but the block telegraph existed throughout the SER main line by the 1850s so there were also block instruments and bells or gongs on the block shelf, there were oil lamps for illumination, the coal fired stove for heating, and the desk for the train register for the booking lad to record the times of the block signals and the passage of the trains. This was the beginning of the signalbox as we know it and which survives with modern improvements in diminishing numbers. This was the beginning of the great leap forward in signalbox development and Saxby & Farmer were involved in several projects during the 1860s including London Victoria, with what was known as the 'hole in the wall' signalbox which was little more than a platform recessed in a wall overlooking the tracks, Brighton and Charing Cross in 1864 and Cannon Street two years later.

Thus by the 1860s the basic ingredients had evolved to provide a simple and safe formula for the operation of trains, with the concentration of signalling controls within a signalbox under the jurisdiction of one man, interlocking between levers to ensure that signals could not show conflicting indications between themselves and between signals and points, and the block telegraph. This was the medium of communication that could provide a space interval between trains instead of the erratic and unreliable time interval system which had fast become the normal operational method.

Resistance to the block system

Anyone who thought that the new technology would be quickly adopted right across the country to improve rail safety was doomed to disappointment. Signalboxes at major stations or junctions were one thing, signalboxes, interlocking, and the block telegraph at hundreds of rural country stations, even on principal main lines were something else. Clearly cost was one factor but the number of train accidents in the 1850s and 1860s was not that high. In 1854–6 the annual average of passengers killed in train accidents was only ten, a rate of around 1 in 10 million passenger journeys. But in 1861 no fewer than 46 passengers were killed in train accidents, 32 of the 56 train accidents that year being collisions involving passenger trains. Of those 46 unfortunate victims, 38 lost their lives in just two major collisions, 23 plus 176 injured in the collision at Clayton Tunnel on the Brighton main

Many of the 1860s signalboxes were characterised by elevated structures on legs with the signals on masts above the roof. This one was at Beckenham Junction but the Brighton line had numerous examples, some of which survived into the 20th century, although in later years the signals were re-located on ground level posts and more in keeping with the geography of the layout. One snag with the high signals mounted above the signalboxes was the difficulty in seeing the arms in fog, especially if the signalbox was located beyond the convergence of two lines at a junction. (National Railway Museum)

line on 25 August 1861, and 15 plus 317 injured when a North London Railway excursion from Kew hit a ballast train shunting at Kentish Town just a few days later on 2 September, the latter arising from a lack of interlocking. It was perhaps a pity that Col Yolland had not insisted on interlocking here as at the nearby Kentish Town Junction when the line opened 18 months earlier but he must have felt that running junctions were more important than crossovers and siding points.

Clayton Tunnel had been worked by a form of absolute block with messages sent from one end to the other by the electric telegraph for about nine years. Here was 'modern' technology failing to stop a major accident. Railway management was split on the desirability of adopting new equipment feeling that it was a waste of money. The time interval system worked well enough provided the policemen and the drivers kept to the discipline of its rules. New equipment would only serve to make staff less attentive.

In the Clayton accident there was an added factor. In the up direction there was a distant signal controlled by the man at the south end of the tunnel to indicate whether the tunnel was clear as an advanced warning of his own flag signal. This signal was based on one of Whitworth's developments and was known as a Whitworth signal. It was a disc distant signal but to ensure that it was restored to danger after the passage of a train it had an automatic replacement feature operated by trains themselves. Alas for modern technology it was not totally reliable and thus not fail safe. The signal was about 300 yards from the south end portal of the tunnel and the signalling was under the control of two signalmen, one at each end of the tunnel, provided with a hut, red and white flags, a single-needle telegraph instrument linked to the opposite end, and at the south end a wheel to work the wire to the distant signal both to turn it to clear and to turn it face on back to danger. The man at the north end also had a semaphore signal at the tunnel entrance although that was not relevant to the accident. The automatic replacement feature of the south end distant signal consisted of a 'treddle' depressed by the train wheel flanges and linked to a vertical arm in a lineside box which when lifted released a horizontal slide bar attached to the signal wire which was pulled to normal by weights and restored the signal to danger even if the wheel controlled by the signalman was still turned to the clear position.

Although the Brighton main line between London Bridge, Victoria, Croydon and as far south as Reigate (today's Redhill), was worked by the block telegraph, south of there to Brighton the time interval system was still in force except through Clayton Tunnel. Three passenger trains were booked to leave Brighton for London on that Sunday morning, 25 August 1861 timetabled to leave at ten-minute intervals, at 8.5, 8.15, and 8.25am. The first, an excursion from Portsmouth, was running late so they actually left, according to a number of witnesses, at 8.28, 8.31 and 8.35, far closer together than claimed by the Brighton stationmaster

and well in breach of the minimum five-minute time interval rules. The procedure for signalling a northbound train through the tunnel was for the man at the south end to send 'train in' by a beat to the left on the telegraph needle which repeated on the north end instrument and rang the telegraph bell there once, as the train entered the tunnel. When it emerged at the north end the man there sent one beat to the left and one to the right to the south end which gave two rings on the bell, this signal being acknowledged by a beat to the right from the south end. That was all there was to it. The telegraph instrument applied both ways with different code beats for both tracks and was not of the pegging type where the needle was held deflected so there was no reminder to either man of what signals had been sent and neither was required to keep a record book to show what times signals were sent and received.

The first train correctly entered Clayton Tunnel with the distant signal showing clear and was telegraphed to the north end as 'train in'. Unfortunately, the replacement mechanism had failed to turn the distant signal to danger. To the horror of the south end signalman, Killick, the second train was seen approaching with steam on and the distant signal still clear and no indication from signalman Brown at the north end that the first train was out of the tunnel. Killick left his hut and waved a red flag towards the oncoming train which passed him and entered the tunnel. Then, at that moment Killick received the 'train out' signal from Brown for the first train and immediately gave the 'train in' telegraph signal for the second and showed a white flag to the guard as the rear of the train passed into the darkness of the tunnel. Meanwhile Killick had managed to restore his distant signal to danger. The evidence of the two signalmen disagreed on what followed. Killick maintained that he asked Brown on the telegraph whether the second train had left the tunnel. Brown thought he was referring to the first train and replied yes. Brown claimed that a message sent by Killick said that the train was not out, to which he replied yes, followed by Killick continuing that 'they are run into each other'. Whatever messages had been sent, as the third train had approached the tunnel Killick thought the second train was out of the tunnel and showed the driver of the third train clear signals. But unknown to Killick, the driver of the second train had in fact seen his red flag despite passing the distant signal showing clear. He managed to stop with the back end of the train about 220 yards inside the tunnel. He had then started to reverse slowly back to the tunnel mouth just as the third train entered at about 25mph. Catastrophe was unavoidable and 23 passengers out of the 589 on the two trains were killed and 176 injured in the collision in the confines of the tunnel.

Capt H. W. Tyler who inquired into the accident was

scathing in his criticisms, not so much of the misunderstanding between the two signalmen but of the Brighton stationmaster who had not observed the minimum time intervals between departures, the lack of the block telegraph between Brighton and Clayton Tunnel, of the inadequate telegraph equipment between the north and south ends of the tunnel, and the lack of registers for recording the times of telegraph signals and the passage of trains through the tunnel. Also for not noting departure times at Brighton, the lack of a semaphore signal at the south portal of the tunnel, and the lack of maintenance of the automatic replacement equipment which should have restored the distant signal to danger. Seemingly it had not been oiled. He recommended the adoption of the block telegraph system which would provide the means of communication to operate a space interval between trains (the block system) and a minimum of three telegraph instruments to be provided for the signalmen at each end of a telegraph section, one for each track to act as a signal to show the state of the line labelled 'line clear' and 'line blocked' arranged so that the needle could be pegged pointing to one or the other, and a third instrument with a bell attached to act as a means for sending messages to ask leave for a train to pass, to receive the reply and to communicate in other ways. Thus where a signalman operated the block telegraph to stations or junctions on both sides of him there would be six telegraph instruments for him to look after.

Here was the foundation for space interval signalling, but like interlocking, was it welcomed with open arms? The reply from the LBSCR company secretary Frederick Slight gives an insight into the thinking prevalent in many railway boardrooms at that time:

'My Board feel bound to state frankly that they have not seen reason to alter the views which they have so long entertained on this subject, and they still fear that the telegraphic system of working recommended by the Board of Trade will, by transferring much responsibility from the engine drivers augment rather than diminish the risk of accident.'

The LBSCR Board did though somewhat grudgingly accede to the recommendation for the telegraph to be installed between Brighton and Hassocks Gate, 'to give it a fair trial', despite the fact that the telegraph was already in operation at the London end of the line.

We have looked in some detail at the circumstances of the Clayton Tunnel collision because it was already being worked by the telegraph to provide a space interval. It failed because it was an island in the midst of operating methods on the approaches which were totally unregulated and even if the regulation time intervals had been observed at Brighton would not have guaranteed similar intervals between the trains as they approached Clayton Tunnel. While the one basic telegraph instrument provided a means of communication between one end of the tunnel and the other, experience was beginning to show that one instrument was simply not adequate and there had to be supplementary instruments to give a permanent display of the state of the line. The official report by Capt Tyler into the Clayton Tunnel accident was demanding for its day and, with his colleague Col Yolland, recommendations following accidents and in inspections of new works hit hard in the pursuit of railway safety. But their hands were tied when it came to new developments in safety. They could recommend, they could persuade, but they could not insist even though Parliament was concerned at safety standards and however much the railway inspectorate huffed and puffed, new signalling and safety developments came slowly.

Chapter 4

THE ACCIDENT EFFECT

BY THE MID-1860s the main line passenger railway in the British Isles was marking its 40th birthday. The operational mileage had reached half of its ultimate total by the early 1900s of roundly 23,000 miles and its passenger carryings were heading for 300 million a year. Its potential as a mass carrier had yet to be developed for, in later years, passenger journeys increased at a rate far and away greater than the increase in mileage open, to a peak of 1,500 million passenger journeys a year in the early 1900s. That of course reflected far more frequent train services and longer trains carrying more people than were run in the 1860s. But in the 1860s most trunk railways had no more than two tracks, one for each direction with extra tracks and sidings at a few major stations where faster trains could pass slower ones. Passenger trains running at up to 50mph, even perhaps 60mph in a few instances like the GWR broad gauge, had to share tracks with goods trains running at no more than 20 to 25mph with heavy loads (150 to 200 tons was heavy for the 1860s considering the small, lightweight locomotives with no more than a tender handbrake supplemented by a handbrake in the guards van). Even with a service of no more than perhaps 20 trains a day in each direction at a main line country station, with speed differentials between passenger and goods or mineral (coal etc) trains, late running, engine defects, breakdowns, and the like and it soon becomes clear that the potential for trains to run within a few minutes of each other was considerable.

With hand-worked points and no interlocking it was very clear from the early days that one set of facing points leading to another track or into sidings, forgotten by a pointsman and left in the wrong position might easily lead to disaster if a train were to be switched to the wrong track. Facing points were thus avoided like the plague except for running junctions at the divergence of routes or at principal stations where additional platforms allowed two or more trains to be at the station together so that branch trains or main line stopping trains could make connection with a long distance express. Goods trains needing to be sidetracked to be overtaken by a faster passenger train normally had to gain access to refuge sidings by drawing forward beyond the siding points which were trailing to the main line, then stopping and setting back through the points into the sidings. At some stations the sidings were on one side of the line only so that a goods train needing to shunt out of the way had to cross from one running line to the other over a crossover. The crossover points between the two main tracks were also arranged to be trailing to the normal direction of running on the main lines so that again the goods train would have to go beyond the crossover and then set back through it to the opposite line, where if no train was due it could wait until the overtaking train had passed on its original track. But if trains were due to pass on both tracks then the goods train would then have to shunt off the opposite line by going forward into the sidings. Then when it was clear for the goods

Fig. 8. *A typical country station layout with basic signals in mid-Victorian years. Signals and points would have been worked by hand levers at the site. As interlocked lever frames spread so a signalbox would have been provided from the 1870s or 1880s either on the platform or probably at the right hand of the station near the sidings, and new stop signals (home signals) would have been installed at the approaches to the station, and later distant signals as well. Compare this layout with Fig. 18.*

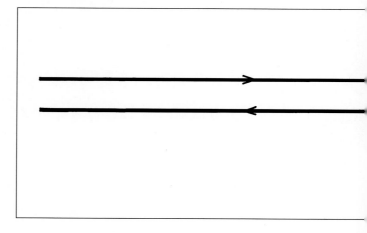

to continue on its journey it would have to reverse the procedure. All this took time and apart from the rudimentary signalling and communications systems which might or might not be available, operating procedures laid down by instructions detailed the minimum times to be allowed for a goods train to be let out ahead of a timetabled more important train, and particularly express and mail trains, so that it could not only reach the next station with a refuge siding but had time to shunt off the main line before the more important train was scheduled to reach there and overtake it.

Staff at intermediate stations and sidings not only had to allow for the normal timetabled trains but also had to be on the watch for extra trains, both passenger and goods, at times of heavy traffic. True, if the general telegraph was available as distinct from the block telegraph some stations at least could be advised that an extra train was to run, the expected time, and the type of train. Even where lines were equipped with the general telegraph, transmission and receiving equipment was often installed only at the principal stations so that local country stations would be kept in the dark unless they had a written or verbal message passed to them by train if there was time or, as we have already noted, by additional or special tail lamps on the train immediately ahead of the special train. During daylight it might have been a red flag or board and at night an extra red light. Trains in any case carried tail signals to show that they were complete, normally a red light showing to the rear and also side lights showing red to the rear and white to the front so that the driver and fireman could look back and see that the train was intact. Locomotives also carried headlights, not for the driver to see where he was going and whether the line was clear, but to provide an indication to others at stations ahead particularly at night as a warning of approach. Usually distinctive lamp positions denoted passenger or goods trains but different colours, as for example green or blue, sometimes in combination with white were used to show the intended route of the train. Practices varied from railway to railway depending on the operating need to distinguish trains in this way.

Working conditions

Railway operation at this period provides a fascinating insight into social conditions of the time and how the various railways treated their employees. Foremost was the point that the railways were public companies created by Acts of Parliament with capital provided by shareholders who put money into the railways for the reward of dividends and an increase in the value of their capital. It did not always work out like that but the expectation was there. Thus railway management always had to recognise that whatever actions they took company profit and shareholders' dividends could not be far from their minds. Operating costs thus had to be kept as low as possible and investments in new capital equipment had to be weighed against an increase in receipts. Would new equipment bring in more receipts without incurring additional costs and make more money for the proprietors?

Regrettably the attitude of too many top railway people in the mid-Victorian years was that additional safety equipment could not be justified financially. The North Eastern Railway for example in 1865 had received estimates of around £38,000 to install the block telegraph throughout its 800 or so route miles which the general manager felt unable to recommend. Others genuinely thought that more safety equipment would lead to greater slackness by drivers and signalmen in carrying out their duties and relying too much on the new equipment. This it must be added, was an attitude which still prevailed 100 years later, otherwise how can one explain the reluctance to provide drivers with added safety aids in the 1960s and later? Discipline among the company's servants, and observance of the rules and procedures were the basis for railway operation as indeed they had to be. The problem was that often procedures and equipment were inadequate. As we noted in the previous chapter, Capt Tyler criticised the system in the Clayton Tunnel collision far more than the men who confused each

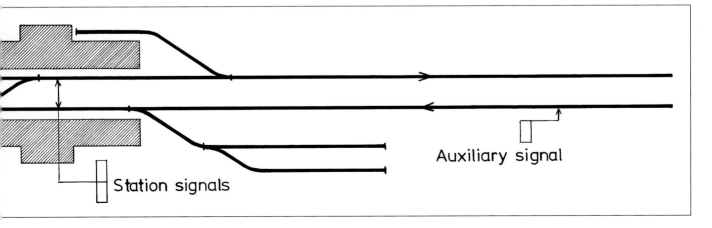

other at the tunnel portals. Tyler also criticised the long working hours of the two signalmen who were just starting a 24-hour shift in order to get a day off and to change turns. Railwaymen then and for many years after often worked long hours and even in the 20th century, while basic shifts were normally no more than about eight hours, staff have often been required to work overtime – indeed at times of staff shortage or extra traffic overtime has been a regular feature and almost incorporated into regular shift patterns. Even today, additional working hours are often still required to get time off and to allow for shift changes for round-the-clock working if relief staff are not available. Certainly in the 1860s, 12-hour shifts were often the norm and staff on lines open 24 hours a day had to cope with day and night working, helped in later years by three eight-hour shift patterns although even then it was often difficult for some signalmen to adjust to night shift working every third week. How many night-time accidents would have been avoided not just in the 1860s but in the following hundred or so years if added safety equipment had been provided as soon as it had been developed and proved? Just how much would LNWR shareholders for example have gained had the company adopted the absolute block system in 1855

London Waterloo was gradually enlarged but almost to the end of the Victorian years was hampered by the restrictions of its four approach tracks. This 1860 view of 'A' box with semaphores taking over from the Martin discs on each side, makes an interesting comparison with the 1890s expansion of the station approaches illustrated later. (National Railway Museum)

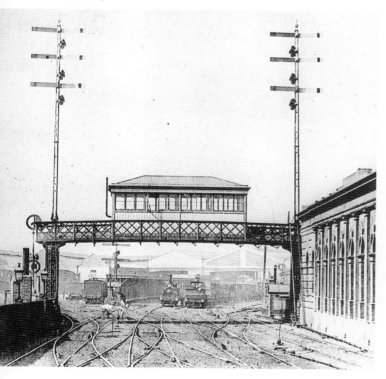

when it installed the electric telegraph for train signalling between Euston and Rugby but as an adjunct to time interval working, and as a result was still appearing in the Board of Trade's accident statistics, including a collision at Harrow in 1870 where damage to engines and stock was extensive and eight people were killed. Thirty more years were to pass from 1860 to 1889, with many more collisions, and 887 passengers killed in train accidents before the reluctance of too many railway companies to adopt new safety equipment was over-ridden by the force of law when Parliament acted.

As the 1860s dawned, signalling on railways was very mixed with the variety of early lineside signals, despite the foresight of George Stephenson who in 1841, wrote to the Board of Trade suggesting that it was desirable to have uniformity of signals. There were rotating discs, rectangular boards, Brunel's disc and crossbar types, fantail boards, and three-position slotted post semaphore arms providing in their different ways the indications to drivers to stop or go on at caution or proceed at speed, apart from hand, flag, or lamp signals. The early types were gradually giving way to semaphores though and Brunel's disc and crossbar signals were largely confined to GWR broad gauge routes with semaphores used on the GWR standard gauge routes particularly in the West Midlands and to the North West. Even on the GWR, as disc and crossbar signals fell due for renewal on broad gauge routes to the West, they were replaced by semaphores.

Block instruments develop

As for the extension of the telegraph system it was here that the railway inspecting officers still encountered resistance from many railways to its adoption for train signalling. Like lineside signals, where the telegraph was used for train signalling block systems it took several forms largely because new developments and improvements even from the same pioneer supplier brought new working procedures.

As we have already seen, the original Cooke & Wheatstone telegraph of the late 1830s had a somewhat cumbersome instrument using five needles deflected to right or left to point along a diamond grid to denote individual letters, and it inevitably needed a multitude of line wires between the instruments. It was this type of instrument that was used for the pioneering GWR telegraph experiments in the 1840s and by a few other railways including the Norwich & Yarmouth line from opening in 1848, not just for general messages but also for authorising train movement between stations on the single track route. This was the first railway to be operated throughout, as distinct from isolated tunnel protection as at Clay Cross, Box, etc, by a form of block telegraph. By the 1860s simpler systems were in use especially Edward Tyer's single-needle instrument in which messages were spelt out by defined movements of the needle to the left or right to represent the letters of the alphabet. The American, Samuel Morse, by 1844 had developed his now world famous Morse code of dots and dashes, or in sound or light short and long pulses, to represent letters for transmission over the telegraph system, which in the needle instruments was denoted by a movement to the left for dot and to the right for a dash, the letter B for example, being represented by a flick of the needle to the right and three flicks to the left to represent the Morse dash, dot, dot, dot. This was the type of instrument used at Clayton Tunnel.

The single-needle instrument had also been developed as a pegging type in which the needle could be held deflected to left or right pointing at a labelled indication on the face of the instrument. This was achieved by retaining the operating handle of the controlling instrument to right or left with pegs, hence the term 'pegging' a block instrument still sometimes used today. This was later arranged so that the handle was retained either by spring pressure on a notch on the handle shaft or by a spring bolt engaging a slot. Sometimes movement of the needle was coupled with operation of a single-stroke bell. The single-stroke bell as a separate instrument had been developed by Charles Walker, the SER's Telegraph Superintendent, by 1851 and from then on bells alone had started to provide a form of communication between SER stations to allow a rudimentary type of block system to be operated. But as new developments came so different sections of line were equipped with different instruments. In the Lewisham accident noted in Chapter 2 bells were used in conjunction with pegging single-needle block instruments. Elsewhere on the SER bells accompanied what was called the correspondence telegraph which was sometimes used to signal trains.

By 1863 Charles Spagnoletti, the young Telegraph Superintendent of the GWR, had devised a disc block instrument in which a disc instead of a needle swung either way between the electromagnets in such a way that the legend 'line clear' or 'train on line' appeared at a window at the bottom of the block instrument face. When neither indication was pegged up the disc hung in the neutral position so that half of each legend appeared, to denote line blocked. The unusual feature of these instruments was that each legend was called up by pressing on a key, one for each indication, which was held down by sideways movement of a wire frame which passed over the key shank. It needed a deft movement with thumb and fingers for a signalman to operate the instrument with one hand. It was first used on the Metropolitan Railway from opening in 1863 and on the GWR although only sparingly from 1864. Once adopted more widely in the following decade it was long lived and this type of instrument survived not only on the GWR until it ceased to exist in 1948 but until recent years.

Also in 1864, Walker of the SER had devised another form of block indicator in which the state of the line was shown by miniature representations of semaphore signals, with two arms one each side of a central post just like some of the full size signals out on the line. The left one was painted red and the right hand one painted white. The red painted arm denoted the section towards the station or signal box ahead and the right hand arm the line from that station. With the red arm horizontal the instrument denoted line blocked or train on line so that the signalman knew that his own semaphore signal outside should show danger. The red arm lowered at 45 degrees denoted line clear to the station ahead and thus his signal outside could also be clear towards that station. The white arm showed the signalman the state of the line coming towards him and he controlled the indication of the semaphore arm at the signalbox or station at the entrance to that section (which would have been a red arm), the white arm on his own instrument repeating that indication as a

Walker pattern two-position block instrument with block indicators for each direction in the form of signal arms. The arm on the left controlled by the box ahead is showing 'line clear', the arm on the right showing 'line blocked', or 'train on line'.

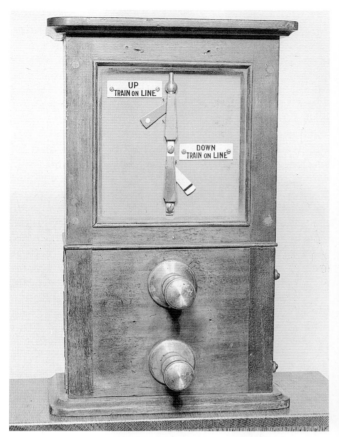

LEFT *Edward Tyer was one of the pioneers of the single-needle telegraph instrument adapted for use as a block instrument with the needle pegged to point at 'line clear' or 'train on line' indications or equivalent wording. Tyer also produced a two-position instrument with signal arms to denote the state of the block section.* RIGHT *After the Abbots Ripton collision in 1876 when snow blocked the arms of the slotted post semaphore signals, the Great Northern Railway, and a few others, adopted the balanced semaphore arm, centre pivoted, and usually known as somersault signals, to avoid any interference from snow. This pair formed Welwyn North up distant signals in the 1930s. (J. R. G. Griffiths)*

reminder of what actions he had taken. Gradually the Walker semaphore block instruments were extended to most of the SER's routes by the mid-1870s and some survived for the next 90 years. Similar instruments are still in use on parts of the old Glasgow & South Western line between Dumfries and Kilmarnock today. Of course, safe operation relied totally on the strict observance of the operating procedures for these instruments and on the signalmen seeing the trains and ensuring that they had actually left the section of line to which the block instruments applied, before giving the 'train out of section' signal to the signalman at the next signalbox to the rear, and having another train sent forward. The human element was very much a part of that operation.

Note that we have used the term signalman, for by

the 1860s, it was becoming recognised on some lines at least, particularly where trains ran fairly frequently, that train signalling was important enough to warrant a man solely devoted to it, rather than a policeman who looked after station security generally. Gradually the role of the policeman as part of railway operation declined and while they have survived as a security force the term policeman disappeared from railway terminology in the sense from which it originated. The police nickname 'bobby', derived from the Metropolitan Police in its newly constituted role in the 1830s under its new chief, Sir Robert Peel (Bobby's men), stuck not merely to the railway policemen of the pioneer railway years but also to the newly evolving signalmen and has continued to the present time.

Like the variety of equipment for both the signals and the new forms of telegraph instruments so the actual methods of operation varied from line to line. In many, the telegraph instruments, if provided at all, were situated in the station office, sometimes in the stationmaster's office, which at the time was the logical place to have them. Usually the fixed signals, fixed in the sense that the signal was a permanent structure rather than a man with flags, if they were provided were somewhere near the station building just a short walk away, and only if points needed changing, would somebody have to walk to the point levers. If there were no fixed signals or if flag or hand signals needed to be given to a passing train to supplement the fixed signal indications, then again the person authorised to give the signal only needed to walk out of the office on to the platform. Problems began to arise when signals and points started to be controlled from levers grouped together in a lever frame, either with or without interlocking, perhaps on an open stage or enclosed in a cabin which might have been at one end of the platform and possibly not close to the station office. Then divided responsibility began to creep in between the person who operated the signals and the person who operated the telegraph. Where new types of purpose-built signalboxes were erected there was usually little problem for the telegraph instruments and the signal and point levers were within the one building worked by one man, as we have seen with the new signalboxes outside London Bridge.

The LNWR two-mile telegraph

One of the first installations of the telegraph on a long length of a major trunk line specifically for train signalling, as distinct from general messages, was on the London & North Western following the plans of Edwin Clark of the Electric Telegraph Company in 1854. Installation started the following year and the system was in operation between Euston and Rugby soon after. It was known as the two-mile telegraph because the telegraph stations were placed more or less two miles apart, not just at the normal passenger and goods stations such as those at Harrow, Watford, Boxmoor (today's Hemel Hempstead), Tring, Bletchley and the like, but also at locations which were never passenger stations. These included Nash Mills (between Kings Langley and Hemel Hempstead), Bourne End (between Hemel Hempstead and Berkhamsted) and Hanslope (between Wolverton and Roade) which, in later years, had signalboxes that not merely survived until the 1960s electrification and resignalling, but one or two notable signalling locations of today which have sweeping crossover junctions between the multiple running lines away from the geographical constraints of station platforms, bridges or other lineside structures.

Telegraph stations were equipped with telegraph instruments, each having two indicator faces and single-needle indicators, one instrument for the up and down lines to the next telegraph station in one direction, and another similar instrument to the next telegraph station in the opposite direction. Note that by this time the terms up and down were coming into general use to denote the direction of trains on each line. In England the up line was usually but not exclusively towards London, although on cross country routes which line was up and which down was a matter of compromise. Each instrument had two operating handles, one for each needle, and the signalmen at both ends of a section controlled movement of the needle.

The centre neutral position of the needle was labelled 'line blocked' and was normally used only for emergencies. When diagonally to the right the needle pointed to 'line clear' and diagonally to the left to 'train on line'. When no train was in the section the needle stood at 'line clear'. The 1855 instructions to signalmen refer to bell signals to call attention of the signalman at the other end, both when a train entered a section and when it left, presumably operated by a separate tapper key, although the instructions are not precise on this. The telegraph needles could be 'flicked' to either side by a quick movement of the operating handle at either end or could be pegged to remain pointing at 'line clear' or 'train on line'. Normally the man at the entry end was required to peg the instruments at 'line clear', and when a train entered the section the man at the exit end was responsible for pegging 'train on line'.

The procedure was straightforward. Unless a train was already in the section between two telegraph stations the line was deemed to be clear and the telegraph instrument would be showing 'line clear'. As a train approached the signalman at the entrance to the section he rang the bell at the telegraph station at the exit of the section and flicked the telegraph needle from side to side. In acknowledgement the signalman at the exit end held his needle over for a second or two which was repeated on the instrument at the entry end. The first signalman then gave two slow and distinct ticks to the left to denote a passenger train or an engine on its own, or three ticks for a goods, coal or cattle train, repeated back by the signalman at the exit end and then he pegged the instrument at 'train on line' showing both on his own instrument and on that at the entry end. When the train passed the telegraph station at the far end and left the section, the signalman there called back to the signalman at the entrance end by ringing the bell and flicking the needle from side to side and when acknowledged, the exit end man held his needle on 'line clear' which was repeated back by the man at the entrance end who pegged the instruments at 'line clear'. The 'line blocked' indication could be displayed either by not pegging the instruments to right or left or could be initiated by train crews or anyone else breaking the telegraph wire at specified telegraph poles where a thin wire loop in the telegraph circuit was taken down to be within arm's reach. The instructions to engine drivers explained how the wire was to be broken in the event of a train breaking down or for an accident. In the telegraph stations if the needles showed 'line blocked' and could not be flicked or pegged the signalman was to assume the worst and place his signals at danger to stop following trains.

The LNWR two-mile telegraph could have been used to institute absolute block working, 'absolute' meaning not more than one train on one line in one section at one time. But it wasn't. For all the expenditure and its potential to take a great leap forward in rail safety all it did was to provide an add on to time interval working, for the system was used permissively, that is more than one train was permitted to be on one line in one section at one time. And not just two trains, but three or four or however many may have been close to one another at a given time. Each telegraph station had a semaphore signal for each direction showing the normal three positions, danger, caution, and clear. Only if the section ahead was clear was the signal to show clear. If there was already a train in the section ahead, then the normal time interval indications were shown on the signal, danger for three minutes and then caution but this indication remained displayed as long as there was a train in the section ahead. If a second train approached less than three minutes after the first had entered the section all that happened was that the danger signal was displayed but the signalman then instructed the driver to proceed at caution into the already occupied section telling him that there was a train on line. If the initial three minute time interval had elapsed the semaphore signal was placed at caution and trains were allowed to enter the section without further advice with drivers expected to slow down in accordance with time interval rules and to expect a train ahead. When a second (or more) train entered the section the signalman called the man at the exit end by the bell to signal the second train on the telegraph even though the indicator was already at 'train on line'. The signalman at the exit end had no option as there was no offering and acceptance procedure as in later years. He unpegged the needle to receive the flicks of the needle to tell him the type of train approaching, repegged it at 'train on line' and recorded details of the trains entering the section on a slate and ticked them off as they passed him and left the section. Only when the last of a group left the section did he telegraph back to say the line was clear. It should be added that the slate had a long life on this line for even as late as 1949 the only way a signalman at the principal terminus, the great London Euston, had of knowing which platform was occupied was by a chalked note on a blackboard!

Even as early as 1856, commenting on a collision between two goods trains at Berkhampstead (the then current spelling) on 13 October 1855, only weeks after the introduction of the two-mile telegraph, Lt Col George Wynne, the Board of Trade's inspecting officer, was scathing in his criticism of it:

'The London and North Western Railway Company have, within the last few months, at great expense, put up a telegraphic communication to all the stations on the southern part of their line, with the professed purpose of signalling their trains between stations.

The object which one would suppose a Railway Company desired to attain in erecting so expensive an auxiliary as the telegraph would be to hinder trains from running into one another, by preventing one train from going on to a certain length of railway, until it had been ascertained that the preceding train had passed off it; such is the mode adopted in working trains through tunnels with the aid of the telegraph, and such is in general the notion conceived by all persons conversant with the subject, when they hear that the telegraph has been established at all stations, as an element for working the train safely; but the London and North Western Railway Company have adopted quite another system, they allow any number of trains to pass on a telegraph length, taking only the ordinary precaution of exhibiting a danger signal for five minutes, and a caution signal for five minutes longer after each train has passed.'

One of his main criticisms was of the inadequate brakes on both passenger and goods trains which meant that the rule requiring drivers to 'have their engines in sufficient command to be able to stop at any moment' was impossible to comply with. Even with a light load the colliding goods train in the Berkhamsted accident could not stop within 600 yards before running into the train ahead which had just finished shunting. In summarising the rules he concluded seemingly with an element of sarcasm:

'I may perhaps have mistaken their application, or overlooked some element of safety they contain; but the view I entertain of the new system, for which very great expense has been incurred, is that the elements of danger are greater than in the old.'

Matters were not helped because the LNWR could not make up its mind on the function of distant or auxiliary signals. As originally devised on the LNWR they showed green when the main station signal was at danger and no signal at all when the station signal was at caution or clear. Then during 1855 the auxiliary signals were ordained to show danger as well, meaning that the line was obstructed or there was a train ahead towards or at the station, but unfortunately no-one thought to issue new instructions at the time to show how the signal was to be interpreted. By 1860 the rules stated quite categorically that auxiliary or distant signals 'are to show the same as the main signals. If the main signal is at danger then the distant must show danger. If the main signal is at all right then the distant must show all right'. No mention though of a distant indication if the main arm was at caution. That, though, was not the final word for by 1870 Rule 50 said that 'distant signals must not be used when the main signals are turned on (danger) merely to indicate that a train is on the length to the next telegraph station; they are only to be turned on to danger when there is a train or other obstruction occupying the line at or near the station'.

The permissive aspect of the two-mile telegraph might have provided communication between stations and given a more positive indication of 'line clear' if the section ahead was free of trains, but as soon as another train was admitted to an already occupied section there was no more safety than with the basic time interval system relying solely on good sighting of a train ahead, and the ability of the driver to slow down or stop his train before catching up or hitting a train ahead. That required better brakes than were available then. It was hardly surprising that collisions between telegraph stations featured fairly regularly if not frequently, showing that the system for much of the time was operated with reasonable safety levels. Collisions occurred at Blisworth in April 1858 involving a mail train running into a goods train, at Atherstone on 16 November 1860, also involving a mail train running into a goods train, though here with purely time interval working and no telegraph, and at Sudbury (Wembley) in December 1865. There, a passenger train ran into the wreckage of two goods trains on the adjacent third line (built in 1859/60 between Bletchley and Primrose Hill to provide an independent track for goods trains to keep them off the main line but worked without the telegraph). Then there was the serious accident at Harrow on 26 November 1870 when an express passenger train rammed the back of goods wagons on the main line, killing the driver of the leading of two engines, and seven passengers, while 41 passengers were injured. To some extent it was an action replay of the 1850 accident because a goods train which preceded the express was to shunt into the refuge siding at Harrow out of the way. It had passed the Harrow distant signal at clear but the main signal was at danger although as he passed the signal unable to stop in time the signalman called for him to shunt into the siding which meant going past the points and backing in. As the driver applied steam a coupling broke behind the rear of the seventh wagon. It was foggy and as the crew tried to recouple the train there was a massive collision as the 5pm express from Euston to Liverpool, Manchester and Birmingham ran into the goods train. Strictly speaking the cause was signals passed at danger primarily at Wembley where all signals were at danger, but also at Harrow where the distant and main signals were at danger for the express, the collision occurring just north of the station. The signalman at Wembley, who had only been employed as a signalman for three weeks after one week's instruction, tried to put down fog signal detonators when he saw the express was not stopping but could not get them on in time.

Lt Col Hutchinson the inspecting officer concluded that the driver of the train engine was not driving with the caution that was needed in foggy weather, and that he might have thought he had seen a clear handsignal at Wembley as drivers were in the habit of paying more attention to handsignals than semaphores. In practice it seems that drivers tended to pass the fixed signals at danger because normally they indicated only that the section ahead was occupied and, in accordance with the rules, they could be verbally cautioned and then instructed to proceed, so why stop? Certainly the working was lax but this Harrow collision was enough and the LNWR agreed to bring the permissive system to an end by adopting absolute block. At last the inspectorate had its way. The LNWR had always claimed that it ran too many trains on the southern end of its line between Euston and Rugby to operate absolute block because it could only function if more than one train could run between any pair of telegraph stations. The report into the 1870 Harrow accident showed that on average there were four trains an hour in each direction and with proper organisation, Lt Col Hutchinson thought this was well within the capacity of an absolute block system.

The Inspectorate's limited powers

One reason why the railways were able to continue with pioneer systems that were unsafe and refused to adopt newly developing safety systems on grounds of cost was that the Railway Inspectorate had no powers of compulsion. Legally at that time they did not even have powers of investigation because the 1840 Regulation of Railways Act provided powers of inspection but no powers to stop openings, and the 1842 Act gave them authority to postpone openings if they were not satisfied as to the safety of the equipment provided, but still did not authorise them to hold inquiries into accidents. However the inspecting officers insisted on accident investigation to make recommendations for future safety, hence the many calls for absolute block working, interlocking, and better brakes, but they had no power to make the railways adopt these measures. All these aspects of their work were given legal sanction in the 1871 Regulation of Railways Act but still no authority to enforce their recommendations. Then a spate of major accidents in the 1870s and 1880s was destined to change attitudes in high places.

On its own 1870 was bad enough, for apart from accidents in which signalling or the lack of it was a cause there were several accidents in which rolling stock faults resulted in derailments. In all that year 66 passengers were killed in train accidents and 1,084 injured. Two months before the Harrow collision, the up 'Irish Mail' was wrecked at Tamworth when the signalman at the north end of the station was expecting a goods train and had his points set from the main line into the loop platform line with his distant signal showing clear and his main signal correctly showing clear into the loop itself. At the south end of the station was a crossover from the loop platform back to the main line but the platform line continued into a dead end siding which terminated just short of a drop into the River Tame. There was no telegraph in operation but it was being installed and although the main signal at the north signalbox was interlocked with the crossover to the platform line, there was no interlocking with the distant signal, which had no separate indication to show that the points ahead were set for the loop. Thus the 'Irish Mail' was diverted to the platform line and through the dead end siding into the river. At least the train had a better brake than many others, operating on most of the coaches. This accident brought the usual remarks about lack of the block system and inadequate interlocking.

In August 1873 an overnight special express bound from Euston to the Scottish Highlands was badly damaged when the rear of the train left the track at Wigan after the 16th coach was derailed on facing points at the approach to the platform, killing 13 people. There were suggestions that the points might have been moved under the train but in fact the points lever was interlocked with the signal lever concerned and there was no evidence to show that the levers had been moved. But as an added precaution the inspecting officer, Capt Tyler, recommended the use of a lock, bolting the point blades firmly home while trains were passing over them, in effect what became a facing point lock.

The miserable tale of woe for the railways in 1870 was not yet over for in December at Brockley Whins, between Sunderland and Gateshead, a facing platform crossover between the two running lines was left set in the wrong position leading to a head-on collision between a down goods train and an up train, killing five people. There was only one platform face here and down trains had to cross to the up side, hence the facing crossover, but there was no interlocking between points and signals. Col Yolland criticised not the unfortunate pointsman who had failed in his duty but the company management who were wholly to blame. They had been warned 15 years earlier of the dangers of heedless action by pointsmen. Interlocking would have prevented this accident and two others, including that at Kirtlebridge in 1872 on the Caledonian main line between Carlisle and Glasgow, when a northbound express hit wagons being propelled on the up line and diverted over a wrongly set crossover to the down line. The other was at Manuel near Bo'ness Junction on the Edinburgh–Glasgow line in January 1874 when signals for an express were clear, at least at first, while shunting was taking place into sidings off the main line, and only placed at danger as the express approached and inevitably could not stop before hitting the goods train which was still partly on the main line. In both accidents there was considerable loss of life, 12 at Kirtlebridge and 16 at Manuel and once again there was a repeat of the call for the block system and interlocking. At Manuel the block telegraph was being installed and was commissioned just 12 days later, but too late to prevent disaster.

Two head-on collisions on single lines which were already equipped with the telegraph, between Norwich and Brundall on the Yarmouth line in September 1874, and on the Somerset & Dorset line near Radstock nearly two years later in August 1876, perhaps suggested to those reluctant to adopt new equipment – and some lines were still worked by time interval without any form of telegraph – that it was not infallible. Both accidents have been well described elsewhere, suffice it to say here that the Norwich accident was caused by misunderstandings between several staff at Norwich resulting in a telegraph message being sent without being signed to Brundall to send a train forward when another had already been sent away from Norwich towards Brundall. The five-needle telegraph still in use might have been adequate in the late 1840s but not in the mid-1870s. As for Radstock, altered passing arrangements were made by telegraph from the office at Glastonbury which was not in direct communication with all the stations but the stations were staffed by inexperienced youths quite unsuited to their jobs. One did not really understand how to work the telegraph, and another had allowed a train forward into the single line section without signalling it on the telegraph or using the block instruments and then accepted a train in the other direction. Clearly something more positive than the telegraph was needed for single line protection. While the wooden staff, or staff and ticket, which we have already met, provided a degree of added security on some lines the challenge was taken up by Edward Tyer who again produced out of his inventive hat a new piece of equipment, the electric tablet instrument which he patented in March 1878 and which will be described in more detail in Chapter 7.

Snow changes block working
How weather conditions came to influence the development of block signalling can be seen in the after effects of a collision at Abbotts Ripton (as it was then spelt) on 21 January 1876, on the Great Northern main line between Huntingdon and Peterborough, a line on which the absolute block system was in use but not by the method familiar today. Following earlier practice with time interval operation the block section was normally clear except when a train was actually in the section. This meant that the signals governing entry to the section were only placed at danger after a train had entered the section ahead to stop any following train. Once the first train had been telegraphed back as leaving the section at the far end the signals at the entry end were again placed at clear regardless of whether another train was due or expected. The block instruments used by the GNR were of the single-needle type pointing to line clear to the right and train on line to the left, and they worked in conjunction with bell signals. Although the signalmen at both ends used the operating handle to send dial messages only that at the

far end of the section actually pegged the instrument. With the instrument pegged at line clear from the box ahead called C, the signalman at box B on receiving the signal from the box in his rear, A, that a train has entered the A–B section gave two beats on the bell to C, the 'be ready' signal. When the train passed B and entered the B–C section the signalman at B called attention with one beat on the bell to C, followed by two ticks of the needle to the left for a passenger train (or three for a goods or cattle train or five for line blocked, the latter after giving five beats on the bell). The man at C acknowledged the ticks and pegged the instrument at train on line. As the train passed C and left the section the man there called attention to B by the bell, gave two ticks to the right on the needle and after acknowledgement by B, C pegged the instrument at line clear. The only way a signalman could stop another train entering the section was to send the line blocked signal to the signalman at the entry end. The train was considered to be out of the section as soon as the last vehicle had passed the main signal post. The signals in use on the GN main line were still the old slotted post three-position semaphores dating from time interval days, but only working in two positions at danger, horizontal, and clear when the arm was almost vertical. Of course, only two light indications were given, red and white.

In the late afternoon of 21 January 1876 a very heavy but fairly localised snowstorm swept north east from the Bristol Channel, no more than about 40 miles wide from north to south, but causing damage to the Great Western Railway, the LNWR, the Midland and reaching the Great Northern by 5pm between an area roughly bounded by Huntingdon in the south to Peterborough and towards Grantham. The snowflakes were large and with temperatures hardly above freezing the snow built up on telegraph and signal wires some of which had a three-inch coating of frozen snow around them which caused wires to break in places. Snow also built up around signals. The first sign of trouble was when a coal train which left Peterborough at 5.53pm for the south failed to stop at danger signals at Holme where it was to shunt out of the way of a following Scotch express. The coal train crew however had seen the signals at clear to continue. The Holme signalman could not contact the next signalboxes at Connington and Wood Walton as they did not have the speaking telegraph, so he block signalled the train to Connington, where it was passed on to Wood Walton and then to Abbots Ripton. There the coal train driver had seen the distant signal at clear with a white light but he was given a red headlamp signal from the signalbox and instructed to set back into the refuge siding. The Abbots Ripton signalman had not cleared the coal train off the block indicator for the up line from Wood Walton and naturally expected the Scotch express, which he knew from telegraphic advice had

left Peterborough 21 minutes after the coal train, to be held at Wood Walton. But just as the front wagons and the locomotive were about to get clear into the siding the Scotch express charged out of the blizzard and hit the front wagons and piled up. Alas the signalman did not immediately respond by sending the line blocked bell and needle signals to the next box to the south at Stukeley to stop any down trains but tried to send a telegraph message to Huntingdon without success. Meanwhile, with great presence of mind, the crew of the coal train took the undamaged engine and with others ran forward towards Huntingdon showing a hand danger signal and were able to warn the oncoming 5.30pm King's Cross–Leeds express just after it passed Abbots Ripton down distant signal showing clear. However, with handbrakes alone it could not stop before hitting the wreckage of the first collision. In the combined wreck 13 passengers were killed and 53 injured. Yet at Wood Walton all the signal levers were at danger for the Scotch express. At Abbots Ripton they were also at danger and so too were the down line levers after the first collision but the second collision, 11 minutes later, was not prevented.

Back view of a somersault signal showing the supporting bracket holding the arm pivot, and the operating rod from the spectacle casting and down rod. (J. R. G. Griffiths)

The weather had played a trump card, for the snow had either blocked the slots in the posts of the semaphore signals and prevented the arms from rising to the horizontal danger position or had masked the red glass with a covering of snow so that the light appeared to be white. Capt Tyler who investigated was sparing in his criticisms of most of the men involved but was critical of the lack of adequate brakes particularly on the Leeds express. His main recommendation was for signals normally to stand at danger and only to be cleared when a train was actually due to run. It led to an abandonment of the open block form of absolute block to a system where trains were offered and accepted before the signals were cleared. It also brought to notice the then practice of giving 'line clear' once the first train was out of the section. In clear weather there only needed to be the thickness of the main signal post between a clear block section and the back of the preceding train. In practice at Abbots Ripton there was a space of only 68 yards from the main signal to the fouling point of the goods train which Capt Tyler felt was too close and he suggested that this weakness should be looked at. In following years a quarter of a mile was adopted as a clearing distance beyond the first stop signal which had to be kept free of obstruction before line clear could be given to the signalbox in the rear. Another result of the Abbots Ripton collisions was the development of a balanced semaphore signal arm, which became known as the somersault type, used by the Great Northern and one or two smaller railways, even abroad in Australia. Isolated examples have survived well into the 1990s.

Armagh and its aftermath

Gradually, by constantly thumping the table, the railway inspectorate was getting safety systems adopted but success was slow and the pressure to adopt the absolute block system, interlocking and continuous brakes, meaning brakes which operated throughout a train, at least on passenger trains, was still falling on a few deaf ears. Brakes were a problem since, in the 1870s, continuous brakes meant a mechanical form in which brakes on several adjacent coaches could be worked from one position. Power brakes operated by vacuum were just seeing the light of day and in America George Westinghouse had developed his quick-acting compressed air brake. Even by the 1880s still there was reluctance by some railways to go for lock, block, and brake as it has been termed. This was especially true of some local and rural lines which were barely profitable. In Ireland the Great Northern Railway of Ireland operated the main line between Belfast and Dublin and a number of branch and cross country lines including one from Armagh to Newry which crossed the Belfast main line at Goraghwood Junction.

The date of 12 June 1889 has gone down in railway history as the turning point when old, unsafe railway operating methods were brought into the full glare of publicity right across the British Isles. At Armagh that morning excited children were boarding an excursion train bound for the coast at Warrenpoint due to leave at 10am. The 15-coach train was composed of six-wheel coaches each weighing about 10 tons, and with a load of nearly 40 tons for passengers, the total weight was around 240 tons including the engine. This was a diminutive 2-4-0 tender engine and it was a daunting task facing its driver, the first $3^1/_2$ miles out of Armagh being on a steep rising gradient of 1 in 82 increasing to 1 in 75. He had asked the stationmaster for an assisting engine but his request had been dismissed with scorn. The train was certainly fitted with power brakes, the simple vacuum type in which a vacuum was created throughout the brake system in order to apply the blocks to the wheels. But this was totally useless if the brake pipes were uncoupled for any reason, and even at this stage in railway development, the time interval system was still in use. The excursion got away at about 10.15am but just yards from the summit of the incline it stopped as the engine just did not have the power to get the train to the top. The general manager's chief clerk, who was in charge of the train, decided to split it into two. The engine would take the first five coaches forward to the next station, Hamiltons Bawn $1^1/_2$ miles on, and leave them, returning for the remaining ten coaches. The handbrake was applied in the guard's van at the back, the vacuum pipe was uncoupled between the fifth and sixth coaches, the screw coupling was unhooked and so too were the side safety chains. The rear part was on its own. As an added precaution stones were placed under the wheels of the back coach but as the engine started with the intention of going forward it must have just set back and touched the buffers. It was enough. The ten rear coaches started to roll back and despite the efforts of the staff they could not be stopped. At a fairly high speed $1^1/_2$ miles back they met the oncoming 10.35am train from Armagh, proceeding under normal time interval rules. It does not need a description to imagine the result other than to say that 78 passengers in the excursion train died, 22 of them children, and 260 were injured. Even the 10.35am train was split in two by the force of the collision and the rear portion started to run back having lost the brake by the parting of the vacuum pipes but fortunately, this was stopped by the handbrakes applied by the guard and driver. The latter had a remarkable escape for his engine overturned and he leapt on to the tender. If only fail-safe brakes had been in use, if only the block system had been in operation, if only an engine of greater power or an assisting engine had been provided.

Parliament had had enough. The 1889 Regulation of Railways Act gave the Railway Inspectorate the backing of the law to order the absolute block system, interlocking, and automatic continuous brakes at least on passenger trains. The Act in itself did not impose these devices for the Inspectorate were able to allow some relaxation where appropriate. At certain large stations passenger trains were permitted to run at low speed under permissive or station yard regulations into platform lines already partly occupied by another train after being stopped and signalled forward by a subsidiary signal. On certain branch lines, mixed trains of passenger coaches and goods wagons were allowed with automatic brakes operating only between the engine and the coaches while the goods wagons were without continuous brakes and a guards van ran at the back.

It was the end of the beginning of railways and the beginning of the basic safety structure for the modern railway which we know today. But it was a long time a-coming for it had taken over 60 years from those pioneer railways at Darlington and Liverpool.

LEFT *Basic signalling in the 1880s at a country station with just a home signal in each direction, a crossover between up and down lines, and not seen in this view, a distant signal for each direction. The home signal seen close to has only a single red spectacle which, in the 'clear' position, has moved away from the light to display a white clear light. From 1892 green was ordained to be the new night-time indication for 'clear' meaning the provision of double spectacles for the two colours. (National Railway Museum)*

RIGHT *Not all semaphore signals served as indicators of whether the block section ahead was clear, or as route indicating signals. On certain lines alongside mountain slopes in Scotland they were used as rockfall indicators. They were linked to wires on the lineside designed to break if rocks rolling down the mountain slope crashed through them and obstructed the line, releasing the arm back to danger.*

TOP *In the last years of the GWR broad gauge, finally taken out of use in May 1892, a West of England express passes a disc and crossbar signal set at danger for the opposite line but its driver has the reassurance of a white (clear) flag held by the signalman out of the signalbox window. Once interlocked lineside signals had become widespread from the 1870s and 1880s, the practice of displaying flag, lamp or hand signals by signalmen did not disappear and they supplemented the indications of the fixed signals. Even in recent times, a wave of the hand more informally often served the same purpose.*

ABOVE *Although GWR disc and crossbar signals survived in the West Country virtually until the end of the broad gauge, often with semaphores interspersed, further east semaphores had become the normal pattern. New semaphores not yet in use and bearing crosses on the arms meaning they were to be ignored are seen here near Old Oak Common for the standard gauge relief lines in the last years of the broad gauge. (L&GRP)*

Chapter 5

THE STANDARDS ARE SET

T HE PASSING OF the 1889 Act did not finally change things overnight but it set a target to complete the adoption of the absolute block system and the installation of interlocking. This was backed by the force of law and the Railway Inspectorate breathing down the necks of the last few railways without these safeguards to ensure that installation was actually in progress and was going to happen. In some cases, even with the major companies, just one or two lines still had to be upgraded for much of the work had already been completed well before compulsion. Indeed, contemporary reports show that by 1889 some 90 per cent of points and signals in Britain were already interlocked to some extent, that block signalling was being observed on nearly 100 per cent of double-track passenger lines and on about 90 per cent of single lines. Also, about three quarters of the locomotive and passenger rolling stock fleet was equipped with some form of automatic continuous brake. The Act was intended to ensure that all companies, large and small, complied with the minimum requirements, but in so doing it also established new standards, many of which are still in force today, and underlined the need for further improvements.

Some standardisation had already taken place. Following a series of accidents and incidents caused by confusion over bell signals between signalmen from different companies using differing bell codes, a standard block telegraph code was adopted in 1884. Likewise, following the accident at Abbots Ripton on the Great Northern Railway in 1876, when slotted signals had become clogged with snow, and with the adoption of block signalling in place of the time interval system most railways had begun to abandon the three-position slotted semaphore signal – horizontal for danger, sloped downwards at 45 degrees for caution, and out of sight vertically within the post for clear – in favour of two-position semaphore signals showing either a horizontal arm for danger or sloped downwards at about 45 degrees (the actual angle varied between companies), for clear. Even on the Great Western the disc and crossbar signal was becoming a

thing of the past. Its standard gauge empire in the West Midlands had always had semaphore signals but even on the last of the broad gauge routes to the far South West, finally converted to standard gauge beyond Exeter in May 1892, semaphores were fast taking over although disc and crossbar examples survived into that decade in the West. By the end of the century they had gone. Surprisingly, a disc and crossbar signal survived into the new century, not on the GWR but on the

Disc and crossbar signals were not uniquely confined to the Great Western. The Somerset Central used them and this one at Midford just survived into the new century as an indication of whether trains had to call to pick up passengers. (L&GRP)

Somerset & Dorset Railway which was run jointly from 1875 by the London & South Western and Midland railways as it linked those two companies at Poole and Bath. The S&D disc and crossbar signals originated from the primitive years, before joint operation, on the Somerset Central Railway. Once semaphores had been adopted by the new partners the disc and crossbar signals had been retained not for block signalling purposes but at a few non-crossing stations on single lines to indicate whether trains booked to 'call if required' had to stop for passengers.

No longer too was there a need then for the green light for caution at night, for the danger and clear indications were, as they had always been, red and white. The use of a green light with the arm at caution on many junction signals dating back through the previous four decades survived in a few places, but in others the night-time 'clear' indication had reverted to white lights, especially as interlocking and facing point locks had reduced the risks of points being incorrectly, or not fully, set. With separate signal arms for each route at facing junctions and signals now located where they applied, at the approach to facing points or short of converging junctions so that drivers were given more precise stopping points when signals were at danger, it was up to drivers to know which way the trains were going and to know the safe maximum speed through the points. It was part of their route knowledge.

As for auxiliary or distant signals which, over the same 40 years, had had a variety of often confusing meanings, being used both as an advanced warning of what the main signal ahead was showing and as a stop signal in its own right, often meaning 'stop before you get to me', or 'stop after you have passed me because there is a train already standing between me and the next signal ahead', a more precise use was beginning to evolve in the 1870s and 1880s. This was a warning of

Fig. 9. Key to the diagrams of signals and track layouts in this book.

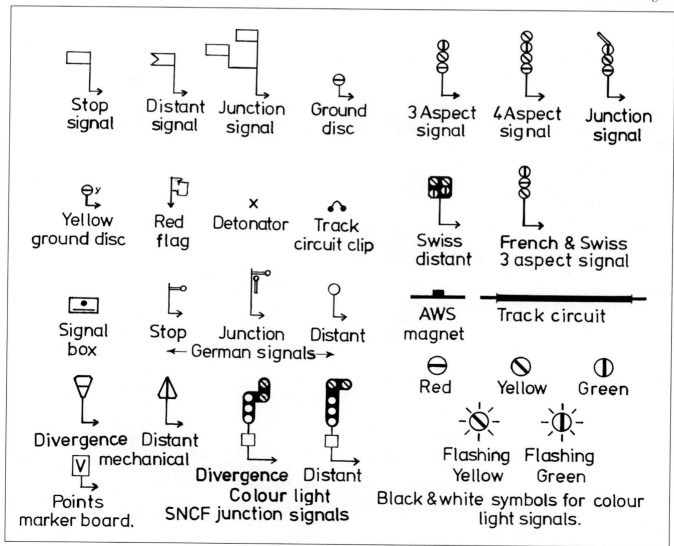

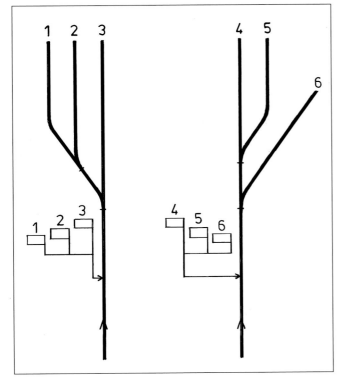

Fig. 10. *Junctions in British mechanical signalling are normally denoted by separate arms for each route with the tallest arm applying to the principal high speed line, and those to lower speed restricted turnouts at lower levels on left or right.*

what the next main signal ahead was showing. With the spread of signals around the layout a signalbox was now often provided with more than one main signal, which was called a 'home' signal, generally approaching a station or junction or remote signalbox not at a station and generally marking the exit end of the block section. Another signal, often called the 'starter', beyond the signalbox, was placed more often than not at the departure end of a station or perhaps at a train's length beyond a diverging junction on each line, and usually marked the entrance to the block section ahead. The distant signal was usually placed at braking distance from the first stop signal to which it applied but could only be cleared when all the stop signals worked from the same signalbox on the line ahead of it were also at clear. In this new more clearly defined function it was given a distinctive shape with a horizontal vee notch cut out of the left hand end of the arm, first seen on the London, Brighton & South Coast Railway at Norwood in the early 1870s and gradually taken up by other railways. The distant arm when horizontal meant 'danger, be prepared to stop at the next signal ahead' and at night showed a red light, just like the stop signals. With the arm lowered to 45 degrees it meant that all the stop signals ahead to which it applied were clear. At night it showed the same

white light as the stop signals in the clear position. Drivers had to know which were stop signals and which were distants, for a red light in a distant meant 'pass me and be prepared to stop at the next signal' but woe betide them if they passed a red light in a stop signal, which meant 'stop in front of me and do not pass'.

As for the construction of signals, already by the 1880s new types had been designed with the arm carried in a cast bracket including a pivot outside the front or side face of the post. The night-time indications were given by a single spectacle carrying a red glass mounted either separately, usually below the arm, or as an extension of the arm on the right hand side of the post, with the lamp behind it. Naturally with only two indications needed on absolute block lines the clear position of the arm moved the spectacle away from the lamp so that the flame of the lamp gave the (more-or-less) white light. By the time of the 1889 Act new standard designs with the spectacle as part of the arm were becoming the usual form. The reliability of the simpler two-position semaphore signal was also improved by the 1892 requirement that all signal arms should be counter-balanced so that they would return to the danger position if the controlling wire broke or was damaged. As mentioned previously, it had already

The role of advanced warning or distant signals was finally clarified in the early 1870s when they were installed on the Brighton line at Norwood. They were given a distinctive vee or fish tail cut out at the left hand end of the arm but were otherwise undistinguished from stop signals in colour or night-time lamp signals. They either stood alone, ostensibly at braking distance from the first stop signal to which they applied, or where signalboxes were close together were carried under the stop signals of the previous signalbox. In this picture of a gantry at Norwood the next signalbox ahead controls several junctions hence the array of junction distant signals. (National Railway Museum)

become standard practice for signals normally to stand in the 'danger' position, rather than 'clear', as had been the earlier practice.

There was though now another factor. Lighting in towns and cities was becoming more widespread and brighter as gas replaced oil lamps and candles, and lights in the streets began to provide illumination. The white light was no longer the preserve of the railways. Approaching a station in a built up area a driver could be faced with several white lights and he had to pick out the one intended for him. Signal lights were often not very bright even though gas light was used much more than might be thought for signals, having replaced oil or even candles at many locations. Taking gas pipes to signals was not cheap even if a main existed at a station, and improvements to oil lamps including incandescent mantles and long burning types, which came in the new century, brought a renaissance for the oil lamp which survives today in signals. The final elimination of time interval working in the early 1890s saw the end of the use of green lights and flags for caution as part of the primary signalling code. There was thus no bar to the adoption of a green light for clear, and gradually, from then on, signals, both stop and distant types, were altered to show a green light when the arm was in the 45 degree clear position, certainly at night and when the lamp was burning in bad weather. This meant of course that then newish signals having a single spectacle with just a red glass had to be given new double spectacles with red and

Some of the branch and cross-country railways built under the less restrictive Light Railways Act of 1896 had simpler signalling than railways built under a specific Act of Parliament. Often their equipment was second-hand or unique. This was a points indicator on the Kent & East Sussex Railway for main or loop lines. (L&GRP)

Stop and distant signal arms showing all the features of the 1880s with just one red spectacle and giving a white light when the arm was clear. This though was the Isle of Man in the 1940s and obviously in no rush to follow the British standards of the 1890s and 1920s. (L&GRP)

usually blue glasses (blue plus the yellowish flame of the lamp is seen as green). The older three-position semaphores, altered to work in two positions, mostly already had double spectacles from which the green caution glass had been removed a few years earlier and it was simply put back. But green remained in use as a caution indication, not in main signals, but in other respects as we shall see later for the next 60 or so years. Although the slotted post type of signal was now being replaced when renewals fell due by later designs, examples managed to survive on a few lines, particularly on former North Eastern Railway routes, for the next 70 years. Rotating disc or crossbar signals did not die out totally as semaphores became standard and a handful could be found controlling sidings, yards, perhaps level crossings, or on industrial sidings into the 1950s.

Let us have a look at the equipment and practices of the mechanical signalling era which were standard

A point indicating signal with the lie of the points denoted by which way the upright arm in the middle was inclined. This signal was at Kerry on the Cambrian branch in Wales. (L&GRP)

An early signalbox at Keymer Junction on the London, Brighton & South Coast Railway, seen here in the transition period towards the new standards of the 1880s/1890s. The lofty, all-timber structure is positioned as close as possible to the junction points, and is clearly designed to give the signalman the best possible view over the adjacent bridge of approaching trains. The connection to the nearby telegraph pole in this view shows that basic block working is in operation, and there is evidence of a point lock on the facing points of the junction, but otherwise there would have been only basic interlocking, with the wires and rodding dropping directly from the levers down the front of the box to run alongside the tracks. The signals are no longer above the signalbox roof but are at the approach to the points. (National Railway Museum)

features, some of which survive today where mechanical signalling is still in use. Even with power signalling, as described later, there was still a need for many features but they were accomplished by different means as will be described. As a simple example the mechanical or electro-mechanical means of train detection have largely been replaced by track circuiting which, despite other more technologically advanced ways of knowing the location of a train, is still the principal method employed in Britain. Some of the equipment and procedures described later in this chapter relate to more recent developments but are dealt with here as part of the general safety add-ons.

Interlocking methods

Interlocking of all levers controlling signals and points in signalboxes was a requirement of the 1889 Act and is still in force today. It is intended to prevent signalmen setting up two conflicting routes at any one time, to ensure that signals can only be cleared when the route to which they apply is properly set and, conversely, that

points and other signals applying to that route cannot be changed once the original route is cleared, so that as far as possible, the risk of collision or derailment is removed.

In manually-worked mechanical signalboxes, interlocking is usually achieved by a system of rods and tappets mounted in a locking room at ground level, beneath the main signal lever frame. Each lever is connected to longitudinally-sliding bars into which notches are cut, and into which sideways sliding locks can fit. Movement of any one lever causes its locking bar to slide and push the relevant locks sideways, freeing some but locking others which, if moved, would allow conflicting movements to be set up. Since no two signalboxes control exactly the same track layout and signalling, every locking installation has to be specially designed and built. In larger signalboxes, locking can be very complicated and, because of the practical mechanical difficulties involved, was often broken down into smaller sub groups. Until the advent of electrically-worked points and signals, the number, size

A general view of a mechanical lever frame. The top half of the levers from the quadrant plate in the middle would be in the upper operating room and everything below would be in the locking room, usually at ground level. Extending diagonally downwards from the framework of the supporting structure is the mechanical interlocking with rows of bars which slide along as levers are moved to lock or release other levers. (National Railway Museum)

and siting of signalboxes was very much dictated by the location and complexity of the points and signals they controlled. The position of signalboxes also had to comply with the Board of Trade's distance limit for mechanically worked points, which was originally 120 yards in the 1870s but this was gradually extended to 350 yards (see Chapter 8). Some lever frames had what was called catch-handle locking because if a lever was locked the catch handle itself could not even be lifted, or if free as soon as the catch handle was gripped it locked conflicting levers. In other designs the catch handle was not locked and could be gripped to the lever handle but the lever shaft was held or freed directly by its locking bar below.

Facing point locks

Not all locking is achieved within the signalbox. One of the greatest fears of early locomotive drivers was of facing points, since the consequences of point blades

being wrongly set or standing open could be extremely grave. For this reason, track layouts in the early days were designed with the minimum number of facing points, but clearly at junctions and the approach to stations their use could not be avoided. Early installations often included point indicators, worked mechanically by the movement of the blades, but because they were of necessity alongside the points, they gave drivers no forewarning if they were wrongly set, and in any case gave no guarantee that the blades would not move with the vibration of a moving train. From the 1870s the Board of Trade therefore required all facing points on running lines used by passenger trains, or leading to lines used by passenger trains, to be equipped with facing point locks. Basically, these take the form of a tie bar between the two point blades in which there are two holes or slots, one for the normal position, the other for reverse, and into which a locking bar can slide to prevent the tie bar moving sideways, and thus the point blades from moving. The locking bar is usually connected by rodding to a separate lever in the controlling signalbox, and is normally engaged in the slot holding the point blades in the normal position. However, when a signalman needs to reverse the points, he first operates the locking lever in the frame (locking levers in some frames are in the normal position in the frame when the points are locked, others – as on the GWR – stand in the reverse position when points are locked) which withdraws the locking bar. He then pulls the lever controlling the points so that they move to the reversed position, then operates the locking lever again and thus inserts the locking bar in the other slot, holding the points in the reverse position. The facing point lock lever is interlocked in the signalbox so that none of the signals protecting the points it works can be cleared unless it is in the locked position and thus the points themselves are locked; the locking on the lever controlling the points themselves would ensure that only the appropriate signals can be cleared. Recent power signalling installations have seen the development of the clamplock in which the switch blades are moved and locked, clamped to the stockrail, in one movement rather than with a separate bolt lock.

Detection

How can the signalman be sure that the point blades have moved fully, or at all, and that the point lock has re-engaged? The answer is by detection, achieved either mechanically or, in more recent times, electrically. The mechanical detector involves at least three interlocking slides, one connected to each signal operating wire, others to the point blades, and so arranged that the appropriate signal wire only becomes free to pull when the points are correctly and fully set for the route to which the signal it controls applies. This is shown in Fig. 11. If a signal applies to a route in which there are

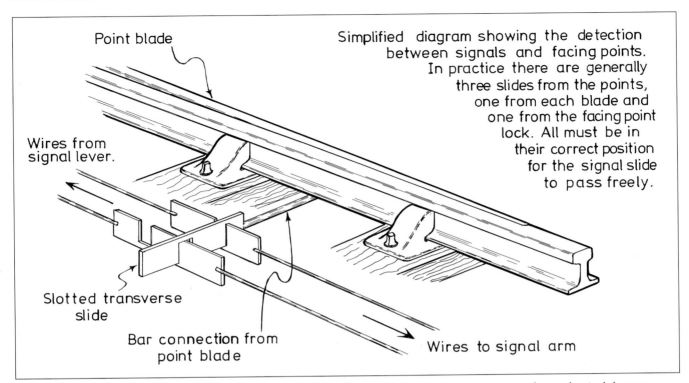

Point blade

Simplified diagram showing the detection between signals and facing points. In practice there are generally three slides from the points, one from each blade and one from the facing point lock. All must be in their correct position for the signal slide to pass freely.

Wires from signal lever.

Slotted transverse slide

Bar connection from point blade

Wires to signal arm

Fig. 11. *The basic arrangement of a mechanical detector.*

two or more facing points, the signal wire must be taken through detectors for each set of points before it reaches the signal it controls. This equipment can be cumbersome and difficult to maintain, particularly in areas of complicated trackwork, and in more recent years, electrical detection used in conjunction with electrical locks in the signalbox, have become the norm.

Fouling bars

Even with facing point locks and detection to ensure that points had correctly responded to lever movements, there was originally nothing to stop a signalman from moving points under a train. This could happen if the points were some distance beyond the signals protecting them, and the signalman could thus restore the signal levers in the frame, releasing the locking after the train had passed the signals but before it reached the points. To prevent this, facing points were also fitted with a fouling bar, which lay alongside the inside edge of one of the running rails but below wheel flange depth immediately on the approach side and part way through the points, and connected by rodding in series with the facing point lock. The mechanism is connected in such a way that the act of reversing the point locking lever to withdraw the locking bar raises the fouling bar into the flangeway. Clearly, if a train was passing, its flanges would prevent the fouling bar from lifting and thus it would be impossible to withdraw the locking bar and move the point blades. Again, in more recent times, track circuits controlling electric locks have taken over the function of fouling bars.

Sequential locking

Interlocking is mainly used to prevent conflicting routes being set up, and to ensure that points and signals are correctly set. It can also be used, in conjunction with other controls, to prevent one train from being inadvertently signalled into the back of another. Known as sequential locking, it only permits the levers controlling the running signals for each line to be pulled in a given order – usually the outer home, the

A close-up view of a mechanical detector with the signal wires operating detector bars passing through the slides from the point blades. (Kenneth Field)

inner home, the starter, the advanced starter, and finally the distant. By also arranging the locking so that each of these stop signals cannot be cleared unless the next signal ahead worked by the same box is at danger, it will be seen that a signal cannot be cleared for a second train until the next signal has been returned to danger behind the first. As we shall see in later chapters, when used in conjunction with track circuits and controls on the block instruments to the next signal box, the risk of a train catching up and colliding with the train in front due to signalman's error is virtually eliminated.

Slotting

We have noted that, because of mechanical constraints, signalboxes needed to be sited within a relatively short distance of the points and crossovers they controlled. In busy, heavily trafficked areas, this often meant that signalboxes were spaced too closely to allow full braking distance from one to the other. As a result the distant signals for one box had to be mounted on the same post or posts as the stop signals for the previous box. In extreme cases, the same distant signal was used for two very closely spaced successive boxes. Clearly, however, some form of interlocking was necessary to ensure that the distant signal for one box was only cleared if the stop signal above it for the previous box was clear, and that in the case of a signal worked by

The detail of slot balance weights at the foot of a stop and distant signal on the GWR. The nearer balance weight is the slot weight. There were other forms of slot mechanism including a scissors type of bracket which would only clear the distant arm when both stop and distant levers were pulled.

Fig. 12. A diagram showing the operation of a conventional mechanical slot on a signal with stop and distant arms to prevent the distant arm from showing clear when the stop arm is at danger. The centre slot weight must be heavy enough to pull the distant arm to clear when it is free to drop, but either of the balance weights pulled to clear from the respective signalboxes must be heavier than the slot weight to ensure that the slot returns to caution or danger when just one of the levers is restored to normal.

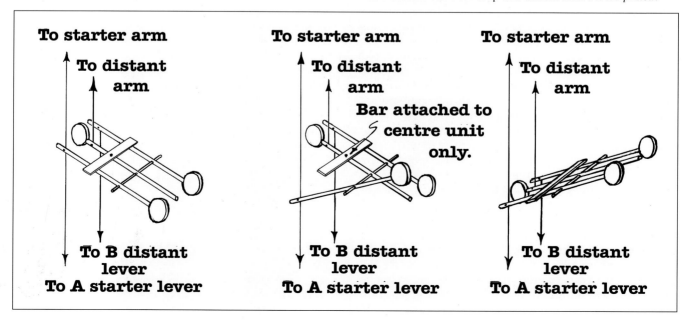

two signalmen, that the signal only cleared when both had pulled their relevant levers. This form of interlocking is known as slotting, and is normally achieved on the signalpost itself by a system of balance weights and a slot bar. The signal arm concerned is not connected directly to either signalbox but instead to a separate counterbalance weight which is held up by two heavier counterbalance weights, one connected to the signalbox controlling the stop signal, the other to the box controlling the distant signal. Only when both signal levers have been pulled will the lighter balance weight drop and the signal clear; as soon as one or other of the levers is restored its heavier balance weight restores the signal to the 'on' position. This arrangement ensures that no distant signal on the same post as a stop signal can be cleared unless the stop signal above it is clear, and that it returns to caution immediately the stop signal above it is returned to danger. In some instances stop signals can be slotted, worked from two signalboxes as a starting signal for one and the home signal for the next.

Treadles

Knowing the exact whereabouts of a train, or whether it has passed a particular point, is clearly of great help to a signalman, particularly at night or in adverse weather conditions. In the early days of electricity, before track circuits were widely used, this was often achieved by the use of a treadle. This took the form of a metal bar fixed against the inside edge of a running rail, rather like a fouling bar but working in the opposite way. A treadle was normally at the same height as the

A typical scene in the British countryside at the end of the steam era. This excursion train to Bognor has just passed Christ's Hospital signalbox, visible behind the last coach of the train, and is entering the block section ahead as it passes the Christ's Hospital starting signal, which also carries the splitting distant signals for the next box ahead, Itchingfield Junction. These signals, which indicate which route is set at the junction ahead, will be slotted with the stop signal so that, even if the Itchingfield Junction signalman pulls his respective levers, the distant signal will not clear unless the Christ's Hospital starting signal is also clear. Note also the treadle on the up line adjacent to the engine, which would give warning to the Christ's Hospital signalman of the approach of a train to his home signal, acting in effect like a berth track circuit. (Derek Cross)

top of the adjacent running rail, and was thus in the flangeway. It had short 'run on' ramps at each end and was pivoted against a spring in such a way that it was depressed by the flanges of passing trains, but returned to the normal position thereafter. When depressed, an electrical contact was broken, and an indication given in the controlling signalbox. Some treadles were actually electrical contact units beneath the rail relying on the vertical movement of the rail as a train passed.

However, treadles can only give local indications because of the practical limit on their length and, as they normally foul the flangeway, are not really suitable for use on higher speed lines, although some railways did so. Their use today is normally restricted to locations where normal track circuits cannot be relied upon, either because the rail conditions are regularly very wet or greasy, or because the section of line is little used and thus the railhead is susceptible to rust.

However, a more modern form of treadle, known as a striker, is now used extensively on non-track circuited lines to detect the passage of trains. They are particularly useful for use in connection with apparatus warning of the approach of trains at rural level crossings on lines which are not fully track circuited. They take the form of a short, spring-loaded arm which normally sits alongside the inside edge of the running rail, and at the same height as the railhead. The passage of a train is detected when the wheels of the passing train depress the arm and break an electrical contact.

Axle counters

However, even this modern form of treadle gives only a snapshot of what is happening as a train passes by, and not a continuous indication. They can be and are used at the entrance to block sections to lock equipment until a train subsequently passes over another treadle or track circuit at the end of the block section, but they cannot prove that an entire train has passed through the section. To do this, axle counters are employed. These are used widely overseas, and now increasingly in Britain and Europe to enable remote control of long single lines and in other locations where perhaps because of dampness in, say, tunnels, track circuiting is unsuitable. Axle counters, as the name implies, count each axle as it passes the detector, today electronic in form rather than electro-mechanical, and another counts the number of axles again when the train passes similar equipment at the other end of the section. The two counters are connected, and unless the second counter counts the same number of axles as the first, the equipment remains locked, because the presumption is that part of the train has remained in the section.

Other reminder apparatus

Despite the march of technology, inevitably there still remain some situations for which the normal signalling equipment does not provide adequate train protection. In these circumstances, or when the equipment fails, the signalman may need to resort to working without the normal protection of the interlocking block instruments. He then needs to be very careful not to forget about a train, and to help him, each signalbox has certain 'Reminder appliances' which he can use in various situations. These appliances usually take the form of a collar which slots over a lever and its catch and thus prevents the lever from being used until it is removed. A signalman might use such a lever collar to remind him of a light engine standing on the main line, or part of a train left in a platform, or a vehicle left at bufferstops. In some boxes, specially labelled collars are provided for use on the levers of points and signals which are disconnected while engineers are at work. Other reminder devices in a signalbox might include an annunciator, in the form of a bell or a buzzer worked by a treadle or track circuit that warns signalmen of the approach of a train when block sections are very long, to remind him, for example, to be ready to close level crossing gates. As we shall see in the next chapter, some signals have plungers which operate indicators in the signalbox to alert signalmen that there is a train waiting and there are other ways of reminding signalmen of a train as provided in the rules.

Another form of reminder is the 'train ready to start' indicator. These are usually provided at large stations to advise signalmen that a train is ready and he can set the route and clear his signals if the line is clear. A plunger or key operated switch for platform staff is normally provided on each platform, and when operated this shows an appropriate indication in the signalbox which is usually extinguished either by the signalman depressing another plunger in the signalbox, or more usually, by clearing the signal for the departing train.

Detonators

Another warning or reminder device, although more for the advice of drivers than signalmen, are detonators. A detonator is a round, flat container, somewhat larger and deeper than a coin, which is packed with explosive and clipped to the running rails and which, when crushed by the passing wheels of a train, explodes sharply with sufficient sound to attract the attention of a driver, even above the noise of the train. Detonators are carried on all trains, and are kept in all signalboxes, and are used, as we shall see in subsequent chapters, to warn of any obstruction on the line, or of emergency speed restrictions. In semaphore signalled areas, they may also be used in fog as an added indication at distant signals, and at home signals protecting junctions. Detonators are placed on the rail while the signal is at danger or caution, and only removed when the line is clear. On busy lines, and particularly on multi-track lines, where it would be dangerous for the fog signalmen – who are usually permanent way staff – to cross the lines in fog, special fog signalmens's huts are provided, with repeaters of the signals and small lever frames connected to detonator placing machines. These machines are mounted on the outside of the running rails, usually on the sleeper end and, when activated, swing one or two detonators into position on the rail head. Some machines had magazine storage of detonators so that as one (or two) were set off; movement of the lever brought new detonators into position. Many signalboxes are also equipped with similar machines, mounted on the track outside the box and worked directly from levers in the box, so that a signalman can instantly alert any passing train to danger.

Normally, detonators are not used for fog signalling in conjunction with colour light signals because their beams are regarded as sufficiently powerful to penetrate even the densest of fog. However, in busy areas where colour light signals are very close to the junctions they protect, and have short overlaps, detonator placers are sometimes provided, working automatically in conjunction with the signal, so that the driver of any train passing the signal at danger is immediately alerted. Today, automatic detonator placers, sometimes working in conjunction with other devices, such as special warning lights, are also used at locations where the incidence of Signals Passed at Danger (SPAD) is high.

Speed restrictions

British railway signalling has always been based on the concept of indicating routes rather than, as in some countries, speed, and for many years, apart from siting distant signals to allow for braking from the highest permissible line speed, little attempt was made to use signals to influence the speed at which trains were driven if the line was clear. Drivers were simply expected to know the topography of the lines over which they worked, where it was necessary to reduce speed, and to control their trains accordingly. Only after Nationalisation in 1948 was the practice of even marking speed restrictions widely adopted, the then-new British Railways adopting the LNER practice of indicating the speed limit at any point on the line with white stencil figures mounted on a post beside the line. But even these, because they were usually placed at the actual commencement of the speed restriction, gave drivers no advance warning of a speed restriction, and a driver coming upon them too fast would have no chance to slow down in time.

As colour-light signalling became more widespread, the practice of approach-controlling the clearance of signals protecting slower speed divergences (described in detail in Chapter 14) tended to enforce speed restrictions over slow speed diverging routes. Otherwise there was little further development for plain line restrictions over curves for example until a series of high speed derailments, culminating in the Morpeth disaster in 1969, when a sleeping car train was derailed at more than 80mph in the early hours of the morning on a curve restricted to 40mph. By this time, the Automatic Warning System (AWS), described later in Chapter 13, had come into widespread use at the approach to signals, and as a result of Morpeth, it was proposed that an illuminated Advanced Warning Indicator (AWI) of yellow figures on a black background should be provided, together with an AWS warning magnet, at braking distance from the restriction. As railways abound in curves and speed restrictions, to keep the number of installations down and thus avoid the possibility of their effectiveness being eroded by the sheer number, it was decided that AWIs should only be provided on lines where the maximum speed was 75mph or more, and the

TOP *Byfleet Junction signalbox, seen in the centre of this view beneath the gantry, had been working trains on the Sykes lock and block system for over 60 years when this picture was taken. The signals themselves are more modern though, with motor-worked distant arms for the next box ahead, and detonator-placers alongside the running rails, worked by rodding from the box, and provided with ramps to protect them from the dangling current collector shoes of passing electric trains. (Alan Williams)*

ABOVE *Co-acting detonators coupled to a starting or advanced starting signal so that they were on the rail head when the signal was at danger and would be exploded if a train passed the signal and entered the block section irregularly. When the signal was cleared the detonators swung away from the rail. (BR, LMR)*

reduction in speed required was more than a third. In the event, this proved not to be enough, and by incredible coincidence, following a further high speed derailment at Morpeth in 1984, also of a sleeping car

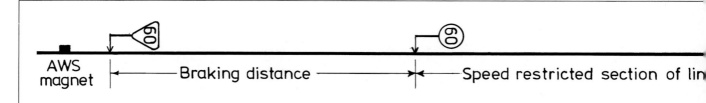

Fig. 13 *Present day arrangement for marking permanent speed restrictions on higher speed main lines. Most speed limits are now marked on all lines but do not always have advanced warnings and AWS magnets unless the restriction is substantially below normal line speed.*

train, and also at night, but this time travelling in the opposite direction, the rules were extended. Although the same curve was involved, with the same speed restriction, the approach was by a series of gradually reducing speed restrictions, none of which individually qualified under the 75mph plus/more than one third reduction rule. However, the rules of gravity are the same, and almost the entire train turned on its side. Now, AWIs are provided on all lines carrying trains above 60mph, even if the required more than one third

There will be no trains for a little while yet in this view of Bopeep Junction near Hastings, because both lines are blocked for engineering work, hence the 'stop' signs and accompanying flashing red lights between the rails on each line outside the box. Note also the latest road-style reflective 20mph speed restriction sign behind and to the left of the signal. (Alan Williams)

reduction in speed is only achieved through a series of lesser stages. AWIs are no longer illuminated and now take the form of black figures on a white background with a yellow edge in an inverted triangle as an advanced warning, all in reflective material so as to be picked out by the now mandatory headlights of locomotives and multiple units. There is also a programme of marking the start of every change of speed limit – increases as well as decreases – with round signs which have black figures on a white background with a red edge, also in reflective material and very similar in style to road speed limit signs.

Permanent speed restriction signs may be relatively new on Britain's railways, but temporary speed limit signs to protect track or bridges under repair, or other engineering work, have been in use almost since the developing years of railways. By their very nature, temporary speed limit signs have on the one hand to be sufficiently portable to enable them to be carried often for some distance, but on the other sufficiently robust as to be entirely weatherproof, as well as able to withstand the draught from passing trains. For many years these signs took the form of short wooden posts

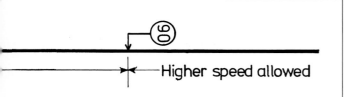

Higher speed allowed

with stencil lettering or figures on a panel illuminated at night from behind with paraffin lamps. The warning sign showed the speed restriction together with two horizontal white lights on a yellow 'fishtail' panel pointing towards the line to which it applied at braking distance from the restriction. For many years the actual start of the restriction was marked with a sign showing a 'C' (for commencement) but in recent years this has been changed to repeat the reduced speed to be enforced. A third sign at the end of the restriction simply shows a letter 'T' (for termination). Originally warning boards were painted green (for caution) which lasted until 1949 when the colour changed to yellow.

As with permanent speed restriction signs, increased line speeds and the availability of new technology has required changes, and once again an accident underlined the need for a rethink. In 1975, the driver of yet another sleeping car train, running at maximum speed to recover time lost earlier, missed in the dark a warning board whose lights had gone out on the approach to Nuneaton, and ran at 80mph onto track restricted to 20mph, becoming totally derailed. It transpired that the old-style warning board had been

converted to work from propane gas so as to give a brighter light, but the supply had run out. Since then, a new, lightweight design of warning board has been developed, electrically lit from batteries, further intensified by lenses and with a flashing mechanism so as to both make the sign more noticeable at night, and to conserve power. This mechanism also has a light sensitive switch to conserve power during hours of daylight. There was some suggestion following the Nuneaton accident that signs at another location had been removed before the planned time if engineering work finished early, or for some reason did not begin at all, and that this confused drivers. As a result, therefore, once installed, signs remain in place for the planned duration, even if the restriction is lifted, but with a diagonal stripe in place of the usual speed restriction figure on the approach warning sign, and the normal line speed on the sign indicating the beginning of the erstwhile restriction. The most important change introduced as a result of Nuneaton was the now mandatory use of a temporary AWS permanent magnet alongside the warning sign to alert

Comparison of advanced temporary speed limit warning boards in use during the 1980s. The older version has the arrow (albeit painted) yellow warning board with white figures on black and is floodlit at night. The later version has the rectangular yellow board with white figures on blue with flashing white lights displayed in the yellow board. Other variations have appeared in the mid-1990s in which the figures are black on a yellow background with a reflective material illuminated by train headlights. (Geoffrey Kichenside)

The driver's view of the sign warning of an emergency speed restriction ahead. In the past, if a speed restriction had to be imposed before drivers could be given written warning, detonators had to be used to alert the driver of each approaching train, but now these conical signs, with black and yellow vertical chevrons and two powerful white strobe lights, one above the other, are used. This sign has been placed just beyond and below the signal, so as not to distract the driver, and is accompanied by the temporary installation of a permanent magnet between the running rails to ensure an appropriate alert is given on the automatic warning system equipment of any passing train. (Alan Williams)

drivers, bringing British practice into line with that long established elsewhere in Europe. Signal engineers were initially concerned that the widespread use of AWS magnets for non-signal aspect purposes might cause confusion in closely signalled areas, and special instructions ensure that proper spacing is maintained.

All temporary speed restrictions are normally listed in special notices issued to drivers each week of which they are required to take note, but occasionally temporary speed restrictions have to be introduced at very short notice – perhaps as a result of track becoming damaged – and on such occasions the rules require that a hand signalman be provided at the warning sign, with detonators to alert the driver of each passing train to the unscheduled restriction. This practice can, of course, be extremely expensive in manpower, requiring as it does round the clock manning, and also tends not to be very well received in residential areas! In recent years, therefore, a special sign has been developed, with an upright as opposed to horizontal panel, with black chevrons on yellow, and featuring two high intensity white strobe lights, one above the other, which are highly visible, even in broad daylight. Such a sign is illustrated in the picture on the left.

Chapter 6

THE
BLOCK SYSTEM

THE BLOCK SYSTEM of signalling, which divides a railway line into successive sections, or blocks, and then in absolute block seeks to ensure that not more than one train occupies any one block section at one time, evolved during the latter part of the 19th century, and became compulsory for almost all passenger carrying lines in Britain from 1889. It is still the basis for operating most railways throughout the world today.

The invention of the electric telegraph had enabled the early railway policemen to send messages along the line about the running of trains in connection with the time-interval system. Later, it was the development of the electric telegraph into specific block telegraph instruments showing the state of the line between adjacent signalboxes that had allowed the progressive introduction of the block system in the 1870s and 1880s. Despite the more recent introduction of power signalling, with colour-light signals and full track circuiting, many lines in Britain, Europe and the rest of the world are still controlled by mechanical signalboxes communicating with each other by block telegraph and bells. Often this is with additional controls and safety devices, and varying methods of operation, although with a common principle.

From the early days of railways in Britain the rule book has been the railwaymen's bible, detailing much of the working methods of train operation, particularly the duties of drivers, guards, signalmen and other staff, together with the procedures to be undertaken both in normal running and when things go wrong. Later, in conjunction with the signalling regulations which describe how the equipment is used and the way trains are to be signalled, the general appendix which adds more instructions on the way, for example, failed trains are to be assisted, or how the braking system is to be used, and the sectional appendices which show special working arrangements at specific locations including such things as running line details, permanent speed restrictions, locomotive restrictions and the like, these books have provided reference to all manner of operating matters, and of course how the block system is to be worked.

The block section

Signalboxes have been needed wherever there are points or crossovers to be controlled, and since most stations have – or had – sidings for freight, most block sections ran from station to station, unless there was an intervening junction also requiring a signalbox. As we have seen, at large junction stations, because of the restriction on the distance from which points could be worked, there were often several signalboxes spaced quite close together. Conversely, where there were long stretches of line without stations or junctions but the length of the block section would have made operation inconvenient (because the frequency of a train service on any line is dictated by the time taken to travel through the longest block section) additional intermediate signalboxes were often provided simply to break the line into shorter block sections. In more recent times, where semaphore signalling and block telegraph working is still in use, most of these intermediate boxes have been abolished to save manpower, their signals being controlled remotely from adjacent boxes.

A block section is defined as the section of line from the most advanced stop signal controlled by one signal box to the outermost stop signal controlled by the next signalbox. Conversely, the section of line from the outermost stop signal of one signalbox to the most advanced stop signal controlled by that same signalbox, and therefore entirely under the control of one signalman, is defined as 'station limits' – even though there may be no station. Subject to certain rules, a signalman can make train movements within station limits without reference to the signalmen in the adjacent signalboxes, and if the track layout and signalling permits it, as explained later, there can be more than one train on the same line at the same time within station limits.

Stop signals are divided into two groups – home signals, which are usually on the approach side of a signalbox, and starting signals, which are beyond, or in advance of, the signalbox. In railway signalling terms 'in advance' and 'in rear' have specific meanings. These

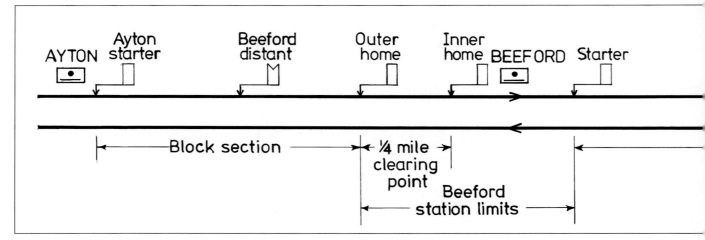

Fig. 14. *Limits of a block section, station limits, and the clearing point.*

London & North Eastern Railway three-position block instruments at Newbridge Junction on the Edinburgh–Glasgow main line. Both are 'pegging' instruments – ie to allow trains to enter the block section approaching the signalbox – and both are showing 'train on line', one for a train from Winchburgh Junction, the other for a train from Saughton Junction. Note also the padlocked release switch with a paper seal for signal No. 24 between the two instruments. To operate this switch, which would release the locking on the signal in an emergency, the signalman had to break the dated and signed paper seal, which would then have to be replaced and resealed by the signal technician.

are best understood by imagining a person standing on a line facing in the normal direction of travel. Everything in front is said to be 'in advance' – and everything behind 'in rear'!

Under normal circumstances, before accepting a train, in addition to the intervening block section being clear, a signalman must have a distance of about ¼ mile clear beyond his home signal. This distance, known as the clearing point or overlap, is provided as a safety margin in case the driver should misjudge his braking and inadvertently pass the signal at danger. (In some countries, a stop signal is deemed to mean exactly that, and no overlap is provided.) The end of the overlap extends into station limits. At junctions and

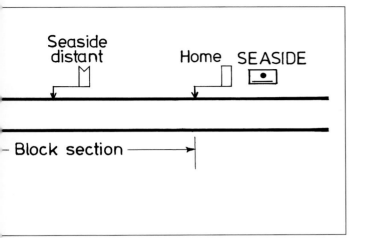

Block section

busy stations where it would be impractical or inconvenient to keep the $^{1}/_{4}$ mile section beyond the home signal clear while a train is approaching, an

An ex-London & North Western Railway three-position block instrument in use at Tamworth on British Railways. Unlike most railways, the LNWR made its own block instruments, and this neat, space-saving design, which incorporated both the pegging and non pegging indicators for a block section in one unit, as well as the relevant block bell and its tapper, was first introduced in the 1890s and is still in use at a few locations today. Notice the two types of signal repeater below the block instruments, lights for the up distant and a miniature semaphore for signal No. 17. (British Railways)

additional 'outer home' stop signal is usually provided, $^{1}/_{4}$ mile in rear of what then becomes the 'inner home' signal so as to provide the necessary overlap without interfering with other movements. These terms are explained in Fig. 14.

Block telegraph instruments
To operate the block system, each signalbox has a block telegraph instrument and single-stroke bell for each block section. Each block instrument has an electrically operated pointer or needle which, when the electromagnetic coils inside the instrument are energised, moves across the face of the instrument. Early block instruments showed only two positions, 'line clear' or 'line blocked', but all modern instruments have three positions, 'line clear', 'train on line' and 'line blocked'. Line blocked is the normal position, and the position to which the needle returns when the coils are de-energised. There are two types of block instrument, known as pegging and non-pegging. A pegging instrument has a handle or knob beneath the face of the instrument which the signalman turns to operate the block indicator needle. A non-pegging instrument has no handle and simply repeats the indication shown by the pegging instrument in the adjacent signalbox, to which it is electrically connected by lineside wires or cables. Before a train can pass from one signalbox to the next, the signalmen in both boxes need to know the state of the block section between them. Each signalbox has a specific block indicator for that section of line; the signalbox in advance of the block section (the exit end) has a pegging instrument, through which the signalman there allows a train to enter the block section and approach his signalbox. The signalbox at the rear of the block section (the entry end) has a non-pegging instrument which displays the same indications as the pegging instrument at the box ahead. The three positions of a pegging instrument are shown in Fig. 15.

Unless it controls a terminus at the end of a line, most signalboxes are the boundary between two block sections, and therefore have two instruments for each running line – a pegging instrument for the block section in rear and a non-pegging repeater instrument for the block section in advance. Most signalboxes controlling a normal double-track line will therefore have four instruments, two of which are operated by the signalman there, but for every additional running line, it would need an additional pegging instrument, and a non-pegging instrument. One bell and one bell tapper or plunger, to send bell signals, is provided at each signalbox for each pair of up and down lines through each block section, so that bell signals for both up and down trains are sent on the same equipment. An additional bell and tapper or plunger would be necessary for each additional running line or pair of running lines for each section. The various bells in any

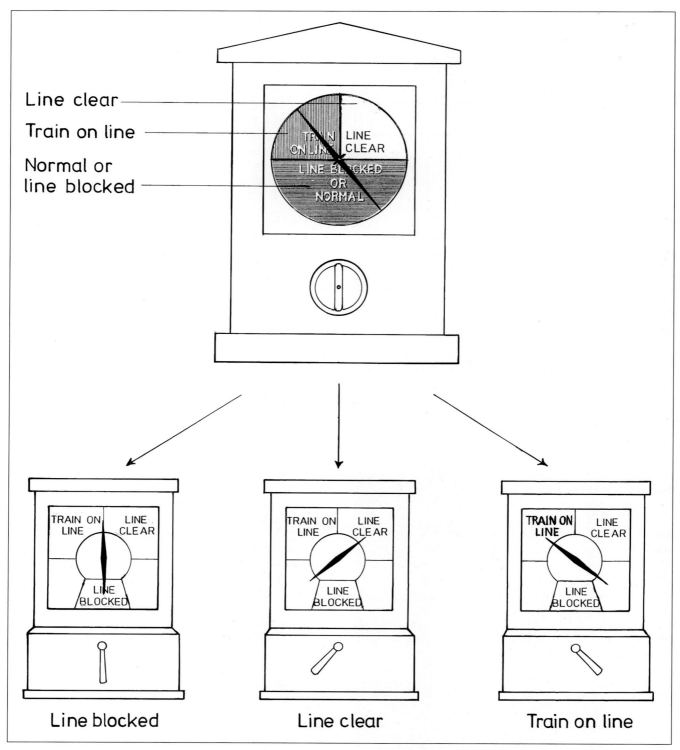

Line clear

Train on line

Normal or
line blocked

Line blocked

Line clear

Train on line

Fig. 15. *The labelling of a fairly standard three-position block instrument face.*

one signalbox are deliberately given significantly differing sounds so as to readily identify which block section bell signals refer to, and thus to reduce the possibility of mistakes. To ensure that bells are really distinctive some signalmen have used add-ons to the bell such as elastic bands or spring clothes pegs.

Signalling a train

So how does it work? The best way to follow the method of block working is to imagine you are in a signalbox at say, Beeford, on a double-track line

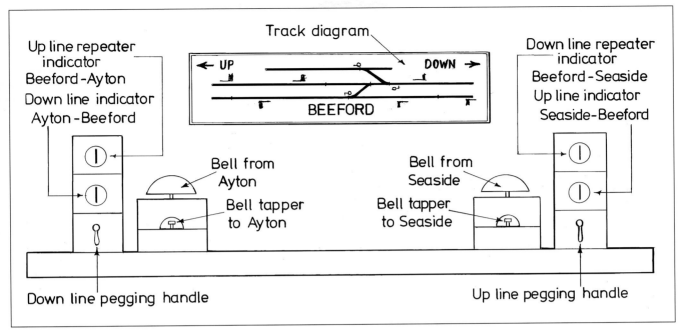

Track diagram

Up line repeater
indicator
Beeford-Ayton

Down line indicator
Ayton-Beeford

← UP   DOWN →

BEEFORD

Down line repeater
indicator
Beeford-Seaside

Up line indicator
Seaside-Beeford

Bell from
Ayton

Bell tapper
to Ayton

Bell from
Seaside

Bell tapper
to Seaside

Down line pegging handle

Up line pegging handle

between Ayton and Seaside signalboxes (see Fig. 16). All signals at all three signalboxes are at danger because there are no trains about, and thus the indicators on the block instruments are all showing 'line blocked' because the line is assumed to be blocked until specifically cleared for the passage of a train. A down stopping passenger train is ready to leave Ayton to run through Beeford to Seaside, so the signalman at Ayton calls the attention of our signalman at Beeford with one beat on the bell, which our signalman at Beeford acknowledges by repeating the single beat back – standard practice, as we shall see, in block signalling work. On hearing this beat, the signalman at Ayton knows his colleague with us at Beeford is ready and sends the 'Is line clear for stopping passenger train?' signal (3 pause 1) on the bell. If the block section is clear and the line beyond Beeford's home signal is clear to the clearing point, our signalman at Beeford accepts the train by repeating the 3 pause 1 signal back to Ayton and moves the pegging handle on the Ayton–Beeford down line block instrument from 'line blocked' to 'line clear', causing the indicator on both his own instrument and that in Ayton signalbox to show 'line clear'. On seeing the indicator move to 'line clear', the Ayton signalman clears his down line signals. When the train leaves Ayton, the signalman there sends the 'train entering section' signal to us at Beeford (2 beats), which our signalman at Beeford acknowledges by repeating the 2 beats signal and moving the block indicator from 'line clear' to 'train on line', which is again repeated at Ayton, where the signalman has meanwhile restored his signals to danger behind the train.

Our signalman at Beeford now has a train running towards him, but before he can clear his signals, he

Fig. 16. *A typical signalbox layout of the block instrument shelf above the lever frame with the track diagram above.*

must offer the train to Seaside by the same procedure. The signalman at Beeford therefore calls the attention of the signalman at Seaside with one beat, which Seaside acknowledges, and if the line is clear through the block section up to his clearing point, the Seaside signalman will acknowledge the 'Is line clear for stopping passenger train?', 3 pause 1 bell signal which Beeford then sends him and puts his block instrument to 'line clear'. If, however, the line is not clear, Seaside will not accept the train by simply not repeating the bell signal back and maintaining his block indicator at 'line blocked'. Our signalman at Beeford, however, knows that his colleague is in his signalbox and aware that Beeford wishes to offer him a train because Beeford has received an acknowledgement of his 'call attention' signal.

However, let us assume that the line is clear, and that the Seaside signalman has accepted the train and moved his block indicator to 'line clear', so that our signalman at Beeford, on seeing his repeater indicator move to 'line clear', can clear his signals. When the train leaves Beeford, our signalman sends the 'train entering section' (2 beats) signal on to Seaside, who acknowledges it and moves his block indicator from 'line clear' to 'train on line'. Our signalman at Beeford restores his signals to danger behind the train, and when it has passed beyond the clearing point and he has satisfied himself that the train is complete by observing the tail lamp on the rear, he sends the 'call attention' (1 beat) signal to Ayton, and when the Ayton signalman acknowledges with 1 beat, our signalman sends the 'train out of section' signal (2 pause 1). When

Ayton acknowledges by repeating this signal, the Beeford signalman moves his indicator back to the normal 'line blocked' position, and is now ready to accept another train from Ayton if the signalman there has one to offer.

Meanwhile, the signalman at Seaside has offered the first train further on down the line, had it accepted and cleared his signals, and in due course, when the train passes his signalbox and he has checked that it is complete, the signalman then calls the attention of our signalman at Beeford with one beat, and when this is acknowledged, sends the 'train out of section' signal (2 pause 1) and, when our signalman acknowledges it, moves the indicator for the Beeford–Seaside block section back to 'line blocked'. If our signalman at Beeford had accepted another train from Ayton, he could now offer it on to Seaside. The detail sometimes varied from railway to railway. Not all used the call attention before giving train out of section, and on parts of the LMS this signal was acknowledged by one beat on the bell. Where signalboxes are close together and the block section therefore short, it is often not practical for a signalman to wait until he receives 'train entering section' before offering the train on to the next box, because signals could not be cleared in time and unnecessary delay would occur to trains. Equally, trains cannot immediately be offered too far down the line, otherwise the line would be cleared too far ahead and delays to other services would result. In these cases, an additional 'train approaching' signal (1 pause 2 pause 1) is sometimes used. In our example, when Ayton sends 'train entering section' to Beeford, our signalman there, who will already have offered the train to Seaside, immediately sends the 'train approaching' signal to Seaside, who then immediately offers the train forward to the next signalbox.

Rule 39(a)/C4.6

If for any reason a signalman cannot accept a train, the signalman at the signalbox in rear must maintain his signals at danger, until the approaching train has almost stopped at his outermost home signal. Thereupon this signal is cleared to allow the train to draw forward slowly past the next signals – possibly an inner home and a starting signal – which are in turn cleared when the train has almost stopped at them, until the train reaches the most advanced stop signal controlling entry into the block section, which is of course maintained at danger until the block section is clear. A driver seeing this sequence of signals clearing, allowing him to slowly draw ahead, will understand that the block section remains occupied. However, in fog or falling snow, when visibility may be limited, and a driver might miss the signal controlling entry into the block section, a signalman may not allow a train to draw forward further than is necessary to bring it within the protection of his

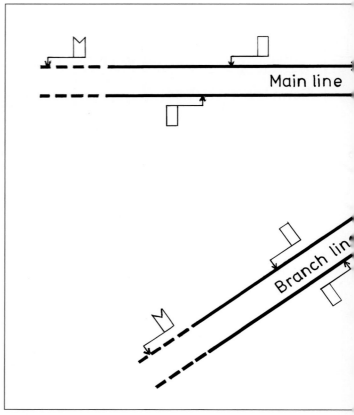

Fig. 17. *The signalling and track layout of a conventional double junction. Many junctions like this were rationalised during the 1970s and 1980s to what were called single lead junctions, see Fig. 32.*

Fig. 18. *The layout and signalling at a typical country station on a double-track main line after the standards were set in the last decade of Victorian years, and which generally lasted until station closures, rationalisation, and resignalling of the 1950s and 1960s. Compare with the basic layout of the 1860s in Fig. 8.*

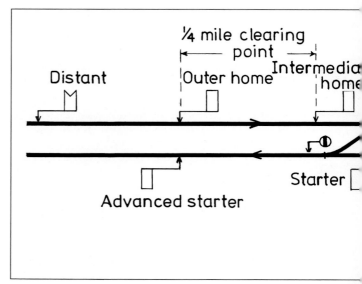

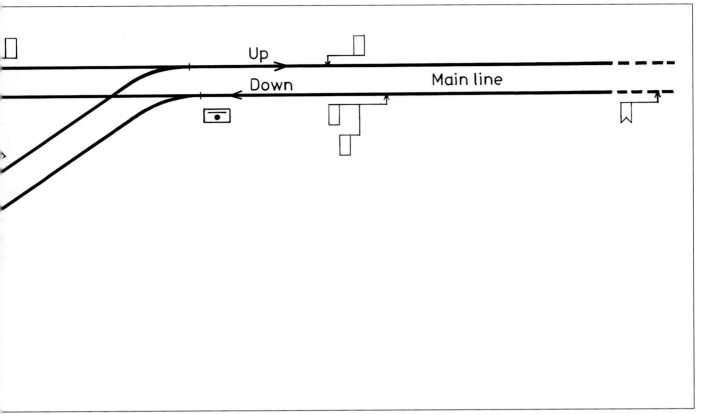

signals. In clear weather, once a train that has been checked has drawn forward to the signal controlling entry into the block section to await acceptance, provided the rear of the train is then beyond the clearing point, the signalman may accept a second train from the rear, which, when it arrives and has been brought almost to a stand at the outermost stop signal, may in turn be brought within the protection of the signals, so that there are two trains within station limits on the same line. The rule laying down this procedure was known as 39(a) in the rule books until the 1960s but as C4.6 from the 1970s.

Rule 55/K3

If a train is brought to a stand on any running line by a signal at danger, the train crew need to assure themselves that the signalman has not overlooked their presence. This they would achieve by the second man or the conductor going to the controlling signalbox within two minutes (but immediately in fog or falling snow) to

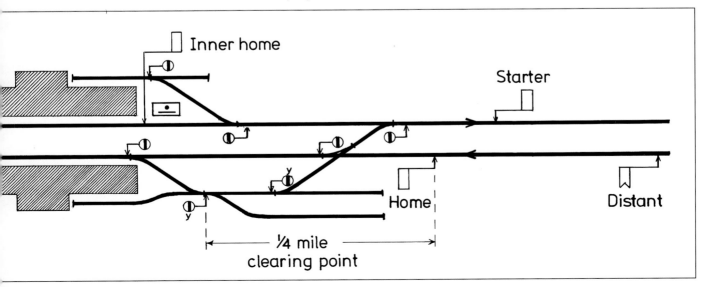

remind the signalman of the situation, to see that the signalman is using the appropriate reminder appliances, such as lever collars, and to sign the train register to that effect before leaving. This requirement also applies to any shunting move brought to a stand on a running line. This procedure, known as Rule 55 until the 1960s and as K3 from the 1970s is probably the most famous rule in the rule book. Its lack of observance in the past lay at the heart of many accidents and was an essential part of the reminder process to stop trains from being forgotten.

Obviously, the procedure can cause further unnecessary delay if the line becomes clear in the meantime, or if the signal concerned is some distance from the signalbox. Many signals are therefore provided with a telephone, or a plunger which, when operated, sounds a bell or buzzer and drops a flap indicator in the signalbox to remind the signalman of the train's presence, and in either of these instances, there is no need for the crew to go to the signalbox, although they must still make use of the equipment within the stipulated time. Signals with this facility carry an indicator as on page 132. The train crew need not go to the signalbox except in the case of long delay if the signal at which they are standing is track circuited, and the signalman thus knows from his illuminated diagram of their presence (or, in the past, if the line was worked on the lock and block system). Such signals are provided with a white diamond-shaped sign as shown on page 130. Many such signals – and almost all on lines with colour light signals and/or using track circuit block – are equipped with signal post telephones, and in more recent times, direct cab to signalman radios have obviated the need for drivers to even leave their cabs, the lineside telephones becoming only an emergency backup. As we shall see in later chapters, on lines where Driver-Only-Operation is employed, driver to signalman radio is a precondition. The other exception to the requirement to go to the signalbox is on single lines, provided the driver of the train concerned is, as we shall see in the next chapter, in possession of the appropriate single line staff, tablet or token. Today a signalbox may be miles away so telephone or radio must be used.

One of the most common reasons for a signalman being unable to accept a train is because of another movement across the running line concerned within the clearing point, usually at a busy station or junction. It may, however, sometimes be possible for a signalman to establish the necessary $1/4$ mile overlap beyond his stop signals by setting an alternative route to that eventually required, and as long as this route is unobstructed as far as its clearing point he may accept a train in the usual manner but maintain his signals at danger until the desired route becomes available.

Block controls

To avoid the possibility of confusion, the times at

which all bell signals are sent or received are recorded in a Train Register book in most signalboxes, as are the times when signalmen come on duty or leave, or of any other incidents affecting the running of trains. Nevertheless, as so far described, the block system is of course open to human error. In early installations, although discipline among signalmen was good and there were remarkably few incidents caused by incorrect block working, it was nevertheless possible for a busy signalman to mistakenly give 'train out of section', clear the block indicator and accept a second train while the first was still in the block section, having perhaps been delayed for some reason. Likewise, there was nothing to stop him, in a moment of aberration, from clearing his signals to allow a train into the block section in advance without getting the acceptance of the signalman at the box ahead.

Inevitably, and particularly as traffic levels increased, putting increasing pressure on signalmen, such errors did occasionally occur, and because of their serious potential consequences, signal engineers were constantly looking to find ways to ensure that trains were properly signalled and could not be overlooked. This was usually achieved by various forms of locking between the block instruments, signals and some form of detection on the track.

Sykes lock and block

One of the most widely used systems, employed by several of the pre-Grouping railways around London to

Fig. 19. The basic arrangement of a Sykes lock and block instrument. The semaphore arm at the top was the block indicator for the section ahead, the top tablet showed whether the starting signal into the section ahead was free or locked, and the bottom tablet indicated whether there was a train in the rear section coming towards the signalbox.

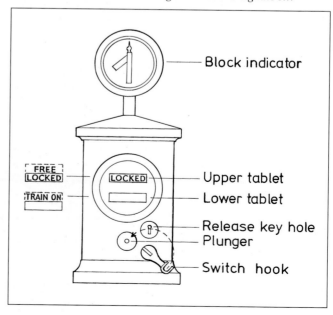

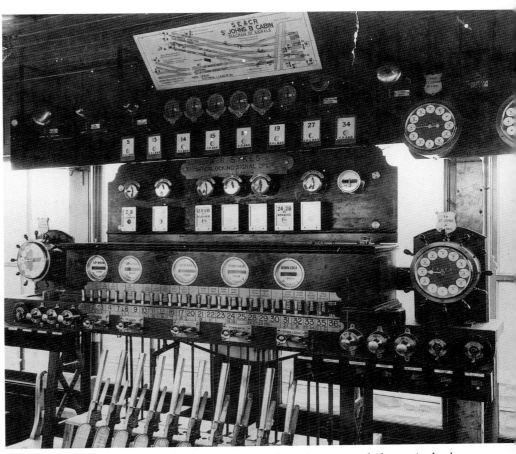

LEFT *Close up of a Sykes lock and block instrument used on the London, Brighton & South Coast Railway. The two-position miniature signal arm block indicator – horizontal for 'line blocked' or 'train on line', lowered for line clear – is at the top. The indicator shows that the signal it controls is 'locked' because there is a 'train on line' (ie in the block section), and the switch hook at the bottom is turned across behind the release plunger, preventing it from being used. (National Railway Museum)*

RIGHT *A fascinating pre-Grouping view of St Johns 'B' signalbox, at Lewisham in the southern suburbs of London on the South Eastern & Chatham Railway, showing the Sykes lock and block indicators above the 26 push-pull miniature sliding levers for the electrically-worked signals, which are themselves above the ten large levers for the points. Also prominent are the Walker electro-mechanical rotary train describers, the 12 different routeing descriptions even then being very necessary on this busy suburban line.*

cope with their rapidly expanding suburban services, and in use until the 1970s, were the various forms of the Sykes lock and block system. This system prevented a signalman from clearing his most advanced starting signal to allow a train to enter the block section ahead until the signal had been electrically released by the signalman at the next box ahead. In turn, the system prevented this signalman from giving such a release until the previous train had passed his home signal, that

signal had been returned to danger, and the train had then activated a treadle to prove that it had passed a certain distance beyond the home signal, usually equivalent to the clearing point. Special combined block and signal indicators were provided to show the state of the block section and whether the signals were locked or free. If a signalbox controlled several signals on the same line within its station limits – say home, starting and advanced starting signals – each signal would be provided with an instrument to show whether it was free or locked.

The method of working was generally similar to that used in conventional block working. If our signalboxes at Ayton and Beeford had been so equipped, and Ayton wished to send a train to Beeford, the Ayton signalman would call attention, and when Beeford acknowledged, would send the relevant 'is line clear?' code, which Beeford would accept by repeating the signal in the usual way. The Beeford signalman would then press a plunger on his home signal instrument, which would cause the indicator on his instrument to change from a blank to 'train on', the indicator for the starting signal at Ayton to change from 'locked' to 'free', and the arm on the two position block indicator to rise. The signalman at Ayton is now free to clear his starting signal, but once he has done so, the indicator for this signal will change back to 'locked' and remain so until

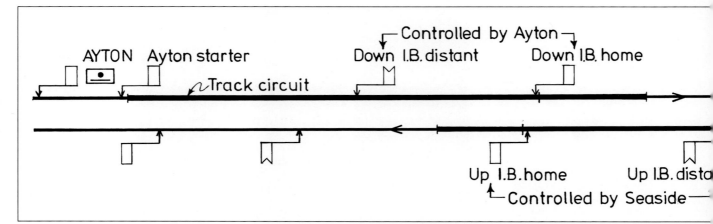

Fig. 20. *The layout of intermediate block signals.*

the train has passed it and worked a treadle, which then changes the indication to 'free' to allow the signalman to return the signal to danger, whereupon it is locked again behind the train, preventing another train from being allowed into the section. Ayton then sends 'train entering section' to Beeford, who acknowledges and turns a special switch hook over the plunger on his home signal instrument to stop it being used. When the train arrives at Beeford and passes over the treadle to release the signals, the indicator there would move from 'train on' to blank and once the signalman there had restored his signals to danger, from 'free' to locked. The Beeford signalman would then send the 'train out of section' signal to Ayton, and when it was acknowledged, remove the switch lock from the plunger, which action leaves the block indicator at Ayton ready for the block section to be used again.

The Sykes system undoubtedly worked well and gave additional assurance and protection to signalmen in busy boxes, but it relied heavily on electric locks and electro-mechanical equipment on signals, and track treadles, and was therefore susceptible to failure, particularly in adverse weather – the very conditions in which reassurance was necessary. A special release key or button was provided to allow signalmen to unlock the equipment if a train was cancelled after it had been signalled, or if there was a failure, but in the latter case, of course, the safety sequence was then bypassed. Often a release could only be obtained by co-operative use of the release key at the two signalboxes at each end of the section. In later years, track circuits or modern lightweight single-arm treadles serving the same function replaced the original treadles.

Line clear release
In many ways, the Sykes equipment was the forerunner of modern electric block controls, but using the then available technology of electro-mechanical locks and treadles which pre-dated track circuits. Nowadays, the

basis of block controls is achieved by the use of two track circuits on each line at each signalbox. One track circuit is situated on the approach to the outermost home signal, and is known as the home berth track circuit, and the other is on the approach side of the starting signal controlling entry into the next block section, and is known as the starter berth track circuit. Electrical locking ensures that the lever for the signal controlling entry to the block section can only be released – and usually only for one pull – when the block indicator for the section ahead is at 'line clear'. In turn, locking also ensures that the signalman at the box ahead can only put his instrument to 'line clear' if the berth track circuit leading up to his home signal is clear, and both his distant and home signal arms are respectively at caution and danger. When a train running through the block section occupies the berth track circuit leading to the home signal, it will change the block indicator to 'train on line' if for any reason

Fig. 21. *Modern block controls provide a check on signalmen's actions rather akin to Sykes lock and block although by different methods. Welwyn control, introduced after the Welwyn Garden City collision of 1935, ensured that one train had passed through a block section with the signals returned to danger and caution behind it before a second train could be signalled.*

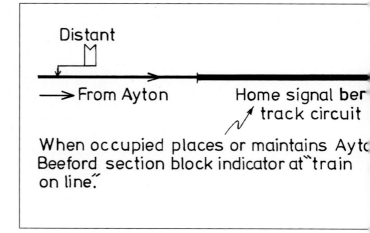

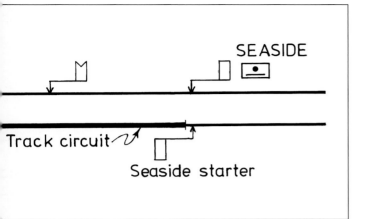

Track circuit

Seaside starter

the signalman has omitted to do so when he received 'train entering section', and while the train continues to occupy the track circuit, the indicator is maintained at 'train on line' even if the signalman forgets there is a train standing there and attempts to clear the block section.

Welwyn control

In some installations, a form of control (known as Welwyn Control because it was introduced after an accident at Welwyn Garden City in 1935) is provided whereby the second track circuit, on the approach to the starting signal, is linked to the block indicator for the section in rear in such a way that, once 'line clear' has been given on the rear section block indicator, it cannot be given again until both the home and starter berth track circuits at the box have been occupied and cleared, thus proving that a train has passed through the rear section. This is shown in Fig. 21. Together with sequential locking, which as we have seen ensures that a signalman must restore his signals to danger before he can clear them again in the correct order, interlinking proving distant and home signal arms are at caution and danger, and 'line clear' release ensure that trains are correctly signalled and that, once signalled, a train must pass through the block

section before a second train can be signalled.

Intermediate block signals

Earlier in this chapter, we saw how the siting of signalboxes was dictated by junctions and station track layouts, and conversely, how on long sections of line without either stations or junctions, intermediate signalboxes were necessary simply to break otherwise very long block sections into shorter sections. Many of these signalboxes controlled no more than a home and distant signal in each direction, with perhaps an emergency crossover. With advances in technology, coupled with the increasing cost of manning what were often simple, very boring and lonely boxes to work, it has for many years been the practice to abolish these signalboxes wherever possible. To avoid lengthening the block section the control of the signals is transferred to the adjacent signalbox, usually the signalbox in rear in each direction. In early installations, the signals remained as semaphores, but because of the distance, worked by electric motors activated by contacts on the levers in the new signalbox controlling them. In most cases, because no mechanical wiring was involved, the distant and stop signal were worked by a single lever, the distant arm only clearing once the stop arm was proved to be at 'clear' by an appropriate contact. In more recent times, it has become standard practice to use two-aspect colour lights for distant and home intermediate block signals (IBS). To illustrate how IBS work, let us assume that, in our earlier example, Beeford signalbox has been abolished and replaced with intermediate block signals, worked on the down line from Ayton, and on the up line from Seaside. Both lines will be continuously track circuited from the most advanced starting signal controlling entry to the intermediate block section to a point about $1/4$ mile beyond the intermediate block home signal, equivalent to the clearing point at a normal box. The actual block section between Ayton and Seaside runs from Beeford intermediate down home signal to Seaside on the down line, and from

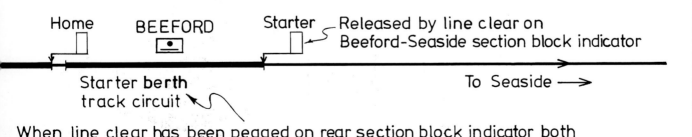

Home   BEEFORD   Starter ⌐ Released by line clear on
                            Beeford-Seaside section block indicator

Starter berth
track circuit   To Seaside ⟶

When line clear has been pegged on rear section block indicator both track circuits must usually be occupied and cleared before "line clear" can be pegged for a second time. The starter must be at danger before the home signal can be cleared.

Beeford intermediate up home signal to Ayton on the up line, as shown in Fig. 20.

To see how the system works, we once again imagine that we are in a signalbox, but this time we are at Ayton. The signalman there has accepted a train from the previous box, and when he receives 'train entering section', provided there is no train in the section to the IBS, he can clear all the Ayton signals immediately, giving the train a clear run as far as the Beeford intermediate block home signal. He then offers the train to Seaside, and if it is accepted, he clears the Beeford intermediate block home and distant signals. When the train passes Ayton, if the line is clear all the way to Seaside, our signalman sends 'train entering section' then, rather than waiting for it to pass the intermediate block home signal into the block section proper. In most modern installations, the track circuits automatically return the intermediate block distant and home signals to caution and danger respectively as soon as the train has passed them, and our signalman at Ayton cannot clear them again until he has received a further 'line clear' from Seaside for the next train.

However, as soon as the first train has cleared the overlap beyond the intermediate block home signal, our signalman at Ayton can clear his signals to allow a second train to run into the intermediate block section towards the intermediate block signal at danger. Then, when the first train has passed Seaside and the signalman there has given Ayton 'train out of section', Ayton can offer him the second train, and if it is accepted, clear the intermediate block signals. In this instance, our signalman at Ayton gives the 'train entering section' signal for the second train only when it has been accepted, not when it passed his box into the intermediate block section, because of course at that time the first train was still in the actual block section.

Special block working

So far, we have seen how the basic block system works. But clearly the system has to be sufficiently flexible to allow for individual local conditions and local operating requirements, and to provide for these, there are both special bell codes and, in some cases, special instructions for working at individual signalboxes. (On some lines, special bell codes are used at the approach to junctions to forewarn the signalmen controlling the junction of the route a train should take – for example, the normal 3 pause 1 bell signal for an ordinary stopping passenger train is often reversed to 1 pause 3 if the train is due to take a diverging route at a junction ahead. Likewise, an express passenger train for a diverging route might be offered to the junction signalbox as 4 pause 4 rather than the usual bell code of just four rings. On the lines of the old Southern Railway where, particularly in suburban areas, tracks were often shared between passenger trains with many different destinations and stopping patterns, but there

was little freight or other special traffic, just as the trains carried special headcodes, so they were offered from signalbox to signalbox by special bell codes, which were routeing codes rather than codes describing the type of train, often designated as branch or main.

Signalboxes close together

Where signalboxes are very close together, and therefore for braking reasons the distant signal for one box must also act as the outer distant for the next signalbox, both signalmen must exercise control over the same signal arm. Although slotting as described in the previous chapter will be used to ensure that the distant signal cannot be cleared if there is a stop signal above it at danger, the working of the distant arm may be by means of bell codes. Let us imagine that our signalboxes at Ayton and Beeford are very close together, and therefore the Ayton distant signal is also the outer distant signal for Beeford. The signal is controlled only from Ayton, and the signalman at Beeford has no physical control over it, but obviously it must not be cleared until Beeford has cleared all its stop signals, including its own inner distant signal. In this circumstance, the normal method of working would be for the Beeford signalman, when offered a train by Ayton, to immediately offer it on to Seaside. If it is accepted, the Beeford signalman can in turn accept it from Ayton, who can then clear all his stop signals and, when given a special bell signal from Beeford to indicate that his signals are also clear, finally clear the distant signal applying to the signals controlled by both boxes. If, however, Seaside cannot accept the train, the Beeford signalman will respond to the offer of a train from Ayton with a further special bell signal (used particularly on GWR lines) of 2 pause 2 pause 2, 'line clear to clearing point only', which the signalman at Ayton must acknowledge before the signalman at Beeford moves his block indicator to 'line clear'. In this case, although the train has been accepted by Beeford, the Ayton signalman must maintain his signals at danger until the train has passed the distant signal, which will of course be locked at caution.

In some busy areas, special indicators are provided in the signalbox controlling the outer distant, either worked directly by the signalman at the next signalbox ahead, by electric contacts on the distant levers in that box, so that the indication only changes from caution to clear when all the signals at the next box, including the distant, are cleared and only then does the first signalman finally clear his distant signal. In more recent times, outer distant signals have been converted either to electrical control of the mechanical arm or to colour lights, and the wiring is so arranged that the signal will only clear if the distant levers in both boxes are reversed – which, of course, because of the interlocking, can themselves only be reversed if all the stop signals are already cleared.

Double block working

When the LMS and the LNER introduced their high speed streamlined trains in the 1930s, to provide adequate braking distance double block working was used ahead of the trains, that is two block sections at least had to be clear. The LMS distinguished its 'Coronation Scot' train with the special bell code of 4-4-4, the same code employed for the royal train although there would not be any confusion between the two. Double block working was also used ahead of, and to the rear of the royal train. It was also used in fog if fog signalmen were not on duty.

The 'warning' arrangement

We have already seen that, before a train can be accepted from the signalbox in rear, not only must the block section be clear, but an overlap, usually of about ¼ mile, must also be clear beyond the outermost stop signal to what is defined as the clearing point to allow for any misjudgment of braking on the part of drivers. In the past, when freight trains were often not fitted with the automatic brake, and were slow-moving and therefore often took some time to pass through block sections, or even had to stop in the block section to shunt or for other purposes, it was inconvenient to keep the clearing point free for a long time, particularly if other shunting or light engine movements needed to take place within the station limits at the accepting box. In such circumstances, provided that none of the trains involved were passenger trains, special acceptance arrangements were authorised.

Because the overrun beyond the home signal could not, in these circumstances, be guaranteed, the driver of the freight train concerned had to be specially warned

An interesting view of Derby West Junction signalbox and the gantry spanning the Midland main line north from Derby in the early 1930s. This is one corner of the triangle with the loop line back to Trent Junction seen going off to the right. The signal heights are unusual. The third and fourth tracks from the left are goods lines going straight ahead so the higher doll with the stop signal at clear refers to the sharply curving passenger line going off to the right. Similarly in the opposite direction the signals on the fifth post from the left apply over the crossover from the goods line to the main passenger line on the left and behind the camera but the straight route is controlled by the lower sixth signal. Note the corrugated signal arms. (LMS)

at the previous signalbox and thus the procedure became known as the 'Warning Arrangement'. If, for example, our signalman at Ayton wanted to send a ballast train due to stop in the block section to Beeford, he would send the 2 pause 2 pause 3 bell signal to Beeford, and provided the line was clear up to Beeford's outermost stop signal, Beeford would respond with a 'Warning Acceptance' of 3 pause 5 pause 5, but would not place his block indicator to 'line clear' until Ayton acknowledged this bell signal by repeating it. The Ayton signalman now has to warn the driver that his train has only been given a Warning Acceptance, which he does by maintaining his signals at danger until the train is closely approaching and therefore running very slowly. The signalman then clears his home signal or signals and shows a steady green handsignal (a green flag by day, a green lamp at night) to the driver, who must acknowledge it before the signalman can clear his remaining signals to allow the train into the block section. A driver would understand that this procedure specifically authorises him to enter the block section

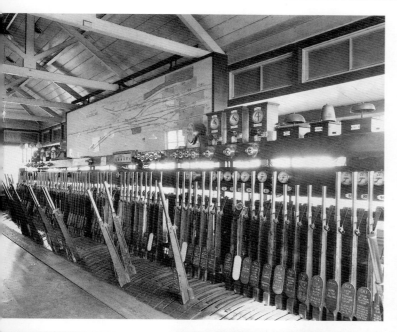

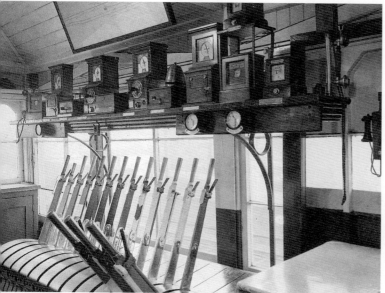

LEFT *The interior of a typical large mechanical signalbox. This one, at Guildford, built by the London & South Western Railway but considerably modified in Southern Railway times, controlled both mechanically and electrically worked points and both semaphore and colour light signals, but all the levers are mounted in a mechanical frame. The track diagram above the lever frame shows all the lines controlled by the box, and carries the track circuit indicators showing the presence of trains in the appropriate geographical positions on the diagram. There are block instruments, block bells and rotary train describers on the block shelf, with beneath them appropriate block bell plungers and 'train ready to start' indicators from the platforms, while behind each of the levers controlling signals there is an indicator to show if the signal is actually 'on' or 'off'. (British Railways)*

BELOW *Part of the interior of Mill Hill Broadway signalbox on the old Midland Railway main line showing the lever frame for the fast lines. Another frame for the slow lines was behind the camera. An older, simpler installation, the track diagram, tucked up in the roof above the block shelf, does not carry any track circuit indicators, these being provided separately by indicators on the crowded block shelf. Of the 16 levers in what was known as a 'knee frame' (because the lever quadrants were above the floor level, at about knee height), the second from the left has been shortened slightly, indicating to the signalman that it controls an electrically worked signal, the down fast colour light distant, and he does not, therefore have to give it much of a heave! The white stripe midway down the fourth lever from the left indicates that the signal it controls is electrically released by 'line clear' from the next signalbox in advance while the downward-facing chevrons on lever No. 9 show that it controls detonator placers on the down line – the chevrons would point upwards for a similar installation on the up line. The block instruments include the Midland's rotary block controls, meaning the handle had to be turned to the three indications in sequence. (British Railways)*

under the Warning Arrangement; if he was being authorised to pass a signal at danger, the rules require him to be stopped and specifically authorised to do so. In some locations, where this form of operation was routine practice, a special subsidiary signal, usually displaying a 'W' was provided beneath the main starting signal permitting entry to the block section.

In these circumstances, a train would be checked in turn at each of the stop signals at the box in question and the subsidiary signal would only be cleared when the train had almost come to stand at it. If the line beyond the accepting signalbox's home signal becomes clear to the clearing point before a train accepted under the Warning Arrangement enters the block section, the signalman at the box ahead sends the 3 pause 3 pause 5

signal (line now clear to clearing point) to the signalbox in rear, and the signalman at that box need not warn the driver and may clear all his signals. Because of the virtual disappearance of slow-moving freight trains, coupled with the decline in the number of in-section sidings with ground frame access, use of the Warning Arrangement is now rare, and usually limited to the working of ballast, engineers' or inspection trains needing to stop in the block section, but is sometimes used in other prescribed circumstances, even for passenger trains.

Permissive block
Another form of special block working is permissive block working. This apparently contradictory concept – of allowing more than one train into a block section at a time – is normally permitted at specifically authorised locations where no passenger trains are involved. It was usually only used on freight lines, or lines used predominantly for freight, often at the approach to large marshalling yards so that successive trains waiting to enter the yard could 'bunch up' behind each other rather than be strung out behind each other in successive block sections, delaying both themselves and

other traffic. Signalboxes authorised for permissive working are equipped with special block instruments which are similar to those used for absolute block working, but in addition have an indicator which is set by the signalman to show how many trains have entered the section. This indicator was sometimes, but not always, repeated in the box ahead. If it was not, the signalman there had to remember also to advance his indicator every time a train was accepted. They were known as tell-tale instruments.

With the exception that, for obvious reasons, with permissive working it is not necessary to have the line clear beyond the outermost home signal to the clearing point (in which case a train is accepted to the home signal only, 4 pause 3), the actual method of working trains is similar to that used with the absolute block system. The important exception is that a signalman can accept a second train while the first is still in the section, and while the block indicator is still showing 'train on line'. This he does by responding to the offer of a second or subsequent train with the 'line occupied acceptance' bell signal (2 pause 4 pause 2) and leaving the block indicator at 'train on line'. When he receives and acknowledges 'train entering section' for the second train, both signalmen advance their counters by one. When a train leaves the block section, after exchanging the 'train out of section' bell signal, both signalmen reduce their counters by one. The block indicator remains at 'train on line' throughout until the last train leaves the section. Thereafter, trains can be worked on the absolute block system if required, or a further batch may be worked permissively. Over the years bell codes changed. On the GWR for example the line occupied acceptance was one beat on the bell.

Special subsidiary signals are usually provided at the entrance to a permissive section. If there is no subsidiary signal the driver is shown a green flag and told to proceed. When a train is admitted to a permissive block section that is clear, the main running signals are worked in the usual way, but if there is a train still in the section, the following train is brought almost to a stand at the signal controlling entry to the section, and then the subsidiary signal, for permissive working, is cleared. Drivers allowed entry to the block section under permissive conditions know that there is at least one train, if not more, probably on the move ahead of them in that section, and that they must therefore control their train in such a way as to be able to stop short of any train in front which itself may have stopped. If a passenger train needs to use a line normally used permissively for freight working, absolute block working conditions must be used, including the requirement for a $1/4$ mile overlap beyond the home signal to the clearing point before a train can be accepted. Permissive working is inherently less safe than absolute block working, and of course many of the modern block controls used in absolute block

signalling cannot be applied to permissive working, and it is now rarely used, although it has been adapted to a few freight lines in track circuit block areas with modern signalling.

Permissive working is allowed however, at some major stations where passenger trains need to stand one behind the other at platforms for connections or where multiple units are coupled together. The trains are not allowed to be on the move at the same time and the first must be at a stand at the platform with room for the second. The second is then brought to a stand at the signal protecting the platform and allowed to proceed forward on sight, on the authority of a subsidiary signal, usually a calling-on signal in mechanical signalling, or a position light subsidiary (see later in Chapter 14) in colour light practice. There was also a method of working in the past where two parts of a train were on the move together. This was in slip coach operation which survived from the last century until the 1960s on a few former GWR services. The rear coach or coaches were detached by the slip guard riding at the front of the slip portion as the train approached a station. The slip guard controlled the brakes of the slip portion and had to keep it back from the main part of the train ready to stop at the platform. Slip working was only allowed if the signals were clear through the

Another standard feature of the mechanical signalling era which has survived into modern signalling, although now becoming very much an endangered species, is the guard's right away flag signal, often accompanied by a blast on his whistle. But with on-train starting bells or buzzers on multiple units, or in some cases driver-only operation, the guard's flag is almost a thing of the past. (Geoffrey Kichenside)

station for the main part of the train. If not, the whole train had to stop. At Reading, special slip distant signals were provided for the information of the slip guard to show whether it was safe to uncouple the slip portion.

Other block working procedures

In addition to block signals and regulations covering the working of trains through the block section between signalboxes, there are also special bell codes and instructions covering both other normal aspects of working and, as we shall see later, emergency working when things go wrong.

We saw at the beginning of this chapter how the tracks wholly within the protection of stop signals controlled from any one signalbox were known as 'station limits' and that within this area, a signalman could generally signal movements without reference to the signalmen on either side of him. However, even within this area, if he wishes to signal a move which impinges upon the $1/4$ mile overlap beyond his home signal to the clearing point, he must first obtain authority from the signalman in rear by sending the 'blocking back inside home signal' bell code (2 pause 4) to the signalbox in rear and, when this is acknowledged, placing the block indicator at 'train on line'. In addition to protecting shunting moves, this regulation would be used at a junction if, for example, to allow another move, points were set towards a route on which a train was standing within the $1/4$ mile overlap. If a shunting move requires all or part of the train to reverse in the wrong direction beyond the home signal, the 'blocking back outside home signal' bell code (3 pause 3) is used.

Fig. 22. *Protection of a disabled train on adjacent or opposite tracks. On high speed lines carrying trains at over 100mph the triple detonators first encountered by an approaching train would be placed at least 1¼ miles from the obstruction, and sometimes are required on both rails to ensure that they are heard in an air-conditioned insulated cab.*

When the shunting move is completed, or points are reset towards a route on which there is the requisite $1/4$ mile overlap, the signalman concerned sends the 'obstruction removed' bell signal (2 pause 1) in the same way he sends 'train out of section' and restores the block indicator to normal.

On lines where signalboxes are not open continuously, signalmen need to inform each other when they are closing or opening their signalboxes. This cannot normally be done while a train is in the block section, but when the section is free, all signals are at danger and the block instruments are at 'normal' or 'line blocked', a signalman sends the closing signal (7 pause 5 pause 5) to indicate to his colleagues in the adjacent signalboxes that he is leaving. Likewise, when he wishes to re-open the signalbox, before moving any levers, the signalman sends the opening signal (5 pause 5 pause 5) to the adjacent signalboxes, and when this is acknowledged, he tests the block instruments and bells (16 consecutive beats, followed by one beat of acknowledgement for each movement of the block indicator during testing).

Even on lines which are open continuously, intermediate signalboxes which are not required throughout the day may be closed, particularly at night, when there is less traffic. When an intermediate signalbox closes, the two adjacent block sections of course become one single, longer section, and the signalmen on each side must be able to communicate directly. This is achieved by the use of a closing switch in the box to be 'switched out'. Let us imagine that the signalman at our box at Beeford, between Ayton and Seaside, wishes to close his signalbox and so make the section between Ayton and Seaside one long section. Usually, he must wait until there are no trains in either of the block sections. Then he sends the closing signal (7 pause 5 pause 5) to both boxes on either side, and on receiving acknowledgement, operates the block closing switch, which disconnects his instruments, and

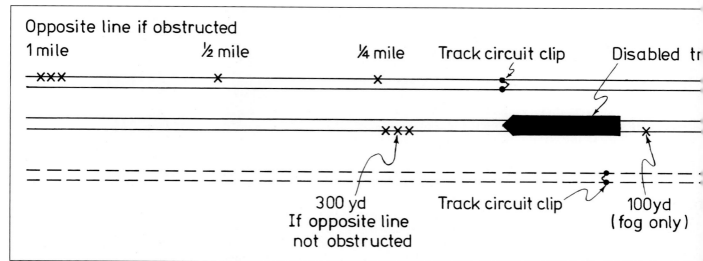

instead directly connects the instruments at Ayton on one side to those at Seaside on the other, and then clears all his signals. If, however, the Beeford box were to be fitted with block controls, including 'line clear' release on his starting signals, the process is a little more complicated, because the signalman must first obtain 'line clear' from the next signalbox in advance in each direction so that he can clear his signals before switching out. In this case, the bell code 5 pause 5 pause 7 is used. Once Beeford has closed, the signalmen at Ayton and Seaside must test their bells and instruments to ensure that they are working properly.

Before reopening his signalbox, the signalman at Beeford must telephone the signalmen on either side to ensure that there are no trains in either of the sections, because he must not switch line if there are, or if 'line clear' has been given. When he is free to do so, our signalman sends the 'opening signalbox' code (5 pause 5 pause 5) to the boxes on either side, restores the block switch to normal, restores his signals to danger, and tests the bells and instruments.

Not all unusual workings were described by 'is line clear?' bell codes. Where banking engines were used to push trains up steep gradients often they were not coupled to the train. So that the signalmen at the top of the climb knew if there was a banker or how many, each banker was advised by the signalman at the bottom of the incline by bell code 2 pause 2 sent following the train entering section signal.

When things go wrong

If, after being signalled, a train cannot proceed for some reason, a signalman can send the 'cancelling' signal (3 pause 5) to the box ahead and restore his signals to danger. Where, however, block controls are in use, it is usually necessary to obtain a release of the equipment by the use of a plunger or key. In many cases these are either sealed and use thereof requires the seal to be broken, or are fitted with a time delay, so as to

discourage misuse. Any such special release must be recorded in the Train Register in the signalbox. Alternatively, if a signalman decides to send an alternative train to the one originally described, or discovers that it has been incorrectly described to him, he can send the 'last train incorrectly described' signal (5 pause 3). In this case, when the signal is acknowledged, he then sends the correct description, but the block indicator is maintained at 'line clear'.

On lines where absolute block working is in force, it is part of every signalman's duty to observe the passage of each train as it passes his box, to ensure that there is nothing amiss, and that it is complete. If it is not he must obviously take immediate steps not only to stop the train, but possibly others on adjacent running lines. If he is too late to stop the train at his own signals, he must send the 'stop and examine' signal (7 consecutive beats) to the signalbox ahead, followed by a telephone call to the signalman at that box explaining the problem. On receiving this signal, the signalman at the box ahead must immediately put his signals to danger so as to stop the train and have it examined. Both signalmen must also take steps to ensure that no trains use any adjacent lines until it can be definitely established that these lines are not obstructed.

Where large areas are controlled by power signalboxes, and trains often do not therefore pass close to the signalboxes controlling them, hot axlebox detectors are often provided at strategic locations to give warning of anything that is overheating as it passes – although such equipment can sometimes be erroneously triggered by the heat of a normally functioning diesel engine that passes. A hot axlebox could lead to bearing collapse and derailment.

All trains on running lines are required to carry red tail lamps, both to indicate that the train is complete and, during darkness or in tunnels, so as to be seen by anything approaching from the rear. On lines using the absolute block system, it is the signalman's responsibility to check each train to ensure that it has passed through the preceding block section complete. If a train passes his box without a tail lamp or red rear lights, he must assume that it is not complete, and send the 'train passed without tail lamp' bell signal both to the signalbox ahead (9 consecutive beats) and to the signalbox in rear (4 pause 5). All the signalmen concerned must stop and caution all trains travelling in the opposite direction. Nowadays, when almost all trains are fully equipped with automatic brakes, the problem is usually nothing more than a tail lamp having fallen off or, at night, the light being extinguished for some reason. But if it appears that the train has been divided he must take immediate action to stop both parts.

Trains very rarely run away, but it has happened, sometimes due to mismanagement of the brake by the driver, and sometimes due to the actions of others,

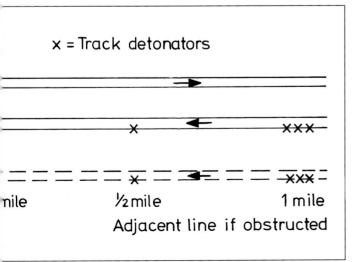

x = Track detonators

½ mile   1 mile

Adjacent line if obstructed

including vandalism, often without anybody on board. If a signalman becomes aware of a train running without authority along a line in the usual direction, he must immediately send the 'train running away in right direction' bell signal (4 pause 5 pause 5) to the signalbox ahead, and prevent any further trains entering the block section until the line is cleared. The signalman at the next box ahead must put his block indicator to 'train on line' and take all steps to stop the train, including putting down detonators if the runaway train is crewed. If, however, there is a train still in the block section ahead of the runaway, he must keep his signals cleared for the first train so as to get it clear as quickly as possible, and then restore his signals to danger, put down detonators and try to direct the errant train from the main line. Throughout this period he maintains his block indicator at 'train on line'. If the runaway train arrives at his signalbox intact, the signalman may then send 'train out of section'.

Should a train run away in the wrong direction, against the normal direction of traffic, the signalman must send the 'train running away in wrong direction' bell signal (2 pause 5 pause 5) to the signalbox towards which the runaway is going. This is, of course, a more dangerous situation; the signalman receiving the signal must do everything possible to stop a head-on collision with any train that may be approaching on the right line, and if possible either turn the runaway train into a siding or across to the right line. If he succeeds in doing the latter, but is unable to stop the train, he then in turn sends the 'train running away in right direction' bell signal to the next signalbox.

If a signalman becomes aware of an obstruction at any time – perhaps something reported to have fallen from a train, a car crashing through the fence onto the line, or perhaps through vandalism – he must immediately send the 'obstruction danger' (6 consecutive beats) signal to the box in rear, place the block indicator for the line or lines obstructed at 'train on line' and either return or maintain all his relevant signals at danger, and put three detonators, 20 yards apart, on the running lines to prevent any train from entering the section. Once action has been taken to stop any approaching trains, the signalman receiving the 'obstruction danger' signal must acknowledge it, and ascertain the reason for it having been sent. If he has already offered a train through the affected block section and had it accepted, he must send the cancelling signal; if, however, a train has already passed into the now obstructed section, he instead sends the 'train running away on right line' signal, whereupon the signalman who sent the original signal must take steps to stop the approaching train short of the obstruction. The 'obstruction danger' signal does not need to be preceded by the 'call attention' signal, and may be sent at any time, irrespective of the state of the block section although some railways had an emergency 'call attention' by a rapid number of bell beats. When the line has been cleared of the obstruction, the 'obstruction removed' bell signal, which is the same as 'train out of section' (2 pause 1) is sent.

In the event of a running line in a block section becoming obstructed – in effect, any running line outside the protection of the signals of a single signal box – it must be immediately protected. In addition to the signalmen controlling access to the lines concerned placing lever collars as reminders on the relevant levers in their boxes, and if possible setting an alternative route, the obstruction – which may be anything from a failed train through a broken rail to a collapsed bridge or culvert or a tree on the line – must be protected by placing detonators on the line. Three are placed, 20 yards apart, one mile from the obstruction or $1\frac{1}{4}$ miles on 100mph plus lines, one at $\frac{1}{2}$ mile, and one at $\frac{1}{4}$ mile. On routes carrying modern trains at 125mph with well-insulated cabs, detonators are placed on both rails.

In the event of any accident or incident obstructing other running lines, obviously the lines affected must be protected as quickly as possible. In track circuited areas, this can be achieved quickly by the use of track circuit clips, which are carried in the cabs of all trains and which are literally clipped across between the two running rails to simulate the action of a pair of wheels on the tracks and thus return or maintain signals at danger. It is vital that any adjacent lines that may be obstructed are protected even before the line on which the train is standing, because whereas the train will be protected by the normal signalling, trains may already be approaching at speed on adjacent lines. It is a sobering thought that, with the modern high speed trains running at up to 125mph, or more than two miles a minute, even if an oncoming train is ten miles away, the crew of a derailed train have little more than four minutes to get out of their train and get the adjoining line protected. Protection with detonators and track circuit clips, and with the added visual indication of a red flag, red lamps and/or a 'stop' board, is provided to protect planned engineering work which obstructs running lines. This is often in connection with emergency single line working, described in more detail in the next chapter.

As modern signalling has progressed, procedures have changed to suit new conditions. In the past a train failure or a divided train in the middle of a block section might mean rescue by an assisting engine or train. This could entail wrong direction running, a procedure requiring strict observance of the rules and the issue of one of four types of written wrong line order. One, form D, was issued by a signalman to allow a train to return in the wrong direction towards him. Today the signalling centre might be 50 miles from the failure so a written order by the signalman is out of the question, and arrangements are made following set procedures by telephone or cab radio.

Chapter 7

SINGLE LINES

MANY OF THE early railways were built only as single lines, and while many were subsequently doubled to give separate tracks for each direction of travel, in more recent years, some little-used double-track lines have been reduced to a single track as an economy measure. Throughout railway history therefore, methods to ensure the safe working of trains in both directions over a single track have been uppermost in the minds of signal engineers and operators – the more so because any failure can lead to a head-on collision. Single line signalling is inevitably more specialised than double line and the developments in single line control effectively form a step by step change related to what has gone before. Thus the modern developments in token, tokenless block, and electronic radio data exchange systems are described here rather than in later chapters which cover the general breakthrough into computer control of signalling.

One Engine in Steam/One Train Operation

Single-track lines are worked on the same block principle as double-track lines – that there should not be more than one train in any one block section at one time – but with additional devices to ensure that trains cannot enter from opposite ends at the same time. The basic principle of single line working is that no train should ever enter a single line section without a specific authority to do so – usually but not always some form of tangible authority such as a staff, ticket, token or key specific to that stretch of line. The simplest form of single line authority is a single wooden or metal staff, engraved with the name of the single line section and kept in the signalbox at the entrance to the section. The driver of any train entering the section is given the staff, and until it is returned, no other train is allowed to enter the section. Clearly, however, the disadvantage is that a second train running in the same direction arriving at the entrance to the block section cannot proceed until another train in the opposite direction returns with the staff. Such rigid use of a single line section in alternate directions is operationally impractical – even if the timetable were so constructed, for it makes no allowance for failures, late running or cancellations – so this 'one engine' method is normally used only for dead-end single lines carrying light, possibly only goods, traffic, where it would be normal for the first train to return before any other wished to use it. Where this form of working is used, there is normally no block working – because there can only ever be one train in use at a time anyway – and any points or crossovers needing to be worked at the terminus end of the line can be worked from a ground frame unlocked by a key on the staff.

Staff and ticket

A development of this method, known as staff and ticket was used in the early days – and on some lightly-used lines for many years. If more than one train wishes to travel through the single line section before any others return in the opposite direction, the signalman at the entry end, having gained permission from the signalman at the opposite end, either by telephone or in most cases on the block instruments, issues a ticket of authority to enter the single line section to all but the last train. He gives the 'ticket' – which is actually a printed form on which he writes the train details and the specific section of line it applies to – to the driver and must show him the staff but does not give it to him. As an added security, the ticket forms are normally kept in a locked box in each signalbox which can only be unlocked by a key on the staff. Each train is worked through the single line section in the usual way, and the driver carrying a ticket surrenders it to the signalman at the end of the single line section who then clears the section for the next train. The last train of any group in one direction carries the staff and no ticket; only when the staff is in the possession of the signalman at the far end of the line can any trains be offered in the opposite direction. Clearly, such a method, which ideally requires block instruments and at the very least a telephone or, in Victorian years a telegraph installation, allows a greater degree of flexibility in the operation of timetables, but it is cumbersome, and still does not allow for out of course running or the unexpected – once a train has been sent through the section with a ticket, another must follow with the staff, even though another train may arrive at the far end wanting to pass through the section in the opposite direction. It is also difficult to incorporate additional block controls or other safety devices in such an essentially ad hoc system, and signal engineers therefore set about devising special block instruments for single lines which would combine greater security with the maximum flexibility of operation.

Electric tablet/staff/token

Various types of electric single line instrument were developed, some using metal staffs, others tablets or tokens, and yet others large keys. Edward Tyer patented his electric tablet instrument in 1878 while the

Despite their everyday purpose, early single-line tablet machines were often housed in impressive wood cases which would have done credit to the furniture-makers' craft. In this fine example, the 'block instrument' part of the machine, housing the indicators and bell and release plunger, is mounted atop a splendid case which, on receipt of a release, and working the side handle, would produce a tablet for the single line section concerned at the bottom slot. (National Railway Museum)

The Webb & Thompson electric staff instrument pioneered on the LNWR in the 1890s and supplied under licence by contractors to other railways. The staff was very heavy, two of which can be seen at the foot of the instrument. Later, a smaller version was produced and in turn the key token, which used a key form of lock rather than the rings round the staff for distinctive configurations.

Webb & Thompson large electric staff was a development of the late 1880s. The electric key token instruments and miniature electric staff followed in the new century. All however worked on the same principle. The two signalboxes at each end of a single line section each have an electric single line tablet, staff or token instrument. Each instrument has a supply of several tablets, staffs or tokens and is electrically interlocked with its twin at the other end of the single line. This is done in such a way that, once a tablet, staff or token has been taken out of one or other of the instruments, it is impossible to obtain further authorisation from either instrument until the first has been restored either to the instrument from which it was first taken, or more usually, the instrument at the opposite end of the line, it having been taken there by the driver of a train passing through the single line section. All single line staffs, tablets or tokens are engraved with the name of the specific section of single

In later years, key token machines became more popular, both because they were easier to handle and were more robust in operation. Here, the signalman at Shanklin, Isle of Wight, holds the key in the lock, awaiting a release from his colleague at the other end of the single line section, while in the magazine below, a dozen or so other key tokens are stored ready for re-use. The machine, by now made of steel, is much smaller, robust and functional than earlier examples. (Geoffrey Kichenside)

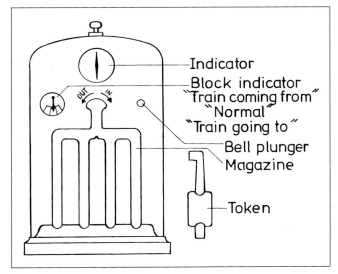

Fig. 23. *The basic electric token instrument.*

Whatever the form of single line authority, whether it be tablet or token, it was usually carried through the single line section in some form of pouch or carrier, usually of leather, with a large holding hoop. This was both to keep it clean and prevent it being lost on the footplate, and to help in the process of passing it to and from the signalman at each end of the section. In this view of Goathland on the North Yorkshire Moors Railway, the crew of a train arriving off the single line section from Grosmont lean out to surrender the carrier to the signalman, who stands arm raised to grab the hoop. Only when this manoeuvre is complete and the arriving train is at a stand can the signalman clear the signals beyond the bridge for a train arriving in the opposite direction. (Alan Williams)

line to which they apply, and whether they are metal staffs, small metal tablets (which usually looked like a large thick biscuit with a hole in the centre) carried in leather pouches, or tokens in the form of a large key, they are always configured in such a way that they will only fit into one or other of the two instruments for the single line section to which they apply. Therefore there is no possibility of them being wrongly inserted into another instrument for an adjacent single line section.

All single line instruments also serve as block instruments and have a magazine in which are stored the supply of staffs, tablets or tokens, a bell plunger, a needle indicator, and a pointer – in effect a modified block indicator. The instruments at each end of a single line are identical. The needle indicator is deflected by the sending of bell signals on the plunger, while, like a block instrument, the pointer has three positions –

The moment of exchange of tokens by hand on the Torbay & Dartmouth line with the driver handing out the token for the section just left by the train and the signalman holding up the token for the section ahead. These are key tokens which are held by a spring clip within the carrier rather than in a pouch. Hand exchange in theory imposed a 10mph limit on the train speed. Higher speeds caused many arm bruises or at worst, injury. (R. E. B. Siviter)

'normal' or 'line blocked', 'train coming from', and 'train going to', as shown in Fig. 23. In earlier patterns the pointer was operated manually but in the final designs it operated automatically as tokens were released and replaced.

Let us now imagine that we are back with our signalman friend at Ayton signalbox, but the line is now single to Beeford, as shown in Fig. 24. If he wants

Fig. 24. *The general signalling arrangement of a single line section.*

to send a train to Beeford, he calls attention with one beat on the plunger, and on receiving a one-beat acknowledgement on the bell, sends the appropriate 'is line clear?' bell signal which the Beeford signalman will acknowledge if he wants to accept the train. However, the Beeford signalman keeps his bell plunger depressed on giving the last beat of this signal, which action keeps the needle indicator deflected and frees the Ayton instrument so that our signalman, who will already have lifted the staff or token out of the magazine into the lock, can turn the staff or token in the lock and withdraw it. This action causes the needle indicator on the instrument in Beeford signalbox to return to the upright position and the signalman there can release the plunger. Our Ayton signalman gives one beat on the bell to confirm that he has obtained a staff or token, the pointer on our instrument at Ayton moves to 'train going to' and that in the signalbox at Beeford to 'train coming from'. The single line is now committed to use by a train from Ayton to Beeford, and the signalman at Beeford cannot remove a staff or token to send a train in the opposite direction, so our signalman can clear his signals and give the staff or token he has withdrawn from the instrument to the driver of the waiting train. When the train departs, our signalman sends the 'train entering section' bell signal to Beeford, which the signalman there acknowledges. The pointer remains in the position as it was after the staff or token was withdrawn. When the train arrives at Beeford the driver gives the signalman there the staff or token, and he passes this through the lock, and sends the 'train out of section' bell signal to us at Ayton which action causes the indicator on the instruments in both signalboxes to return to the 'normal' or 'line blocked' position. The single line is now ready again for use by another train from either direction.

If tablets or tokens are used, to make sure they do not get lost or damaged – because obviously a lost token, or one which is damaged and will not therefore fit back into an instrument, effectively renders the system unusable – they are usually carried through the block section in a leather pouch attached to a large metal hoop. As well as being more difficult to lose this also makes handling easier. Although rules require trains to slow down to less than 10mph to exchange

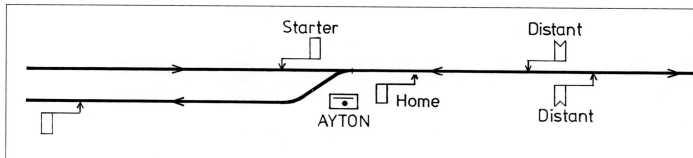

The manual exchange of tablets or tokens was no problem at stations where trains were in any case scheduled to stop, but at signalboxes away from stations, usually at junctions, or on lines which were used by non-stopping expresses, the need to slow to the crawl necessary for manual exchange caused unnecessary delay, and so various types of automatic tablet-exchanging equipment were developed. One type is pictured here at Crossmichael, near Castle Douglas on the now-closed Portpatrick & Wigtownshire Joint line from Dumfries to Stranraer. Provided the next single line section ahead of the approaching train was clear, before the train arrived at his box, the signalman would obtain, in this case, a tablet from his machine, place it in the pouch and clip it to the apparatus seen here, before retreating to his box. Meanwhile, the crew of the train would have clipped the pouch for the section they were in, to a similar device mounted on the nearside of their cab. When this equipment engaged with the lineside mast shown here, the existing pouch was deposited and the new one for the section ahead collected. This simple but robust equipment enabled exchanges to take place at speeds of up to 60mph in all weathers, day or night, and allowed the considerable acceleration of services over long single-line routes. (BR, LMR)

Most single lines were and are, by definition, lightly-used secondary routes, often in rural areas, with perhaps only a handful of trains each way a day. The passing places on many of these lines were often managed by a single porter-signalman, who both supervised the station work, often including selling tickets, as well as working the single line instruments and the associated signals. At such stations, the signalbox was often on the platform, for obvious reasons as close as possible to the station buildings, and in some installations, like the one pictured here at Mayfield on the former Oxted–Eastbourne line, was little more than a large ground frame in a fenced area on the platform. The associated single line instruments were in the adjacent booking office for security. (National Railway Museum)

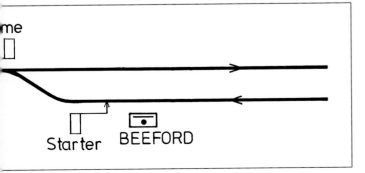

tablets or tokens with a signalman, or even in some circumstances to stop, it still requires care to collect a pouch from a driver for the section he is just leaving and to hand him another for the section he is just entering from the lineside, particularly at night or in adverse weather conditions. Almost all signalboxes on single lines control passing loops – there wouldn't really be much point in having them otherwise, except perhaps to break up really long single line sections, but even then they would only be of use for following trains in the same direction – and such signalboxes tend to have periods of intense activity. This occurs when trains arrive from both directions to pass each other and is interspersed with long periods of complete inactivity while trains are running through what can be very long, single line block sections. As with double line block signalling, signalmen on single lines must ensure that there is a $1/4$ mile overlap beyond their outermost stop signal before accepting a train, and must maintain it while a train is approaching. This means that, unless he has an outer home signal as well as an inner home, which is unusual on single lines except at the approach to junctions, a signalman at a passing loop on a single line must have the lines in both directions clear up to their respective starting signals before being able to accept trains from both directions at the same time. All the signals – which in any case will almost certainly be interlocked to ensure that signals for opposing directions cannot be cleared at the same time – are maintained at danger until the first train to arrive is at or nearly at a stand at the home signal, whereupon it is cleared to allow the train to run into the station. Only when the signalman is satisfied that the first train is safely at a stand within the passing loop may he clear his signals for the train in the opposite direction.

Station limits at passing places on single lines run from the outermost home signal in any one direction to the most advanced starting signal in the same direction, both of which may be on the single line, the former at the approach to the passing loop, and the latter beyond it. Shunting moves onto the single line within station limits without a staff or token are usually permitted, provided such a move does not infringe the overlap to the clearing point of an approaching train. If, however,

By the 1960s other methods of controlling single lines were being used more widely. London Transport's short Chesham branch was given track circuits throughout and the whole line was worked from a route setting push-button panel in the then new Amersham signalbox. At the entry to the single line section double co-acting starting signals were provided. In some ways this feature has been taken up in the 1990s where SPAD (signal passed at danger) signals are provided ahead of a main signal in risk positions so that if a train goes past the main signal at danger the SPAD signal just ahead, normally dark, immediately displays flashing and steady red lights as an extra warning.

a locomotive needs to shunt outside the protection of a home signal, it may be necessary for the signalman to send the 'blocking back' bell signal to the next signalbox and obtain a staff or token from the instrument while the move takes place. When a train is travelling on the single line away from the signalbox concerned, a shunting move into the single line section may be made behind it without blocking back, provided such a move is completed before the train clears the single line section. If it is not complete by the time the signalman at the other end of the section sends 'train out of section', the signalman controlling the shunting move must immediately send the blocking back bell signal.

Tokenless block

Although the electric staff and key token systems are still in use on some lines, faster schedules and growing safety awareness, coupled with advances in electronics, have seen the progressive introduction of various forms of 'tokenless' single line working which do not require the use of a physical staff or token for each single line section, and therefore dispense with the need for signalmen to leave their signalboxes to exchange them and for trains to slow to a crawl or even a stand at each passing place purely for this purpose. Some long-distance single track main lines such as the Midland & Great Northern, the Somerset & Dorset, Highland and on the Glasgow & South Western were equipped with automatic tablet or token exchange apparatus which allowed the exchange to be made at express speeds up to 60mph.

The earliest forms of tokenless block involved interlocking the block instruments with appropriate signals at both ends of the single line, but because it was essentially an electromechanical system, the difficulty of connecting boxes often many miles apart made it rather cumbersome to install. More recently, some lines have been worked on the direction lever principle, whereby conventional block instruments are used in conjunction with master direction levers in the signalboxes at each end of a single line section. These levers are electrically interlocked with each other so as to determine the direction of travel over the single line – rather like the pointers on a staff or token instrument – and depending on their position, either free or lock the signals allowing entry into the block section at their end through the mechanical interlocking in their own signalbox. In the signalbox at the opposite end of the single line section they also either lock or free the corresponding signals there through the similar direction lever in that box. To run a train, both signalmen must have their levers set for the same direction of running, thus automatically locking at danger all the signals for movements in the opposite direction.

More recently still, and especially on single lines in

areas controlled remotely from power signalboxes, track circuits have been installed throughout the single line section, interlocked with the signals controlling the entry into the section – which would almost certainly be multiple-aspect colour lights – and with a direction switch on the control panel in the signalbox. This is the modern equivalent of a direction lever, with which the signalman or men can select the desired direction of travel.

Switching out an intermediate signalbox on a single line worked by electric staff or token systems is complicated but not impossible, because the tokens will only fit the instruments at each end of the section to which they apply. Closure is achieved by the signalman at the signalbox to be switched out obtaining a token from both the sections in each direction and inserting them in a closing instrument which releases a long section token which fits long section instruments at the further ends of the two short sections. By its nature closure can only take place with a train at the signal box to be closed. As part of the closure procedure a 'king' lever is operated which locks one track of the passing loop as the line to remain in use, and frees the interlocking for the signals in both directions for that line to be cleared together.

There remain a number of secondary lines which are still controlled by mechanical signalboxes – or if not from local panels rather than large power boxes – which are not fully track circuited, often because the sheer distances between passing loops makes continuous track circuiting an expensive option. In the 1960s, British Rail developed a form of tokenless block for use on conventionally signalled lines without full track circuiting which employs modified standard block instruments, a short track circuit at the entrance to the single line section, and a further track circuit or treadle at the opposite end. The block instruments have an acceptance switch with 'normal' and 'accept' positions, a plunger for sending bell signals, and a block indicator which can show 'normal' or 'line blocked', 'train going to' and 'train coming from' indications. The starting signals are released for one clearance only by the indicator moving to 'train going to'. Each instrument has a cancelling key and a sealed cancelling plunger; if for any reason a train fails to start after it has been accepted, the signalman can simply turn the key and cancel the acceptance. If however, the train enters the single line section, locking all the equipment, and then for some reason returns to its station of departure, once the train has cleared the single line, both signalmen must break the seal on their plungers and depress them simultaneously to restore the indicators on their block instruments to 'normal'.

Let us imagine that tokenless block has been installed on what is now a single line between Beeford and Seaside. To send a train to Seaside, our signalman at Beeford calls attention with one beat on the bell in the usual way, which Seaside acknowledges. Beeford then sends the appropriate 'is line clear?' bell signal to Seaside which, if the signalman there wants to accept the train, he also acknowledges and puts his acceptance switch from 'normal' to 'accept'. The Beeford signalman presses his bell plunger for about five seconds, which moves the block indicator at Seaside from the normal to the 'train coming from' position, and the Seaside signalman responds with a similar five-second plunge, which moves the Beeford indicator from 'normal' to 'train going to'. This also releases the lock on the Beeford starting signal, which our signalman can now clear.

When the train enters the single line, Beeford sends Seaside the 'train entering section' signal but there is no further movement of the block indicator. However, as it enters the section, the train passes over the entry track circuit (or in some cases a treadle) and in so doing locks the block indicator at 'train going to' in Beeford, and at 'train coming from' at Seaside, until it has passed through the single line section, occupied and cleared the corresponding entry track circuit at the other end of the single line at Seaside, and passed beyond the overlap of its home signal. Once it has arrived, the Seaside signalman sends Beeford one beat on the bell, and then, when it is acknowledged, restores his acceptance switch to normal, which puts his indicator from 'train coming

Honiton signalbox on the Salisbury–Exeter line as converted in the mid-1960s to operate WR pattern tokenless block over the single line on each side, using block instruments and direction switches with an open block procedure, entrance and exit track circuits and treadles, and colour light signals, with reversible working on the principal loop track. The old lever frame was adapted for the new layout with the levers working colour light signals having shortened handles. (Geoffrey Kichenside)

from' to normal, and sends 'train out of section' to Beeford, again depressing the plunger for about five seconds on the last beat to restore the Beeford indicator from 'train going to' to normal. The Beeford signalman acknowledges this signal, and the clearance of his indicator, and the line is now ready to be used again in either direction.

The Western Region of BR further developed this form of tokenless block into an open block system, particularly for use on the Salisbury to Exeter line, which was reduced from double track to single as an economy. Open block working is highly unusual, particularly on single lines, and caused some apprehension among staff at its outset. Under this system – which was intended to cut down signalmen's workload so that they could also undertake other duties such as selling tickets – trains are not offered or accepted in the conventional way. There are no block bells, only block instruments supported by signalbox to signalbox telephone. Standard block instruments are used, but showing 'normal', 'train accepted' and 'train in section' indications. The normal bell plunger is replaced by a train offer plunger, and there is also a 'train arrived' plunger and again a switch with 'normal' and 'accept' positions. Trains are expected to run as shown in the timetable, and any out of course running has to be agreed between signalmen on the telephone.

This time, since the system was developed specifically for the Salisbury to Exeter line, we will visit two actual signalboxes, at Gillingham, west of Salisbury, and Templecombe, the next passing place. If the next train is timetabled to run between Gillingham and Templecombe, and the section is clear so the instruments are normal, the signalman at Templecombe will put his acceptance switch in the 'accept' position. When he is ready to send the train, the signalman at Gillingham will check that his acceptance switch is in the normal position, and then press his offer plunger. Provided the acceptance switch at Templecombe is still switched to accept, and the track circuits at the entry and exit proved to be clear, the block indicators in both signalboxes move to 'train accepted', which releases the starting signal at Gillingham and locks the starting signal for the other direction at Templecombe. When the train occupies the track circuit at the entry to the single line section, the indicators in both signalboxes automatically move to 'train in section' and are held in this position until the train occupies further track circuits and is clear of the single line at Templecombe. When the signalman there is satisfied that the train is complete, he restores his acceptance switch to the normal position and presses the 'train arrived' plunger, which restores the block indicators in both signalboxes to normal. It will be seen that, with this arrangement, both signalmen do not have to be in their respective signalboxes at the same time in order to signal trains from one end of the section to the other, thus releasing

them for other duties between trains if necessary. Another feature of the Salisbury–Exeter signalling is that, because full braking distance between the home and starting signals is not provided at all locations, even when the line is clear, some home signals are maintained at danger and released only when the train is closely approaching. Also, because it was envisaged that signalmen would not always be available in their boxes, the circuitry is arranged so that if a signalman at the exit end of the section becomes aware of an obstruction after he has accepted a train but cannot then contact the signalman at the entry end, the restoration of his acceptance switch to normal will cause the starting signal at the entry end of the section to revert to danger.

No-signalman token

On some long single lines carrying relatively few trains a day, but still needing some form of signalling, signalboxes have been abolished and 'no signalman' token working has been established. Under this system, drivers themselves work modified token instruments which are normally housed in locked cupboards on the platforms at each passing place. On arrival at the station, a driver inserts the token for the section he has just left into the instrument for that section, and obtains another from the instrument for the next section by pushing a plunger which, if there are no tokens for that section out at the time, enables him to remove it. Thereafter, both instruments for the section are locked until the token is restored to one or other of the instruments at each end of the section. On such lines, the facing points are not controlled in the usual way, but are set, usually for left hand running, and electrically detected, with a white or in some cases yellow light showing towards the driver if the blades are correctly set. These indicators, which are rather like single aspect colour light signals, are positioned to allow a driver to stop short of the points if the light is extinguished. Such points are trailable in the opposite direction of travel, and controlled by hydraulic action to restore them to normal; they are subject to relatively severe speed limits in both directions. Because of both

Fig. 25. *The basic layout of signal boards and signs at a passing loop operated by RETB. The points are trailable and self restore using stored hydraulic energy.*

the time taken for a driver to exchange tokens at each passing place, and the need for reduced speed through pointwork both on arrival and departure, this system is not suitable for more heavily trafficked lines, or where higher running speeds are necessary. On such lines there are no conventional signals, but in addition to the point detection lights, there are red 'stop – obtain token' boards at the exit end of each passing loop, boards depicting a distant arm at caution – in effect a fixed distant – at the conventional braking distance from the facing points at each passing place, and special 'train clear of loop' boards beyond the station so that drivers know they can begin to accelerate.

Radio Electronic Token Block (RETB)

In Scotland, north of Inverness, on the Cambrian lines from Shrewsbury to Aberystwyth and Pwllheli, and in East Anglia, a development of the no-signalman token system, but using radio, has been introduced. Known as Radio Electronic Token Block (RETB), it utilises radio transmitters/receivers mounted in the cabs of trains using the line which can communicate with solid state interlocking – SSI (see Chapter 16) – in the control centre. There is no other external block equipment at passing places, but as with 'no-signalman' working, points are trailable with hydraulic self-restoration to normal and electrically detected, and there is similar

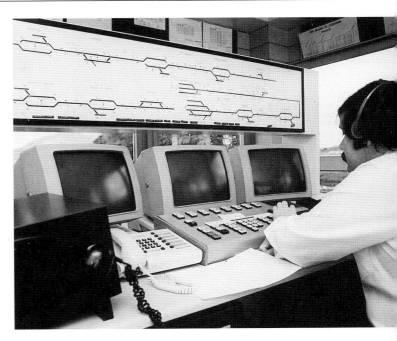

Radio electronic token block (RETB) has enabled the cost of running rural single lines to be reduced drastically by doing away with intermediate signalboxes and worked lineside signals, and by allowing trains to be worked at any time of the day or night without the need to open signalboxes specially. Pictured here is the RETB controller at Banavie, near Fort William, who controls the entire West Highland line from north of Crianlarich to Mallaig, a distance of over 100 miles, with seven intermediate passing places, and several remote sidings. His equipment enables him electronically to authorise trains to enter each single line section by communicating with the cab-borne equipment depicted which shows that the locomotive in which it is installed, is authorised to run through the single line section from Loch Eil to Glenfinnan. Once this authorisation has been given, the electronic equipment ensures that no other authority for this section is given until the original authority is rescinded by the driver on arrival at the next passing place. Drivers can also speak to the controller by radio, to ask for a token, make other position reports or to arrange any out of course or emergency arrangements to be set up quickly. (British Railways)

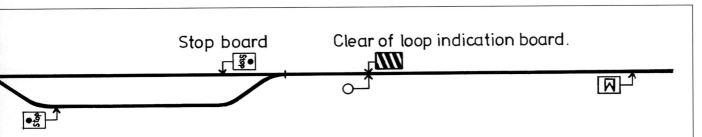

Stop board   Clear of loop indication board.

There are no worked lineside signals on RETB-controlled lines, but a sign equivalent to a fixed distant warns drivers of their approach to a passing place, and as this picture shows, each passing place has the equivalent of a fixed stop signal which requires drivers to stop and obtain permission by radio electronic token to proceed into the next single line section. Just visible in the background between the sign and the locomotive is the back of what looks like a single-aspect colour light signal. These are in fact not signals in the normal sense, but show a white or yellow light to drivers approaching passing loops to indicate that the self-restoring stored hydraulic energy facing points are correctly set. At some locations position-light elevated shunting type signals serve the same purpose. (British Railways)

the request into the SSI, and instructs the driver to press a 'receive' button on his cab radio unit. Further data exchange takes place between the SSI and the cab radio unit, and the appropriate 'authority' – in effect a radio token – appears on the cab display unit. When this appears the driver formally acknowledges receipt of the token for the section and may now proceed. Once the SSI has given such an authority, it will issue no further authorisation for this section of line until the same cab unit has surrendered the 'radio' token.

On reaching the next passing place, the driver calls the controller to advise him that he has arrived, is clear of the single line section, and would like to give up the token. The controller acknowledges the message, instructs the SSI to receive the token, and asks the driver to press a 'send' button on his cab radio equipment, which enables a further data exchange to take place, removing the authority for the single line from the cab display. The driver reports that his display is now clear, and the SSI can issue another authority for the section of single line if so required. When the train proceeds into the next section with a new token, on passing the 'train clear of loop' board the driver radios to control to confirm that his train is clear of the loop.

A more developed version of RETB, known as Advanced Radio Electronic Token Block (ARETB) has been developed and is already in use overseas. Essentially, ARETB uses transponders to allow the train to report its position automatically by radio; as the locomotive or power unit passes over a passive transponder mounted on the track, train-borne equipment interrogates it and reports back to the control centre the transponder's unique code together with the train identifying code. If the train has a valid electronic token for that section the control centre transmits back an authority to continue, but if it has not, no confirmation code is transmitted back to the train, and the brakes are automatically applied. Transponders can be mounted anywhere, each programmed with a unique identity, wherever it is required to identify the position of a train, but there are normally four in each single line section. The first is located just beyond the loop points, at the very

signage. At rural junctions, points are powered and drivers can select which route they require by pressing appropriate platform plungers.

All trains using lines where this system is employed must be equipped with the appropriate cab radio display processor equipment. The driver of a train arriving at the entry to the first single line section would call control by speech transmission and ask the controller to enter the train identification into the system. The controller initiates the necessary data interchange between the SSI and the train, and as a result the train is allocated a unique code. The driver then asks the controller for the token to the next passing place. If the line is clear, the controller enters

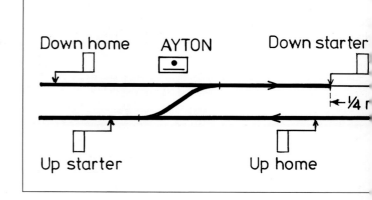

beginning of the section, and the second just beyond the 'limit of shunt'. The remaining two are located in similar positions at the other end of the single line. As the train passes each transponder, if the line is clear, authority to proceed is confirmed. On passing the last transponder at the end of a section, the driver receives a warning that he is approaching the limit of his authority to proceed. Using this system, coupled to a solid state interlocking and VDUs showing the position of trains, it will be seen that single lines over a wide area can be controlled from a central point without the need for any lineside signals or moving equipment. It can, however, also be further developed with remotely controlled points and signals to provide full centralised control.

Emergency single line working

It is sometimes necessary for single line working to be instituted on lines which are normally double track, with each line normally carrying trains in only one direction. Such use of one line for trains in both directions may be planned so as to enable engineers to renew the other track, or perhaps repair a bridge, or it may be introduced in an emergency as a result of a derailed train, or perhaps a landslip or broken rail. In either case, there are clear instructions for the introduction and operation of single line working involving the appointment of a pilotman, who acts as a human temporary staff or token for the section of line being used in both directions. (Indeed, if a single line staff or token is lost or damaged, so that the instrument cannot be used, similar working by pilotman must be introduced on normal single lines until the instrument can be used again.)

The pilotman must be easily recognised, and in Britain it is usual practice to wear a red armlet on the left arm, carrying the words 'Pilotman' in white. In an emergency a red flag can be tied to the arm if a pilotman's armband is not available. No train is

Fig. 26. *Single line working past an obstruction, when one line of a double-track route is obstructed by a failed train or engineering works.*

allowed to enter the temporary single line section without the pilotman, unless two or more consecutive trains are due to run through the section in succession without any others returning, in which case the pilotman personally authorises each train to enter the section, and then rides on the last himself. Such operation is of course a human version of the staff and ticket system, with the pilotman himself acting as the staff, and his verbal instructions replacing the ticket of authority. In some cases, particularly when the timetable is subject to last minute alteration, a locomotive may be provided to carry the pilotman from one end of the section to the other. In such cases, the locomotive carrying the pilotman is coupled ahead of the train engine.

Single line working cannot simply be arranged between signalmen – it must be authorised by a senior responsible person. To do this, that person has to address special single line working forms to the person appointed pilotman, and the signalmen and others concerned at both ends of the proposed temporary single line section. If the single line section is to extend further than beyond two adjacent signalboxes then the forms have to be addressed also to any signalmen in intermediate signalboxes that are open, or may be opened, during the single line working. All these forms must be signed by the pilotman, and he also has to obtain the signatures of all others involved at both ends of the section acknowledging receipt of the forms before he can allow a train to use the line in the wrong direction. It is also his responsibility to ensure that all points which are normally trailing points, but which become facing points as a result of the single line working, are correctly set, clipped and padlocked before any trains pass over them. It is therefore normal practice for the pilotman to use the last train through the section in the normal direction to deliver the forms, obtain signatures and thus set up single line operation.

We have seen earlier, in the section on emergency working, that detonators are used to alert drivers to danger, or to protect trains which are derailed or immobilised in the block section. Likewise, detonators are used to protect staff and equipment working on the

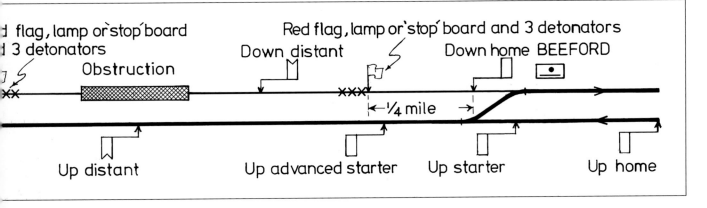

section of line of which the engineer has possession. Let us imagine that engineering work has been introduced on the down line between Ayton and Beeford – that is, on the line normally used by trains running from Ayton to Beeford – and that trains in both directions are being worked over the other, up line. Some $1/4$ mile, or a train's length, beyond the crossover which is to be used to cross trains to the unobstructed line, three detonators are placed on the rail some 20 yards apart, together with a red flag or 'stop' sign and, at night, a red lamp. Beyond the obstruction, three more detonators, together with a red flag, 'stop' sign and lamp, are placed the same distance in the rear of the crossover which trains will use to regain their proper line, as shown in Fig. 26. If at all possible, block working is maintained during single line working, with down trains signalled on the down line instruments, even though trains in both directions are using only one line. In cases where the indications on block instruments are controlled by track circuits, it may be necessary for the signal technicians to specially release the instruments to allow block working to continue.

The method of operation is for a train arriving at Ayton in the down direction to be authorised to draw forward past the home signal to stand just beyond the crossover leading to the unobstructed line. Then, when the pilotman is satisfied that there is no train in the section in either direction, the signalman has, if possible, obtained 'line clear' on his block instrument, and the points are properly set and locked or clipped, the driver is authorised to set back across the crossover onto the 'wrong' line. When the points have been restored and locked or clipped, the train can resume its journey. The pilotman either travels with the driver through the section or, if another train is to follow, authorises the driver to proceed through the block section in the 'wrong' direction to Beeford, where it will stop short of the crossover leading back to its proper line to drop the pilotman, who will ensure that the crossover is properly set, before he authorises the train to continue on its way. During this time, a train would not normally be permitted to approach Beeford from Seaside on the up line unless there was sufficient overlap beyond Beeford's outermost up home signal to allow the movement to take place without infringing the clearing point. In some cases the Warning Arrangement is used. If for any reason block working on the usual instruments cannot be maintained, telephones are used for block working, and in the complete absence of any communication, time interval working is adopted under a clearly defined procedure, and not the free-for-all of Victorian time interval methods.

In areas with multiple aspect signals controlled from a central power signalbox, where the signalman may be many miles from the actual site of the single line working, the signalman may instruct the pilotman by telephone. In such circumstances, of course, clarity of messages and a clear understanding between all those involved is paramount. A signalman's agent may be appointed to act at the site on behalf of the signalman at the signalling centre. The pilotman must obtain new signatures if any of the signalmen or other staff change shift during the course of the single line working, and before normal working can be restored, he must withdraw the single line forms from all concerned.

In recent years on busy lines, it has become the practice to install facing crossovers at intervals between the up and down lines specifically to speed up single line working during engineering work or other blockages of the line, and on some lines, simplified bidirectional signalling, known as SIMBIDS, has been installed. This normally takes the form of fully controlled and interlocked signals for the crossovers, but without intermediate signals on the 'wrong' line so that trains can be switched to the opposite track without the need for a pilotman, but the headway between trains is much increased (see also Chapter 16).

Preserved railway operation

A phenomenon of the last 40 years has been the preservation of numerous branch lines by enthusiast groups and operated as tourist attractions. They cover both former BR standard gauge lines closed as unremunerative as conventional common carrier lines, and one-time independent narrow gauge lines originally built for carriage of specific traffic – slate for example – which then ceased, usually meaning line closure in its original form. Although these lines are operated by enthusiasts, often with volunteer labour, staff must be highly professional and properly trained to enable trains to be run safely. Nearly all are single lines and are required by the Railway Inspectorate to follow the procedures established for their forebears though with allowances for different operating needs. The Light Railways Act of 1896, passed to allow less restrictive construction and operation of rural branch lines, was useful in this respect on many preserved railways which are also keen to re-create the old time systems of semaphore signals and staff or token working. Others work to one-train-operation principles without full signalling and with points padlocked from a key on the staff for the line. In contrast, the Torbay & Dartmouth line in Devon, more a means of transport than a preserved branch, has colour light signalling and track circuit block. However, the most advanced preserved line in signalling is the 15in gauge Ravenglass & Eskdale Railway in Cumbria which uses radio block with speech messages from trains reporting their position at passing loops and requesting permission from the controller to proceed into the next section. Although not really related, this system formed a useful exercise in train-to-signalbox radio in mountainous terrain, pre-dating RETB, and the discrete BR cab-to-signalbox radio network.

Chapter 8

ELECTRICITY MAKES ITS DEBUT

UNTIL THE TURN of the last century it could be fairly said that railway signalling equipment was mechanical in concept, with wires used to link signal levers with signals, at least as far as the bottom of the signalpost, and rodding to transmit lever movements to points and facing point locks. As has been seen in Chapter 5, nearly all the allied components, including means to detect trains had a largely mechanical element, and the signalbox lever frame itself was almost entirely composed of purely mechanical parts. Even communication between the signalman and shunters in the yard or station staff, was frequently mechanical with a lever working a bell or gong by direct wire pull with coded bell signals to denote the various messages that the signalman wanted to convey, or for the yard staff to reply.

Another element in railway signalling had been used right from the early days, not always reliable at first but developed gradually into an important ingredient in safe railway operation, and that was electricity. Without it the electric telegraph could not have been envisaged and indeed, the world would not be the place we know today. But with its development from low voltages given out by primitive cells to a major power source by the end of the 19th century, generated on a large scale, not in itself a primary form of power, but obtained by harnessing water, or using the force of steam, to turn generators, it was destined to play a major role in everyday life and not least on the railways. Alas, it took years before many railway managers could see advantages in adopting new electrical equipment as an aid to train operation. Often cost was a factor and many devices were only installed following recommendations after an accident which might have been prevented had such equipment been in place beforehand. Such attitudes hardly changed in Victorian years when, as we have already seen, there was often reluctance to adopt the absolute block system, interlocking, and continuous brakes. Regrettably, in the 90 or so years since then, the attitude of too many railway decision makers has still not changed and in later chapters we will chronicle

recent instances, even in the 1990s, where cost has been a major factor in the slow progress of, or total reluctance to adopt, more advanced safety devices, and not always on the part of the railway operators.

Allied to the mechanical developments in railway signalling in mid-Victorian years was the development of the telegraph instrument into the block instrument in its various forms from the ideas of those involved in the telegraph systems of the different railways and industry. Already we have seen how W. R. Sykes developed in the early 1870s a combined electrical and mechanical form of block system using treadles on the line to detect the passing of a train and sending an electrical signal to the signalbox to apply or release locks on block instruments and signals. The first use of the Sykes lock and block system was in 1874 (and in this context 'lock' meant locking the block system with the signals not the interlocking between levers of the pre-1889 years with the battle of minds for lock, block and brake) when it was installed on the London, Chatham & Dover Railway between Shepherds Lane, Brixton, and Canterbury Road Junction on the busy main line out of Victoria. James Forbes, the LCDR General Manager wanted it installed out in the country where, if it failed it would cause little harm, but the railway inspectorate who had got to hear of it pressed the case for use in a busy area. For once, even before the 1889 Act, their view prevailed. It was patented a year later. Undoubtedly this was one of the factors which lay behind the reluctance of railways to put in new equipment since licence fees would be due to the patentee. Yet here was a remarkable safety add-on to the block system since in normal working it proved that a train had run through the block section and had cleared a specified point beyond the protecting signal, and that signal had to be returned to danger before the block instrument could be cleared back to the signalbox in the rear for another train to be signalled. Its use was called for following the accident at Ludgate Hill in November 1875 and again over the following years, but it was installed only gradually on the LCDR reaching Dover by 1882. It was used by a few other

ABOVE *By the end of the Victorian era some major stations had reached the extremes of what could be provided by mechanical signalling. This gantry, just outside St Pancras station, included shunting signals below the main arms and with separate arms for each route gave 42 signals in both directions which presented drivers with a complicated array of lights at night. (BR, LMR)*

BELOW *In May 1892 Waterloo 'A' signalbox was enlarged to control the increased number of approach* tracks which, with both ways working as the trains approached the platforms, called for nearly 50 arms on these brackets. Waterloo was then totally rebuilt between 1914 and 1922, resignalled in the mid-1930s and again in the early 1990s, and from 1994 has been served by international 'Eurostar' trains to and from Paris and Brussels through the Channel Tunnel. These trains use tracks which, in the context of this photograph, would be to the left of the signalbox. (National Railway Museum)*

ABOVE *The famous gantry at Rugby after it had been duplicated with sky arms in the late 1890s in readiness for the construction of the viaduct carrying the new Great Central Railway London Extension, the early stage works for which had just started and which, when completed, provided a patterned background to the lower arms preventing a clear view from a distance. The LNWR made the GCR pay the cost of the new gantry. (National Railway Museum)*

BELOW *Even though standards were set towards the end of the last century there were detailed differences between some signals from railway to railway, particularly with shunting or subsidiary signals. The Great Western used backing signals with two holes in the arm but the Scottish companies made use of the scissors or crossed frame arm, as here at Perth, with the right hand arm applying to wrong direction shunting moves to the opposite line. The signals are seen in 1961, just before resignalling with colour lights. (Geoffrey Kichenside)*

railways, particularly urban lines with frequent services as for example the Metropolitan District in London, the Mersey in Liverpool, and eventually parts of the Great Eastern, Brighton, and London & South Western railways. The Waterloo & City underground line in London used it from opening in 1898. But the other railways out of London ignored it despite its safety features.

Even before devising his lock and block system Sykes' fertile mind had produced his first electric signal repeater in 1864 with a miniature semaphore arm in an instrument at Herne Hill relaying the working of the 'distant' signal from the Tulse Hill direction. In 1872 he experimented with electrically operated signals at Victoria (Metropolitan District Railway) and a decade later had installed electrically powered shunting signals upstairs in Victoria LCDR station. He had also developed a fouling or interlocking bar which, purely by mechanical linkage with the signalbox, locked the appropriate levers when a train, engine, or vehicle was standing over the bar with the wheel flanges depressing the bar. All this time, from 1863, Sykes was employed by the LCDR but on the formation of the Joint Managing Committee with the South Eastern Railway in 1899 Sykes left to form the world renowned signal engineering firm of W. R. Sykes Interlocking Signal Co. Ltd.

Lock and block on the underground

Sykes was not the only engineer looking at lock and block, for the first of London's deep level electrified tube railways, the City & South London, from opening in 1890 used the Spagnoletti lock and block system with rail treadles as part of a station-to-station manually operated block system. This included oil lit semaphore signals at the platform end at stations and oil lit lanterns in tunnels approaching stations. Although the second London tube line, the Waterloo & City, also the second to have electric traction, was signalled by Sykes lock and block with mechanical signalboxes at Waterloo and Bank stations, on plain line between the two stations there were electrically operated signals. They consisted of little more than vertical spectacles with red and green glasses held in the clear position by a solenoid unit operated by a plunger from the signalboxes. When the train passed over a treadle an electrical contact was broken and released the signal to danger. Remarkably the W&C trains were fitted with a device to prevent a signal from being passed at danger, achieved when a wiper arm on the leading car brushed an energised rail which tripped the train's circuit breaker and applied the brakes.

Automatic signalling
on the Liverpool Overhead

The first moves towards an automatic signalling system came a few years before the opening of the Waterloo &

City Railway, not in London but on the Liverpool Overhead Railway from opening in 1893. This was a standard gauge railway carrying lightweight electric multiple-unit trains nearly all the way on viaduct along the seven miles of Merseyside docks from Seaforth in the north to Dingle in the south. The line was equipped with electrically operated semaphore signals fed by 50V batteries controlled through lineside contact boxes engaged by wooden striker arms on the last coach of each train. As a train proceeded so the striker arms operated contacts within the boxes, breaking the electrical connections to place the signal behind the train to danger, and making connections at certain contact boxes to place signals further back at clear through a circuit which proved that signals protecting the train were actually at danger. After a few years the railway inspectorate was not entirely happy with the system and block working was added in 1897, but six years later the automatic system was re-equipped to operate from the 500V main with contact bars between the rails replacing the lineside contact boxes. Now the signals were restored to danger by mechanical depression of the contact bar by a shoe on the train to break lineside electric circuits or clearing signals further back by electrifying a bar from another shoe under the train linked to the traction feed. Right from the start the semaphore signals had electric lamps with twin bulbs in parallel to ensure that if one failed the other would still show a light. A form of automatic train stop was added in 1917 in which a wire brush under the train engaged a bar on the track which was earthed if the signal was at danger and energised a solenoid on the train which tripped out the circuit breakers and applied the brakes. But following two collisions within a month in 1919, after an impeccable record, the railway inspectorate demanded a more modern system. In 1921 most of the line was resignalled with alternating current track circuits and for the first time in Britain, daylight colour-light signals with the red and green indications given through separate units by lights only. The lights were sufficiently intense to be seen a long way off even in the brightest of sunshine. Unusually by the standards of later practice, the red light unit was above the green. This system lasted until the line closed at the end of 1956.

Developing automation on the Underground

Back in London, the Central London Railway the third of the deep level tube lines, opened in 1900, was unremarkable in its signalling. It was worked by manual lock and block signalling from signalboxes at each station with semaphore starting signals mounted on the tunnel headwall at the departure end of platforms, with a vertically moving spectacle signal carried in a frame on a horizontal pivot in the tunnels approaching stations. But the signals were fitted with electric lamps. The City & South London, by then ten years old, was also given electric lamps for its signals but the original lanterns moving in a horizontal plane had been replaced by vertically moving spectacles with the movement powered by compressed air controlled through electrically operated air valves, the electro-pneumatic system. This of course needed a compressed air main to serve the signals and other equipment which was air-operated.

Yet another step forward occurred just a few years later when the Great Northern & City Railway, opened early in 1904, had automatic signalling controlled by track circuits and treadles but the signals were given by lights only in fixed lighting units, one with a red glass and one with green. This was the first use of a colour-light signal though within the confines of a tunnel. When the first of the tube lines built as part of the new London Electric Railway, the Bakerloo, Piccadilly and Hampstead lines were opened in stages from 1906, it was almost a step backwards, for although on plain line the signalling was automatic, controlled through track circuits, the signals were of the vertically moving spectacle type which, astonishingly, were oil lit. In hindsight, 90 years on, it seems remarkable that oil lamps were still employed for signalling on a new underground electrified railway which clearly had electricity available at stations for lighting.

The vacuum incandescent light bulb had been developed in America by Thomas Edison in the late 1870s and by Joseph Swan in Britain soon after, and

Electro-pneumatically operated spectacles giving the colour indications for early colour light signals on the London Underground. The spectacle plate moved vertically in front of the lamp source. Although electric lamps were already used in railway signalling this type of signal, provided for the opening of the Baker Street & Waterloo Railway in 1906, had oil lamps. (London Transport)

was quickly used in an experimental installation to light the new Savoy Theatre in 1881 and around the same time to provide street lighting in Godalming, the latter powered by a small hydro electric installation on the nearby River Wey. The underground stations themselves were lit partly by light bulbs and partly by arc lamps. Were light bulbs perhaps so unreliable at that time that they were not considered cost effective against the long established oil lamp, especially as incandescent burners had just been introduced for oil lamps and gas mantles? As we have just seen, the LOR and W&C had used electric lamps from the 1890s. Some railways were using gas lighting for signals but clearly there were differences of opinion on the merits of the different forms. While the London Underground lines eventually adopted electric lamps in the housings behind the spectacles because the oil lamps often blew out with the draught from passing trains, the oil lamp for semaphore signals on the main line surface railways survives to this day where such signals are still in use. It contrasted so much with the other technical developments adopted by the LER such as electro-pneumatic operation of signals and train stops, and track circuits, which set the pattern for much of the signalling on the London Underground network from then on. The moving spectacle signals were superseded by multi-lens colour light signals from the 1920s but the moving spectacle units did not finally disappear until 1946. But track circuits were another thing altogether for they formed the basis for a totally new approach to the detection of trains and the prime element in what was to develop towards total automation in railway signalling. A new era had begun.

Track circuits

So far in this chapter we have concentrated on the part played by electricity in railway signalling on the newly emerging urban electric and largely underground railways of the years between 1890 and the First World War, largely because the first of those railways was opened in 1890 itself. But, in the same period, electricity was also beginning to have a more important role on the main line railways in the control and operation of signalling and not just in the means of communication between signalboxes. The track circuit was to become an important feature, not perhaps as much as it might have been in the early schemes, but soon with its potential fully realised for controlling signals not just automatically but safely.

The track circuit in its simplest form consists of a section of line, perhaps a few hundred yards long, possibly less, possibly more, with the rail joints at both ends of the track circuit section provided with insulated fishplates to prevent the electric circuit reaching the rails beyond (in later chapters we shall describe jointless track circuits of recent times and also look at the equipment needed to pass traction current across insulated joints on electrified lines). A battery feeds a low voltage supply of electricity into the two running rails usually at the exit end of the section and at the entry end a feed is taken from the rails into the coils of a relay. When the track circuit section is clear the current passes from the battery along one rail, into the relay which is energised, and back through the other rail to the battery. When the wheels of a train occupy the track circuit section they short circuit the electricity by returning it direct from one rail to the other and back to the battery without reaching the relay. The relay coils are thus de-energised and the relay contacts to other equipment are changed. It is like a person switching a light switch on and off but with the person's hand replaced by an arm controlled by an electro-magnet. A resistor is permanently in the circuit at the battery end to ensure that the battery is not damaged when the wheels pass the current straight back. This is the normally-energised type of track circuit. There are other types, a few applications for normally dead circuits so that the train energises the relay when the section is occupied (although this form is not fail safe and cannot be used for train detection on its own), and over the years since it was first used the detail has varied in respect of type of current – direct or alternating – and the voltage and in other respects. In recent years electronics have played a part so that track circuits might not be simple detection circuits but can be coded to pass information to the train. But that is to jump well ahead in signalling progress.

The track circuit was originally devised in America in 1872 by one William Robinson and knowledge of it spread to Great Britain where the imaginative William Sykes (who else?) was trying one out at Crystal Palace in 1876. It was not entirely successful for much of track circuit technology, such as insulation and ballast resistance, had still to be learned. But even by 1880 following an accident at Nine Elms Junction, the inspecting officer's recommendation included the observation that the accident would have been prevented by track circuits already used in America. The plea fell on deaf ears at least at first. Then in 1886 Sykes tried again on the LCDR with a track circuit at St Pauls near Blackfriars, and a decade later the Great Northern had equipped Gasworks Tunnel just beyond the King's Cross station throat. It was slow going though. One of the problems was that many coaches were fitted with Mansell wheels. Mansell was the carriage superintendent of the South Eastern Railway in its early years and by 1848 had developed a carriage wheel made of hardwood segments round the wrought iron axle and held together by an iron tyre. With steel instead of iron the Mansell pattern wheel was used by most railways in Victorian years right to the end of the century. They ran quietly but with wooden centres they were very effective insulators and would not operate track circuits unless modified with

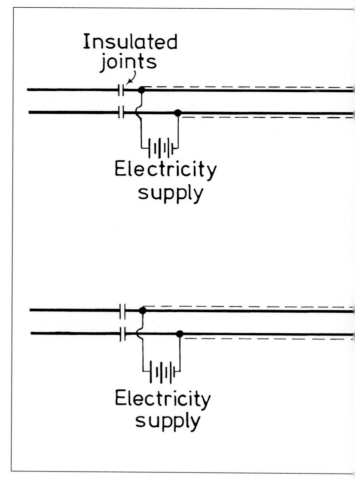

Fig. 27. *Diagram showing the operation of a simple track circuit with no train present at the top, and with a train at the bottom.*

bonding between the axle and the tyre on both wheels. This meant calling coaches into workshops and spending money which, as we have seen, was not a thing which many companies liked to do. But track circuits were not necessarily a pre-requisite of power operation.

Power operation
The first moves towards power operation of main line signalling took place just as the 19th century was drawing to a close. There were basically three forms, the all-electric type, the low-pressure pneumatic type and the electro-pneumatic type. The essential feature initially was that the power system was employed simply to replace the direct wire pull between lever and signal or the rodding between lever and points and facing point locks. In the all-electric system the lever in the signalbox operated electrical contacts which completed electric circuits through cables to electrical equipment which operated the signals and points. In the low pressure pneumatic system the lever changed

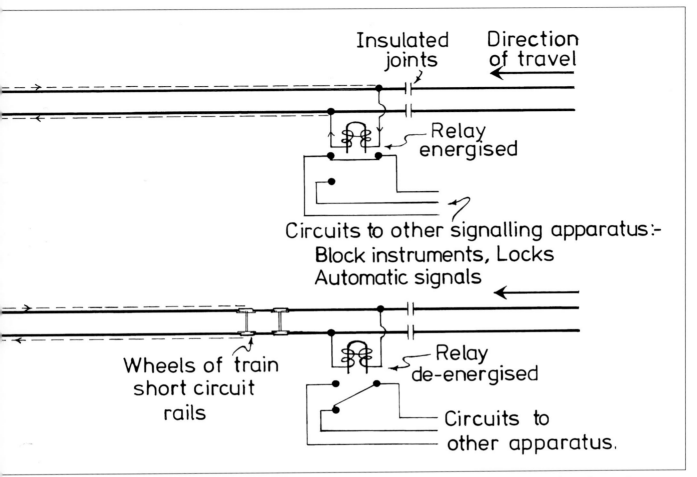

Insulated joints

Direction of travel

Relay energised

Circuits to other signalling apparatus:-
Block instruments, Locks
Automatic signals

Wheels of train short circuit rails

Relay de-energised

Circuits to other apparatus.

the internal valves in an air valve to direct compressed air in pipes to air valves at the signal or points which changed position to admit the compressed air to the operating cylinders. The control pipes carried compressed air at a lower pressure, 7lb/sq in for example, compared with the main air feed pipe to the operating cylinders at around 15lb/sq in. In the electro-pneumatic system the lever operated an electric circuit from the signalbox to the points or signal where an electrically controlled air valve fed the operating compressed air to the cylinder. There were advantages and disadvantages in all three systems depending on the availability of the electricity supply, or a compressed air main and compressor, the size of the layout and its complexity, and to a large extent, the whims and personal likes and dislikes of the engineer in charge. At the turn of the century they were the days of rivalry.

The LNWR all-electric system
The first of the main line power installations were seen at Crewe Gresty Lane (all-electric) on the LNWR and at Granary Junction (electro-pneumatic) at Spitalfields just outside Liverpool Street on the Great Eastern. It was a photo finish for first place but by all accounts

The early LNWR all-electric power lever frames first seen at Crewe Gresty Lane in 1899 had double banks of levers. This view shows the interior of Crewe North Junction. Normally block working was still employed to the signalboxes on each side. (BR, LMR)

they were both complete by mid-January 1899, with the LNWR Crewe installation probably winning by a short head. But Granary Junction was the first electro-pneumatic scheme. In the LNWR all-electric type the lever frame had been miniaturised with the hand gripped part of the lever protruding no more than about six inches above the top of the frame. Behind the lever shaft was a catch handle controlling spring loaded blocks which fitted against stops on the frame top to hold the lever in the correct positions, just like the long mechanical levers. On a point of detail, LNWR mechanical levers normally had the catch handle in the form of a ring in front of the lever pivoted to the down rod behind the lever, and needed a two-handed operation to move the lever. With a vertical catch handle behind the lever a single hand could grip the catch handle squeezing it against the lever proper to lift the blocks away from the frame stops while the lever was being moved. The first LNWR power frames had two levels with a second row of levers above and behind the front row but spaced between them so that the $3^{1}/_{2}$ inch spacing between the levers in each part of the frame (compared to $4^{1}/_{2}$ inch spacing of mechanical levers) combined in the back part of the frame to become $1^{3}/_{4}$ inches. The bottom part of the lever

The Great Eastern embarked on power operation at the same time as the LNWR but used electro-pneumatic operation in its first signalbox at Granary Junction and here at Whitechapel, with control through rotary handles rather than levers. (National Railway Museum)

formed a tee pivoting in the centre with down rods from one part of the tee linked to the electrical contacts and from the other to the mechanical interlocking connections. Outside on the line, the signals, normal LNWR semaphores, were operated by solenoid motors and originally the points were operated by magnet units later changed to rotary electric motors. Points levers included a check lock position in mid-stroke so that they could not be pulled or pushed fully home which would release the interlocking on related levers until the points themselves had fully responded and were locked and detected. This action completed a circuit back to the signalbox to release the electric lock and free the lever from the check lock position. But there were no track circuits in this pioneer LNWR power installation, and signalmen still had to see trains pass. The system was so successful that the LNWR decided to use all-electric operation, though with detailed modifications as for example with single row lever frames, at other major centres in the following years. This included Euston–Camden in 1905 but excluding, let us hasten to add, Euston station itself which had to wait until BR days in the early 1950s for modern signalling. The rest of Crewe was completed by 1907 and Manchester London Road (today's Piccadilly) by 1909.

Pneumatic pioneering

The Granary Junction installation used rotary levers rather than ones which were pulled, and indeed with power operation, there was no real need to have a lever which looked anything like what had become the conventional mechanical signal lever whether miniature or otherwise. All that was needed was some means to make or break electrical circuits or with direct pneumatic systems a device to open or close air ports in valves. Thus with these pioneer power installations other forms of operating methods appeared but for ease of working inevitably they had handles attached to whatever device was used. But the signal lever in miniature form always seemed to predominate, and not always miniature, for in some signalboxes where power operation was introduced to part of the equipment full size levers were altered at the bottom end to change electrical contacts rather than pull a wire or rodding directly. Yet again in some pioneer power installations points remained mechanically worked from full length levers while signals were power controlled from switches or slides in contact boxes above the lever frame with mechanical linkage to interlocking below the main part of the frame. Some signalboxes with Sykes lock and block had this arrangement.

In 1901 came the first power signalling installation which, combined with developments in following years, was to be the precursor of what today we would describe as modern signalling. The small country station at Grateley on the LSWR West of England main line between Basingstoke and Salisbury was chosen as the location of a new power signalling installation using the low pressure pneumatic system. The station was being enlarged to provide a new up side loop outside the up platform to accommodate trains on the single-track Bulford branch which was to run parallel to the double-track main line and, with other alterations to the layout, brought the need for a larger signalbox. The British Pneumatic Signal Company supplied a 70-slide operated pneumatic frame although not all slides were in use and some of the signal slides operated more than one signal. This was achieved by taking the control pipes to the points concerned where selector valves, worked from the air cylinders of the points, directed the air supply to the appropriate signal depending on the lie of the points. Naturally the slides were interlocked mechanically in the signalbox so that once a signal slide was pulled to the clear position it locked the points in the correct position. Thus points could only be moved when the appropriate signals were at danger and provided they were not locked by other points, just as in mechanical practice. So far, the Grateley installation was little different except for the means of operating points and signals than other signalboxes. It was the next stage, completed later that year, that moved signalling development forward, for between Andover Junction and Grateley the section was divided by automatic pneumatic semaphore signals controlled by track circuits. They were on trial and a close watch was made on their operation both by the LSWR signal engineers and the railway inspectorate for this was the first example of what today would be called track circuit block. Those signals controlled by track circuits were of course not purely pneumatic since the track circuit relay operated another circuit which controlled the electro-pneumatic valve which fed compressed air to the operating diaphragm.

Seemingly the system worked well both in the application of pneumatic control to points and signals and in track circuit operation for in the following year the LSWR embarked on further installations, firstly at Salisbury where two new signalboxes equipped with pneumatic control were built for the enlargement of the station layout, though without track circuits, and then in 1904 the four-track main line between Woking and Basingstoke including the latter station but not the former. Here was a real test for the new automation, for although signalboxes with pneumatic controls were provided at intermediate stations to control running crossovers and access to goods yards, in between were lengths equipped with automatic pneumatic semaphores controlled by track circuits. The intermediate automatic signals had stop and distant arms since, as far as possible, the signals were spaced to provide even length automatic sections. The signals at one point were at adequate braking distance from the next signals ahead so the lower distant signals gave

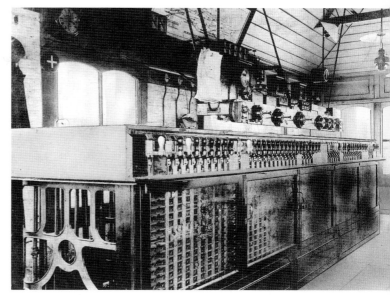

The LSWR first tried the low pressure pneumatic system for operating signals and points at Grateley in 1901. During the following years the system was adopted for larger installations. This is the interior of Salisbury West signalbox showing the push-pull handles. Behind the glass doors is the mechanical interlocking. (National Railway Museum)

Undoubtedly the most notable pneumatic installation on the LSWR was the section of automatic and semi-automatic signalling between Woking and Basingstoke in 1904. With most signals carried on fairly evenly spaced gantries like this one, stop and distant arms effectively formed three-aspect signalling. This, and the NER Hall system, pre-dated by almost 30 years the first of the major automatic colour light signalling schemes of the Southern and LNER in the 1930s. Note the fogman's hut between the centre tracks and the magazine detonator placers in the foreground. The distant arms have the Coligny Welch indicator alongside. With upper quadrant arms the system survived until 1966. (National Railway Museum)

The down line signals approaching Basingstoke with co-acting upper and lower arms for sighting beyond a bridge. The operating cylinders of the low pressure pneumatic system can be seen just below each arm. (National Railway Museum)

A low pressure pneumatic point operating cylinder showing the slides with the zig-zag cut out to operate the links to the switch blades. (National Railway Museum)

timely indication of the position of the next stop signal – the first example of three-aspect signalling, albeit with semaphores.

The low pressure pneumatic frame at Brookwood in its last years. As part of the Bournemouth electrification of 1967 colour lights took over and with a simplified layout, the signalling was controlled from Woking. Note the array of signal repeaters, lamp indicators and point repeaters. The block indicators on the left are for the Alton branch. (National Railway Museum)

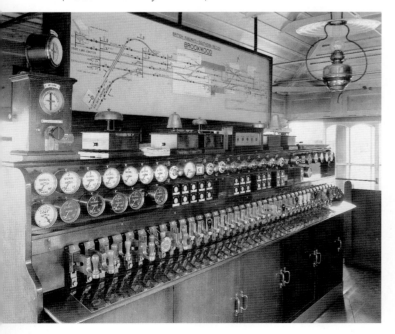

The automatic signals were spaced in such a way that the signals for both main and local tracks for both directions were carried on the same gantry, with the lattice structures spanning all four tracks. The normal position of the arms was at clear unless a train was occupying the section, or in the case of the distant arm, two sections ahead, a reversion to the practice before the 1876 Abbots Ripton collision, although from a safety viewpoint the LSWR semaphores were not working in slotted posts and they were powered by compressed air so it was unlikely that snow would have impeded operation. Certainly in the 63 years during which they were in use until replaced by colour lights for the 1967 electrification to Bournemouth there was never a reported case of snow causing a wrong side failure. The LSWR added more pneumatic installations at Staines and around Clapham Junction but they and the pioneer Grateley area system, had relatively short lives. The purely pneumatic system was not adopted widely and was largely supplanted by the rival electro-pneumatic or all-electric systems then and later when the pneumatics had reached the end of their lives.

The Hall system on the NER

A year after the LSWR Woking–Basingstoke automatic signalling was commissioned a second length of main line automatic signalling was brought into use, this time on the North Eastern Railway part of the East Coast main line over the 12 miles between Alne and Thirsk, north of York. It was known as the Hall system after its inventor. Again, track circuits were used together with semaphore signals, but there the resemblance with the LSWR system ended, for the signals were operated by carbonic gas derived from bottled supplies at each location, controlled by electrically operated gas valves, and the signals normally stood at danger. They were approach controlled to clear by a complex series of relays linked to the track circuit sections ahead and bringing other batteries into the circuit so that, provided the line ahead was clear, the signals for an approaching train would be operated to the clear position by the gas valves feeding gas to the operating cylinders before a driver would see the appropriate distant signal. Then as a train passed the signal it would return to danger behind it. If a second train approached before the first had cleared the section, track circuit occupancy of the first train would prevent the signals protecting it from clearing even though the second train might have reached the approach track circuits calling for the signals to clear. Clearly thoughts of Abbots Ripton must have been in the minds of the NER in opting for the normal danger position of these signals. Although the NER installed other power signalling, at Newcastle for example, there were no further examples of track circuit block like that used between Alne and Thirsk.

Point operation limits

The Great Western, not to be outdone, dabbled with power operation but largely with isolated installations and mostly lacking any giant leap forward into new technology with one notable exception, route setting, which will be described in Chapter 11. The GWR's first essay into electric control of signalling was at Didcot North Junction in 1905 followed by a new electric installation at Yarnton just north of Oxford. Electric operation as on the LNWR simply took over the link between lever and signals or points.

There were no track circuits in these early GWR schemes but, as on other railways, there were benefits in point operation, which was no longer tied to the restrictions of the railway inspectorate requirements. When points were first operated from lever frames, largely from the 1870s and egged on by the railway inspectorate in pressing for interlocking, there were fears in some quarters, and rightly, that long lengths of point rodding might not be absolutely positive in moving the point blades fully home against the stock rail, a potentially very dangerous situation in the case of facing points. The Wigan derailment in 1873 had shown that. Even with facing point locks the lock bolt might confirm that the blades were fully home but the bolt could not be expected to give the final push if the blades were standing just out of proper alignment because the rodding had not been able to transmit the full throw, since the bolt would be partly obstructed by the stretcher between the blades forming the lock mechanism and could not enter the slot cleanly. Even with expansion cranks reversing the rodding movement from push to pull or vice versa to allow for hot or cold

weather expansion or contraction it was reckoned that limits should be placed on the length of point rodding between signalbox and points. From the mid-1870s the limit was 120 yards but gradually the restriction was relaxed as it was found that initial fears were over cautious. By 1900 another 80 yards had been added but with power operation there was no mechanical link and the limit was really governed by the ability of air pipes or cables to carry the controlling medium without reduction in pressure or drop in voltage which would affect safe operation, and the return of indications proving the lie of the points to the signalbox. The new power installations in some cases replaced perhaps two or even more old signalboxes which may have been provided simply to control points and related signals because they were beyond the imposed limits for working from one signalbox. The only restriction on the areas controlled by the new power signalboxes if they were not given track circuits was on the length of line which could be seen by the signalman looking out of the windows. It was no use giving him control of points 400 yards away if he could not see the trains on them.

The Great Western made a small advance in 1907 when it tried out track circuits to divide a long block section without adopting automatic signalling, and at the same time saving the costs of operating and maintaining small signalboxes provided for little other purpose than as a block post. This was the intermediate block system, the equipment and operation of which was described in Chapter 6. The first GWR installation was at Basildon between Goring and Pangbourne on the Paddington–Bristol main line with Pangbourne controlling the down line signals at Basildon and Goring controlling the up lines. Yet despite the obvious advantages of the system installation was inconsistent, not only on the Great Western but other railways as well, and many manned (or should it be 'personnel' as some were worked by signalwomen?) intermediate signalboxes survived for many years after.

Isolated power points and signals

Another small step towards power working was the use of electrically operated points in isolated locations which enabled signalboxes that had been provided solely to overcome the mechanical limits, to be closed, or provided the opportunity to improve operation. Almost from the beginning of time on the railways refuge sidings had been provided at some stations to allow goods trains to shunt off main lines to be overtaken by faster passenger trains. Inevitably with the abhorrence of facing points the points to the sidings were trailing to the normal direction of running on the main line. As we have seen, goods trains had to run past the points and set back, in itself perhaps a hazardous operation, particularly as the points were not usually fitted with facing point locks. It was

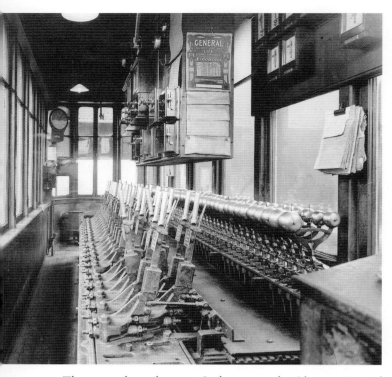

beginning to be realised that this was a time consuming operation and since locked facing points and interlocking had reduced the danger potential of being switched to the wrong line (we are not going to say 'eliminated', as we shall see later) or being derailed by points not fully home, it was possible that fewer delays would be incurred if goods trains could run straight into goods loops off the main line, stop when clear inside to be overtaken by a following passenger train, and when that had cleared the section ahead to go straight out on to the main line again without having to reverse.

However, to accommodate the usual length of goods train the points at one end would almost certainly be beyond the limits for mechanical operation, even with the further relaxations of distances to 250 yards, and to 350 yards by 1925, which has remained to this day. Only where a signalbox was built specifically to control a loop by being situated roughly half way along, and

The power lever frame at Stobcross on the Glasgow Central underground line, contained in a very narrow signalbox, had small versions of the normal heavy duty mechanical levers. (National Railway Museum)

Glasgow Central was given electro-pneumatic power signalling in 1907 controlled from this massive signalbox situated on the Clyde bridge. Like many power signalling schemes of this period the electro-pneumatic system merely replaced the wires from levers to signals and rods to points. All the other mechanical signalling components remained, including the mechanical fouling bars linked to mechanical facing point locks seen here in the points at the bottom. (National Railway Museum)

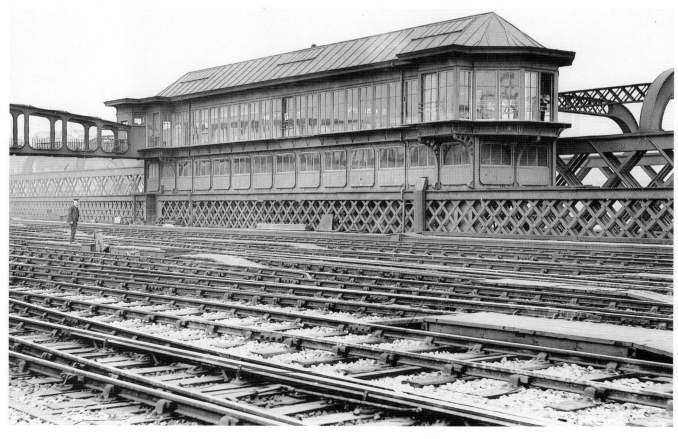

thus having the limit in both directions, was total mechanical operation possible. Where a single-ended refuge siding was converted to a through loop then the points at the new end would either need to be worked by a new signalbox (expensive), a ground frame (inconvenient), or they could be worked electrically. This might be done from batteries but another way was by the use of a hand generator, often used in developing countries but seen occasionally in Britain for controlling loops and possibly the relevant signals, and also for passing loops on single lines or remote junctions as in Ireland. The generator was powered by the signalman turning a handle with one hand at a rate of about one revolution per second while, with the other, he pulled or pushed the lever slides to operate the equipment. A special battery circuit was employed at signals to provide the small amount of current needed to energise holding off coils once the generator supply had done the heavy work of moving the arm to the clear position. But batteries were used to work junction points for the Verney Junction branch in what was described at the time as 'long distance operation', 600 yards from Quainton Road box on the former GCR main line in 1923. The up trailing points were sprung and not worked and the whole area between the box and the junction was track circuited.

Power operation of signalling at the end of the last century and in the first decade of the 20th century, might today seem very pedestrian in its effects. It was applied sparingly and employed a wide range of equipment, sometimes combined, as in the LSWR track circuit block and pneumatic signalling, sometimes to ease the workload of the signalman in pulling heavy levers operating points at their maximum mechanical distance or signals perhaps $^3/_4$ mile away, as seen in the purely power replacement for mechanical linkage and no other additional safety aids as on the pioneer LNWR electric installations. There was also the massive (for those times) power signalling scheme installed at Glasgow Central in 1907. While the signalman might have been spared the physical effort of pulling a heavy mechanical lever, much of the object of power signalling was to allow signalboxes to control larger areas (then as now) so that the signalman would in practice have to look after more trains. In contrast, the first developments in automation on urban and underground railways, and in signals with lights only, were beginning to point the way forward. But before then other factors, including a major collision when an overnight Scotch express (how many Scotch expresses were involved in accidents, and why were they always known as 'Scotch' rather than Scots or Scottish?) rammed the back of two forgotten light engines near Hawes Junction on the Settle & Carlisle line in 1910 with calls for track circuiting as a result, and the First World War intervened. Other signal engineers came to prominence and more American ideas to add to those signalling developments which had already crossed the Atlantic, were tried out which meant that British signalling between 1910 and the mid-1920s was to take a few new routes in its development although some proved to be dead ends.

Chapter 9

WHICH
WAY AHEAD?

WITH THE AFTER effects of the 1889 Act hardly a decade old, and only a few years since the completion of the changeover to a green light for the night time clear indication for stop and distant signals, for the white light clear indication just hung on into the new century on one or two lines, it might be thought that the new standards would have been set to last. But towards the end of the first decade of the new century

For about 25 years from the 1890s, this was the standard that had been set, seen here in GWR form with this bracket at Birmingham Snow Hill in this case with the arms powered electrically. Both stop and distant arms were painted red on the front face with the white stripe or vee, although one or two railways had a black stripe on the front, as well as the back of the arm. At night the distant signals showed the same red or green lights as the stop arms. (National Railway Museum)

came moves which culminated in a radical rethink of the whole future of British signalling which, in the early 1920s, literally turned upside down much of what had gone before. This stemmed from what was seen by some in the signalling industry, both within and outside the railways, as the unhappy use of a red light at night for both stop and distant signals when at danger.

Distant confusion
The role of the distant signal had gradually been clarified from the 1870s onwards as a signal giving early advice to a driver of the indication of the stop signals at the next signalbox ahead, rather than being an outer stop signal in its own right as was the practice on some railways before then. With the development of interlocking the distant signal lever could only be pulled to clear when the locking on it was released by the prior clearance of the home and starting signals and any extra stop signals to which it applied, and similarly the distant had to be returned to danger before the stop signals ahead could be put back. This meant that if the distant signal was clear then so too were the stop signals (assuming they had not been put back to danger in an emergency after the train had passed the distant signal) all showing originally, white lights, but from 1892 green lights. But with all signals at danger they all showed red lights with the conflict at night of the distant signal saying 'pass my red light but be prepared to stop at the next signal', and all the stop signals saying 'stop at my red light'. Moreover, if the home signal was cleared to allow the train to draw up to the starting signal still at danger the green light meant 'pass me' while the red light at the starting signal said 'stop at me'. Yet a green light in the distant meant 'line clear at signals ahead, proceed at speed'. So there were conflicting meanings of both red and green lights depending on which signals they were in. Safe working thus depended entirely on the driver knowing which signal was which, and knowing every detail of the track, points, and speed limits. It was ingrained into every driver but he carried a great weight of responsibility in knowing where he was and

RIGHT *The LNWR distinguished its signals for slow or goods lines with a ringed arm as here at Nash Mills on the main line out of Euston where the signalbox controlled only the slow lines with an up goods loop. The fast lines had only distant signals for the next boxes ahead, at Kings Langley and Boxmoor. The distant arms are red but with a white vertical stripe rather than a vee. In LMS days intermediate block signals replaced the signalbox here. (L&GRP)*

MIDDLE *All three of the Southern lines in pre-Grouping days used the Coligny-Welch distant signal indicator to the right of the arm, like this signal on the South Eastern & Chatham.*

BOTTOM *The Coligny-Welch distant signal indicator had a reflective vee illuminated from the signal lamp alongside the spectacle end of the arm to identify distant signals on some railways. It needed to be kept clean otherwise its reflective properties faded.*

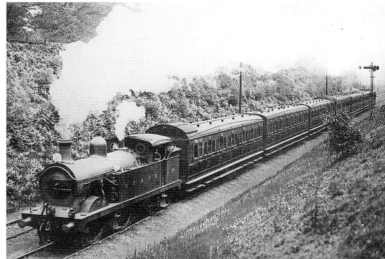

interpreting what he saw into the handling of the train. To do them justice, few accidents were caused by drivers mistaking an absolute stop signal for a distant signal.

Some railways though, felt that the risk was there and endeavoured to give drivers added advice by identifying distant signals using the Coligny-Welch distant signal indicator. This was an extension of the lamp housing to the right of the spectacle with a reflecting white fishtail illuminated from the main lamp appearing alongside the red or green spectacle at night. By day a distant signal was easily identified by the fishtail notch cut out of the left hand end of the arm. The Coligny-Welch distant signal indicator was not universally used and indeed was found largely on the three railways south of London, the Great Eastern, and just one or two in the north of England. It had its drawbacks. For a start it had to be regularly cleaned since the reflecting surface soon faded when covered in dirt. The Furness Railway distinguished its distants by flashing red lights given by AGA gas lamps. But most railways continued to rely on their drivers' ability to know where they were.

Yellow for distants on the District and upper quadrants on the Metropolitan

The next moves came not on the main line railways but down in the murk of London's Inner Circle sub surface line operated jointly by the Metropolitan and Metropolitan District railways (usually known just as the District) which was being resignalled as part of electrification with automatic sections controlled by track circuits. In 1907 the District started to use yellow for its distant signal arms and a yellow light for caution, followed a year or so later by the Metropolitan which did the same on the northern half of the Inner Circle. Once the Metropolitan had completed resignalling on its inner London section it turned its attention to what it called the main line, from Baker Street to Harrow. From the 1880s the Harrow line had

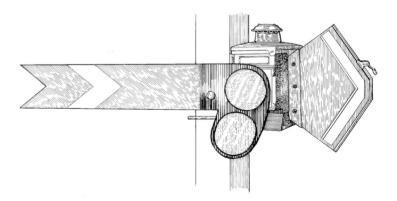

been signalled with absolute block using Spagnoletti instruments. Its semaphore signals were unusual in having a balancing arrangement with an extension of the arm to the right beyond the spectacle to help even out the weight on each side of the pivot, doubtless with the Abbots Ripton accident in mind which had happened only a few years before the line was completed to Harrow. By 1911 the original signalling was deemed to be life expired for the electric trains and the Metropolitan started to install track circuit block on plain line, using ac track circuits, but the signals were of a new type. While they still denoted danger, stop, in the horizontal position, for clear they rose to 45 degrees above horizontal. Not only that, the distant signal arms were painted yellow and showed a yellow light for caution and green for clear. Purely automatic signals were painted in a distinctive style with stop signals having red, white, red horizontal bands, and distant signals yellow, black, yellow.

Stop and proceed

The need to have automatic signals distinguished lay in the fact that there had to be a way of overcoming a fault which held an automatic stop signal at danger. If a signal remained at danger because of a problem in the electrical circuits then a train coming to a halt at the signal might be kept there for some time and the train service would grind to a halt. At a manned signalbox, the signalman could call to a driver and give a verbal instruction, or display a flag, or take action to move the train on. Until the signal lineman reached a faulty automatic signal on these early automatic schemes there would have been nobody to tell the driver what to do. So an emergency procedure was devised to allow stop and proceed working at automatic signals. This permitted a driver after waiting for a prescribed period, usually one or two minutes, to restart and continue through the section ahead at low speed ready to stop

Once other forms of signal had been developed the Great Western was extremely reluctant to use anything other than its traditional lower quadrant semaphores, an attitude which continued for more than 40 years after the GWR had ceased to exist at the end of 1947. However, it was the first to try a three-position upper quadrant semaphore with track circuit control, in 1914. This was on the down main leaving Paddington and is seen here in the 1920s, just alongside the third coach, in the vertical clear position.

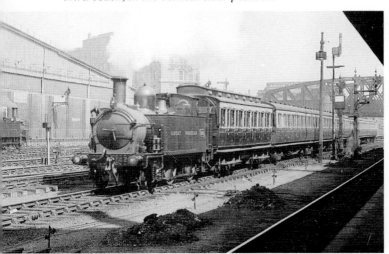

short of any obstruction, which might be another train, or a broken rail if he could see it, or even a physical obstruction which had fallen on to the line. On the other hand the fault might be due to nothing more than a bad relay contact preventing the circuit from functioning and the train would reach the next signal showing clear. Over the 80 or so years since these early automatic signals were introduced, stop and proceed working in clearly defined circumstances has been part of underground, urban and main line operation, but at times has led to collisions because the driver of the train going forward past a signal at danger has not kept speed low enough to stop if a train ahead was suddenly encountered at a stand, initially unsighted. Indeed, until recent years drivers were not required to demonstrate their judgement of what was meant by proceeding at caution as part of training or re-examination in knowledge of rules. As we shall see in subsequent chapters, one or two signalling schemes of later years actually embodied stop and proceed operation in the signal aspects.

Three-position signals – new style

The yellow light for caution had been seen in America from the turn of the century in semaphore signals which gave three indications: horizontal, 'danger – stop', with a red light at night, lowered at 45 degrees with a yellow light at night, called the approach indication, meaning 'proceed but be prepared to stop at the next signal', and lowered to at least 75 degrees or more with a green light at night to indicate 'clear, proceed'. Even in America though, there had been colour changes for, as in Britain, the original colour code had been red for danger, green for caution, and white for clear. By 1908 a new pattern signal had evolved with the arm raised above horizontal to 45 degrees for the approach indication with its yellow light, and raised to a vertical position, with the green light at night for clear. These signals known as upper quadrants, as distinct from lower quadrants which dropped below horizontal for the proceed indications, gave a much better spread of arm angles with clear being vertical and thus 45 degrees further on from caution. In the lower quadrant American three-position signal the arm did not reach the vertical position like the British three-position slotted signal used in time interval signalling. One or two American railways still did not use the yellow light for caution, preferring to display red and green lights side by side for caution, as did at least one railway in Australia. The American signals, like most of those in Britain had the arm facing away from the track, but in America right hand running was and is the rule on double track so that signals were placed to the right of the line with the arm facing away to the right of the post. British practice has usually had the signal post to the left of the track for left hand running, with the arm facing away from the left side of the post, although for sighting purposes on curves signal posts are sometimes placed to the right of the track.

Like many American signalling developments it was not long before the three-position upper quadrant semaphore signal found its way across the Atlantic and was anglicised, not only with the arm to the left of the post but with the lamp housing also to the left since the swing of the arm towards the vertical took the spectacle in an arc upwards to the left of the post, and not vertically on the right of the post as in what was becoming the traditional British lower quadrant signal. The first three-position semaphore signal in Britain was somewhat surprisingly, installed by the Great Western Railway at Paddington in 1914. (Perhaps in the light of the Great Western's reluctance in the following 30 odd years to have anything to do with signals which did not have semaphore arms operating in the lower quadrant the word surprisingly should be changed to astonishingly!) It was in the nature of a one-off, located on the down main line as a sort of advanced starting signal, working automatically to indicate the line situation for two sections ahead soon after down trains left the station.

Two years later the Great Central Railway installed a group of eight three-position upper quadrants at Keadby on a new section of line on the Doncaster–Grimsby route, including a lifting bridge across the River Trent. There were four on the up line and four on the down and partly working automatically in that they returned to danger as a train passed, from track circuit control through electro-pneumatic equipment.

Proposals for revolution

This installation was the brainchild of the GCR's signalling superintendent, Arthur Bound, who was way ahead of his time in his thinking. In 1915 he had stunned the railway establishment in a paper to the Institution of Railway Signal Engineers (IRSE) in which he called for the replacement of manual block signalling by track circuit block and automatic signals on plain line, more track circuits through interlocked areas at stations and junctions, and an automatic system for preventing drivers from passing signals at danger. His reasons for thinking this way arose from the number of accidents caused by signalmen's errors in operating the block system thus giving false clear signals to drivers, and those caused by drivers going past signals at danger. But his prime conclusion was that British signalling practice should change to a speed signalling system to tell the driver the speed of the route set ahead at junctions and not specifically the way he was to go. So far-reaching were the calls in Bound's paper that the Institution, then only in its infancy, needed two more meetings to discuss the proposals including the suggestions for three-position semaphores

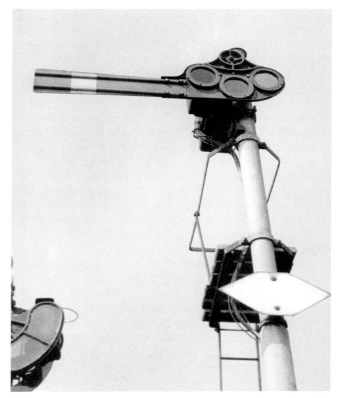

A British three-position upper quadrant semaphore from the First World War period installed near Keadby on the Great Central Railway. Note the tapered corrugated arm which was powered by a topmast electric motor. It was photographed in 1967, shortly before removal. (BR, ER)

and the use of the yellow light at night for caution. Certainly Arthur Bound was controversial and stirred up a hornet's nest between the traditionalists who could see no need for change and were quite happy that a red light in a distant signal meant what it said – stop at the next signal, and those who had a broader vision on how signalling could be developed.

Perhaps the massive double collision, in all involving five trains, at Quintinshill on the Caledonian main line between Carlisle and Glasgow in May 1915, with 225 dead, the highest toll in any British accident before or since, which happened just before the second of the IRSE discussion meetings on Bound's paper, might have brought home some of his proposals to the disbeliever. Track circuiting would have locked the signals at danger and protected the local train which had been shunted to the up line and then forgotten by the signalmen who cleared the signals for a troop special, with a down sleeping car express running into the wreckage of the first collision. Fire broke out in gas lit coaches and engulfed the three passenger trains and part of two goods trains standing on the loop tracks on each side. Following his own ideas Bound then installed the Keadby three-position semaphores and in 1917 converted the night-time indications of the ordinary lower quadrant semaphore distant signals between Marylebone and Neasden to yellow lights when at caution, although the arms themselves remained painted red with the usual fishtail end and white chevron.

Three-position signals at Victoria

While all this was going on, the South Eastern & Chatham Railway was embarking on the resignalling of its part of Victoria station in London with a complete three-position semaphore signalling installation from Grosvenor Road over the half mile or so into the terminus. Work was delayed by the First World War but it was commissioned at the end of 1919. The whole layout was controlled by one signalbox taking over the work formerly done by two, with a 200 'lever' power frame controlling signals and points on the all-electric system. The levers were in fact slides with vertical handles at the outer end, alternate handles pointing up and those in between pointing down so that while the slides were close together there was ample room for the signalman's hand to grasp the handles to pull them out or push back. The whole area was track circuited and through points track circuits were used for route locking instead of locking bars attached to the facing point lock. The signals displayed what were now the standard three-position indications – horizontal danger, inclined up at 45 degrees for caution, be prepared to stop at the next signal, and vertically up for clear, with the corresponding night indications of red, yellow, and green lights respectively. In truth there were only two signal sections on the up lines and three on the down to which the three-position signals applied but at least it showed what could be done with a single arm signal giving an indication of what the next signal was showing. As was said at the time, one arm with one motor could do the same thing as two arms with two motors using conventional lower quadrant two-position semaphores.

With the variety of routes available beyond certain signals only single arms were provided, working with route indicators. Shunting signals were unique for they also worked in three positions. They were in the form of white discs face on to trains, with a painted signal arm across the disc. Like the main signals the arm was horizontal for danger, diagonally raised as the disc turned through 45 degrees, meaning shunt into the section ahead which might be occupied (allowing vehicles to be attached to or detached from a standing train) for which purpose the track circuits were not taken into account although points were locked and detected, or with the arm vertical as the disc turned through its final 45 degrees, meaning shunt through the next section (with the track circuits proving the section was clear) into the following section, the shunt signal there showing at least a caution indication. A special feature above the lever frame was an aid to signalmen

with diagrams of the layout with the lever numbers showing the points and signals to be operated for specific moves. These were in addition to the track diagram of the whole layout which included indications of track circuit occupancy.

Illuminated diagrams

Diagrams of the track layout showing signal and point positions and numbers had become part of the signalbox equipment once layouts were concentrated in lever frames. Now, with the development of track circuits it was possible to show the position of trains as they occupied and cleared track circuits in progressing through the layout. Not all the early power signalling schemes, even if they had track circuits, displayed the train position on a track diagram, the other way being to have an indicator which took varying forms showing line clear or line occupied, usually on the block shelf near or above a lever to which it applied. The first illuminated diagram had been seen on the London Underground at what was then known as Mill Hill Park, (today's Acton Town on the Piccadilly and District Lines) brought into use in June 1905. It established a style on London's Underground which became the standard with the tracks on the diagram normally lit in white, with the section occupied by a train, dark with the lights out. Eventually on the main lines track circuit indications on track diagrams were usually shown by red lights, lit to denote the presence of a train.

Three-position signals
on the Ealing–Shepherds Bush line

Hardly had the Victoria three-position installation been completed when another was brought to fruition, this time with the Great Western having another dabble, not entirely on its own account but in conjunction with the Central London Railway tube line. The GWR had built a new 3 1/2-mile line from Ealing to Wood Lane near Shepherds Bush via North Acton. This provided a link from the West London Railway with its connections to the railways south of London to the Great Western High Wycombe and Birmingham line at North Acton, and to the relief lines on the main West of England and South Wales route at Ealing Broadway. There was an existing connection which gave this same facility at Old Oak Common, but goods trains in particular to or from the West London line had to cross the main lines on the flat. The new Ealing & Shepherds Bush Railway gave an alternative route without crossing the flat junction of the main line. To open up the area for passengers and to encourage new housing the Central London was to extend its electric trains to Ealing Broadway from the existing terminus at Wood Lane, for which purpose the GWR installed a centre electrified third-rail, the system then used by the Central London. Signalling was of the three-position semaphore type, and only three signalboxes were provided, to work Wood Lane Junction with mechanical points, North Acton Junction with mechanical points, and Ealing Broadway. Here the station points were worked from electro-pneumatic machines controlled by the District Railway signalbox and the crossover from the Shepherds Bush line to the GWR relief lines from the GWR signalbox after a co-operative release lever had been pulled in the District Railway signalbox, together with a slot release by the GWR signalman on the appropriate signal.

All the three-position semaphores were worked by power, those at Wood Lane by electro-pneumatic operation, and the remainder by all-electric motors. The signals on plain line worked purely automatically by track circuit block and as such they were distinguished from controlled signals by having pointed ends, the reverse of the fishtail, with a corresponding white chevron pointing away from the post on the otherwise red arm. This identified to drivers signals where stop and proceed rules applied. Some signals, including those at Ealing Broadway, had telephones to the signalbox because of the difficulty in getting to the box. Once again the night time indications were red – danger, yellow – caution, and green – clear. Yellow was obviously coming to mean caution, whatever the view of the traditionalists. The last signals leading to the dead end platforms at Ealing Broadway only cleared to the caution position. Signals at junctions had a separate arm on its own post for each route. Shunt signals only had two positions, with a red bar on a white disc diagonally up on the left for clear. Surprisingly the three-position semaphores had long-burning oil lamps, yet two-aspect fog repeaters placed 200 yards on the approach side of main signals not only gave their indications by lights only, yellow when the main signal was at danger, and green when the main signal was at caution or clear, but had electric lamps switched on by the signalman during fog. All the main signals were accompanied by electrically powered ground trip apparatus with the arm raised when the signal was at danger to stop a train from passing. (See Chapter 13 for a more detailed description.)

Position light signals

There was another form of three-position signal which made a tentative appearance at this time on one or two lines including the Metropolitan, and the London & South Western which had one at Waterloo. This was in the form of a position light signal with the indication given by rows of usually white or yellow lights. The signal consisted of a display of four lights arranged horizontally for danger, diagonally up for caution, and vertically for clear shown against a backing plate. The third light from the left formed the pivot and was always alight. There were just a handful of these signals and they were not perpetuated as main signals, although as we shall see, position lights were later

adopted for junction indicators and for subsidiary signals.

Speed signalling and a fourth indication

By 1920 there were thus three areas where three-position upper quadrant semaphores were in use plus the example at Paddington. Were Arthur Bound's ideas coming to fruition elsewhere? More to the point, what were the implications of three-position semaphore signals? So far they merely indicated danger, caution, and clear and in the Ealing & Shepherds Bush installation had separate arms for each route at facing junctions just like conventional signals. The caution position merely saved the use of a separate distant signal arm. But what was to happen if signals had to be closely spaced so that there was insufficient braking distance from a signal at caution to the next one at danger? It would be possible to show caution on the second signal back as well as the one preceding the signal at danger, but that in itself could be misleading if a second train was running close behind the first, since the second driver might see several signals at caution and then not be able to stop in time at one at danger because the first train had stopped further ahead.

Already in America, this possibility had been overcome by using a second arm below the main arm to give what was called the 'approach medium' indication with the upper arm at caution displaying a yellow light and the lower arm vertical giving a green light. The next signal would display the top arm at caution showing a yellow light and the bottom arm at danger showing a red light. Finally the next signal would have both arms at danger showing a red light. This sequence gave what we would call preliminary caution but this was also embodied in the American signalling code introduced in 1913 which primarily devised speed signalling indications at interlockings. The same caution over clear meant reduce to medium speed, but with speed signalling the position of the arms one above the other on the same post denoted different speed bands, the top arm applying to the straight high speed route, the second arm down applying to the medium speed route, and the third arm down applying to the low speed route. Thus if the middle arm was at caution and those above and below were at danger it denoted proceed at caution on the medium speed route. It also meant that a driver could be faced with an array of lights, in this case red, yellow, red displayed vertically. In Belgium, which had then recently adopted three-position signals, distant signal arms also formed part of the system so that while three-position stop signals could show danger, caution, and clear, the three-position distant arms showed horizontal for caution, with a yellow light, raised diagonally to 45 degrees for attention, with a yellow and green light side by side, and vertical for clear with a single green light. The attention indication was the preliminary caution preceding a stop signal displaying caution and could provide the fourth indication if signals were closely spaced. Sometimes the distants were mounted below stop signals and the two arms together had the same meanings, ie both arms horizontal, one red light – danger stop, stop arm at caution diagonally up and the distant horizontal, one yellow light – caution, the stop arm vertical and the distant arm at 45 degrees up, yellow light alongside green – attention, and both arms vertical, one green light, clear proceed. But these signals were not used as speed indications at facing junctions since separate signals were normally provided for each route, as in British practice.

The potential for complicated semaphore signalling with three-position signals was certainly there, but so far no British scheme had had to face the question of a fourth indication for closely spaced signals to give adequate braking distance over two signal sections, and no British scheme used the three-position arm as a speed signal. Then there was the question of the colour to be employed for the caution night-time indication. Yellow lights were used in the three-position signals, and yellow for conventional distant signals at caution had already been seen, although the great majority of British distant signals still showed a red light when at danger (as the caution position was still called by many when referring to the arm when horizontal). It really had to be sorted out for there were voices for change and voices for keeping what was already a standard. Certainly there had been no problem in drivers identifying a yellow light by comparison with a red light, by night or in fog or through smoke. If anything, smoke or fog tended to darken yellow towards orange or even red but this was effectively erring on the side of safety. There was some criticism of yellow as being close to green in the spectrum but in practice this has never been an obvious problem.

The IRSE's signalling proposals

The professional institution, the IRSE, set up a committee to examine the whole question in 1922. It could not be considered by individual railway companies because any one railway would have its own ideas, apart from the fact that Parliament had just completed legislation to amalgamate the individual railway companies into four main groups although excluding the London Underground railways and a few others.

The IRSE committee consisted of nine leading signal engineers from three of the four newly emerging group companies (but without anyone from what was to become the London Midland & Scottish Railway), the London Underground, and from firms in the railway signalling industry. It was perhaps unsurprising that the chairman was Arthur Bound, newly appointed as Signal Engineer of the London & North Eastern Railway Southern Area. The committee examined all the options, not just of the different types of signal but the effect of new types of signalling on traffic operation and the complications that might arise in different locations if three-position semaphores were adopted.

The then existing type of manual block working meant that before a second train could be given a clear distant signal, a mile or so before it reached the signalbox, the previous train would had to have passed beyond the clearing point ahead of the first of the stop signals at the next signalbox ahead. The signals there must have been returned to caution and danger and the block telegraph signals exchanged to clear the first train from the block section and for the second train to be accepted. If the first train had not cleared the section then the distant signal at the previous signalbox would remain at caution for the second train which would have to slow down ready to stop at the home signal and then crawl from home signal to starting signal, and possibly advanced starting signal with green lights at night leading to red as we have seen already. With three-position signals each signal acted as a warning for the next.

By the late 1920s distant signals were changing colour from red to yellow arms on their front face with a black vee stripe and a yellow light at night in the caution position. This is a GWR co-acting distant signal with upper and lower arms for sighting purposes. (National Railway Museum)

Another two-arm distant signal near Wells, Norfolk but not with co-acting arms. In this case the top arm is the distant signal for the next box ahead but because it is a passing loop on a single line the arm is fixed at caution. The lower arm which is worked, is a gate distant for an intermediate level crossing and tells the driver whether the crossing gates are open or shut for the train or whether a gate home signal is at danger or clear. Not all level crossings had a home signal. (National Railway Museum)

The committee's majority report, which was so thorough that it was not published until the end of 1924, rejected the use of three-position semaphores altogether and came down firmly in favour of colour-light signals by day and night with three aspects, red – danger, stop, single yellow – caution, be prepared to stop at the next signal, and green – proceed, all right. Where signals had to be spaced at less then braking distance then a fourth aspect was recommended. The committee examined the possible use of green and yellow together which could be given by a three-aspect head if red was in the middle, but felt it invited misinterpretation and opted for double yellow displayed vertically which meant that a fourth light unit would be needed to obtain the four aspects. Moreover double yellow was fail safe in that if one of the lights failed the signal would go to the more restrictive single yellow. As to the meaning of double yellow the

committee's choice of phrase seemed to be drawn from Belgian and speed signalling language, 'Attention – run at medium speed'. In more recent years the meaning has been more precisely defined as 'preliminary caution, be prepared to find the next signal at caution'.

The committee's endorsement of colour light signalling and its implicit acceptance of yellow for caution meant that yellow would also have to be adopted for semaphore distant signals, with yellow painted arms with a black fishtail chevron near the left hand end and a yellow light at night when the arm was in the horizontal position, henceforth to be known as the caution position. The new proposals were embodied in the Ministry of Transport's requirements from 1925, (the Ministry of Transport was formed in 1919 having taken over the regulatory function for railways including the railway inspectorate from the Board of Trade). At last, nearly 100 years after the first passenger railways, drivers now had a distinctive warning signal. The abandonment of three-position

By the late 1920s the lower quadrant semaphore began to go out of fashion although it survives in a few places today, 70 years on. In its place was the two-position upper quadrant signal first seen on the Metropolitan Railway in London about 1909 and recommended as the future standard in the mid-1920s. The arms were lighter and the construction less weighty since the arm would return to danger automatically if a wire broke. These examples of stop and distant arms on the LNER are mounted on tubular steel posts. (LNER Publicity)

In Ireland, lower quadrant semaphore signals virtually remained standard both in Northern Ireland and in the Republic although LMS pattern upper quadrant semaphores were installed on the Northern Counties line at Larne. In the Republic, CIE, the Irish Transport Company in the 1960s, painted many semaphore stop signal arms in vivid Day-Glo orange-red to make them more visible. This gantry signal, seen in the 1950s, was situated at the approaches to Cork Glanmire Road (Cork Kent from 1966) on the Great Southern & Western line from Cobh and Youghal. (Geoffrey Kichenside)

upper quadrant semaphores as a future standard meant that two-position semaphores could be made to work in the upper quadrant, still indicating danger when horizontal but denoting clear with the arm raised to 45 degrees or a little more above horizontal. Arms could be much lighter without the heavy balancing needed to return lower quadrants to danger if a wire broke. An upper quadrant arm would simply drop by gravity to the danger position.

Already daylight colour-light signals had been used on the Liverpool Overhead Railway in 1920, and a year or so later on London's Metropolitan Railway. But in 1923 even while his committee was contemplating the future of signalling, Bound presided over the first use of daylight automatic colour-light signals on a main line. Commissioned on the Great Central line between Marylebone and Neasden in 1923 this was part of the work being undertaken with the new Wembley Stadium loop, just after the GCR had become part of the LNER.

The new automatic signalling provided a three-minute headway between trains. Two of the other committee members, W. J. Thorrowgood, the new Southern Railway Signal & Telegraph Superintendent, and his Assistant, W. Challis, were anticipating the report's recommendations for they were pressing ahead with new four-aspect colour-light signals between Holborn Viaduct and Elephant & Castle. These were controlled from miniature lever frames at Holborn and Blackfriars signalboxes which replaced seven mechanical signalboxes. The new signals were commissioned in March 1926, just 15 months after publication of the IRSE report.

But change did not come overnight. Many railways only started to repaint distant signals and provide the yellow caution spectacle from the mid-1920s and the work was not complete until early in the 1930s with odd examples surviving a little longer. The three main three-position upper quadrant signalling installations were not perpetuated and compared with traditional signalling did not have long lives. The Victoria installation lasted until June 1939 when it was replaced by a new colour light scheme, the Ealing–Shepherds Bush signals were replaced by standard London Transport colour lights in 1948, but the handful of signals at Keadby lasted well into the British Railways' era, until the 1960s. Although the new standards were intended for country-wide adoption they were used by only three of the four new group companies and, in their own way, by the London Underground railways which came into a new organisation, London Transport, in 1933. The Great Western Railway, despite its foray with three-position semaphores otherwise remained so conservative in its outlook that it would have virtually nothing to do with upper quadrant semaphore signals and did not adopt the new four-aspect colour light code or the standard method of displaying the three aspects. The attitude in respect of semaphore signals not only lasted to the end of the GWR as a private sector railway in 1947 but to the present day on its successor organisations through the BR years where semaphore signals have survived. Even in the 1990s, in Cornwall lower quadrant semaphores were still being put in as renewals became due.

The recommendations in the IRSE report were so sound and simple in concept that the basic signal aspects have remained unchanged to this day, 70 years on and will remain so as long as there is a need for lineside signalling. However, as will be described in later chapters with the simple aspects trying to be all things to all men and in more recent years attempting to be block signals, route signals, speed signals, all in one, some of the meanings have become blurred.

Chapter 10

POWER OPERATION EXPANDS – THE SOUTHERN WAY

THE SOUTHERN RAILWAY undoubtedly led the way into power operation during the 1920s for, following its initial four-aspect colour light signalling scheme between Holborn Viaduct and Elephant & Castle completed in March 1926, another much larger conversion was in hand at Charing Cross and Cannon Street. Plans were also well advanced to continue resignalling past Borough Market Junction, the convergence of the Charing Cross and Cannon Street routes, and on through London Bridge towards New Cross on the former South Eastern & Chatham main line, henceforth to be known as the Eastern Section, and from the main London Bridge terminus of the London, Brighton & South Coast Railway (renamed the Central Section) towards New Cross Gate. Colour light signals, largely four-aspect on Eastern Section tracks, and mostly three-aspect on the Central Section, with track circuit block, would take over from the old signalboxes with their Sykes lock and block equipment and semaphore signals.

The whole scheme was allied to electrification initially of the Eastern Section suburban routes on the SR's new standard third rail dc system with the running rails used for traction return as in use on former London & South Western (Western Section) suburban routes, and planned by the SECR. Already some of the tracks on the Central Section route into London Bridge terminus were electrified but on the 6,700 volt 25 cycle ac overhead conductor system favoured by the LBSCR, the first section of which had been inaugurated over the South London line between London Bridge and Victoria in December 1909. Even though a further section of electrification on the ac overhead system was commissioned to Coulsdon in 1925, plans were soon in hand to convert the ac lines to dc third rail as part of the Southern's great electrification scheme and the last of the overhead system was taken out of use in favour of the dc third rail system in September 1929.

The system of electrification could of course affect the signalling equipment, particularly track circuits, since the type of track circuit used was dependent on the type of traction supply. Generally, lines electrified

with direct current had alternating current track circuits to ensure that stray currents from the traction supply, especially from an electrical fault, could not falsely energise the track relay to give a track clear indication when there was actually a train standing or running on the track circuit. Similarly, with alternating

The Southern Railway wasted little time after the production of the IRSE report in 1924 recommending the adoption of four-aspect colour light signals, in pressing ahead with them. The first, seen here at Blackfriars Junction, were brought into use in March 1926 between Holborn Viaduct and Elephant & Castle in conjunction with third rail electrification. Like their semaphore predecessors still in use in this photograph, junction signals had separate indications for route diversions ahead. (National Railway Museum)

current traction at that time direct current track circuits were normally used which would not respond to stray alternating current. This was not always so since the pioneer London Underground lines, with dc traction had special dc track circuits with double polarised relays designed so that they could not be energised by a fault current. As we shall see in later chapters in BR days, the re-introduction of high voltage ac traction supplies, the combination of ac and dc electrification on the same tracks, and the development of three-phase alternating current traction supply on trains brought immense problems in track circuit technology to ensure that false operation could not occur. But for the following 40 years from the 1920s, generally speaking, it was ac track circuits for dc electrification and that was the Southern way of doing it. The track circuits could be either single rail or double rail, the former with one of the running rails insulated into sections for track circuit purposes, the latter with both rails insulated. With electric traction utilising the running rails for the return path of the traction supply, and both rails insulated, some means had to be devised for passing the dc traction supply across the insulated joints. This was done by an impedance bond at the insulated joint, linking the rails on each side of the insulation which allowed the dc return current to pass but inhibited the ac supply of the track circuit. On the London Underground with third and fourth rail electrification the return traction current was taken by the centre fourth rail while the running rails were not in the traction circuit. On purely steam operated lines there was no restriction and track circuits could be either ac or dc, depending on the type of installation and the availability of supply. As we have seen already, in its simplest form the track circuit was fed from rechargeable cells with low voltage of no more than two volts passing through the rails. In the case of the LBSCR's ac electric lines, they were signalled by Sykes lock and block so that the track circuit type was not a major factor.

The new signalling between Charing Cross, Cannon Street and Borough Market Junction was commissioned in June 1926, and two years later almost to the day, new signalling was brought into use through London Bridge and on towards New Cross and Bricklayers Arms Junction. That historic location was just a stone's throw from Corbett's Lane, where the old London & Croydon Railway diverged from the London & Greenwich Railway which we saw in an earlier chapter had its curious red and white route signals, and Bricklayers Arms Junction itself with its junction semaphores of 1843. By the 1920s the area had become a spread of multiple tracks. Then, in 1929, colour light signals were taken on through New Cross to the Lewisham area where the Eastern Section lines diverged into several branches and loops.

Several of the old mechanical signalboxes had their functions taken over by the new power signalling, and while a few new mechanical lever frames were installed – Metropolitan Junction for example, where the west curve from Cannon Street joined the line towards Charing Cross and a spur linked the Charing Cross line to Blackfriars, with points operated mechanically but with the full size levers adapted to work circuit controllers for the colour light signals – miniature lever frames were provided in the new or re-equipped signalboxes to work points and signals electrically. Borough Market Junction, controlling four tracks paired up, up, down, down, from the London Bridge direction splitting into four for Cannon Street and two to Metropolitan Junction on the Charing Cross line, had just 35 levers, but London Bridge, a new three-storey signalbox, had a massive 312-lever frame, weighing 23 tons, supported by the middle floor, even though the signalmen worked the levers standing on the top floor. The main reason for its size was the mechanical interlocking which inevitably, since the signalbox controlled both the six Eastern Section through tracks, including the crossings of up and down tracks over each other further out, and the ten-track terminus of the main station with the approach lines, was extremely complex. The Eastern Section through platforms, moreover, had seven tracks which converged to four to Borough Market.

Despite its small size, Borough Market Junction was one of the busiest signalboxes in the country with an average of over 1,000 trains daily and, with virtually alternate trains, certainly during the busy commuter periods, crossing the paths of trains in the opposite directions as up trains for Cannon Street competed for the flat crossings with down trains from Charing Cross. At Borough Market speeds were low and most trains were not doing more than about 15mph as their wheel flanges squealed round the sharp check-railed curves on the bridges over the streets below. In the down direction from Charing Cross the home signal gave little more than 15 yards overlap to the fouling point of the nearest up Cannon Street track crossing in front of it and, in clear weather, the Borough Market Junction signalman could allow a down train from Charing Cross to enter the section from Metropolitan Junction to that home signal even though a train was passing through the junction across its path. In fog, manual block working was introduced between Metropolitan Junction and Borough Market so that if an up train was signalled across the junction to Cannon Street a down Charing Cross service would be held at Metropolitan Junction until accepted by Borough Market Junction and signalled with a clear run through and unusually for colour lights in fog, Borough Market's down home signal from Charing Cross had a fog-signalman.

Of course, with such an intensively used section of line it was inevitable that trains would at times be stopped to

wait for the clearance of a conflicting move and the presence of the double-track bottleneck on the Charing Cross line over the 300 yards or so to Metropolitan Junction on an otherwise four-track route did not help. The secret of working at Borough Market was for the signalman to wait until he could see the whites of the driver's eyes before he cleared the signal, for in that way he was not holding another train awaiting the passage of the first which might not actually be coming for a few more seconds. It was not like that in the regulations but that was the way it worked in practice. It was a pity that

One of the busiest signalboxes but one of the smallest on the Southern's Eastern Section mid-1920s resignalling was Borough Market Junction, just west of London Bridge where Cannon Street tracks diverged from the Charing Cross line. Speeds were low but often the two signalmen had to handle four trains at once. In this late 1960s montage top left is the interior showing the 35-lever frame and the train describers; top right, four together; bottom left, one for Cannon Street and one approaching from Charing Cross with just a 15 yard overlap beyond the home signal; bottom right, one each way on the Charing Cross line and one from Cannon Street. (Geoffrey Kichenside) the SR did not totally reorganise the tracks between New Cross and Borough Market to avoid the dozen or so flat crossings where up and down lines crossed each other several times as they were rearranged from pairing by route or use at New Cross to pairing by direction through London Bridge station and Borough Market and back to pairing by use from there to Charing Cross. That did not come for another 50 years when London Bridge and the surrounding lines were resignalled again in 1975, and trains to and from Cannon Street used the two northernmost tracks and those on Charing Cross services were allocated the southernmost pair with corresponding reorganisation between London Bridge and New Cross, eliminating many of the conflicting crossings.

Miniature lever frames

The miniature lever frames of the first of the new signalboxes, as just mentioned, at London Bridge had mechanical interlocking, the Westinghouse style K frames. However, a new development was incorporated in the miniature lever frame at North Kent East Junction where the Greenwich line left the New Cross tracks, for the interlocking was achieved using electric locks on the slide bars attached to the levers; the Westinghouse style L frames. The locks consisted of an electro-magnet unit which when energised attracted an arm linked by a rod to a latch which engaged slots in the lever slide bar. When energised, the arm and rod lifted the latch out of the slide bar slots to free the lever and, for the electro-magnet to be energised, all the other levers related to that lever had to be in their correct positions making all the right electrical connections. Some of that Westinghouse L frame from North Kent East went for further use on the Torbay & Dartmouth Railway in Devon after its first owners had finished with it when the 1975 London Bridge resignalling was complete.

Colour lights on the main line

The London Bridge area resignalling from 1926 to 1929 was just the start, for colour light signalling, track circuits and power operation was effectively the future standard for the Southern on its intensively worked routes, partly in conjunction with new electrification and partly to renew old life-expired signalling. By no means all the new electrified routes were given new signalling and once away from the inner London areas the existing signalling continued in use on most lines. When it came to Britain's first main line electrification on the Brighton line in 1932/3 (the North Eastern's planned York to Newcastle electrification after the First World War never actually happened) that too was given new signalling over much of the route with colour light signals being installed between Coulsdon North and Brighton via the Quarry line avoiding Redhill. While some signalboxes had new miniature lever frames much

A *three-aspect signal on the Brighton line at Earlswood. Notice the 'pigs ears' giving a sideways indication of the aspect displayed if a train is too close to the signal for the driver to see the main beam. (Southern Railway)*

of the signalling was controlled by existing mechanical signalboxes suitably adapted although several were designed to be closed unless they were required for point operation as for example when goods trains needed access to yards. At other times a 'king' lever could be pulled which set the running signals to work automatically purely by track circuit operation. The 36 miles from Coulsdon to Brighton formed the longest length of colour light signalling in the country in 1933 and the scheme set the pattern for future development for only seven signalboxes needed to be open all the time in that distance.

Sykes accidents speed resignalling

So it went on, with resignalling schemes for Waterloo

and parts of the Western Section main line at Woking, the Portsmouth line at Guildford, Haslemere and Havant, and another major London scheme at Victoria covering both the Eastern and Central sections of the station. To an extent this scheme had to be started fairly quickly following a major collision at Battersea Park in 1937 when a relief signalman tied himself up with the lever locking of the Sykes lock and block in trying to signal a South London train out across the junction to the up local line. He had tried to pull the signal slide before setting the points but could then not restore the slide which he had been able to pull part way, and could not clear the signal. The signalman cut the seals and put his hand into the Sykes locking case to lift the lock by hand to get his release but somehow, whatever he did, he also released the block indicator to 'clear' for the up local line from the next signalbox, Pouparts Junction, although a train was standing at his home signal and still in the block section. The Pouparts Junction signalman, with 'line clear' on his block instrument, signalled a following train into the section which, in the mist and drizzle of that April morning, collided with the back of the standing train and 12 passengers were killed. The official report makes interesting reading for it shows just how busy the signalman was and the pressure under which he was working. In one peak hour the Battersea Park Junction signalman would handle 65 trains on four main tracks and two branch (South London) tracks. Each train required five bell signals, operation of the Sykes plunger, movements of the Sykes switch hook, and the operation of three signal slides, and for South London trains changing of points as well, at least 14 signalling actions for every train, more for others, making a total

of over 900 signalling operations in one hour by one man! And that was apart from telephone calls, setting the train describer indications and any out of course operations. Did anyone ever calculate the signalman's workload and the psychological effect of such pressure? The signalman was blamed for the accident but he was trying to untie himself to keep the traffic moving and somehow managed to release other locking on the block system. But was the system itself examined? The inspecting officer, Col Mount, thought it was time for modern signalling to take over and within 18 months a new power signalbox at Battersea Park had been commissioned. In 1939 Victoria itself was resignalled with two signalboxes, one for the Central Section and the existing Eastern Section signalbox from three-position semaphore days was re-equipped to work colour light signals.

By then the Southern was turning its attention to the remaining mechanical signalling on the Brighton main line, forming a Y-shaped gap between the power signalling at London Bridge and Victoria, and the existing Brighton line signalling from Coulsdon southwards. These routes still had LBSCR semaphore signalling and Sykes lock and block but the Second World War intervened and it was hardly the time to start new signalling projects. The Southern, being south of London, was right in the path of air attacks and its

Most of the Southern's resignalling schemes between the 1920s and the 1950s included several new power signalboxes with miniature lever frames and eventually, magazine type train describers. This is the interior of Gloucester Road Junction between Croydon and Selhurst, one of the new boxes in the early 1950s scheme to complete resignalling between London and Brighton (except for Redhill). (BR, SR)

signal engineers had a hard enough job maintaining and repairing signalling damaged by bombing. Soon after the end of the war, in 1946, the Southern announced that resignalling of the gap was to be put in hand and it was commissioned in stages between 1951 and 1955 bringing colour lights and power control to the complex of junctions at Balham, Streatham and in particular Croydon where a series of flying junctions already segregated the rearrangement of local and main tracks and the West Croydon line. Curiously, Redhill remained an isolated outpost of mechanical signalling because the 1932 colour lights bypassed it on the Quarry line taking in all four tracks south of Earlswood, the next station south of Redhill. From 1955 colour lights existed from Coulsdon to London but poor Redhill had to wait for the next total resignalling in the area in the 1980s before it too got its colour lights and power operation.

The completion of the London–Coulsdon gap with colour light signals did not come in time to stop another major collision arising from a signalman's

The 1936 resignalling on the Western Section from Waterloo to Hampton Court Junction introduced the three-lamp position light junction indicator to the Southern, in this case at Wimbledon with routes to left and right from the up local line, and a subsidiary signal for access to Durnsford Road depot. Mostly existing signalboxes were retained and adapted to work the new signalling. (Southern Railway)

blunder with the Sykes lock and block system in October 1947, just three months before the Southern Railway ceased to exist. The signalman at Purley Oaks forgot a train standing at his starting signal, out of sight in fog, and even though his rear section instrument was correctly locked at 'train on line' he thought it had failed and used the release key to free it and accept a following train. With the signals cleared for it this train rapidly caught up the standing train which had moved on and, in the subsequent collision, 31 passengers and the driver of the second train died. It was not to be the last collision caused by misuse of the Sykes release key for much the same thing happened in December 1955 at Barnes Junction on the Western Section Waterloo–Richmond line. On this occasion it allowed an electric multiple unit to run into the back of a goods train, much of which caught fire, resulting in 13 deaths.

Position light junction indicators

The early 1950s Southern resignalling on the Brighton line continued the same practices of the 1930s, with signalboxes equipped with miniature lever frames. There had been detail changes in the colour light signals themselves though. In the late 1920s' schemes junction signals were given two (or more) three- or four-aspect heads side by side to signal trains towards diverging routes. Only the head concerned had a proceed aspect, that is the left hand head for a left hand route, and the other heads for the routes not set showed a red aspect, which meant a train would be passing a red light as well as a proceed yellow or green light. By the time of the Waterloo resignalling in the mid-1930s it was felt undesirable for a train to pass a red light so only one main head was provided showing the usual three- or four-aspect lights. Any divergence to the left or right was indicated by position light indicators, usually above the main signal head. These showed a row of three white lights diagonally upwards to the left for the only or last left hand divergence, horizontally to the left for a first (out of two) divergence to the left or diagonally down to the left if there was a first out of three divergence. There were three similar positions to the right for tracks diverging to the right. Trains routed on the principal track, which was usually straight ahead, had no position light route indicator. In low speed areas where one signal might lead to several routes or platform lines, theatre type route indicators showing letters or numbers were used alongside the one signal head to amplify the information to the driver. By combinations of small white lights different letters or figures would denote the route the train was to take provided the signal was showing a proceed aspect.

The original four-aspect signals were arranged with the lights showing yellow at the bottom, then red, then the second yellow, and green at the top. In the 1930s

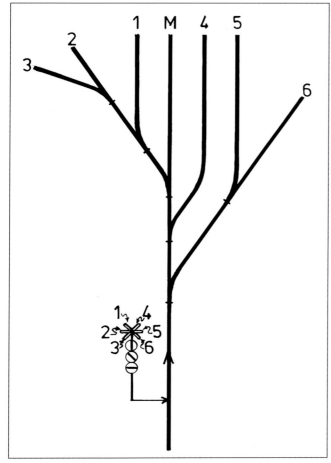

Fig. 28. *Colour light junction signal showing the route indicating position light displays in relation to track layouts. With points set for the main line 'M', no route indication would be displayed.*

Inside these Southern signalboxes, behind the miniature levers, were rows of lights. There were four vertical lights behind a lever controlling a four-aspect signal which displayed the same indications as the signal out on the line to show that the signal had responded either to the lever having been pulled to clear, (but coupled to the track circuits to display what the signal was actually showing), or had returned to red as a train had occupied the track circuits beyond, even though the lever might still be in the clear position. The signal lever would have to be restored to danger and re-pulled before the signal could clear for a second time and then only if the track circuits were clear. If they were not the electric lock on the lever would not allow it to be pulled. Normally, controlled signals returned to danger by track circuit operation. Only automatic signals, or semi-automatic when working automatically would clear from red to a proceed aspect automatically. Behind points levers were two lights, one displaying a letter N when the points were normal and the other a letter R when the points were reversed as a repeater to confirm the actual lie of the points. The illuminated diagram was essential in these power signalboxes since the signalmen could not directly see all the trains under their control. Lights, sometimes white but in later years normally red, were illuminated for each track circuit section occupied by a train on an otherwise plain track diagram.

At some locations, as here at Waterloo in the mid-1930s scheme, low speeds allowed the use of theatre type route indicators with letters or figures formed from combinations of white lights, in this case 'MT' – Main Through. Note the shunting disc, floodlit from above and without night-time colour aspects. (Alan Williams)

new signals had the red at the bottom, then yellow, the green, and the second yellow at the top, an arrangement which is still standard today. Some of the four-aspect signals on the early Eastern Section schemes were arranged with the lamps in a cluster around a circular back shield. The two yellow lights were arranged top and bottom, the red to the right and the green to the left. They were not perpetuated. Another feature of the Waterloo signals and also used for a couple of decades elsewhere, was what was known as 'pigs ears', a small shaded light alongside the main lens of each colour angled towards the track to which it applied. It allowed a driver of a multiple-unit electric train or indeed any motive power unit with the cab at the front end, to draw right up to a signal at danger and he could see the aspect displayed even though he was not in the line of sight of the main lens. By the 1960s the main lenses incorporated a small section which threw some light towards a train standing alongside out of view of the main beam, and the 'pigs ears' went out of use.

Magazine train describers

Inevitably, as these colour light schemes from the 1920s to the 1950s covered what were then quite large areas with one signalbox controlling several miles of line, including the supervision of automatic sections on plain line, the signalmen needed to know what trains were approaching and where they were to go. The Southern's three main constituent companies had used the Walker rotary describer which consisted of an instrument rather like a large clock face with destination labels rather than clock figures set around the dial and with a single hand. Walker we have met before for he was the South Eastern's telegraph superintendent in mid-Victorian years. On the sending instrument each destination position had a handle on the outside of the case and when one was pulled the hand would rotate to stop against the required destination, and was repeated on the receiving instrument at the next signalbox ahead. This type of instrument was used on the early SR power resignalling schemes, but by the mid-1930s something more was required since several trains might be on an automatically signalled part of the line between adjacent signalboxes. A new type of describer was devised in a rectangular case with a vertical list of destinations or descriptions. The sending instrument had a button against each pressed by the signalman to transmit the description to the receiving instrument at the next signalbox and a white light was illuminated in the

SGE rotary train describer used on parts of the Southern, with a white light against the description disc concerned. It was a development of the Walker pattern in which a pointer powered by clockwork and controlled by electric impulses rotated around the face to point to the required description. (Southern Railway)

The Southern's power signalboxes were given illuminated track diagrams in which train position was shown by lights along the tracks concerned. This is the diagram of the new Cannon Street signalbox built to replace the original so catastrophically destroyed by fire in March 1957. Even though it replaced equipment 30 years old the new box was of similar type with a Westinghouse L frame transferred from the London Midland Region where it had been spare during the Second World War. Remarkably, the new signalbox was commissioned just nine months after the fire. (BR, SR)

sending instrument to show the last description sent. The receiving instrument had a similar vertical list of descriptions but three vertical rows of lights for first, second, and third train approaching, the lights being normally out except for those actually showing the details of an approaching train. Normally the instruments could store more descriptions than the first three, up to the maximum number of trains that could be between the two signalboxes ready to move into the display as soon as the receiving signalman cleared the

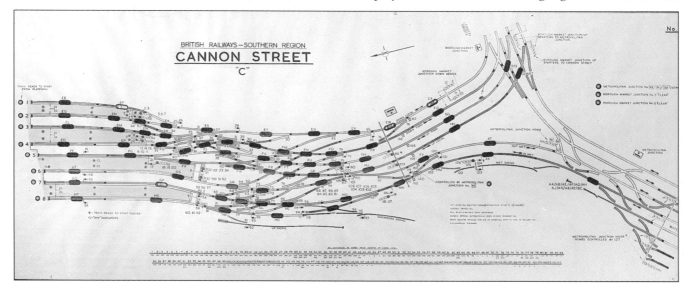

PRE 1890 SIGNALS
Early Rotating Board Signals

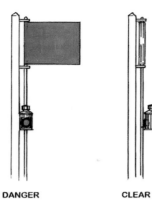

DANGER   CLEAR

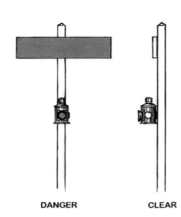

DANGER   CLEAR

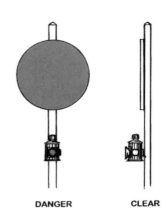

DANGER   CLEAR

GWR Disc & Crossbar with
Fantail Curtains at caution
and Disc at clear

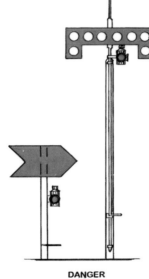

DANGER

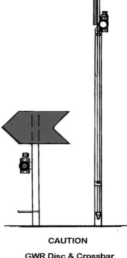

CAUTION

GWR Disc & Crossbar
with Fantail Board

CLEAR

LSWR MARTIN DISC

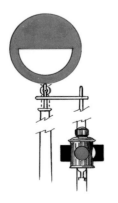

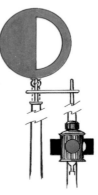
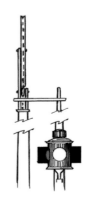

DANGER BOTH WAYS   CLEAR FOR LEFT HAND   DANGER FOR LEFT HAND   CLEAR BOTH WAYS
                                 TRACK, DANGER   TRACK, CLEAR
                           OPPOSITE DIRECTION   OPPOSITE DIRECTION

PRE 1890 SIGNALS
Early Semaphore Signals

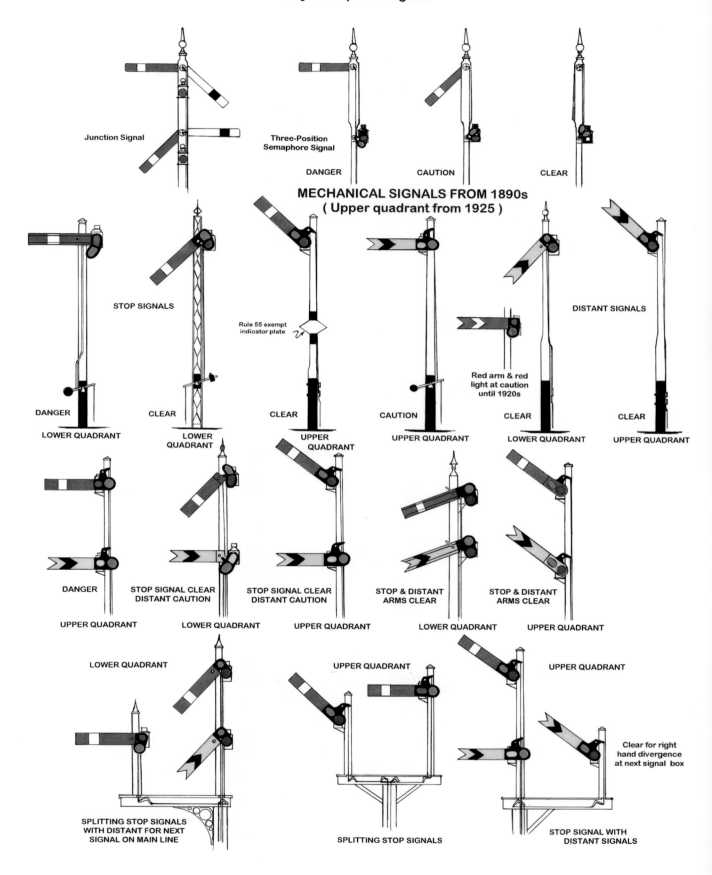

Junction Signal

Three-Position
Semaphore Signal

DANGER

CAUTION

CLEAR

MECHANICAL SIGNALS FROM 1890s
(Upper quadrant from 1925)

STOP SIGNALS

Rule 55 exempt
indicator plate

DISTANT SIGNALS

Red arm & red
light at caution
until 1920s

DANGER

CLEAR

CLEAR

CAUTION

CLEAR

CLEAR

LOWER QUADRANT

LOWER
QUADRANT

UPPER
QUADRANT

UPPER QUADRANT

LOWER QUADRANT

UPPER QUADRANT

DANGER

STOP SIGNAL CLEAR
DISTANT CAUTION

STOP SIGNAL CLEAR
DISTANT CAUTION

STOP & DISTANT
ARMS CLEAR

STOP & DISTANT
ARMS CLEAR

UPPER QUADRANT

LOWER QUADRANT

UPPER QUADRANT

LOWER QUADRANT

UPPER QUADRANT

LOWER QUADRANT

UPPER QUADRANT

UPPER QUADRANT

Clear for right
hand divergence
at next signal box

SPLITTING STOP SIGNALS
WITH DISTANT FOR NEXT
SIGNAL ON MAIN LINE

SPLITTING STOP SIGNALS

STOP SIGNAL WITH
DISTANT SIGNALS

MECHANICAL SIGNALS FROM 1890s
(Upper quadrant from 1925)

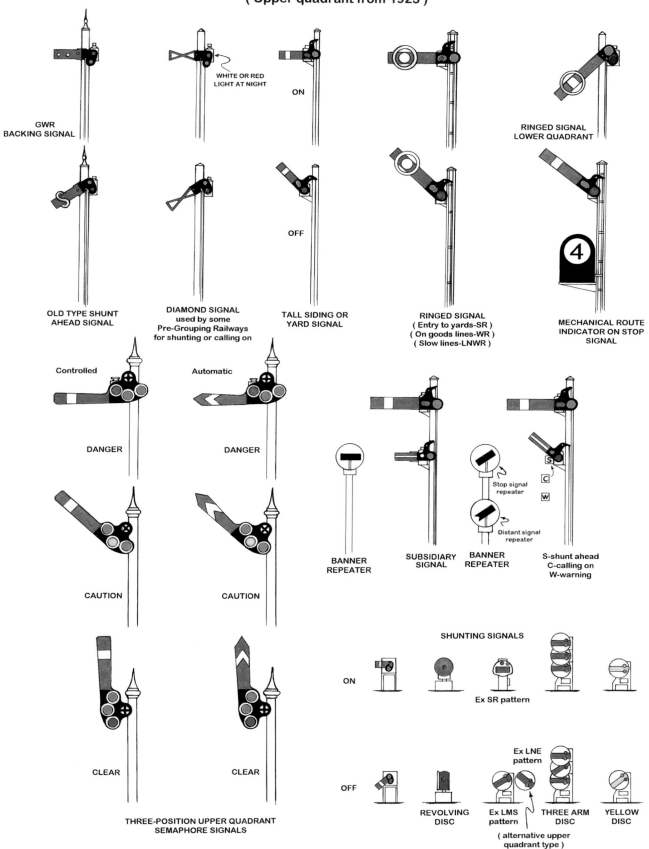

GWR
BACKING SIGNAL

WHITE OR RED
LIGHT AT NIGHT

ON

RINGED SIGNAL
LOWER QUADRANT

OLD TYPE SHUNT
AHEAD SIGNAL

DIAMOND SIGNAL
used by some
Pre-Grouping Railways
for shunting or calling on

OFF

TALL SIDING OR
YARD SIGNAL

RINGED SIGNAL
(Entry to yards-SR)
(On goods lines-WR)
(Slow lines-LNWR)

MECHANICAL ROUTE
INDICATOR ON STOP
SIGNAL

Controlled

Automatic

DANGER

DANGER

CAUTION

CAUTION

BANNER
REPEATER

Stop signal
repeater

Distant signal
repeater

SUBSIDIARY
SIGNAL

BANNER
REPEATER

S
C
W

S-shunt ahead
C-calling on
W-warning

CLEAR

CLEAR

THREE-POSITION UPPER QUADRANT
SEMAPHORE SIGNALS

SHUNTING SIGNALS

ON

Ex SR pattern

Ex LNE
pattern

OFF

REVOLVING
DISC

Ex LMS
pattern

(alternative upper
quadrant type)

THREE ARM
DISC

YELLOW
DISC

COLOUR LIGHT SIGNALS

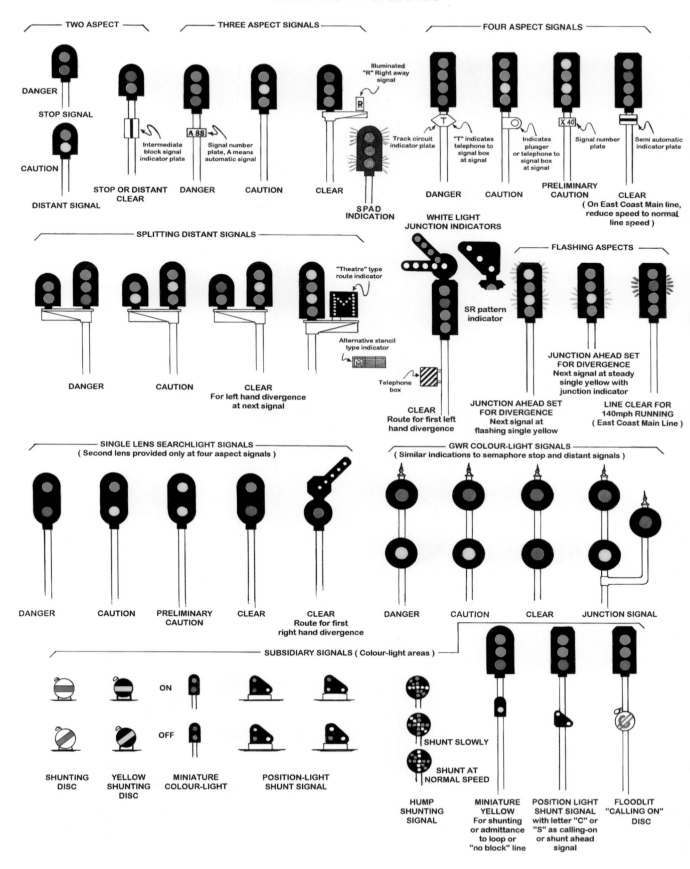

TWO ASPECT

DANGER

STOP SIGNAL

CAUTION

DISTANT SIGNAL

STOP OR DISTANT CLEAR

Intermediate block signal indicator plate

THREE ASPECT SIGNALS

DANGER

Signal number plate, A means automatic signal

CAUTION

CLEAR

Illuminated "R" Right away signal

Track circuit indicator plate

SPAD INDICATION

FOUR ASPECT SIGNALS

DANGER

"T" indicates telephone to signal box at signal

CAUTION

Indicates plunger or telephone to signal box at signal

PRELIMINARY CAUTION

Signal number plate

CLEAR
(On East Coast Main line, reduce speed to normal line speed)

Semi automatic indicator plate

WHITE LIGHT JUNCTION INDICATORS

SR pattern indicator

SPLITTING DISTANT SIGNALS

DANGER

CAUTION

CLEAR
For left hand divergence at next signal

"Theatre" type route indicator

Alternative stencil type indicator

Telephone box

CLEAR
Route for first left hand divergence

FLASHING ASPECTS

JUNCTION AHEAD SET FOR DIVERGENCE
Next signal at steady single yellow with junction indicator

JUNCTION AHEAD SET FOR DIVERGENCE
Next signal at flashing single yellow

LINE CLEAR FOR 140mph RUNNING
(East Coast Main Line)

SINGLE LENS SEARCHLIGHT SIGNALS
(Second lens provided only at four aspect signals)

DANGER

CAUTION

PRELIMINARY CAUTION

CLEAR

CLEAR
Route for first right hand divergence

GWR COLOUR-LIGHT SIGNALS
(Similar indications to semaphore stop and distant signals)

DANGER

CAUTION

CLEAR

JUNCTION SIGNAL

SUBSIDIARY SIGNALS (Colour-light areas)

ON

OFF

SHUNTING DISC

YELLOW SHUNTING DISC

MINIATURE COLOUR-LIGHT

POSITION-LIGHT SHUNT SIGNAL

SHUNT SLOWLY

SHUNT AT NORMAL SPEED

HUMP SHUNTING SIGNAL

MINIATURE YELLOW
For shunting or admittance to loop or "no block" line

POSITION LIGHT SHUNT SIGNAL
with letter "C" or "S" as calling-on or shunt ahead signal

FLOODLIT "CALLING ON" DISC

COLOUR LIGHT SIGNALS, SOME DEVIATIONS
(LMS speed signalling 1932)

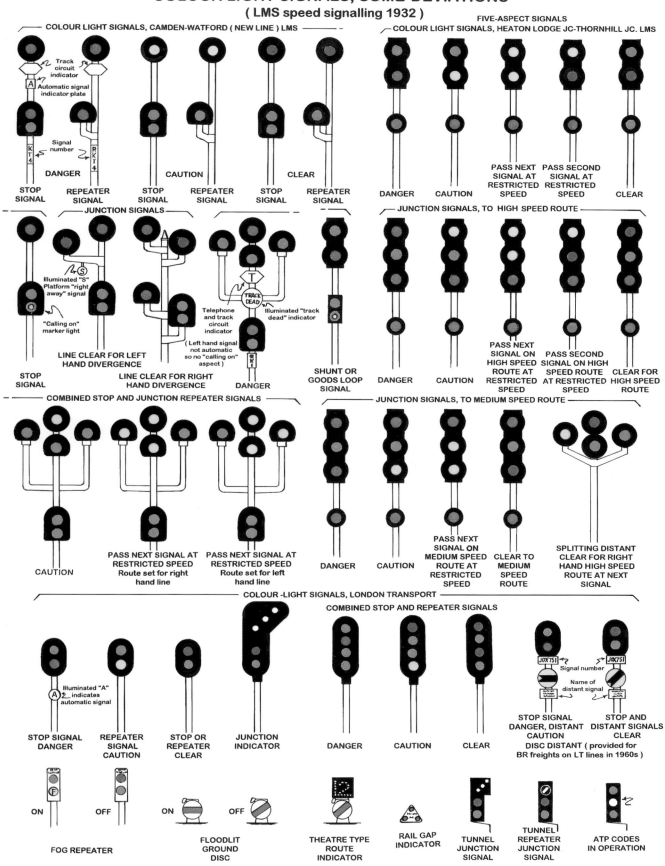

FIVE-ASPECT SIGNALS

—— COLOUR LIGHT SIGNALS, CAMDEN-WATFORD (NEW LINE) LMS ——

—— COLOUR LIGHT SIGNALS, HEATON LODGE JC-THORNHILL JC. LMS ——

Track circuit indicator

Automatic signal indicator plate

A

Signal number

K T 4   R K T 4

DANGER

STOP SIGNAL | REPEATER SIGNAL | STOP SIGNAL | REPEATER SIGNAL | STOP SIGNAL | REPEATER SIGNAL

CAUTION

CLEAR

DANGER | CAUTION | PASS NEXT SIGNAL AT RESTRICTED SPEED | PASS SECOND SIGNAL AT RESTRICTED SPEED | CLEAR

—— JUNCTION SIGNALS ——

—— JUNCTION SIGNALS, TO HIGH SPEED ROUTE ——

Illuminated "S" Platform "right away" signal

"Calling on" marker light

LINE CLEAR FOR LEFT HAND DIVERGENCE

Telephone and track circuit indicator

Illuminated "track dead" indicator

TRACK DEAD

(Left hand signal not automatic so no "calling on" aspect)

STOP SIGNAL

LINE CLEAR FOR RIGHT HAND DIVERGENCE

DANGER

SHUNT OR GOODS LOOP SIGNAL

DANGER | CAUTION | PASS NEXT SIGNAL ON HIGH SPEED ROUTE AT RESTRICTED SPEED | PASS SECOND SIGNAL ON HIGH SPEED ROUTE AT RESTRICTED SPEED | CLEAR FOR HIGH SPEED ROUTE

—— COMBINED STOP AND JUNCTION REPEATER SIGNALS ——

—— JUNCTION SIGNALS, TO MEDIUM SPEED ROUTE ——

CAUTION | PASS NEXT SIGNAL AT RESTRICTED SPEED Route set for right hand line | PASS NEXT SIGNAL AT RESTRICTED SPEED Route set for left hand line

DANGER | CAUTION | PASS NEXT SIGNAL ON MEDIUM SPEED ROUTE AT RESTRICTED SPEED | CLEAR TO MEDIUM SPEED ROUTE | SPLITTING DISTANT CLEAR FOR RIGHT HAND HIGH SPEED ROUTE AT NEXT SIGNAL

—— COLOUR -LIGHT SIGNALS, LONDON TRANSPORT ——

COMBINED STOP AND REPEATER SIGNALS

Illuminated "A" indicates automatic signal

A

J0X751   J0X751

Signal number

Name of distant signal

STOP SIGNAL DANGER | REPEATER SIGNAL CAUTION | STOP OR REPEATER CLEAR | JUNCTION INDICATOR | DANGER | CAUTION | CLEAR | STOP SIGNAL DANGER, DISTANT CAUTION | STOP AND DISTANT SIGNALS CLEAR

DISC DISTANT (provided for BR freights on LT lines in 1960s)

F

ON | OFF

ON | OFF

FOG REPEATER | FLOODLIT GROUND DISC | THEATRE TYPE ROUTE INDICATOR | RAIL GAP INDICATOR | TUNNEL JUNCTION SIGNAL | TUNNEL REPEATER JUNCTION SIGNAL | ATP CODES IN OPERATION

FIXED SIGNAL BOARDS

PERMANENT SPEED RESTRICTION

ORIGINAL "MORPETH WARNING"
ADVANCE WARNING
at braking distance
(Floodlit & with AWS)

LNER and BR CUTOUT
SPEED LIMIT FIGURES
at commencement

PRESENT DAY SPEED RESTRICTION

ADVANCE WARNING
AT BRAKING DISTANCE

COMMENCEMENT

AWS BOARDS

COMMENCEMENT OF
AWS GAP
(at major stations)

END OF AWS GAP
(at major stations)

CANCEL AWS WARNING ON
SINGLE LINE AT TEMPORARY
SPEED RESTRICTION FOR
OPPOSITE DIRECTION

DISTANT MARKER
BOARD

← Instructions to be
carried out before
proceeding

STOP BOARD

BASIC SIGNALLING BOARDS
(RETB, no signalman token etc.)
1970s onwards

CLEAR OF LOOP
BOARD (RETB)

TEMPORARY SPEED RESTRICTION

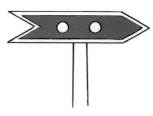

WARNING
(green until 1949
yellow from then)

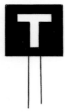

COMMENCEMENT

TERMINATION

WARNING
PRESENT DAY

COMMENCEMENT

PRESENT DAY

TERMINATION

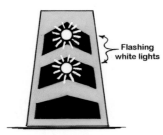

Flashing
white lights

EMERGENCY SPEED
RESTRICTION INDICATOR

OTHER MECHANICAL SIGNAL SYSTEMS

FRENCH

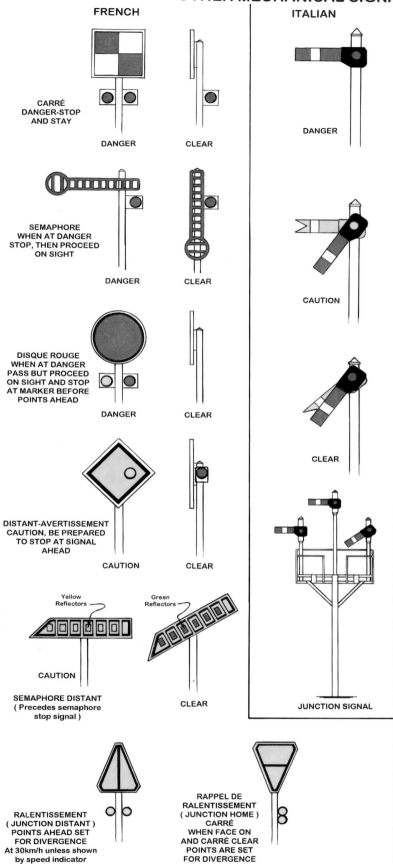

CARRÉ
DANGER-STOP
AND STAY

DANGER   CLEAR

SEMAPHORE
WHEN AT DANGER
STOP, THEN PROCEED
ON SIGHT

DANGER   CLEAR

DISQUE ROUGE
WHEN AT DANGER
PASS BUT PROCEED
ON SIGHT AND STOP
AT MARKER BEFORE
POINTS AHEAD

DANGER   CLEAR

DISTANT-AVERTISSEMENT
CAUTION, BE PREPARED
TO STOP AT SIGNAL
AHEAD

CAUTION   CLEAR

Yellow
Reflectors   Green
                   Reflectors

CAUTION

SEMAPHORE DISTANT
(Precedes semaphore
stop signal)   CLEAR

RALENTISSEMENT
(JUNCTION DISTANT)
POINTS AHEAD SET
FOR DIVERGENCE
At 30km/h unless shown
by speed indicator

RAPPEL DE
RALENTISSEMENT
(JUNCTION HOME)
CARRÉ
WHEN FACE ON
AND CARRÉ CLEAR
POINTS ARE SET
FOR DIVERGENCE

ITALIAN

DANGER

CAUTION

CLEAR

JUNCTION SIGNAL

GERMAN / SWISS / AUSTRIAN

STOP SIGNALS HAUPTSIGNALE

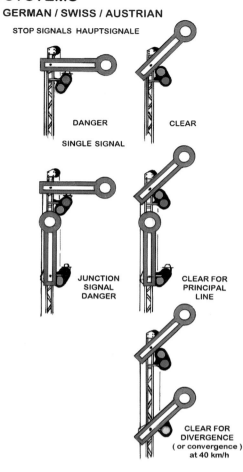

DANGER   CLEAR

SINGLE SIGNAL

JUNCTION
SIGNAL
DANGER   CLEAR FOR
                PRINCIPAL
                LINE

CLEAR FOR
DIVERGENCE
(or convergence)
at 40 km/h

DISTANT SIGNALS VORSIGNALE

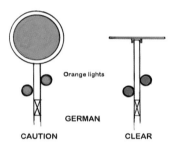

Orange lights

GERMAN

CAUTION   CLEAR

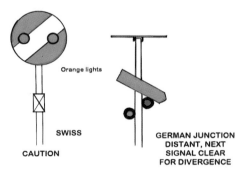

Orange lights

SWISS

CAUTION

GERMAN JUNCTION
DISTANT, NEXT
SIGNAL CLEAR
FOR DIVERGENCE

OTHER COLOUR LIGHT SIGNAL SYSTEMS

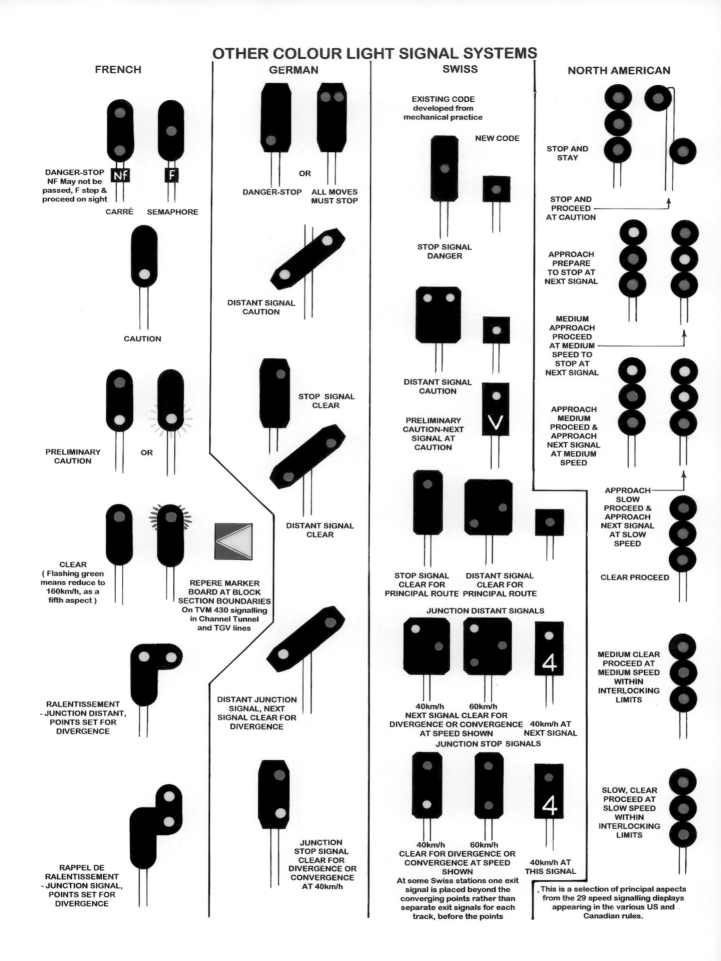

FRENCH

DANGER-STOP
NF May not be passed, F stop & proceed on sight

CARRÉ   SEMAPHORE

CAUTION

PRELIMINARY CAUTION   OR

CLEAR
(Flashing green means reduce to 160km/h, as a fifth aspect)

RALENTISSEMENT - JUNCTION DISTANT, POINTS SET FOR DIVERGENCE

RAPPEL DE RALENTISSEMENT - JUNCTION SIGNAL, POINTS SET FOR DIVERGENCE

GERMAN

OR

DANGER-STOP   ALL MOVES MUST STOP

DISTANT SIGNAL CAUTION

STOP SIGNAL CLEAR

DISTANT SIGNAL CLEAR

REPERE MARKER BOARD AT BLOCK SECTION BOUNDARIES
On TVM 430 signalling in Channel Tunnel and TGV lines

DISTANT JUNCTION SIGNAL, NEXT SIGNAL CLEAR FOR DIVERGENCE

JUNCTION STOP SIGNAL CLEAR FOR DIVERGENCE OR CONVERGENCE AT 40km/h

SWISS

EXISTING CODE developed from mechanical practice

NEW CODE

STOP AND STAY

STOP SIGNAL DANGER

DISTANT SIGNAL CAUTION

PRELIMINARY CAUTION-NEXT SIGNAL AT CAUTION

STOP SIGNAL CLEAR FOR PRINCIPAL ROUTE   DISTANT SIGNAL CLEAR FOR PRINCIPAL ROUTE

JUNCTION DISTANT SIGNALS

40km/h   60km/h
NEXT SIGNAL CLEAR FOR DIVERGENCE OR CONVERGENCE AT SPEED SHOWN   40km/h AT NEXT SIGNAL

JUNCTION STOP SIGNALS

40km/h   60km/h
CLEAR FOR DIVERGENCE OR CONVERGENCE AT SPEED SHOWN   40km/h AT THIS SIGNAL

At some Swiss stations one exit signal is placed beyond the converging points rather than separate exit signals for each track, before the points

NORTH AMERICAN

STOP AND STAY

STOP AND PROCEED AT CAUTION

APPROACH PREPARE TO STOP AT NEXT SIGNAL

MEDIUM APPROACH PROCEED AT MEDIUM SPEED TO STOP AT NEXT SIGNAL

APPROACH MEDIUM PROCEED & APPROACH NEXT SIGNAL AT MEDIUM SPEED

APPROACH SLOW PROCEED & APPROACH NEXT SIGNAL AT SLOW SPEED

CLEAR PROCEED

MEDIUM CLEAR PROCEED AT MEDIUM SPEED WITHIN INTERLOCKING LIMITS

SLOW, CLEAR PROCEED AT SLOW SPEED WITHIN INTERLOCKING LIMITS

This is a selection of principal aspects from the 29 speed signalling displays appearing in the various US and Canadian rules.

first train off the instrument as it passed, when the lights would step forward, the second becoming the first and so on. These instruments were purely on a signalbox to signalbox basis and each box would have a receiving instrument to show what was approaching and a sending instrument to describe trains onwards to the next signalbox. In some places on less busy lines equipped with track circuit block, there were no describers and trains were 'belled on' between signalboxes with a code ring on emergency block bells to indicate a route or class of approaching train, not in the form of offering and acceptance but simply as an advice.

Architectural styles

Although not directly related to the signalling equipment the architecture of the Southern's new signalboxes from the 1930s well into BR days was quite distinctive. While many existing boxes were re-fitted with power equipment – the Southern, ever conscious of controlling costs, never threw anything away which could be re-used even to the extent of using old rails to build signal posts – new signalboxes had to be built in various places to replace life-expired structures or where the existing signalbox could not be given up for re-equipping before resignalling. One of the signalboxes at Waterloo Eastern Section for example, redundant from the mid-1920s resignalling, is still giving service today at Ryde St Johns Road on the Isle of Wight. While new traditional, mostly timber or brick and timber signalboxes were built for the early power schemes, from the mid-1930s until the 1950s the Southern produced some fairly standard, what might

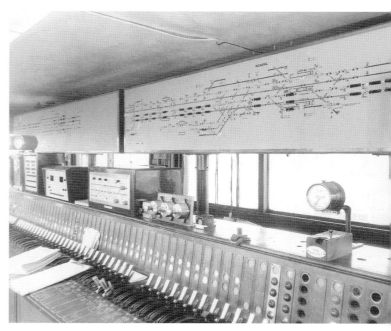

One of the last Southern signalboxes to retain miniature levers, which lasted until 1997 with indications of the 1920s era, was Woking seen here after the 1967 electrification to Bournemouth but with a new illuminated diagram including four-character train description apertures (see Chapter 14) as well as track circuit indications. It also has a small entrance–exit panel (also see Chapter 14) to control the down line junction at Brookwood to the Alton branch. (BR, SR)

be called Art Nouveau designs, differing perhaps in details but all more or less a standard shape with a long rectangular ground floor for the equipment and staff accommodation and an upper operating floor rising from the centre portion like the superstructure of a ship, with a flat roof and semi-circular ends with ample windows all round the operating room, giving rise to a nick-name of glasshouse boxes.

The newly built Southern signalboxes between the 1930s and 1950s were quite distinctive in style with the operating floor upstairs with semi-circular ends to the structure, looking for all the world like an ocean liner. The style was also used for a few new mechanical boxes. (BR, SR)

Chapter 11

POWER OPERATION EXPANDS – THE OTHER WAYS

THE SOUTHERN'S RESIGNALLING programme, starting so soon after the IRSE report in the mid-1920s, and lasting so far as the basics of the equipment are concerned for the next 30 years into British Railways days, certainly set new standards. None of the other three main line companies had anywhere near as much modern signalling. But to be fair, the other three companies did not have the widespread density of suburban traffic and frequency of trains over complex routes, even compared with the longer distance services of the South Coast expresses of the Southern. Only the former Great Eastern suburban network from Liverpool Street matched anything that the Southern had and that was from just one London terminus. The Fenchurch Street to Shoeburyness line of the London Midland & Scottish Railway might have had the frequency but only with a procession of trains all going over one main line and a lesser loop. The Glasgow suburban area, had it been under the control of one railway instead of two, might have matched the Southern with unified command and the same type of dynamic Southern management. As it was, unified command, and certainly electrification had to wait until well into the British Railways' era in the 1960s. In the 1930s it was steam trains, and mechanical signalling on most lines other than Glasgow Central itself which had one of the early power schemes from 1907 and naturally, with semaphore signals. Elsewhere in London to the north and west the Underground worked a large chunk of the suburban traffic and like the Southern, had standardised on track circuit block, colour light signals and power operation, usually through electro-pneumatic equipment from a series of signalboxes located at or near the junctions they served. But as we shall see in Chapter 15, despite the use of power control, London Transport, which took over responsibility for the Underground lines in 1933, remained wedded to mechanical interlocking for many years even though other ways were coming to the fore.

Route-setting levers on the Great Western
The Southern's power boxes from the 1920s, with miniature lever frames, worked on the one lever, one function principle just like their mechanical counterparts. For a signalman to set a route he had to operate the appropriate point levers if the points were not already lying in the correct position and always assuming that they were not already locked by track circuit control or by another conflicting route set previously. Only then when the route was confirmed to be free for use and the points correctly set and locked could he clear the signal lever. But with power operation it was possible to have one lever to do the whole operation. In an earlier chapter, we have described the primitive attempts at what we would call route setting whereby one lever set the points and cleared the signal, as far back as 1856. It was not real route setting but a device to make the signals show clear for the same track towards which the points were set, as a precursor of interlocking. In France, soon after the turn of the century, great minds were concentrated on ways of making a single lever do more than one function by moving in more than one plane and contacting different equipment mechanically and electrically and by so doing was able to control points and signals in the one movement.

Just after the First World War the firm of Siemens, German in origin but with a British offshoot which was getting well into British railway signalling, had devised a route setting system, a combined effort by L. G. Ferriera of the company and R. J. Insell, signal engineer of the Great Western Railway. This was translated into a proposal for resignalling the GWR's station at Winchester, later known as Cheesehill or Chesil, on the Didcot, Newbury & Southampton line. In 1923, the new system was commissioned to control the station and its siding connection. It was a simple layout with a double-track passing loop from the single line approaches from each direction, a crossover to a siding on one side and a headshunt extension from one of the platform lines with crossover connections. Semaphore signals were retained but were worked electrically. A 16 miniature lever frame was provided to do the work which would normally have required 32 levers, thus saving on lever frame length which, for any new installation, would need a smaller signalbox, and thus a saving in cost. At Winchester where the whole layout could be seen by the signalman there was no need for full track circuiting but track circuits were provided through the points since they replaced mechanical locking bars.

Behind the levers were vertical lamp displays, not entirely to depict signal aspects as in the Southern power signalling, but to show the state of the equipment at the different stages of operation which at the end of the operation displayed whether the signal was at danger or clear. The lights from top to bottom were, red, green, amber and white. Each signal, whether for running or shunting, had its own lever. The levers had four positions on the quadrant, position 1 – normal with the signal at danger, no route set and with the red light displayed, position 2 – a check lock when pulling the lever towards clear, position 3 – a check lock position when restoring a lever to danger, and position 4 – reverse with the route set, the signal clear and a green light displayed. When the signalman wanted to set a route he pulled the appropriate lever from position 1 to position 2 where it was check locked. An electric current was then fed to the track circuits to prove that they were clear and if they were the red light was then extinguished and the white light was lit. The sequence circuits then switched the point motors on if they were not in the correct position and when detected set and locked, the check lock on the lever was energised to release the lever, being indicated to the signalman by the white light being replaced by the amber light. The signalman could then pull the lever to the full reverse position which fed the signal motor concerned to lower the arm to the clear position, which was confirmed to the signalman by the amber light being replaced by the green light. To restore the signal to danger the lever was moved from position 4 to the check lock at position 3. The signal arm went back to danger and, provided the route was confirmed to be clear of the train, the white light appeared and the check lock released to allow the lever to be fully restored to danger when the red light would again be shown. If any vehicles were detected as still being on track circuits then the lever would not be released by the check lock at position 3. The main running points stayed in the position in which they were last set but trap points protecting the exit from sidings etc were restored to their trap position.

Winchester GWR, on a lightly used cross-country route, hardly warranted a power route signalling installation but clearly was a guinea pig for something larger. Indeed, four years later it came when Newport (Mon) on the South Wales main line was resignalled with two route setting power frames on exactly the same principles, with the east end signalbox commissioned in 1927 and the west end in June 1928.

The Great Western did not embark on widespread power operation and even though it tried route signalling at Winchester and Newport, its more conventional power operation was largely confined to its principal stations at Birmingham, Bristol, Cardiff and Paddington. This is the interior of Paddington Arrival signalbox with its draw slide frame, one part controlling the arrival platforms of the main line station and nearer the camera, the controls for the suburban station. (National Railway Museum)

This was a much more complex layout involving a core four-track main line with crossovers, access to sidings, bays and the like. But the operation was identical although at Newport the lines were track circuited throughout and there was a certain amount of slotting between levers in each box where control overlapped. Block working remained between the two signalboxes.

That was to be the end of the Great Western's adventures into the world of modern ahead-of-the-time signalling, for although it again trod the path to power signalling in the 1930s it was in a very conservative way and with little consistency. Paddington station and its immediate approaches were given power frames in three signalboxes in 1932/3 using draw slides operated by handles, even then with one frame having electric locking and the other two mechanical locking. Cardiff, a year later was equipped with two Westinghouse L pattern miniature lever frames in East and West boxes, one of which with 339 levers, was larger than the Southern's London Bridge box. Bristol, another year later, reverted to handles operating slides. Nowhere was power operation used to its full extent by having one box to control the entire station as was perfectly feasible given the size of the Southern's London Bridge operation at that time. It seemed that because the GWR had always had (since the development of major signalboxes) at least two signalboxes to control the larger stations – most of the principal GWR stations had East and West signalboxes except at Birmingham where they were North and South – why change with power operation?

The GWR approach to colour-lights

Outside on the line the new colour light signals certainly were nothing like those recommended by the IRSE in its 1924 report. Where were the four-aspect signals or even three-aspect showing a simple red, yellow, or green? Yes, there were signals giving indications by lights only, but no, the Great Western did not want to change from the traditional night-time semaphore signal lights to ensure that drivers were always presented with the same indications whether in colour light or semaphore areas. So the Great Western's

After its essays into upper-quadrant three-position signals at Paddington in 1914 and on the Ealing–Shepherds Bush Railway in 1923, the GWR retreated into its shell and stuck doggedly to lower quadrant semaphores to the end of its existence in 1947, and influenced BR Western Region signalling for another 40 or so years after that. But this oddity appeared at Oxford seemingly using adapted lower quadrant arms in the upper quadrant. The Great Western ran one of the safest railways in the world with standard equipment dating from the end of the last century. If it seemed conservative then its safety record showed there was no real need for change. (BR, WR)

colour light signals consisted of stop signals showing just red or green, and distant signals showing just yellow or green, and where a caution indication was wanted at a stop signal, simple; place a stop signal head over a distant signal head and you get green over yellow for caution and green over green for clear. And that was not all. The colour light signals were of the searchlight pattern in which the different colours were given from one lens with one light by a swinging spectacle with red and green or yellow and green filters in between, controlled by an electro-magnet, energised when the green light was wanted and de-energised for the danger or caution aspect. The heads were distinguished by enormous circular back plates much larger than those used by the other companies. The GWR always had to be so different. Even though these colour lights were actually extended down the main line from Paddington towards Acton they were controlled by the existing boxes which retained absolute block working and just a modicum of isolated track circuits where the signalman could not readily see the trains or for simple block controls. Certainly there was no attempt at track circuit block except on the engine and carriage lines between Paddington and Old Oak Common carriage and engine depots which were given 'normal' three-aspect colour light signals, but which allowed permissive working since only empty trains or light engines normally used those lines. Bristol Temple Meads also had a few conventional two-aspect signals with separate light units. That was virtually the end of GWR power signalling development. It could be argued why change? After all, the Great Western with its automatic train control, which will be described later, ran a very safe and efficient railway, the best in the country according to many. But from then on well into BR days the Great Western and its successor Western Region largely stuck to lower quadrant semaphores and mechanical signalling. There was an oddity in an upper quadrant signal at Oxford which looked almost as though it was nothing more than an upside down lower quadrant. There were occasional closures of intermediate signalboxes simply used as block posts and replacement by colour light intermediate block signals but not a lot else, at least until the 1950s.

Early LMS ventures into power signalling

Similarly, the LMS was not noted for too many power signalling schemes. It had inherited the LNWR Crewe type power installations but for the first few years after the 1923 Grouping, the country's largest railway did very little to improve its signalling technology. Indeed for six years it did not even have an all-line head of department in the signal engineering field. Until 1929 the signal and telegraph engineering departments were not even recognised as being sufficiently important to warrant a totally unified independent organisation and the old signalling superintendents of the major pre-Grouping constituents of the LMS were appointed as assistants under the divisional engineers. On the telegraph side, the people who looked after block instrument and telephone maintenance and installation were responsible to the electrical engineer. Then, on 20 May 1929, a new signal engineering chief was appointed, no less than Arthur Bound who we have met before with his advanced ideas on signalling practice. Alas, with the tight financial control during the 1930s imposed by the President of the LMS (the LMS adopted an organisational structure akin to American ideas) Sir Josiah Stamp, an economist not given to spending money unless he could see a return, Bound was not able to express his ideas on a wide scale. However, as we shall see in the next chapter, he did manage to try a few new ideas.

It was inevitable, before Bound's arrival, that with the pre-Grouping men still effectively running their old patches, though having to submit plans for anything new to the general superintendent for approval, that change was not going to come quickly. For those first six years lower quadrant signals were still being put in for new work and renewals, and anything like the Southern's schemes was not even contemplated. There was one major scheme beginning to come to fruition as Bound arrived, devised by the Manchester divisional engineer, for resignalling at the twin stations of Manchester Victoria and Exchange. This Victoria was the former Lancashire & Yorkshire station with through platforms carrying trains east–west between Liverpool, Southport, Blackpool etc and Leeds, York, and Hull. Just on the south western corner was the London & North Western's Exchange, mostly terminal platforms although one formed a through platform with Victoria to hold the record as Britain's longest platform, 2,194ft in length. Two new power signalboxes, at Deal Street and Victoria West Junction, replaced six old mechanical boxes while some of the retained adjoining boxes were adapted to work with the new signalling as what today we would call fringe boxes. Two-, three-, and four-aspect colour light signals were employed, controlled by all-electric miniature lever frames in the two new boxes, together with track circuits. But it was not track circuit block for although the track circuits automatically restored the signals to danger as a train passed, normal manual block working was retained. The block instruments were unusual in that they did not display the usual 'line clear' and 'train on line' indications by a telegraph needle but instead, by lights on a panel just above the lever frame – green for 'line clear', red for 'train on line' and no light for 'line blocked'.

The signals themselves were very similar to those on the 1920s Southern schemes even to the use of circular cluster type heads which were used in tight locations or where the signals were above the line to bring the lights nearer to drivers' eye level. Also like the early Southern signals, the main running junctions had separate signal heads for each route which in some cases meant three heads side by side including the cluster type. At the low speed approaches to the platforms junction signals had route indicators of the optical projector type in which a light shone through a stencil to project a letter or number on to a screen display seen by the driver when the signal was showing a proceed aspect. A choice of up to 13 different route indications could be accommodated. Some of the running signals approaching the stations did not have a green light and displayed only red, yellow, or double yellow or even only yellow for proceed to reinforce the speed limits.

Unlike the Southern which used power worked disc shunting signals, the Manchester Victoria/Exchange scheme had miniature colour light shunting signals, showing red for stop and green for clear although two of them were three-aspect signals, not to control movement over two sections but to allow a movement into a headshunt with the yellow aspect, and out on to

The LMS undertook a few power signalling schemes in the 1920s and 1930s but they did not match the ambitious schemes of the Southern. These signals at Glasgow St Enoch dating from the early 1930s, show some of the features of the time with calling on and colour light shunting signals beneath the main aspects. (LMS)

the main line with the green aspect. While the miniature levers were not route setting some were not entirely one lever, one function, for they were at normal in the centre of the quadrant and pulled for one signal or pushed for another, usually for shunting signals controlling opposing movements over the same crossover for example. The whole scheme was completed in 1930.

Irish oddity

The LMS, through its inheritance of the Midland Railway, had interests in Ireland. Irish signalling had always followed British practice as indeed it had to since it was all part of the United Kingdom until 1921, although there were subtle variations to suit the more rural location of many lines. Of course, the Irish railways generally, with their multitude of sparsely used branch and cross-country lines, were even less well endowed than British lines and could not afford to embark on later resignalling programmes once they had installed the basic equipment called for under the 1889 Act. Today it is different, for with the rail system now confined to a few strategic main routes, modernisation and new signalling technology in the Irish Republic has at times been ahead of the railways in Britain.

In the 1920s the LMS had its responsibilities in Northern Ireland and undertook resignalling at Belfast York Road, terminus of the lines from Larne, Portrush and Londonderry. It was only a small scheme and employed simple two-aspect colour light running signals, not even as multiple aspect signals, for one stop signal was followed by another stop signal with only a two-aspect distant preceding both of them as a

Both the LNER and LMS embarked on programmes during the 1930s to replace semaphore distant signals on principal main lines with colour lights, usually moved further out to increase braking distances for faster running. Some of the signals were mounted close to the ground with the heads slightly inclined up like these examples near Hatfield. (LNER)

warning, exactly as in semaphore practice. There was also a modicum of track circuiting. But it was the shunting signals which were most unusual since the aspect included a route indication, not in the usual way by a letter or number but by lights. Each signal had a display panel of up to nine lights. At the top in the centre was a single lamp for the red aspect. Below it was a horizontal row of white lights with as many lamps as there were routes from the signal, up to four. Below them was a horizontal row of an equivalent number of lamps for the green aspect. At danger only the red light was shown. As soon as the signal was cleared the red light was extinguished, all the white lights were illuminated and a single green light was shown beneath, in the left hand unit for the first route to the left, in the second for the second route and so on, with the white lights acting as a position reference for the single green light depending on which route was set ahead.

Isolated colour light distants

As for the major part of the LMS, Bound at least gave an edict that upper quadrant signals were the standard semaphore pattern henceforth. Often, this was with upper quadrant arms and fittings mounted on existing wooden or other type posts although even with the rapid spread of upper quadrant signals, lower quadrants survived many more years in quantity until the 1950s and a few, as at Chester, until the 1980s. Semaphore distant signals on the principal main lines were however, soon to become a dying breed for Bound set in motion a programme to replace them with isolated colour lights, isolated because they were single-colour light distants in otherwise semaphore areas. They did not normally replace semaphore distants where a distant arm was situated below a stop arm. Their meaning was very similar to the semaphore distants. They were installed for a number of basic reasons. First, with the increasing speed of principal expresses in the 1930s, braking distances from the distant signal to the first stop signal to which it applied needed to be increased so signals had to be moved further out anyway. Secondly, a colour light distant did not need the heavy pull of a mechanical lever and wire which would have been increased with distants now $3/4$–1 mile out on some of the faster sections on falling gradients. Thirdly, the lights were more arresting, particularly at night, than oil lamps and lastly, colour light signals did not usually require fog-signalmen during fog. (That though was to be sorely tested at Harrow a couple of decades later as we shall see in Chapter 13.) Some were at ground level rather than on posts.

Normally the colour light distants showed the same lights as a semaphore distant at night, yellow for caution and green for clear. But on multiple track sections where there were crossovers between fast and slow lines, the distants could show double yellow (since they were three-aspect signals capable of showing single yellow, double yellow or green) when the crossovers were set for a fast to slow movement or vice versa with the appropriate semaphore home signals clear for the divergence and on into the next section. The meaning of double yellow in this instance was not that laid down after the IRSE 1924 report 'Attention, proceed at medium speed' but 'Pass next signal at restricted speed and if applicable to a junction may denote that the points are set for a diverging route over which a speed restriction applies'. In truth it was effectively doing nothing more than the older semaphore distants had done in these locations because splitting distants were often provided for the fast to slow line crossover movements, just like a route junction. That was fine until one September morning in 1945 when the Perth–Euston overnight sleeping car train approached Bourne End, between Berkhamsted and Hemel Hempstead. Engineering work had closed the fast lines at Watford, a little further south, and up fast line trains were being switched to the up slow line at Bourne End over the 20mph crossovers. The semaphore home and starting signals were clear for the move and the distant was showing double yellow. Quite how the engine crew interpreted the double yellow, assuming they saw it, was never discovered for they were among the 38 dead in the wreckage of the train which took the crossover at about 50mph. The use of the double yellow in this situation was abandoned soon after and the colour light distants showed just two aspects, single yellow or green, the second yellow light became a standby lit only if the bulb of the main yellow light failed. Today colour light signals usually have double filament bulbs certainly in the red aspect, and probably in the yellow as well, so that if one filament fails the other is switched on and an alarm is given to the signalman or technician that the bulb needs changing.

Little development on the LMS

As for great LMS colour light schemes in the 1930s, they did not happen. The recession held back investment, schemes were drawn up and shelved, although some colour light schemes went ahead as for example, Camden to Wembley with the main running lines converted, but controlled from existing signalboxes, and Crewe station area in 1940. Liverpool Lime Street had to wait until 1947 when it was completely resignalled, while Euston had to wait another five years until BR days before it too had modern signalling. Until then it hardly had a track circuit and the only way the signalmen in No. 2 signalbox knew which of the departure platforms was occupied was by chalking up a note on a blackboard! Shades of the reminder slates for the two-mile telegraph in the 1860s. When Euston did eventually get its new

signalbox it was very much like those of the Southern 25 years before, with miniature levers, one lever, one function. It even had the first, second, third train magazine type of describer though of more advanced

BELOW *Euston station was crying out for resignalling in the 1930s but it had to wait until 1952 before it was comprehensively resignalled with electro-pneumatically controlled points, colour light signals and full track circuiting. It was all worked from a new power signalbox with a Westinghouse style L miniature lever frame and magazine type train describers. The first describers were temporary and two years later new pattern magazine describers including automatic clearance were installed. But the new signalling lasted only twelve years and it was done all over again as part of the 25kV electrification in 1965. This is the interior of the 1952 signalbox. (BR, LMR)*

BOTTOM *Close up of the 1954 train describer for the up slow line at Euston. (BR, LMR)*

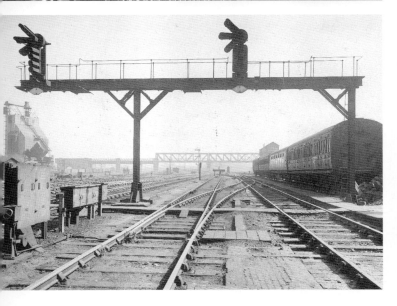

TOP *Night-time exterior shot of the 1952 Euston signalbox. (BR, LMR)*

MIDDLE *The interior of Crewe South power signalbox commissioned early in the Second World War. It included rotary train describers and maintained block working with the normal block instruments to adjacent signalboxes. At least 18 block instruments are visible in this picture. (National Railway Museum)*

BOTTOM *Elsewhere on the LMS colour light signals were installed in isolated clusters or individually at principal stations, controlled by levers in the existing signalboxes. Euston itself had a few before the 1952 resignalling and Rugby, as seen here looking south to the GCR viaduct in the background, was given some during the Second World War. The right hand signal remarkably is within the fouling point with the siding connection. (LMS)*

pattern. A Southern signalman would have been quite at home with the Westinghouse L frame. There were other dabbles into colour light signalling as at Rugby, but major resignalling schemes elsewhere on former LMS lines, with total re-equipment, had to wait until the British Railways Modernisation Plan of the mid-1950s and the subsequent electrification of the West Coast route. If anywhere matched the dense Southern network on the LMS in England it was the former LYR suburban complex around Manchester. But apart from Manchester Victoria itself one looked in vain for complete route resignalling on the same scale as on the SR and the old ways persisted; indeed on a few lines they still do.

The LNER's leap forward

The London & North Eastern was the least endowed of the four Group companies when it came to financial investment but at least it knew how to create publicity with its high speed streamlined trains of the 1930s and the capturing the world's speed record for steam traction. Its prime route, the East Coast Main Line was fairly flat and had long lengths with few curves which invited high speed, although several of its principal stations, Peterborough, York and Newcastle for example, had tortuous approaches. Like the LMS it too started to replace semaphore distant signals with colour lights on its main routes. Despite undertaking considerable track improvements, widenings for example between York and Northallerton and on the Great Eastern line to Shenfield, it also undertook several major power resignalling schemes and marshalling yard improvements which required specialised signalling. But it was the one company which took the great leap forward in signalling technology, overtaking the Southern and developing the new standards in the 1930s which set the pattern for the control of new signalling for the next 50 years. Although the LNER adopted the new colour light code and used three- and four-aspect multi-light signals it also used the single lens searchlight type with an added yellow lens when double yellow was needed in a four-aspect signal. The LNER also introduced the five-light junction indicator.

Within a couple of years or so of the Grouping, it was involved in the resignalling of Cambridge station with all-electric control from a slide frame but with lower quadrant semaphores. But that was the last of the old style power signalling schemes with semaphores on the LNER. By the early 1930s work was in hand on widening the East Coast Main Line to mostly four tracks between York and Northallerton. The section between Alne and Thirsk was used by the NER for its automatic electro-gas semaphore signal installation of 1905 and by the 1930s was outdated. A. E. Tattersall, signal engineer of the North Eastern area of the LNER, and who had been on the IRSE committee to study the future of signalling in 1922, had similar ideas to Arthur Bound who was then signal engineer of the LNER's Southern area. From then on he was to be at the forefront of signalling developments. For the new

Close detail of a searchlight signal on the Clacton line. The semi plate shows that the signal can work automatically but will be controlled when the level crossing gates are across the line. The box with diagonal stripes near the bottom of the post is the signalpost telephone to the supervising signalbox. (BR, ER)

The London & North Eastern made the greatest strides towards modern signalling in the 1930s. It seemed to prefer the single lens searchlight signal with the colours given by a colour filter swinging in front of the main lamp. These are signals at Fenchurch Street with shunt ahead signals, illuminated from behind, below the main searchlight aspects, and at the foot of the bracket are upper quadrant ground discs. (LNER)

signalling between York and Northallerton he proposed to have automatic colour light signals controlled by track circuit block or by thumb switches on a track diagram at certain of the retained intermediate signalboxes needed to operate points which were still to be controlled mechanically. At Thirsk a new type of control was to be employed with route setting switches placed on the track diagram in banks against the signal to which they applied. If one signal could lead to three routes then it had three switches alongside. The interlocking though was of a new pattern controlled entirely by relays. The circuits were so designed that when the signalman turned a switch to set up a route from one signal to the next, the electrical circuits could only be made if the track circuits were clear and no other conflicting route was already set, points were set and locked and then the signal cleared. After all, if only electrical circuits were to be switched why was it necessary to have a signal lever? An ordinary electrical

The Eastern and North Eastern Regions of British Railways continued to use searchlight signals, as here in 1962 on the newly electrified Clacton line. This is a four-aspect example with the second yellow for the double yellow aspect given by the normally dark upper lens. (BR, ER)

switch was all that was required. The Thirsk control area was not large but the lines were track circuited and indicated on the diagram and the trains were described by bell code. Many of the automatic signals were arranged to be approach lit to save power, by track circuit occupation of an approaching train before the train reached the sighting point. A year or so later Leeds West was resignalled with a similar switch panel, and by 1938 another one was being brought into service at Hull.

The 1930s was a busy time for the LNER's signal engineers for in 1932 King's Cross had been resignalled with a miniature lever frame and colour light signals followed by Fenchurch Street in 1935, and by Edinburgh Waverley West and East in 1936 and 1938, both with miniature frames of over 200 levers. In the context of Thirsk these were conventional schemes very similar in principle to those on the Southern and at Manchester Victoria. There were just two more developments in the 1930s to add to the ingredients of the new style signalling mix. Northallerton was given a new relay interlocking and one control switch panel but the essential difference here was that the track diagram

not only showed where the trains were by track circuit lights, it also showed by a row of white lights along the tracks concerned which routes had been set up by the operation of the thumb switches. Unlike miniature or full size levers which, if a conflicting route was already set it would be locked either mechanically or by the mechanical part of an electric lock so that a signalman would know immediately if he could not pull the lever, the thumb switches were free to be turned regardless of whether the route was available. This was a criticism of some of the more conservative signal engineers. In the first thumb switch panels the signalman would have to search in case another switch was already holding a conflicting route or had inadvertently not been returned to normal. At Northallerton he could see what routes were already set and the white route lights confirmed to him that the points and signal had responded to his operation of the thumb switch.

Northallerton was just completed and brought into service on the very day when the Second World War started, 3 September 1939. Having seen the success of relay interlocking and switch panels the LNER was eager for more – Doncaster, York, the Great Eastern from Liverpool Street and the latter scheme included electrification. But alas the war delayed it all. In between bombings and repairs, though, doodles on backs of envelopes or even proper drawings were developing ideas which were to be taken on to fruition once the war was over. These were not just for thumb

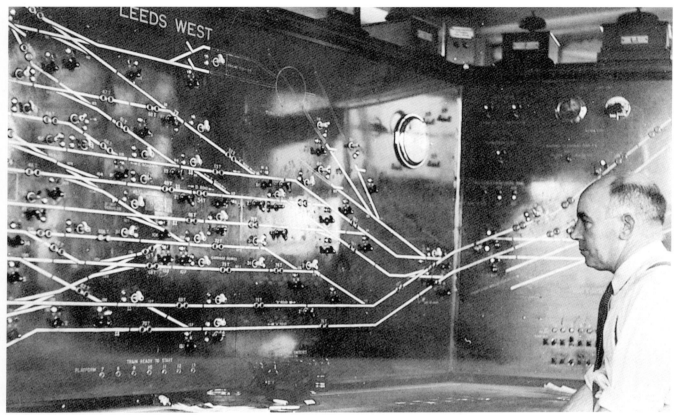

The LNER set the pattern in the 1930s for relay interlocking and control panels rather than miniature levers. Thirsk was the pioneer with a route setting panel and it was followed by this panel at Leeds West with the switches setting individual equipment. Points on the diagram had a pivoted strip which showed a continuous line for the route actually set. (LNER)

switch panels either. On the Cheshire Lines Railway, one of those curious joint concerns involving the LNER and LMS, at a place called Brunswick alongside the Liverpool docks on the approach to Liverpool Central from Manchester, a small resignalling scheme had been commissioned in 1937 and hardly noticed by the outside world. It only involved a short length of double track splitting to three tracks with a few crossovers. The method of control was by operating push buttons, one on the diagram near the signal concerned and another button on one of the routes to which that signal applied. If the signal led to two tracks then the signalman pushed the second button on whichever track was the one to be taken by the train. The tracks were shown as white lines on the dark background of the case but the points had a swinging flap controlled by an electro-magnet which confirmed which way the

points were set by completing the white line along the track for which the route was set and breaking the white line on the route not set. On a complex track layout the advantage would be that the signalman would have just the one button at the entrance to the signal section instead of a bank of thumb switches, and his hand would go along the track he wanted, to the exit button – so much easier to see and operate. It was appropriately known as the NX (entrance–exit) system. The era of the panel signalbox had arrived.

Chapter 12

SOME DEVIATIONS

ONCE THE PROPOSALS for a new colour light signalling code had been accepted in the mid-1920s it might be assumed that the new three- and four-aspect signals would have become the invariable standard for the foreseeable future. With the virtual world wide acceptance of the standard light colours of red for danger, yellow for caution, and green for clear, it might also be thought that there would be little need for too many variations.

We have already discussed the two schools of thought on speed signalling versus route signalling around the First World War period and the introduction of three-position semaphore signals to Britain with their potential for multi-arm displays for speed indication. In those countries where speed signalling was the chosen method, and especially the United States, colour light signals replacing semaphores were well in evidence by the 1930s and speed signalling was developing in a number of countries previously with less formal operating methods, especially where US influence was a factor. With colour light signals of the searchlight pattern with red, yellow and green aspects given through one lens by each signal head, and up to usually three heads on one signal post plus a bottom marker light, a variety of combinations could be given. In recent years, with flashing aspects even more variations can be provided, and by the 1980s there were something like 18 or 19 signal aspects in the speed signalling codes of some East European railways and in the United States. In Canada there are no fewer than 29 signal aspects, covering approach to an interlocking area and passage through it. Whether all these variations could be simplified is open to question but on one occasion a driver on the Government of Ontario rapid transit service which shares tracks with main line freights, when asked if he knew of all the detailed differences between the signal aspects replied, 'Yup, if we've got a green we go, if we've got yellow we slow down, and if its red we stop!' Not perhaps a reply to warrant ten out of ten since many of the combinations include red and by their position relevant to the other colours have a speed indicating function.

The Mirfield speed signalling

There was one man on a British railway, whom we have met before, Arthur Bound, from 1929 signal engineer of the LMS, who was still looking for his ideal signalling system. Although conventional three- and four-aspect signalling had been commissioned by the LMS at Manchester Victoria and Exchange more or less coinciding with Bound's arrival from the LNER, in 1932 Bound resignalled a short three-mile section of

The Heaton Lodge–Mirfield speed signalling installation included signals with three searchlight heads plus a marker light at the bottom. This signal is displaying four lights, red at the top, double yellow in the second and third lights and the red marker, meaning 'be prepared to find the next signal ahead on medium speed route at caution'. (Kenneth Field)

quadruple track in the Mirfield area on the former Lancashire & Yorkshire Railway Manchester–Normanton route with a form of speed signalling. It was not all speed signalling for some of the junction signals had separate bracketed signal heads side by side as in conventional signalling. Also, the splitting distants had separate heads side by side, although used in such a way that the main centre head between two side heads was always the one which applied to the train regardless of which way the train was to go. The signals were of the searchlight pattern and stop signals normally had two or three main lights mounted

Side view of a three-light signal plus marker in the Mirfield system. The marker light could change to a slow speed proceed signal at yellow to allow movements into a yard or loop. In this example there are two subsidiary signals below the marker red. (Kenneth Field)

Various forms of speed signal at Mirfield. (Kenneth Field)

vertically on the post, and below them a marker light usually displaying red unless the main light was showing green. On signals with two main lights the top was the auxiliary light to provide a second yellow, for the system followed the 1924 recommendations in that context. The second light provided the red, yellow and green aspects, and the bottom light was the marker. Signals with three main lights had the auxiliary second yellow as the middle light and the top and third lights gave the red, yellow and green aspects. Again there was a red marker at the bottom.

For a through run at maximum line speed on the straight route the top light gave the indications, red, yellow, green and with the second light the double yellow. All this while the third light down was showing red and the marker red was also alight unless the top lamp was showing green. For a clear for main line indication the driver saw from top to bottom green, the auxiliary out, red, and the marker out. If the points were set for the diversion calling for a speed restriction either to a parallel track or at a route junction, the third light down was the one which was used showing yellow or green and with the second light the double yellow aspect. This time the top lamp was showing red all the time as was the bottom marker. So for a diversion through the points, whether to right or left was not indicated on these signals, the driver was faced with a vertical display of red, green, red if the line ahead was clear for at least three sections, or red, double yellow, red, if clear for two. A fifth aspect was introduced at some signals, yellow over green meaning 'Attention, pass second signal at restricted speed', used where signals were even closer than provided for with a double yellow to give adequate braking distance. In this instance the sequence for successive signals was yellow over green, double yellow, single yellow, red. Bound was obviously not worried about the conclusions of his 1924 committee when they were considering what display should be given for the fourth aspect, in that yellow and green might be open to confusion.

The distant signals approaching the end of the new signalling and followed by semaphore junction signals had the twin light display in the centre head for red (since they were also stop signals controlled by the previous signalbox), yellow, double yellow, or green, and single lamps on each side, lower than the top main light of the centre unit, displaying a single yellow or out. With the signals ahead clear for the principal high speed route the centre head showed green and if it was the left hand route, then the right hand light showed yellow. If the principal route was the right hand one then the centre light was green and the left hand light showed yellow. The junctions offered a multiple choice of routes and the variations on the distant indications were obtained by using double yellow or green on the main centre unit with either left or right single yellow to give four variations of route. But this was not true speed signalling since the display to drivers at night appeared just like a normal splitting colour light distant. Although these signals were also stop signals they did not have a marker light as the next signals ahead were semaphores and marker lights were only used where following signals were of the multiple aspect colour light type. The marker light itself acted as a slow speed signal in its own right since at one or two locations where facing connections led into sidings or yards, the marker changed from red to a small yellow, the lights above being at red, and therefore provided a low speed authority to proceed.

The lines between Heaton Lodge Junction and Thornhill LNW Junction through Mirfield provided a variety of route and parallel junctions of different speeds, thus giving Bound the opportunity to devise different signals and aspect combinations for each feature working within given principles. The aim was to provide more information and to simplify the aspects given to drivers but in hindsight, the installation did no more and proved to be more complex than what came a few years later. The Mirfield signalling might have been a trial but it was not repeated for main line use although it lasted until May 1965 when it was replaced by standard colour light signals and track circuit block. Track circuits had not been part of the block signalling in the 1932 scheme, for the existing signalboxes were retained and signalled trains using conventional block instruments.

Automatic calling-on on the Camden–Watford line

Bound, though, had other ideas up his sleeve and concurrently with the Mirfield signalling was introducing colour light signalling with continuous track circuiting and largely automatic operation on two of the LMS suburban routes. One of these was the existing 'New Line' from Camden to Watford Junction, forming the fifth and sixth tracks serving closely spaced suburban stations alongside the four-track West Coast Main Line. The other was the newly built tracks from Barking to Upminster alongside its existing LMS-owned London, Tilbury & Southend line. The new line to Upminster was electrified on the third and fourth rail system and was to be used solely by District Railway electric trains. The Watford New Line had already been electrified on the third and fourth rail system in stages between 1917 and 1922 and was used by LMS electric services from Broad Street, Euston, Rickmansworth and Croxley Green to Watford and by Bakerloo Underground trains between Queen's Park and Watford. There was a triangle between Watford High Street, Bushey and the connections to Croxley Green and Rickmansworth to allow through working between the branches and London, and at Willesden Junction there were connections to the line via Hampstead Heath. At Harrow there were reversing sidings which required the signalbox there to be open for part of the day. Otherwise, apart from the connections to the main line and North London line at Camden, at Queen's Park for the connections to the Bakerloo line, and the terminus at Watford Junction where the signalboxes had to be open, most of the line was worked automatically by track circuit block.

The signals were of the searchlight pattern, basically of two aspects with stop signals showing red and green and repeaters, just over a train's length on the approach to a stop signal, perhaps surprisingly showing red, yellow and green. Stop signals proper were accompanied by ground train stop trip apparatus. All signals except those leading to other types of signalling (whether semaphore or London Transport) were provided with lower marker lights, those on stop signals being vertically below the main light, and those on repeater signals being offset to the left. A second lens showing a small yellow aspect was situated immediately below the red marker of stop signals and this was one of the unique features of the system. If a train had to stop at a stop signal showing double red lights (main and marker) when working automatically, provided the first track circuit immediately beyond the signal was clear, a timing relay would change the red marker to the miniature yellow aspect as a calling on indication after a train had been at a stand for about one minute. The main signal above remained at red but the trip arm dropped to the clear position and the train could proceed at caution. In this way a train could approach a repeater signal showing red. The rules required a train in these circumstances to stop at the repeater, if still showing double red, wait one minute, then pass the signal and proceed cautiously and in this

A repeater signal with the marker light offset to the left on the Camden–Watford local dc electric line, also known as the New Line, of the LMS. (BR, LMR)

A junction signal at Croxley Green Junction on the Camden–Watford New Line. Although the line to Watford High Street to the right carried most of the traffic, the left hand route to Croxley Green and originally Rickmansworth was regarded as the main route, hence the higher position of the left hand signal. Only the right hand signal has a call-on aspect below the marker light since the left hand route was not equipped for automatic operation. (LMS)

instance there was no trip arm to clear.

The calling-on procedure was valuable in keeping trains moving in the event of a technical fault in the signalling circuits but more often than not it came into operation simply by operating delays. Some of the older LNWR electric trains had only single doors at each end of the coaches and at times of heavy traffic took two or three minutes to unload and load so that a following train would often be right behind it at a stand waiting to enter the platform. In a similar way, a Bakerloo Line train with sticking sliding doors could be overtime at a station so that a following train could be entering the platform as the first one was leaving. As for a delay of several minutes there could soon be a queue of trains buffer to buffer, which was almost inevitable with a peak hour service of trains every two minutes or so, certainly between the 1930s and the 1970s.

There were, though, dangers in fog, for the calling-on system operated without regard to weather conditions and one of your authors on numerous occasions saw a succession of trains departing and arriving at the same

time and at the same platform in thick fog, and at speeds hardly within the description of 'caution' for the conditions. The rules provided for the guard to go back and put down detonators 100 yards behind a standing train detained in fog during a delay but this was impracticable in normal working under stop and proceed conditions. While the system was largely accident free, in its last few years there were, perhaps not surprisingly, three major collisions. The first was near Watford on 16 October 1962 and then, between Willesden and Kensal Green, remarkably 24 years to the day, on 16 October 1986. Both involved LMR trains which ran into and crushed the back car of Bakerloo trains. The other one was within two months of the first, on 5 December 1962, also at Willesden but on the down line and there was less damage. If the Railway Inspectorate ever had doubts on the safety of stop and proceed working, the last quarter of 1962 certainly brought it to the fore with no fewer than four accidents caused by a lack of caution and awareness in stop and proceed working, the two just mentioned, one in the November on London Transport's District line near Victoria and the last – a major accident – near Coppenhall Junction on the West Coast Main Line between Winsford and Crewe on Boxing Day. Here, the up 'Mid-day Scot', running under stop and proceed rules because signal telephones had failed, rammed the back of a train from Liverpool, resulting in 18 fatalities.

In effect, the call-on arrangements on the Camden–Watford line meant that when in operation the section concerned was being worked permissively which, when it was installed, was not quite the intention. The automatic call-on invited the driver to go forward as a right and without any action on his part to acknowledge the invitation. At least with other stop and proceed working, involving going past an automatic signal firmly at danger, being tripped by the train stop equipment on a line so equipped, and re-stopping and then the driver having to take a positive action in resetting the train mounted trip arm, not only took more time but instilled a question in the driver's mind, 'am I justified in going past this signal at danger in accordance with the rules?' It was then up to the

driver to decide what action he would take, although even this procedure has led to major accidents on the London Underground where the onward movement of the train was not at the caution required.

In normal working the Camden–Watford signalling was basically a two-aspect system for, unless a train had passed a stop signal at danger, it would not encounter the next repeater showing red. It was not a speed signalling system and at junctions there were two signals bracketed side by side although if one led to other types of signalling there was no marker or call on aspect. There were a few unusual signals, particularly those acting as distants for the Watford triangle. These were like the Mirfield scheme distants in that they had the main head in the centre capable of showing red, single yellow, double yellow (with an auxiliary light) and green, and on each side were single lights for providing the splitting distant indication. The lights on the right gave a single yellow with the main aspect at double yellow or green for the principal route to the left and vice versa if the principal route was to the right. These signals also had marker lights and the call-on yellow, while the one at Bushey also had a 'track dead' indicator to denote that the current was switched off beyond. If the track dead signal was lit it was an absolute stop indication for electric trains. A few repeater signals also had track dead indicators and because of that they had double red marker lights, one offset to the left for normal use as a repeater and one vertically below the main aspect when the track dead indicator was alight.

Bushey down platform starting signal also served as the distant for the junction signal in the previous illustration. When the next signal was clear towards Watford High Street the main aspect showed double yellow and the left hand light a single yellow. Below the top signal heads are a section gap indicator which, when illuminated, meant that the traction current was off in the next section, below that was the red marker and the bottom light was a calling-on yellow aspect. (Geoffrey Kichenside)

An Irish oddity. This rectangular board signal with a red stripe which worked in the same plane as a conventional semaphore, was the up home signal at Inchicore approaching Dublin on the Cork main line. (Geoffrey Kichenside)

It was possible to see three danger signals behind a train since one stop signal would not clear until the train ahead had passed beyond the overlap of the next stop signal ahead so that, until the train had got to that overlap, two stop signals and the intervening repeater would all show the double red aspect. A few stop signals in closely signalled areas were actually three-aspect signals in their own right while at Watford Junction, the yellow calling on aspects on the home signals were used to allow a second train into an already partly occupied platform.

The Upminster line signalling was much the same as the Watford line but both remained as isolated examples of an interesting variation. With the proliferation of lights they must have been more costly than a conventional two- or three-aspect system. The Upminster signalling lasted until electrification and resignalling of the adjoining LT&S main line in the early 1960s when it was totally segregated from the LTS line and given standard London Transport signalling. The Camden–Watford signalling, with some alterations including automatic operation at Watford in the early 1970s, lasted almost to the end of the 1980s when it was resignalled with conventional three-aspect signalling with multi-lens heads. With train stops but without the automatic calling on feature, control was from a new panel in the existing Willesden main line power signalbox.

Bound's ideas were certainly different and at the time of their introduction, all more or less together in 1932/3, they gave drivers a little more than the then existing standard colour light signalling elsewhere. This was certainly in a more complex way than the information given to drivers by the new standard junction indicators introduced a few years later. Moreover, the practice of trains passing signals showing a red light, even though the relevant one for the train was at yellow or green was becoming less in favour. Therefore, with a junction indicator rather than a separate colour light head for each route, the one set of colour light aspects applied to all trains and for new work meant that trains no longer had to pass a signal with a red light as part of its display. The use of red lights as positioning and marker aspects in the Mirfield speed signals could not be overcome, and for that reason as much as any other, meant that standard three- and four-aspect signalling continued to hold its position.

Variations on a theme

Over the years there have been other deviations, not in the systems as a whole but more in the way signals have been presented to drivers, largely arising from tight clearances or obstructions which limited sighting of what would be termed normal signals. This was especially true in station areas where roof canopies or overbridges gave the signal engineers little room to mount their equipment where, for example, crossovers were provided part way along a platform or platform starting signals had to be placed beyond a bridge. The Great Western Railway was noted for its variety of short arm semaphore signals and some were centre pivoted with the spectacle on the left of the pivot with the red glass within the arm and the green above it. At Worcester it provided discs as main running signals under the station roof, not the discs of disc and crossbar days but rather akin to a larger version of a shunting disc with a white circular plate having a red stripe painted across it, naturally horizontal for danger and inclined down for clear. They were accompanied by normal sized shunting discs below for shunting moves.

Other railways also used shortened arms in restricted locations. Even in BR days, when electrification on the 25kV overhead system normally meant resignalling with colour lights which had to be placed out of reach of the overhead wires and with wire screens to prevent signal engineering technicians carrying out maintenance from any danger of touching the traction catenary, there were a few instances where semaphore signals continued in use. To keep the arms within the obligatory protecting wire cage they were shortened.

Well into the nationalised BR era as different parts of the railway were transferred from one Region to another, the new administrators used their own

This Great Western pattern lower quadrant semaphore stop and distant signal served as Weybridge up local starter on the Southern's main line to Waterloo. It replaced a life-expired LSWR signal for a few years in the 1960s until commissioning of colour light signalling, seen here installed but not yet in service, in 1967. The roof canopy over the platform and the bridge pier prevented a clear view of an upper quadrant signal. (Geoffrey Kichenside)

The unusual colour light signals on certain platforms at Birmingham New Street were necessary for restricted clearances. They were three-aspect searchlight signals, one for each side of the island platform with separate position light shunting signals, but had a combined theatre style route indicator and combined right away indicator at the bottom. Since the tracks on each side of the platform merged just beyond the island only one train could leave at one time. (BR, LMR)

equipment for renewals or for complete resignalling. It might be thought that with one nationalised entity standard equipment would be used throughout the system but in the signal engineering field each Region still had a largely free hand in its own practices which did not really start to disappear until the business structure of BR was established in the 1980s. This accounts for how Great Western style lower quadrant semaphore signals began to appear on what had been LMS lines newly in the Western Region and in contrast, upper quadrants on former GWR lines. It also explains the continued use of GWR lower quadrant semaphores even in the 1990s on former GWR routes, but the installation of a GWR signal at Weybridge on the Southern Region in the 1960s, for a few years before total resignalling with colour lights, was one of those cases where sighting prevented the use of an upper quadrant arm and the Southern no longer had spare lower quadrants of its own.

Even in modern colour light practice there are deviations from the standard upright three- or four-aspect multi-lens signal head. At Birmingham New Street in the 1960s a combination of low platform covers and restricted width at the platform end brought the production of some unique signals. There was one casing displaying searchlight type three-aspect signals for both lines on each side of the platform, position light shunting signals and single theatre route indicators and right away indicators depending on which signal was clear. At a few places in the 1990s, Paddington is one example, where overbridges restrict the driver's view of signals and the multi-lens display has been split, with the red separated from and alongside the remaining lights. The white light junction indicators have also been mounted alongside the three-aspect head and over the red aspect. In another variation the head has been mounted horizontally although provided with only three aspects so any problem with double yellow does not arise. These oddities have arisen because the single lens searchlight signal which would have solved the problem was no longer to be specified for new work from the early 1990s. While there are lineside signals there will always be a few locations where signals will have to be different even though the aspects displayed will be standard.

Chapter 13

AUTOMATIC TRAIN CONTROL AND WARNING SYSTEMS

The safety control loop

As signalling methods and equipment became more clearly defined in the last three decades of the 19th century, a safety control loop became established in which signalmen communicated with each other through the bells and indicators of the absolute block system to ensure that block sections were clear ready for trains to proceed. Signalmen communicated with drivers by clearing signals to tell them it was safe for trains to enter block sections and drivers, seeing the signals at clear, set the controls of their engines so that the trains would run at the right speed through the block sections.

That was how it should have been and most of the time it actually was like that. The whole thing depended on everybody in that control loop doing the right thing every time but human nature being what it is, inevitably at times somebody made a mistake, and the result was often a train accident. Signalmen could make mistakes in the operation of the block system either by giving 'train out of section' because they thought a train had passed and accepting another into a section already occupied by perhaps a broken down train, or on multiple track lines, clearing the wrong block instrument, or becoming confused about the bell signals and clearing signals without the proper exchanges of the 'is line clear?' procedure. In 1876 William Sykes, as we have already seen, made a start on his later well-known lock and block system which, with electric control of locks on signals and block instruments involving the trains themselves operating treadles as they passed along the line, locked and released the equipment and reduced the chances of signalmen's errors by forcing them to adopt specified methods of working. The Midland Railway adopted the rotary interlocking block system which again, in a different way, required the signalmen to work the block instruments and signals in a pre-determined manner to lessen the possibility of a mistake.

In the 1920s and 1930s as described in Chapter 6, other block controls were added – interlinking to prove that distant signals had been put back to caution before line clear could be sent to the signalbox in the rear for a following train. Sometimes this also applied to home signals as well, with line clear release on the most advanced starting signal so that it could not be pulled to clear unless the block indicator for the relevant section ahead was displaying line clear. There was an added control on some lines to give that release for one pull only of the advanced starting signal lever, and sequential locking so that the successive stop signals on one line controlled by one signalbox had to be pulled in order, outer home, inner home, starter, and advanced starter, and if the advanced starter had been left at clear after the previous train, then for the next train the starting signal could not be cleared. With track circuits approaching the home signal and another at the starter these features added up to Welwyn control which proved a train had passed through the block section before another could be signalled. That in normal working virtually eliminated signalmen's safety errors. And remember, interlocking between levers had already ensured that in normal working signals and points had to agree and conflicting signals could not be cleared at the same time.

We stress the words 'in normal working'. We have already mentioned three cases where signalmen defeated the protection of the Sykes lock and block system either by using the release key or button (which had to be employed for certain specified instances but not in the situation of the day) thinking that the system had failed when it was correctly locked. There were cases when trains were flagged over points thought to be correctly set but the signal was locked when in fact another lever was holding the interlocking and trains were derailed or sent forward into a collision. But this was abnormal working where the human element intervened to upset the protection provided. There have also been technical failures as at Lichfield on New Year's Day in 1946 when all the laws of interlocking would seem to have been over-ridden. A crossover remained set for a move from the up fast line into the up platform loop after a local passenger train had arrived at the platform, even though the signalman had worked the levers to unlock the points and reset them for the straight run on the fast line and relocked them. The signals were then cleared for an express fish train to run up the fast line and overtake the local train, but with the crossover still set for the loop the fish train collided at speed with the back of the local train and demolished three of the four coaches with heavy casualties. It was found that the facing point lock and fouling bar links had been obstructed by frozen ballast, the facing point lock bolt had not withdrawn from the lock and the point rodding had bowed when the signalman restored the point lever. While the levers were in their correct positions, thus releasing the interlocking on the signals, the points had not actually moved and were lying set for the crossover move. There was just one other chance that the detector at the points would hold the home signal arm at danger, but having seen a clear distant the driver would not have been expecting to see the home signal at danger and was unlikely to have had time to stop even if he had seen this signal. Proving the indication of the signal arm while used in interlinking was not part of the interlocking between mechanical home and distant signals.

So the third element in the safety control loop now comes into the picture, the driver's interpretation of the signals displayed to him. A single distant signal can be at caution or clear. A stop signal can be at danger or clear. Has the correct indication registered in the driver's mind or has he interpreted the signal as what he was expecting to see and not what it was actually showing? On multi-tracked lines has he identified the correct signal applying to his train or mis-read a signal applying to a train on an adjoining line. In most cases drivers have read the signals correctly and acted properly in controlling their trains. But in just a few cases, and compared with the millions of train journeys and the millions more signals correctly interpreted by drivers it is only a few cases, drivers have made mistakes and run past signals at danger to cause some of the worst accidents in the whole history of railways in both terms of damage to trains and equipment and in casualties.

Fog signalling

Just as in the 1870s there were those initial moves to add equipment to signalboxes to reduce or avoid signalmen's errors so there were the first thoughts about ways of reducing or avoiding drivers' mistakes. In fact, almost from the dawn of railways people had been inventing ways of reinforcing the lineside danger signals with a warning in the cab and literally hundreds of patents were taken out in the last century, but most were impracticable and few stood any chance of success. Many proposed using devices to sound the engine whistle from trackside equipment as, until the development of continuous automatic brakes, there was little else which lineside equipment could act on, for many locomotives in late Victorian years had no more than a hand brake on the tender and in an emergency the driver reversed the locomotive and applied steam to slow down more quickly. The quest for an add-on device to give a cab indication of a lineside signal was largely to help a driver locate signals in fog and not so much a general aid, for in clear weather, even by night, a driver was expected to know

Track trip arms of the North Eastern Railway's mechanical fog signalling apparatus, devised by Vincent Raven in 1894.

where he was and to keep a sharp look out for signals. Traditionally in fog, railways in Britain relied on detonators to assist drivers to locate distant signals and selected stop signals with fogmen, usually from the permanent way staff, stationed at the signals and putting a detonator on the rail when the signal was at danger or caution and displaying a hand lamp signal to repeat the indication of the arm. 'Fog' also included falling snow.

A fogman's life was not very pleasant – on his own, usually out in the elements, sometimes with a small hut as a sort of shelter, perhaps with a brazier for warmth and with only what he had managed to take with him to eat or drink and often on duty for a whole night – cold, damp, freezing in a blizzard, probably after he had been doing trackwork the previous day. He risked life and limb taking a detonator off the rail when the signal cleared, listening intently for the muffled sound of an approaching train which he could not see. But it was a system that has lasted until recent times where semaphore signals survive.

North Eastern mechanical cab signalling
In 1894, Vincent Raven of the North Eastern Railway locomotive department (he later became chief mechanical engineer of the NER), and a colleague devised a system for sounding a whistle in the cab from ground apparatus near signals. The ground unit, which was connected to the signal wire had its own balance weight to ensure that it went to the warning position if the wire broke, consisted of a rod passing under the rails to which was attached two trip arms, originally in the form of an inverted U shaped bar but later a forged T bar, standing vertically above rail level in the warning position. When the signal was clear the arms were lowered and made no contact with the locomotive so that no signal was passed to the cab. The locomotive equipment consisted of a vertical striker arm with a rounded bottom edge which hit one of the raised arms of the ground equipment. The striker rod lifted and operated a valve which admitted boiler steam to a dedicated whistle in the cab as a warning indication of a signal at danger. The ground equipment was fitted at both distant and stop signals although there was no difference in the cab warning, and as just mentioned, there was no indication for a signal at clear. The whistle continued to blow for a warning until reset by the driver which repositioned the striker arm. The pair of ground trip arms was needed to allow for engines to be either way round although quite why a central trip arm could not have been employed is difficult to understand. On locomotives with a steam brake only, just the whistle was given, but on locomotives with Westinghouse air brakes not only was the whistle given from the compressed air supply of the brake but a brake application was made by releasing compressed air from the system until the driver cancelled the warning.

The first installation was tried out at Merrybent Junction on the Darlington–Barnard Castle line in 1894 and it was introduced gradually to other lines two years later. By 1901 Raven's fog signalling apparatus was being installed on the East Coast Main Line north from York. It had its limitations for if a trip arm on the ground broke no cab indication was given, and the same warning whistle was given for both stop and distant signals. As far as the first was concerned the number of failures was remarkably small but they were nevertheless wrong side failures. As for the second, in 1921 proposals were advanced for fitting stop signals with a trip arm in the vacant centre line position and equipping locomotives with a second striker to match, operating a second whistle of a different note. However the LNER which inherited the Raven system at the Grouping in 1923, did not pursue the latter feature and did not extend the system. By the 1930s it was being taken out of use even though many new LNER locomotives in the North East had been equipped with the cab equipment.

NER electrical cab signalling
Not content with his mechanical fog signalling system, Raven was behind another more sophisticated scheme tried out on the East Coast Main Line between Durham and Bensham in 1907. It was an electrical system and in essence very much a precursor of the thinking behind the intermittent forms of today's automatic train protection, of which more later. The track equipment consisted of centrally positioned ramps and additionally, at the triggering position, two side ramps just outside the right and left hand rails. The triggering position was about 100 yards on the approach side of distant signals, but at the distant signal was another single centre ramp, and further ramps at intervals from there to the home signal where there was another ramp and further ramps at the following stop signals up to the most advanced starting signal. The locomotive equipment consisted of steel brush contact arms in the centre and wheeled contact arms on the right and left hand sides. The cab indication consisted of a semaphore arm and two pointers, between them capable of pointing to one of four numbers. As the locomotive passed the trigger position the centre and two side contacts set off a warning by raising the semaphore arm to danger and setting a bell ringing. For safety, any one of the three trigger ramps independently could set off the warning. This was the driver's prompt that he was approaching a distant signal. There was a ramp at the distant signal and if the signal was clear the semaphore in the cab dropped to the clear position and the bell stopped. If the distant signal was at caution then the bell continued and the cab semaphore remained at danger. The driver could stop the bell by operating a cancelling lever. At the intermediate ramps the equipment was updated so that if a train had passed

the distant signal at caution, meaning that the stop signals ahead were probably at danger, and they had then been cleared, at the next intermediate ramp the cab semaphore would be set to the clear position. Similarly, if the signalman had to restore the signals to danger in an emergency as the train approached, an intermediate ramp would set off the warning sequence. The ramp at the home signal was extra long to allow for an engine to come to a stop on the ramp if the signal was at danger. When the signal cleared, the cab indication would also clear in certain conditions. At junctions, when the signals were clear the system operated the cab pointers to denote which route was set; figure 1 denoted the first route to the left and so on.

A prime feature of this system was that at all times it effectively acted as a distant signal and would only give the clear indication when all the relevant stop signals were at clear. After passing a distant signal at caution the intermediate and home signal ramps would only give clear indications when the home signal and the starter and the advanced starter, if provided, were showing clear. Thus a train standing at a home signal at danger could not receive a clear indication unless the signals had been cleared into the block section ahead. If a signalman wanted to bring a train forward inside the home signal to draw up to the starting signal which was still at danger, the cab equipment semaphore would still show danger. So the signalman was provided with a tapper related to the home signal which when pressed and released sent an electrical signal to the home signal ramp and flicked the cab semaphore up and down as a form of call-on indication. It was an ingenious system but cost was an important factor for the locomotive equipment alone was five times higher than the mechanical striker system. Apart from the two trial installations, the second being a modified form on the Richmond branch, it got no further and by the 1920s was dismantled.

Great Western automatic train control
After Raven's original system was devised and slowly installed there was no rush by other companies to install cab signalling. However, an accident on the Great Western in June 1900 when a Paddington–Falmouth express ran past signals at danger and rammed the back of a local train standing at Slough causing considerable damage, killing five passengers and injuring 35, set off thoughts at Reading along the same idea as Raven. Charles Jacobs, the telegraph assistant, made a start soon after the Slough accident with ideas for using a ramp on the track rather than Raven's trip arms. There was no real progress though, until the newly formed signal and telegraph department was established in 1903 when the principal assistant, Robert Insell, joined with Jacobs to evolve a workable scheme. There has always been controversy as to who actually made the first proposals for a GWR form of

audible cab signalling as it was then called, and many would give a chargehand in the department rather more of the credit. As in many railway technical developments it was often the departmental head who got the acknowledgement and in many cases filed the patent rights, rather than the man who actually guided the pencil across the back of the proverbial envelope outlining the initial ideas. In any case, if lowly minions came up with new ideas good enough to adopt it was often held that they were company servants and any work they did was for the company. In the same way, the chief mechanical engineer always took the credit for new locomotive designs whatever work might have been done by the lesser mortals in the drawing office. In the case of technology developments it might not have been fair, but it was the system.

The GWR system used a ramp with an inverted steel T bar in the centre of the track, mostly about 45ft long sloping up at the approach end and down at the exit end with a flat centre section about 12ft long, $3\frac{1}{2}$in above rail level. The ramp was not exactly parallel to the rails and was arranged as a slight diagonal, $1\frac{1}{2}$in each side of the centre line to avoid wearing a groove in the locomotive pick up shoe. They were placed at the approach to distant signals. When a signal was at caution the ramp was dead but when the signal was clear the ramp was electrified at 16 volts negative polarity. The locomotive equipment consisted of a shoe housed in an assembly at the front end, normally standing to within $2\frac{1}{2}$in of rail level so that as it rode up and along the ramp the shoe lifted. This broke an electrical circuit from a self contained battery powered system on board. When the ramp was dead the breaking of the electric circuits on the locomotive released an electro-magnetically controlled valve and admitted steam to a special whistle in the cab and the display of a label 'danger' in an aperture of the cab equipment. The latter was soon discarded. The whistle could be silenced by the driver lifting a cancelling handle which reset the engine's electrical circuits. If the signal was clear the electrified ramp passed current through the lifted shoe which maintained the special whistle valve shut but also sounded a bell as confirmation of a clear indication. That was the initial system which was tried out on the Henley branch early in 1906. It proved to be reliable and later that year was installed on the Yarnton–Fairford branch, a single line where trains would need to pass over ramps for the opposite direction which would not need to give a cab signal. Of course, the shoe would still lift so the ramp was suppressed by being fed with opposite polarity current which held the steam-valve for the whistle shut but did not operate the bell. The change in current polarity on the ramps was controlled either by the direction levers for some sections which released the large Webb & Thompson electric staff, or by contacts on the other single line control systems used on the branch, the table or token instruments. So confident was the GWR signal engineer that it would work that the distant signals themselves were removed, and the ramps placed at the distant signal locations so that the cab indications were the only advice given to drivers.

It was soon realised that the steam valve was not the best of equipment to have in an electric control box because it induced corrosion. Therefore the system was redesigned to work in conjunction with the vacuum brake system fitted to GWR locomotives in which air was admitted through a siren into the vacuum brake pipe thus giving an automatic brake application when a distant signal was at caution. Again, the driver could cancel the caution warning to silence the siren and stop the brake application. Further movement of the train was then totally in the driver's hands but at least he had received a warning as the train approached the distant signal, and in fog, that was a major step forward. Unlike the Raven system, the driver had a positive clear indication and would not be in the dark as on the NER, wondering if he had passed a signal with a broken trip arm.

The Fairford branch equipment proved itself and the GWR extended it to the main line between Reading and Paddington which was equipped by 1910 though keeping signals. But progress was slow since cost was, as usual, a factor and it took just over 20 years to complete the installation of what was now called automatic train control (ATC) to all the GWR's main lines and most of its branches. The GWR even tried to sell the system to other railways but without much success, just one small installation on the Wirksworth branch being tried by the Midland Railway.

There were a number of experimental variations of GWR ATC including ideas for multi-ramp locations before the First World War which, with various combinations of polarity, could have given a number of cab indications. Split ramps using different polarity never got very far, and an actual demonstration of a stop signal ATC was shown to the Railway Inspectorate in 1917, although it was not pursued. There were a number of trials with a mechanical system on locomotives to eliminate the battery and the need for recharging but they were not adopted widely. In the 1930s, modifications were made to a number of locomotives working London suburban and local goods trains in which the ATC pick up shoe could be locked up in a retracted position to allow the locomotives to work over the electrified lines of London Transport where the shoe might have come into contact with the centre return rail of the four-rail electrified system. In theory the shoe ought to have cleared the middle rail by one inch but with wear and tear and without precision in the height of the conductor rail it was found that it might have been possible for the shoe to contact the rail and receive some of LT's traction return current. While LT used the 600V dc system, the return rail was at 150V below earth potential. To overcome this the shoes fitted to the locomotives concerned were lifted to a high position and clipped up automatically by running over a $4^1/_2$in high dead ramp remaking the engine's electrical circuits to hold off a warning in the high position. On leaving the four-rail section the engine passed over an electrified high ramp in which the ramp current powered an electro-magnet to release the clip and the shoe dropped to its normal running position.

The GWR ATC system remained as a warning system at distant signals, with the ramps generally placed 440 yards on the approach side of isolated distant signals, and at the location of combined stop and distant signals on the same post. Later, in BR years when a new form of automatic train control was introduced in the 1950s, with a change of name to the automatic warning system (AWS), the GWR ramps were gradually moved closer to distant signals to a nominal standard 200 yards from the signal of the new BR type. Before then, in 1946/7, there had been further experiments with GWR ramps to give a different caution warning for the double yellow preliminary caution colour-light signal then at long last being thought about on the Great Western. It was achieved by using a reverse polarity current on the ramp to the normal negative feed used for the clear indication, and a horn with a different note to the siren was added in the cab so that both sounded for the double yellow warning and a brake application was initiated until the cancelling handle was operated. The first trial was made with a GWR diesel railcar on the Henley branch (just 40 years after the first cab signalling experiment there) and then a ramp was modified on the main line at Twyford with high speed steam runs, one reaching 100mph. The ATC responded perfectly with the double horn/siren. The system was not adopted however, for just ten weeks after the final trial run the GWR as a legal entity disappeared into the newly nationalised British Railways although the spirit of the Great Western lived on, as we have already seen. As for GWR ATC, it was the best known of the early systems and the one which survived the longest, and in BR days was further modified for use with diesel locomotives and multiple units. It gave the GWR an enviably high standard of safety over many years.

There was just one major disaster in GWR days caused by incorrect interpretation of a caution warning, at Norton Fitzwarren in 1940. The driver of the overnight 9.50pm Paddington–Penzance train left Taunton on the relief line with the main line on his right and with the signals at Norton Fitzwarren clear for the main line. The relief and main lines converged just beyond the station. Somehow the driver thought the signals were for him and cancelled the ATC warning. It was only when an express newspaper train began to overtake him did he realise his mistake with only 300 yards or so to go before his train reached trap points set for a dead end to protect the main line. The driver survived but 27 passengers died in the derailment. There was one other accident following a lack of action after an ATC warning in BR days when an express train took a crossover from the main to goods line being used for passenger trains near Didcot too fast in 1955, and much of the train overturned down an embankment with heavy casualties. But these were the exceptions. Gradually, in BR days, the GWR ATC system was taken out of use as the BR pattern AWS replaced it, generally during major resignalling. The last operational GWR ramps remained in BR service until the end of 1975 in the Hereford area, just 70 years after the system was devised, but a few survive on preserved lines.

The Reliostop system

Returning to the pioneering days of ATC systems there was still little development on other railways. The Great Central had tried a system approaching Woodhead in 1903 in which track circuits were used to induce red and white signal lights and a miniature semaphore arm in the cab, though without any warning siren or any control over drivers' actions. It was not sufficiently robust even though the idea was well ahead of its time. The Great Central tried again from 1915 when Arthur Bound, in conjunction with the chief locomotive draughtsman, devised a purely mechanical/pneumatic system for use at distant and stop signals. It was known as the Reliostop system and like Raven's electrical system, had a trigger point about 300 yards before reaching a distant signal. The trigger point and distant signals had a short side-mounted ramp a few inches above rail level just within the train clearance on the left of the track. The trigger ramp was fixed to engage the locomotive equipment but the distant ramp was moved in (for caution) and out (for clear) in conjunction with the distant signal wire. The ramp engaged a vertical trip arm on the locomotive which was guided inwards by the ramp when at caution. This acted on a pneumatic valve linked to a siren and the brake and admitted air to the vacuum braking system to provide the warning, which the driver could cancel. Though there was no clear indication at a distant signal, the driver would know he was approaching a distant signal by the permanent warning given by the trigger ramp.

The equipment at stop signals was different. The lineside equipment was situated a few yards beyond the signal and in the normal course of events should not have been engaged unless a locomotive passed a signal at danger. It was beautifully simple. The lineside unit was equipped with a pivoted arm a few inches long, retracted when the signal was at clear, but pointing horizontally at a right angle to the track when at danger. The locomotive unit was situated above the

arm of the distant warning arm and consisted of a fixed arm and just above it a sprung arm kept horizontal by a wooden peg supported by the lower fixed arm. If the locomotive passed a danger signal the lineside arm would simply knock out the peg holding the upper arm on the locomotive, that arm would drop and admit air straight to the brake system for a full brake application which the driver could not cancel. It could only be reset after the train had stopped when the driver could lift the arm and insert a new peg. The Reliostop system was installed between Marylebone and Northolt Junction and from Neasden Junction to Harrow but again, the 1923 amalgamation stopped further use because the LNER, having inherited five systems in use or tried out on its constituents, did not want to expand any of them without studies to find the best system – and to find the money to pay for more widespread use.

Other experimental ATC systems

Two other ATC systems were tried out by the Great Eastern Railway. The GER installed trial lengths on its Palace Gates and Ongar branches equipped with the Sykes electro-mechanical system which, like the GWR pattern, used a long ramp but there was no battery on the locomotive so that the bell for clear sounded only while the locomotive shoe was on the ramp. The caution warning was produced by mechanical linkage from the shoe to a valve which opened the train pipe to atmosphere through the siren. In 1920, three years before the amalgamation, the GER tried out the Reagan system of ATC at Fairlop on the Hainault loop from Woodford, running then to Ilford. Again it used a long ramp and with polarised relays on the locomotive could provide full speed, caution and stop indications controlling the driver's actions. The system was combined with track circuits so that even if manually controlled signals were wrongly set at clear the track circuits, unrelated to signal controls, would detect a train occupying the section so that the ATC system would give caution and stop signals to an approaching train.

A more advanced form of ATC, devised by an Australian engineer, A. R. Angus, was demonstrated at about the same time on the Dyke branch of the LBSCR. Its first trial in England was, remarkably, on the West Somerset Mineral Railway in 1912/3 and it had also been tried in Russia and Sweden. It was way ahead of its time for in the trials on the Dyke branch it had been developed to use induction for transmission from track to train. The rails were track circuited with normal low voltage dc which was first used to scan the section to ensure that it was clear. Low voltage alternating current at about 5–10 volts at a remarkably low frequency of 5 cycles per second (today called Herz – Hz) was then fed through the rails and picked up by a receiver situated between the wheels of the locomotive. The weak current detected was amplified on the engine and used to give a whistle warning and to act on the regulator and brake. The train could not move unless alternating current was detected. It was claimed the system could be used for speed control at speed restrictions as well as for signal indications. But once more, it was not adopted.

What type of control?

During the 1920s it was becoming more apparent that automatic train control was a far more desirable aid to everyday operation than simply as a guide to signals in fog. With all the various systems in use or under trial, and with many more subject to patent applications, whatever their potential, which was the best system to be adopted as a national standard? Moreover, should such control be installed just at distant signals or at all signals? And what about improvements to the signals themselves? Even following the Ais Gill collision in 1913 the railway inspectorate pressed for more widespread work on a standard form of ATC but did not push the case for the Great Western type. In the early 1920s the Ministry of Transport, now the railway regulatory authority, established a committee under the chairmanship of Col Sir John Pringle, Chief Inspecting Officer of Railways, to examine the whole question of ATC in order to reduce the numbers of accidents caused by drivers running past signals at danger. The team which reported in 1923 came up more with an expensive wish list of what was desirable rather than what was feasible, bearing in mind that the railways would have to pay for it. The prime requirement was for warning control at distant signals and train stop control at stop signals, the latter being considered of greater importance. The committee's findings were not entirely practicable though and a second committee was set up in 1928, again under the leadership of Sir John Pringle, to review progress and to have another look at the first report. Its findings, produced in 1930, had been simplified and recommended the adoption of ATC generally, improvements to signals, especially the adoption of colour lights, and more block controls to prevent signalmen's errors. While recognising the GWR ATC system, the committee noted the first moves to a non-contact system using magnetic induction.

The Hudd system

The Strowger-Hudd system employed magnets between the rails to induce the commands to the locomotive equipment. This was installed at distant signals and used two magnets, first a permanent magnet which triggered the locomotive equipment to a warning indication with horn and brake application on every occasion, and the second an electro-magnet about 50ft further on which, if the signal was clear, was energised to cancel the warning horn and stop the brake application that had been started by the permanent magnet. If the distant signal was at caution the electro-

magnet was not energised, the horn continued to sound and the brake application made until the driver acknowledged the warning and operated the cancelling handle which reset the system.

While the Hudd system did not distinguish between the sound for caution (long horn) and that for clear (short horn) an essential improvement over the GWR system was the visual indicator in the cab. This consisted of a circular all-black display for a signal at clear, and a black and yellow spoked display after the driver had acknowledged an ATC warning reminding him that the last signal was at caution. The locomotive equipment for Hudd was fairly simple as there was no locomotive electrical circuit but only an armature-operated pneumatic valve. When the engine passed over the permanent magnet the poles of the armature were attracted to open the vacuum pipe to atmosphere through the horn, but when passing the energised electro-magnet or when the driver acknowledged the warning, the armature on the engine was reset to close the valve and stop the brake application and horn. It was purely a magnetic/pneumatic system.

After the second Pringle report the LMS and Southern railways each tried experimental Hudd units in 1931/2 and both found it successful. However, the Southern felt its money would be better spent on providing more colour light signalling which was another of the Pringle findings. The LMS did nothing at the time but five years later decided to use the system on the London, Tilbury & Southend line which, with its proximity to the River Thames, suffered badly from fog and was a fairly self-contained route. With the intervention of the Second World War, it took ten years to install the system which was completed just a few months before Nationalisation in 1948. The LNER was interested but did nothing until after the major collision at Castlecary on the Edinburgh–Glasgow line when it decided to use the system on that route. Only a few locations had received the track magnets before the Second World War stopped further progress and it was not resumed afterwards.

BR Automatic Warning System

As a new era dawned with the Nationalisation of what had become British Railways in 1948, the newly formed Railway Executive soon took the long awaited step (from the Railway Inspectorate's view) of adopting automatic train control generally. The Executive was unhappy about extending a system that was already 40 years old if it took on board the GWR mechanical contact pattern ATC for new installations on other lines. The Hudd system appeared to be successful on the LTS line but it too had disadvantages, particularly the same audible horn for both caution and clear, even if they were long and short notes. Both systems had features which had been proved in service and it seemed logical to combine the best elements of the

GWR and Hudd systems, namely the GWR horn and bell indications and the Hudd magnetic induction from the track. Initially, the BR proposals did not include the Hudd visual indicator. With magnetic induction, to obtain the bell signal for clear needed a power supply from a battery on the locomotive as on the GWR pattern. The first trials were conducted on the East Coast Main Line between New Barnet and Huntingdon in which Hudd permanent and electro-magnets were retrieved from store in Scotland, unused from the pre-war Edinburgh–Glasgow ATC plans, together with Hudd locomotive receivers and GWR cab equipment. The track magnets were placed at 5ft centres, much closer together than on the LTS Hudd scheme, the permanent magnet first to trigger the warning followed

Some of the signals involved in the double collision at Harrow in October 1952. The nearer signal is the up slow home signal, the right hand arm of which was clear for the 7.31am Tring to Euston to cross from the slow to the fast line. In the background is the up fast home No. 2 signal passed at danger by the Perth train together with home No. 1 behind the photographer. (Geoffrey Kichenside)

The horrific results of the double collision at Harrow & Wealdstone on 8 October 1952 in which 112 people died. Automatic train control, as it was then called, would probably have prevented it but only the Great Western had adopted ATC widely during the preceding 40 or so years. Just one other line at that time had ATC of a new pattern, the LMS line to Tilbury and Southend.

by the electro-magnet to cancel it if the signal was at clear. It was not that simple though and many problems emerged during these early trials. Magnet technology had improved no end during the Second World War and new aluminium cobalt alloy permanent magnets were much more powerful than the long bar Hudd type, to an extent that a new magnet only $4\frac{1}{2}$in long was needed. This could be mounted vertically so that only one pole was inducted to the locomotive unlike the Hudd system where both poles played a part. With the smaller permanent magnet and the electro magnet also vertical with its casing taken down into the ballast the new magnets were still closer, at 2ft 6in centres fixed over three sleepers. The earth's magnetic field also played a part in the new design for it was found that better results were obtained in the electro-magnet if the poles in the two magnets were reversed from the Hudd system.

While the trials were in hand the Harrow disaster occurred on 8 October 1952 in which three trains collided, with 112 passengers killed and 157 injured. An up overnight sleeping car train from Perth, the same service that was involved in the Bourne End derailment seven years earlier, on a misty morning did not slow down after passing a colour light distant signal at caution, and ran past the semaphore outer and inner home signals at danger and into the back of a standing local train. Within a minute or so a down express ran into the wreckage. If anything was to focus attention on the need for automatic train control this was it. With television news coverage, the entire country saw the devastating results in much more detail than had ever been given by newspaper photographs or cinema newsreels of earlier rail accidents. Press coverage was enormous and when details leaked out of ATC trials on a train from King's Cross just nine days later, the press was out in force and the one thing which stood out in the photographs was the visual indicator in the cab which had been included despite the edict from on high that it was not needed.

By the time the Chief Inspecting Officer of Railways, Lt Col G. R. S. Wilson, produced his report into the Harrow accident a year later he was able to say, that once he approved the new standard form of BR automatic warning system (AWS) as it came to be called, it would be installed in a five-year programme to the principal main lines. It would then continue on other lines as resources became available in following years. But it was to be three more years before the system gained official approval and several years more before technical developments would allow the Southern to accept the system on its electrified lines. There were technical problems relating to the traction supply and its effect on the AWS magnets, and hardly had the system got the go-ahead in 1956 when there was another major disaster a year later. Ironically, this was on a Southern electric route with colour light

The cab equipment of BR standard ATC, or AWS as it was to be known, consisted of a bell for clear and a horn for caution, an acknowledgement handle, and prominent in this photograph, the visual indicator showing all-black after passing a clear distant signal or spoked yellow and black as a reminder that the driver had acknowledged a caution warning. (BTC)

signals, when the driver of a Cannon Street–Ramsgate steam train, running in thick fog, did not see two signals when approaching St Johns which displayed double yellow and single yellow, and passed the next signal which his fireman saw at red just before the train collided with the back of a standing electric train, 138 yards ahead. The collision brought down a heavy girder overbridge on top of the wreckage. Both trains were well overcrowded and it was hardly surprising that 90 people died and over 170 were injured. Almost certainly, AWS would have prevented such an accident. Thus in two accidents alone within a space of five years, over 200 passengers had been killed and more than 350 injured, to a greater or lesser extent, all for the want of a cab warning system about which the railways, with the principal exception of the GWR, had been prevaricating for over 40 years.

AWS did come in the late 1950s though, and by the following decade had been adapted to work on

An A4 class locomotive passes over the track magnets of the BR AWS system. The receiver on the locomotive is triggered by the first permanent magnet to give a warning but if the signal is clear the electro-magnet is energised and transmits a clear signal to the locomotive equipment. (BTC)

Installing track magnets of the BR AWS system. The electro-magnet is in place and the initial permanent magnet is being lifted into position just ahead of the protective ramp. (BR, LMR)

Southern electric routes and on the newly electrified West Coast Main Line along with multiple aspect colour light signalling. The magnets were normally placed about 200 yards on the approach side of the signal to which they applied. Nevertheless, AWS still followed the original principles of giving only caution or clear indications, and in multiple aspect signalling for any aspect other than green the caution warning was given, as it still is, and that has raised new problems as forecast in the past by many opponents of cab signalling, ATC or AWS, call it what you will. This is the danger of repetitive cancellation when a second train running fairly closely behind a first, gets double yellow after double yellow with AWS warnings at every one which the driver duly acknowledges. Then the first train stops, the second train gets a single yellow and then a red, with the same AWS warnings which the driver again acknowledges but it does not register in his mind that he is approaching a red signal and too late, runs past into collision with the train ahead. It also introduced the problem of what has become known as 'ding-ding and away' collisions which to an extent, have been allied to unconscious AWS acknowledgement. Here, a train arrives at a station with the platform starting signal showing red because of another conflicting train move ahead so that the driver will have acknowledged at least two and possibly three AWS warnings before coming to a stop in the platform. The AWS magnets for the starting signal will usually have been 200 yards on the approach side of the signal so that after making the acknowledgement of the warning the train stops for station work. The passengers are on, the doors are closed and the guard gives the double ring on the starting bell or buzzer, or the platform staff give the right away and the train restarts. But the signal is still at danger, and without properly checking the signal, the driver starts away and into collision. In the last three decades there have been a number of accidents from these causes arising from the combination of simple two-indication AWS and multiple aspect signalling. In his report on the Harrow collisions, Lt Col Wilson stated that AWS must always be regarded 'as an auxiliary to personal observation of the signals, and not as a substitute for it'. We shall be looking at the ideas for overcoming problems of unconscious cancellation in a later chapter on automation.

Just before leaving this chapter on automatic train control, we have described in detail the various forms of warning given to drivers at distant signals and have mentioned proposals for some form of controls at stop signals. On the main line railways stop signal control has not been adopted widely although the systems devised by Raven and Bound have been noted. In Chapter 8 we mentioned the early signalling on London's Underground railways on which it was recognised that some form of positive stop control was essential to prevent an underground collision which, in the confined space, would be far more devastating than on open line. The main form of control was and still is the train stop trip arm with ground equipment consisting of an arm which, when the signal is at danger, is in an almost vertical position a few inches above rail level and just outside the right hand running rail. If a train runs past the signal at danger the ground arm engages a corresponding pivoted arm mounted on the leading bogie and pushes it back and in so doing cuts the current to the traction motors and opens an air valve to apply the brakes. After the train stops the driver can reset the arm by pulling on a cord which restores the arm to the running position. When the signal is clear the ground arm is lowered to below rail level and allows the train to pass without being stopped by the trip. Some of the early ground apparatus had a mechanical link to the signal, while later ones were operated by electric motors or electro-pneumatically. BR itself uses the trip arm system on three of its routes, between Camden and Watford on local lines also shared with London Underground trains, Moorgate and through the Mersey Tunnel on its Wirral line, and a few other trains in steam and diesel days have been so fitted for working on London Transport lines.

Having gone past a signal at danger equipped with a train stop under stop-and-proceed rules or emergency running during engineering work, the train trip arm has to be reset before the brakes can be released. On London Transport at that time it meant the driver leaving the cab, carefully avoiding conductor rails and pulling the resetting cord. This 1956 view shows the procedure being put into practice at Hatch End on the Bakerloo Line service to Watford LMR. (Geoffrey Kichenside)

Chapter 14

THE PANEL
BOX DEVELOPS

IN THE 50 years from the end of the Second World War to the mid-1990s railway signalling in Britain has undergone a sweeping transformation. It has gone from the largely mechanical signalboxes controlling semaphore signals with a manually worked block system and just a tiny proportion of power worked signalling in the 1940s to the extensive power installations of today with track circuit block and the semaphore signal very much an endangered species. Mechanical signalling and semaphores still survive on BR even in the new world of privatisation and are now owned by a new organisation called Railtrack, giving information about the line ahead to drivers employed by train operating companies. Today, semaphore areas are largely in isolated, widely spaced pockets – Cornwall (where even in the 1990s GWR type lower quadrants were still being installed), South Wales Valleys (where upper quadrant semaphores made their appearance on a former GWR line at East Usk near Newport in 1992 because GWR parts were no longer available), the North of England, and Scotland.

We have already seen how power signalling developed from the turn of the century to the Second World War, and how following the adoption of the new four-aspect colour light code in 1925, the Southern pressed ahead with resignalling at its London terminus stations and the Brighton and Portsmouth main lines. But it was the LNER which set the pattern for what followed with its route relay interlocking in its new signalling at Thirsk, Leeds, Hull and Northallerton in the 1930s. The war delayed further progress but by the end of the 1940s, the Liverpool Street–Shenfield electrification scheme had been completed and was accompanied by resignalling which included a new breed of signalbox – the panel box, developing the themes already established by the LNER but on a larger scale. Much of the signalling at intermediate stations on the line out to Shenfield was from existing signalboxes adapted into what were known as hybrid boxes. These retained mechanical operation of points by the old style levers but controlled signals from switch panels, usually mounted above the lever frame. The most complex

areas were given new panel signalboxes although they were of varying types supplied by different contractors. Just as in the last century, when a number of signalling contractors became prominent in the field of mechanical signalling and in inventions of new safety devices which later became commonplace, so too in the second half of the 20th century have a number of contractors been noted for their involvement in British Railways resignalling schemes and related to specific developments. While common principles have evolved, very often exact methods of achieving the end result have been different. Moreover with private sector industry being what it is there have been the inevitable takeovers, mergers and the like over the years with a trend towards international conglomerates so that to label specific projects with company names as the principal contractor might not do justice to sub contractors or to the right divisions within a single organisation. With the introduction of computers into railway signalling a new generation of 'signal engineering contractors' (but in reality firms well versed in computer technology) has stepped into the long line of names involved in railway signalling.

Liverpool Street–Shenfield, 1949

The largest of the new signalboxes in the Shenfield electrification scheme was naturally that at Liverpool Street itself, able to signal 318 individual routes and taking over the work formerly handled by two mechanical boxes. It was the first route relay interlocking at any major terminus in Britain and with the smaller installation at Bethnal Green it was equipped with a one control switch (OCS) panel. The switches related to individual signals and were placed in their geographical position on the track diagram at their signal location. The switches were of the rotary pattern with up to eight positions, one for each route controlled from that signal. Operation of the switch set the complete route to the next signal, checking that track circuits were clear and that no conflicting route had been set already, changing points as necessary, and when they were proved to be in the right position and

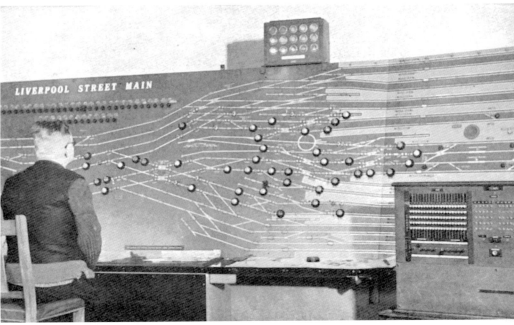

LIVERPOOL STREET MAIN

LEFT *Some of the signals for the Liverpool Street–Shenfield scheme were searchlights but multi-lens signals were also used, as here at Bow Junction, with a three-aspect signal with position 1, 2, and 4 junction indicators. (BR, ER)*

RIGHT *After its first ventures into relay interlocking with control panel operation in the 1930s, the Second World War delayed further expansion by the LNER into this form of control until the resignalling for the Liverpool Street–Shenfield electrification of the late 1940s. The new colour light signalling for the Liverpool Street station area and its immediate approaches was controlled from the new signalbox there which had three panels, one for the suburban lines, one for the main lines and one for the electric lines (the southernmost pair of tracks carried that designation). This is the panel for the main line tracks and platforms in the centre of the station. The route switches were spaced out geographically along the track diagram. (BR, ER)*

locked the signal cleared. The switches were not subject to any locking and were free to be turned at any time, but a route would only be set provided the track circuits were free and that no other conflicting route had already been set.

The new boxes at Mile End, Bow, and Stratford were given entrance–exit panels termed the NX system as a trade name by manufacturer Metropolitan Vickers–GRS Ltd. Today, NX seems to have passed into the language as a generic term for entrance–exit panels in much the same way as the name of a well-known brand of vacuum cleaner is often used rightly or wrongly to describe carpet cleaners generally. In the entrance–exit system the signalman turned a thumb switch situated on the track diagram alongside the signal it controlled and pressed a button on the track along which the train was to proceed, usually near the next signal ahead. Like its OCS counterpart the

interlocking relays would only set the route if the track circuits were free and no conflicting route had been set. The routes set were shown by movement of a point repeater on the track diagram in the form of pivoted elongated triangle at the points which, with magnetic operation switched from one side of the particular track to the other, gave the signalman a continuous visual line of the route set against the dark green background colour of the panel. At Goodmayes the Westinghouse OCS panel used a white light display along the portions of track with a route set up. All the panels showed track circuit occupation.

At first, each of the signalboxes had magazine type train describers but by 1952 the new permanent automatic train describers had been installed. These showed by a combination of letters denoting the class and destination of a train displayed in a panel above the track diagram a description which, once inserted into the system at Liverpool Street, was transmitted automatically from signalbox to signalbox. Moreover, this was transferred between instruments from one line to another if a train was switched say, from the down main to down electric lines. At that time the designation of tracks in and out of Liverpool Street was 'suburban', 'main' and 'electric', even though the main lines were electrified for local electric trains, and the electric lines were also used by steam trains. Signals were of both the four-aspect multi-lens type and searchlight pattern, the latter with an extra lamp unit to give the double yellow aspect, depending on location.

York, the largest relay interlocking
While all this work was going on in London, the North Eastern Region as the former North Eastern Area of the

LNER had become, was completing work on resignalling at York with what was then the largest relay interlocking in the world. It was an OCS installation controlling not only the station area but the lines 1½ miles south to Chaloners Whin Junction where the East Coast route to Doncaster diverged from the Leeds and Normanton route, and a mile or so north to Skelton Junction, a total of 33 track miles including loops, sidings, etc. In all it was able to set up 825 routes, nearly three times that of Liverpool Street, and took over the work formerly carried out by eight mechanical signalboxes with a total of 868 levers, including the very large York Locomotive Yard box

with a straight row of 295 levers. The indication panel was so large that it was formed of four panels angled around one side of the operating floor and quite impossible for the signalmen to reach the upper part. Thus the control switches were arranged in vertical banks on consoles in front of the indication panel. As on the GE main line from Liverpool Street, automatic train describers were provided, mounted above the indication panel and providing descriptions to and from the boxes at the extremities of the York control area.

In course of time these would be known as fringe boxes, a term adopted widely where existing signalboxes, mechanical or isolated power boxes became the adjacent boxes to a major power signalling area. Track circuiting usually extended to and from those boxes so that there was no manual block working and the signalmen in the major power boxes were not required to see – indeed they often could not see – the tail lamps of trains passing them to ensure the trains were complete, as required in boxes working manual block. Automatic train describer circuits often started or finished at the fringe box. In the direction away from the power box the fringe box usually worked the absolute block system with the normal exchanges of

LEFT *When York station was resignalled in the early 1950s the new relay interlocking replaced eight mechanical boxes including the largest, Locomotive Yard, with a straight run of 295 levers, the interior of which is seen here. Some of the block instruments were above the levers, others behind the signalmen on the desks to the left. (National Railway Museum)*

BELOW *The exterior of Locomotive Yard signalbox at York. (National Railway Museum)*

bell signals and block instrument indications, and telephone descriptions if need be.

'Control'

The York OCS power box was designed to be worked by four signalmen and a traffic regulator, compared with the staff for eight mechanical boxes, all working independently and relying on telephone communication for traffic regulation with adjoining signalboxes or 'Control' – that all-embracing office either hated or loved by signalmen all over the country. The Control Office was originally devised by the Midland Railway in the pre-First World War years to improve train operation and stop freight congestion because nobody knew what trains were running and where they were. By reporting train movements from strategic signalboxes to Control, the controllers knew where the trains were, and by knowing how many wagons were on a train and which sidings and loops were occupied, and which engines were hauling which trains, the control office system was able to have an overview of all the traffic on a route or in an area and whether extra trains were needed and how they were to be fitted in. On some railways, the control offices largely concentrated on freight traffic, while on others they had a more widely embracing role in train regulation as a whole, instructing signalmen to give this train precedence at a converging junction over that one, or to hold that train for a late running connection. Other railways left the train regulation function to the signalmen and as to holding connections, that was a

decision for the station inspector or stationmaster. The introduction of the power signalbox with wider control areas and with a traffic regulator as a supervisor began to nibble away at regulation decisions previously taken in the control office.

The other factor was staffing. Look at that level of signalmen, just four men plus a regulator on duty on a shift to control all the trains through York and its approaches. That was just one of the parts of the equation in the costs of a resignalling scheme such as this. The aim of any resignalling, apart from the need to renew life-expired equipment, was to obtain economy of operation, greater productivity from the staff, savings in train operating costs by fewer delays, and easier maintenance. It might not always be possible to obtain all benefits in all areas. Large power signalling schemes might need fewer signalmen but maintenance staff might have to be increased. Other factors in later years included simplification of track layouts, fewer tracks, fewer points, greater capacity with colour light signals on the remaining tracks although as we shall see, that did not always result in greater safety.

Interior of the new signalbox with relay interlocking at York, dating from the early 1950s. It controlled a total of 33 track miles. It was of the one control switch (OCS) type where each route from signal to signal was controlled by one switch and if several routes lay beyond a signal each had its own switch. The switches can be seen in banks on the console beneath the signalmen's hands. The track diagram had track circuit indications and at the top are the train describer displays. (BR, NER)

The 1955 Modernisation Plan

While these former LNER schemes were going ahead, despite their leap into new technology, the other Regions (as the former railways had become), continued for a few more years with more conventional equipment, miniature lever frames still being employed on the Southern on its new Brighton line signalling through Croydon, and the London Midland with its new Euston power box, which a year or two after opening was also fitted with automatic train describers from Camden, although not quite so advanced as those at Liverpool Street.

Quite where railway modernisation was to go was in abeyance for a few years until March 1955 when the BR Modernisation Plan was announced. No less than £1,240 million was allocated for new diesel locomotives and multiple units, electrification of certain routes including the East and West Coast main lines from King's Cross and Euston respectively to the north, extension of electrification on the Southern and resignalling of many routes with power operation, the signalling element being allocated £105 million. This was the impetus needed for the start of a programme for wholesale resignalling on many routes and as it progressed, it brought advances in technology, particularly in the late 1950s with remote control

Fig. 29. *The new power signalboxes for the opening stages of the West Coast electrification from Manchester to Crewe in 1959, introduced new pattern train describers in which a four-character train description code consisting of a figure for the class of train, letter for the destination area, and two figures for individual train number or route number in the case of local trains, was displayed on the track diagram and stepped from aperture to aperture in line with track circuit occupation. There were various methods of achieving the displays and included edge-lit perspex and miniature cathode ray tubes.*

developments, train describers, the introduction of electronics and then a decade or so later computers. Initially these were for information gathering and dissemination, but then gradually they moved into the control of signalling. By the 1980s solid state technology and then computers had entered the world of interlocking and that was a whole new ball game as we shall see in Chapter 16.

The first of the new signalling allied to route improvements was for the start of the London Midland electrification south from Manchester to Crewe as stage 1 in 1959. This was followed by Liverpool to Crewe and then progressively south to Euston by the end of 1965. The new signalboxes at Manchester London Road, (although the station was renamed Piccadilly) and Sandbach, both with OCS panels, introduced new terminology into signalling like 'remote controlled satellite interlockings', and 'four-character train describers'. Right from the beginning of interlocking in 1860, the interlocking frame was part of a signalbox. A signalbox had levers and those levers were mechanically interlocked by equipment in the lower half of the frame under the floor. But with relay interlocking, the relays that provided the safety function preventing conflicting routes from being set together and ensuring that signals and points agreed, did not have to be right under the control panel. Indeed, it would have been difficult to put them under the panel except for the smallest and simplest of control panels and the new style panel boxes by intention were not normally to be small and simple if they were to provide the benefits of scale. So relays went into relay rooms alongside the operating floor or underneath it. The connection with the panel controls was by electric cables which meant in practice that the relay room could be sited in a location away from the operating room or one control panel could be linked to more than one relay room.

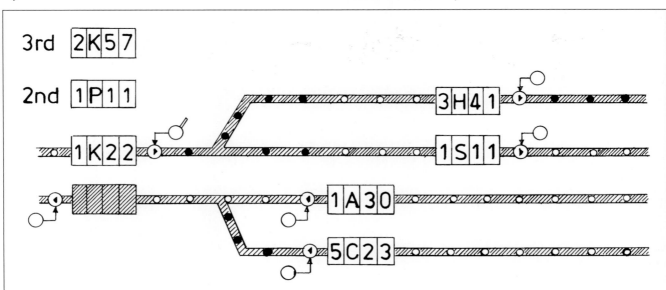

TOP *The architectural styles of the first of the 1950s Modernisation Plan power signalboxes were not over inspiring and many were just rectangular boxes utilising then new prefabricated constructional methods. This was Manchester London Road controlling the renamed Piccadilly station and its approach routes. It was replaced in 1988 by the New Manchester Piccadilly signalling centre. (BR, LMR)*

MIDDLE *The Modernisation Plan resignalling schemes involving relay interlockings, went in a series of steps as far as control methods were concerned. This signalbox at Wilmslow was what might be called the first generation of standard control consoles, the one-control switch type in which all the switches for the various routes beyond a specific signal were banked in vertical rows. The train describer apertures can be seen along the track diagram. (BR, LMR)*

BOTTOM *Smallest of the Modernisation Plan power signalboxes was that at Weaver Junction, where the Crewe–Liverpool route diverged from the West Coast Main Line. This utilised an entrance–exit panel but the train describer displays were on a separate panel. It was intended that the interlocking here would eventually be incorporated into a larger scheme controlled remotely but it lasted until 1997 when its controls were taken over by nearby Hartford Junction. (BR, LMR)*

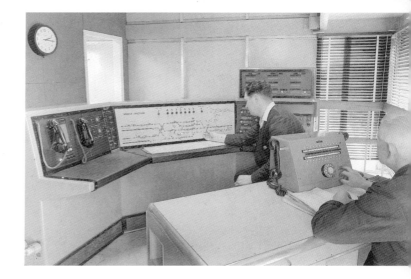

Most railway routes sub-divide into areas with points and crossings either between parallel tracks or at route junctions or stations, or with links to sidings and yards or depots, where interlocking is needed. These are interspersed with lengths of plain track with signals controlled automatically from track circuits without any need for interlocking. While some of the satellite interlockings were worked by direct wire from the control panel, newly emerging forms of remote control systems had begun to make their appearance in which one pair of wires could carry numerous instructions by using different carrier frequencies for each circuit, each being scanned in turn on a time basis to link the transmitting and receiving ends. If in the scanning cycle, which was undertaken in milliseconds, a change was detected in the status of one of the input circuits, as for example the route setting buttons had been operated to set up a route from one signal to the next, the transmission, which included an address code, sent that information to the corresponding output equipment in the remote relay room, causing the relays for the route in question to initiate the setting sequence. When the route had been set and the signal cleared, the relay room sent back the junction information through the return equipment to the control panel to show that the relay room interlocking equipment had responded. The process was known as time division multiplex (TDM) and it was to become the basis of the remote control of distant relay rooms and the means by which signalbox control areas were to become so large. Another form of remote control, frequency division multiplex (FDM) could carry simultaneous transmission instructions over a single pair of wires by using different frequencies for the individual circuits. TDM

The relay interlocking at Willesden commissioned in 1965 showing the plug in relays. Some schemes had free-wired plug bases but many relay interlockings of that time made use of what was called geographical circuitry in which pre-wired sub bases were arranged with the relays in their geographical positions for the equipment they controlled. (BR, LMR)

was normally used for route setting while FDM was used for such functions as ground frame releases, and control and supervision of automatic signalling.

An interlocking was now an entity in its own right but needed a control panel somewhere to control it. Larger signalling control areas meant more problems if things went wrong and as a back up many remote interlockings had their own emergency stand-by control panels which could be switched in and operated on the spot if there was a major failure in the link from the main signalbox. They also had technician's panels so that in the event of a fault the technician could see what was displayed on the panel and also had fault alarms and indications to show what had gone wrong. Satellite interlockings within a mile or so of the controlling signalbox would normally have been direct wired, that is one wire pair for each function, but at greater distances then it was more economic to use a remote control link which needed vastly fewer wires.

The train describers in the new Manchester London Road signalbox, and the other boxes controlling the electrified line to Crewe, also took a step forward almost literally from the automatic describers used at Liverpool Street and down to Shenfield seven years earlier. The new displays were in apertures on the track diagram along each line in the signal sections concerned. The four-character alpha numerical code forming the train number included an initial figure to denote the class of train based on the traditional train classification numbers (1 – express passenger, 2 – ordinary passenger, 3 – parcels or empty trains, 6, 7, 8, freight trains with varying brake power and loads etc), a letter to denote destination area, and two figures to give a unique train number or in the case of local trains a route number. Once fed into the system at the starting station by the signalman operating buttons on the panel, the four-character train number would pass from aperture to aperture along the signalbox track diagram following track circuit occupation. When the train reached the end of the control area for that signalbox it disappeared from the last aperture and stepped

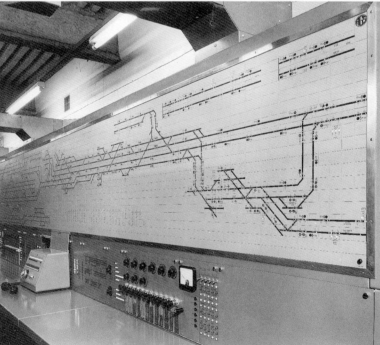

Many of the larger power signalboxes of the 1960s had separate technician's panels for fault finding when equipment failed and by a process of elimination could narrow down the faulty unit for replacement. This one was at Saltley which was unusual at that time in having no remote interlockings and with vital fail-safe links to remote parts of its control area. In some of the latest signalling centres with computer technology a print out or display will alert the technician to which component needs replacement so making fault finding so much easier. (BR, LMR)

automatically to the next signalbox ahead where, if it had the same type of equipment, the description again stepped from aperture to aperture.

Despite these developments they were not adopted universally across BR because each Region had its own signal engineering department with a fair amount of autonomy at that time. Moreover the time factor in progressing plans for a new scheme had an effect, for in the late 1950s and early 1960s the type of equipment provided in new signalboxes depended to a large extent on the current thinking and practice at the time the scheme was approved. This was nowhere more obvious than on the Southern Region for the first phase of the Kent Coast electrification via Chatham (the former LCDR routes) which involved resignalling including London area lines. Three new power signalboxes out of the eight commissioned for that scheme in 1959/60 will serve to illustrate the variations, for Shepherds Lane near Brixton was given a miniature lever frame, Beckenham Junction had an entrance–exit panel, and Chislehurst Junction had an OCS panel. But none of them had the new style four-character train describers on the track diagram like the contemporary LMR signalboxes and they continued with the magazine describers. These were still being installed by the Southern two years later for Kent Coast phase two covering the former SER line via Sevenoaks, Tonbridge, and Ashford, although at least the new boxes for this part of the scheme had entrance–exit panels.

Entrance–exit panels become the standard

During the next two decades the entrance–exit type panel became the norm, although there were variations in that some had combined control and indication panels and others had a separate control panel, either in independent consoles or in front of the main indication panel. The Western Region continued the early practice of using a rotary switch for the first movement by the signalman in starting to set a route and then pressing a button to say which route was wanted. In most other entrance–exit panels the initial switch had become a button and moreover, each button except the first and last on a panel, had a dual function as an exit button for the previous section and an entrance button for the forward section. In setting a route a signalman would press an entrance button, then the exit button for the route to be set, that button was then pressed a second time as an entrance button and then the next exit button on the required route was pressed, and so on.

Apart from the route setting buttons the panels included individual three-position point operating switches, normal, auto, and reverse with the switch left in the centre auto position to allow route setting buttons to be used. Occasionally signalmen needed to operate points individually. Other switches or buttons provided releases for ground frames or for level

At the end of the 1950s and into the early 1960s the Southern Region resignalling schemes were caught in the various advances in technology and practices as described in the text. The new signalbox at Tonbridge, seen here, for the second stage of the Kent Coast electrification of 1961 had an entrance–exit panel but had magazine type train describers. It also controlled Paddock Wood station six miles away by direct wire circuitry instead of remote control. Just over 30 years on, in the early 1990s, Tonbridge was again resignalled but under the control of the new Ashford IECC.

A close view of part of the Nuneaton entrance–exit panel showing the route setting buttons and four-character train describers at Abbey Junction. The buttons with a single solid arrow on the button head are entrance buttons, the ones with an open arrow are exit buttons and those with two arrows are both entrance and exit buttons, first pressed after a preceding entrance button, and then pressed a second time as an entrance button for the next section ahead. The buttons marked 'A' are for setting signals 2 and 4 to work automatically when points 202, 203, and 204 are set for the straight route. (BR, LMR)

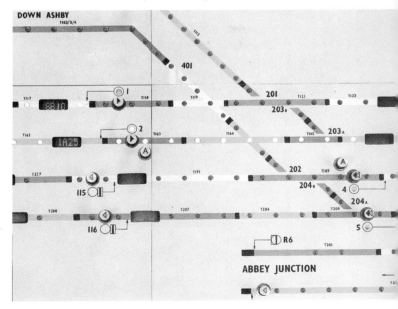

New centralised power signalling schemes brought new thinking on level crossing operation. At some locations signalboxes were converted to crossing boxes to operate full barriers on site, at others barriers were controlled from distant power signalboxes with closed circuit television (CCTV) supervision. On less important roads automatic half barriers (AHB) were used as here, with the barriers lowered automatically after a yellow/flashing red light sequence to road users. After the major level crossing collision at Hixon AHB in 1968 when a train hit a low loader carrying a transformer, more stringent rules for installation and operation were introduced in 1970. (BRB)

crossings where they were controlled by a signalbox at the site but which had been reduced in status to a crossing box, or in conjunction with closed circuit television, full barriers could be controlled direct from the panel. With a rolling programme to eliminate old style gated level crossings that needed someone on site to control the gates and the railway signals, converting them to automatic half barriers or, on lightly used lines/roads, to automatic open crossings, power boxes gradually took over the supervisory role for such crossings within their control area. Road users wishing to cross the lines with exceptional loads or animals were required to telephone the signalbox for permission. As to the panels themselves the early ones had the track diagram depicted on large sheet sections with the apertures for lights and controls cut out, but later the modular mosaic type became general in which small plug-in units with plain line, point sections, control button sections, etc were mounted on a grid to form the complete track diagram. The modules varied in size according to the supplier but typical was the Integra Domino type at 40mm square. The advantage of the plug-in units was the ease of making alterations to cater for later track changes.

Many automatic signals had emergency restoration buttons on the panel to allow the signalman to place them to danger in the event of trouble. In contrast, many controlled signals at junctions were given an auto button on the panel which, when operated, allowed the signal to work automatically for the principal route until such time as the signalman wanted to use the junction points for the other setting and cancelled auto working. White route set lights became standard so that signalmen could see what routes had been set for trains and red lights replacing white showed which track circuits were occupied by trains.

Ground and shunting frames

The reference to ground frame releases emphasises the changing role of the signalbox from the 1960s in that with more centralised power operated control, cost was a vital factor. Not all points and signals used only occasionally came under the direct control of the new power signalboxes even though they were within its overall control area. Emergency crossovers for example, between up and down lines, would not normally be used from one week to another. In the days when practically every station had its own signalbox then these crossovers were directly worked. So too were connections from goods yards and sidings to the main lines even if they were only required perhaps once a day by the local pick-up goods. It was hardly economic to provide all the relay and possibly remote control equipment for full relay interlocking covering a siding or yard used once a day or an emergency crossover perhaps once in six months. These connections were therefore directly controlled by ground frames, or by what were known as shunting frames at the site, often the former mechanical signalboxes adapted for a new role but without any all-day function controlling the regular signalling. The ground or shunting frame would have a king or release lever which, when in its normal locked position, secured all the other levers so that points were set for normal running moves. The king lever was electrically locked and was released by the signalman in the power box operating the ground frame release switch. That could only be done provided no conflicting route was already set or in use on the panel. Once the ground frame release had been given that in turn barred the setting of any conflicting routes. The person operating the ground frame, who might be a shunter or train crew, could then operate the levers to work points (and related signals if provided).

Emergency override controls

Another feature of the newly emerging modern power signalboxes controlling remote relay interlockings by electronic systems was the override control. In the event of a failure of the remote control system between the signalbox and the distant interlocking it would not be

With centralised power signalboxes it was not economic to work the points and signals directly that gave access from main lines into little used goods yards and station sidings. Instead, some existing mechanical signalboxes were retained and adapted to work the siding and yard connections locally or new shunting frames were built, as here at Harrow. While the distant power signalling centre controlled through moves on the main running lines, when a button had been pressed or a switch turned to release the levers in the shunting frame, any conflicting main line signals were locked at danger. (Geoffrey Kichenside)

Where only one or two connections were involved, or for emergency crossovers between up and down lines, a small ground lever frame was all that was needed as here at Bushey. A 'king' lever (or here the middle two levers) in the ground frame would be released electrically from the main power signalbox, in this case Watford, and when pulled would release the interlocking for the points, and in some ground frames, the relevant signals. The levers in this frame are of the LNWR pattern with ring catch handles in front of the lever. The levers themselves have been capped with plastic to prevent rusting in the open air. (Geoffrey Kichenside)

possible for the signalman to set routes there or to receive indications. To avoid 'stopping the job' the signalman could operate override switches on his panel for the interlocking concerned which by-passed the failed communication link and established selected routes to work in automatic mode for principal services, which at least kept trains running. At some remote interlockings a local panel could be switched in to take over from the central panel, but this required someone who was competent to be available locally. One or two of the later power signalboxes were provided with duplicate remote control links to the satellite interlockings using separate routes for each system and override facilities were not deemed to be

necessary. The Waterloo area resignalling of 1989 is an example where this has been done.

Ever larger signalling control areas

During the 1960s and 1970s most of the principal main lines were resignalled with centralised power signalboxes. Control areas grew as remote control techniques were adopted more widely, but above all because miniaturisation of relays, now fast becoming the plug in type, and the gradual introduction of electronics and later computers, particularly for gathering and distributing information, train describers for example, meant that more equipment could be accommodated in a given size of building. Euston and

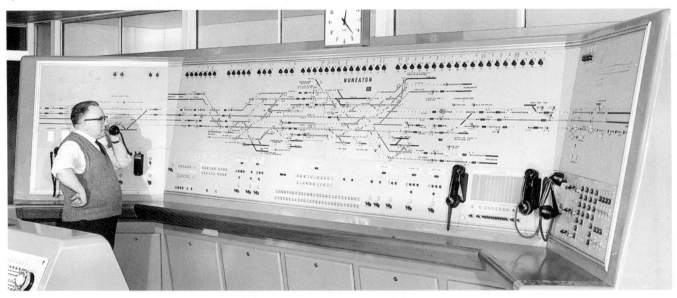

ABOVE *Although entrance–exit panels eventually became the fairly standard style of control they varied in details. Nuneaton had a combined control and indication panel. (BR, LMR)*

BELOW *Watford, by contrast, had a separate control console, the left of the two, with the indication panel standing back to show routes set, track circuit and train describer indications. (BR, LMR)*

Birmingham New Street signalboxes built as part of the LMR electrification in the 1960s both had space to spare in the relay room within the signalbox because small electrical equipment had become available after the box structure had been started.

The resignalling ball was really rolling by the 1960s. For the extension of electrification of the West Coast Main Line, the LMR announced plans for eleven new signalboxes, or signalling control centres as they were fast becoming. The term 'signalbox', with its connotations of an oversize wooden or brick garden shed with lots of windows, was hardly the right description for an air-conditioned, carpeted office with control consoles. This included a new control centre, as

Out on the line old and new signals have to stand alongside each other until the resignalling is complete. Where the old is still in use as here at Harrow in 1964 with the semaphore up starter, the new, Watford's four-aspect colour light signal WJ5, has a shield covering its lamps which remain invisible to drivers even though they may be working inside for test purposes. (Geoffrey Kichenside)

Resignalling schemes usually entailed a fair amount of upheaval especially when trains had to be kept running while stage work was commissioned. Sometimes temporary signalling had to be used when old mechanical signalboxes stood in the way of new realigned tracks and had to be demolished before new permanent tracks and signals could be installed. But some survived until the final changeover and then the old boxes, often with several decades of history behind them, had to go as here at Rugby No. 1. Equally, and particularly on the central parts of the West Coast Main Line between Nuneaton and Crewe, old mechanical signalboxes, several with structures or some equipment dating back almost to the turn of the century or even earlier, remain in service having been adapted to work modern signalling. (BR, LMR)

just mentioned, at Euston, barely eight years after the completion of the 1952 resignalling which had taken two decades to reach fruition but that scheme was not suitable to work with 25kV electrification. Immunisation became the new in-word, meaning to provide track circuits and other equipment that could not be falsely operated by stray 50Hz traction current. At Euston and right down to Watford that meant track circuits which could not be affected both by the dc return traction of the 'New Line' local tracks and the 50Hz of the 25kV main line system. Usually a track circuit frequency of $83\frac{1}{3}$Hz was employed which avoided the harmonics of 50Hz.

The Southern proposed to operate its entire Region from just 13 signalling centres, while the Western Region without any electrification proposals, pressed on with new signalling schemes, first with fairly small areas at Plymouth and Birmingham Snow Hill and then with larger schemes covering the main lines from Paddington to Bristol and South Wales, and by 1987 the West of England main line via Westbury to Exeter.

Meanwhile, the whole of the West Coast main line had been resignalled as part of the electrification,

Hand signalling with flags is sometimes employed during engineering work particularly if points are disconnected or locking disarranged. In some major resignalling schemes flag signalling was employed on changeover day when mechanical signalling had been removed and colour-lights had not been brought into use, as here at Harrow in 1964 when Watford power signalbox was being commissioned. During the changeover telephone block was used. (Geoffrey Kichenside)

Not all developments in signalling during the last 40 years have been for colour light signals and track circuit block. Here on the Newport–Shrewsbury line experiments were carried out with solar power for electrical AWS equipment at this distant signal near Craven Arms in the late 1970s. (Geoffrey Kichenside)

completed in 1974. North of Crewe saw some large control areas at such signalling centres as Warrington and Preston which contrasted to the earlier schemes south of Crewe to Nuneaton which had signalling controlled entirely from hybrid signalboxes where some of the existing mechanical boxes had been adapted to work new signalling. Some of those hybrid boxes are still in service and a few have structures which are well over 100 years old, with some of the surviving mechanical equipment almost as old. There were also contrasts in the modern power signalboxes built for the initial LMR electrification with one of the smallest entrance–exit panel boxes in the country at Weaver Junction, controlling little more than the running junction between the West Coast Main Line from Crewe heading for Warrington, and the Liverpool line. One of the largest is at Birmingham New Street, built in the mid-1960s, it took over the work of more than 30 mechanical boxes and today is one of the busiest signalling centres controlling a fairly compact area in Britain. Astonishingly, 30 years later it was designated as a listed building, worthy for its mid-1960s architecture!

However, nothing south of the border could compare with the vast schemes in Scotland where the new centre at Motherwell controlled the whole of the West Coast route from just north of the English border to the outskirts of Glasgow. Also, the Edinburgh signalling centre, completed in 1981, controlled a massive 230 or so route miles from the border near Berwick upon Tweed almost to the River Tay at Cupar in the north, and half way to Glasgow in the Forth-Clyde valley. In all just over 500 single-track miles are under Edinburgh's jurisdiction while on the English part of the East Coast Main Line, resignalled between the mid-1970s and 1991, just five signalling centres, at King's Cross, Peterborough, Doncaster, York and Newcastle, control nearly all the line from London to the Scottish border where it meets the Edinburgh control area. Three small control centres, at Morpeth, Alnmouth and Tweedmouth, re-equipped with modern controls and indications have been retained to work the numerous level crossings which are unsuited to automation.

The new signalling centres at York and Newcastle, completed in 1990/1, which replaced not only the previous 1950s power signalboxes at those locations but also many other signalboxes intermediately, were not of the same generation as the others on the route which pre-dated them. York and Newcastle entered the computer age and are known as Integrated Electronic Control Centres (IECC) and the interlockings use solid state technology. These developments are described in Chapter 16.

Even by the 1980s, information technology had developed to such a degree that train describers through processor control could be used to provide all sorts of detail, such as automatic train reporting to management offices with train delays printed out. Also, information supplied to stations for train indicators which by then, were in the form of television screens, and signalmen's enquiries on train running. No need for a signalman to telephone a neighbouring box, 'How's the 1.20 doing Jack?' with the reply, 'just got him offered from the junction'. Now it was possible for a signalman to key in a train number to the teleprinter and in seconds a print out would show the whereabouts of the train by reference to the nearest signal number even if it was in the control area of a neighbouring signalling centre, for the train describers were linked as one system.

Whatever modern technology has been introduced over the last half century there is little doubt that power based signalling has a shorter life than its mechanical predecessors. This is largely because electric cable insulation begins to deteriorate and small electrical components are not as robust as mechanical signalling parts which are often heavy steel castings. Some of the 1950s and 1960s power signalling was replacing mechanical signalling dating back to the past century, yet much of that power signalling has itself been replaced within 30 years. An added factor is that technology developments have brought new types of equipment which can bring both maintenance savings and better operation, whereas mechanical signalling was mechanical signalling whether in the 1890s or the 1950s. The leap forward has been from mechanical to power operation, and within power operation from simple electric techniques such as electric locks and relays, to micro-processors.

Waterloo – the last great panel scheme

Probably the last major resignalling scheme to use what might be termed conventional relay technology and a large entrance–exit panel was that provided for the

TOP *During the 1970s control centres for power signalling schemes became ever larger. On the East Coast Main Line Doncaster controls from Stoke Tunnel, between Peterborough and Grantham, north to a point almost half way between Doncaster and York in a large combined operating and indication panel, made up of a matrix of small plug-in panel sections. (BR, ER)*

ABOVE *Doncaster signalling centre controls several level crossings, some from the main panel, but five from a separate panel where the operator has repeater track diagrams, and the controls and monitors for the CCTV supervision of full barriers. (BR, ER)*

Waterloo area resignalling completed in 1989 with the actual control centre sited at Wimbledon. This was despite the advances towards solid state interlockings and computerisation of controls used on other schemes going ahead at the same time but, like some resignalling

Just three signalling centres control the main lines between London and Brighton. Victoria, seen here, looks after much of the complex of suburban routes in South London, London Bridge takes in the route towards Croydon and many of the South East suburbs, and Three Bridges controls the rest of the Brighton line from the Croydon area to the coast and many of the branches. A number of new features were beginning to appear in these 1970s schemes. Victoria included VDU monitors displaying portions of the track diagram for the supervisors, and Three Bridges included some reversible working and automatic junction setting. (Geoffrey Kichenside)

three decades before, the equipment in a particular scheme depended on the length of time it had been in the planning and approval stages and what was current then. The Waterloo scheme did at least include automatic route setting at certain junctions with the trigger taken from the train describer, processors for the TDM remote control system and the timetable computer database. Entrance–exit panels for new work are by no means a thing of the past for they are also being installed for modernisation of other signalling in the 1990s such as on the Waterloo–Southampton main line as part of the South West Investment Strategy for Signalling (SWISS) scheme which is likely to be on-going well into the next century.

Wimbledon control centre and its remote interlockings, and the new signalling centre at Crewe, completed four years earlier in what was known as a 'big bang' operation when the entire station was closed for several weeks while old tracks were removed, new ones installed, and the new signalling completed, set a pattern architecturally by using portable type or permanent industrial modular buildings at lower cost than buildings designed and constructed specifically for the purpose. This meant that the operating room was on the ground floor, but then since signalmen do not need to see the trains does it matter? The traditional upstairs operating room was merely following what had been standard on mechanical

boxes when it was necessary for the signalmen to see the trains.

Resignalling in the Highlands
Before leaving this survey of panel signalboxes of the latter half of this century it is worth a comment that not all modern resignalling schemes were large or complex. Some involved closing one signalbox and adding either intermediate block signals or automatic signals and transferring supervision to a neighbouring box. But one line, where something more was needed, was the Highland main line between Perth and Inverness. This had been double track for much of its life but was singled with occasional passing loops following the Beeching cuts in the early 1960s. By the end of the 1970s traffic needs were outstripping the line's capacity and a second track was restored between Blair Atholl and Dalwhinnie, a distance of 24 miles. Between those stations each track was divided into three sections with two intermediate block sections and one absolute block section worked by manual block. Each line was track circuited through the IB sections and the IB sections themselves were controlled by the signalbox to the rear so that Blair Atholl controlled the down line and Dalwhinnie the up. An emergency crossover was provided at Dalnacardock, the first IB section from Blair Atholl with a release for the ground frame given by both signalboxes. Except for the stop signals at each station which remained as semaphores, all other signals between them were two-aspect colour lights with separate distant and stop signals for the IB signals and the distants approaching each station.

Further north, over the 40 or so miles between Kingussie and Culloden Moor, which remained as a single line but with three new passing loops added to the existing four, track circuit block was installed controlled from the signalbox at Aviemore. Although the loops, except at Aviemore which retained most of its semaphore signals, were given colour light signals it was not MAS in its full meaning. Each passing loop was signalled in the same way with 40mph turnouts from the main to loop tracks and with both main and loop signalled for running in both directions. At the approach to a passing place was a two-aspect distant signal at braking distance from the home signal, a three-aspect colour light with a junction indicator, and this was followed on the loop line only by a two-aspect starting signal. There was no corresponding starting signal on the main line and for a train routed on the main track a green on the home signal was the driver's authority to proceed into the next single line section. When trains were to pass the first to arrive was signalled into the loop after passing a yellow distant, the home signal approach controlled from red to yellow with the junction indicator illuminated, to a stop at the starting signal showing red. The second train was signalled by the main line and could pass through without stopping, and when clear of the rear section the first train could be signalled out of the loop. Because there was no corresponding main line starting signal, the loop starting signals were approach lit for the specific direction of an approaching train signalled into the loop, otherwise the driver of a train on the main track would see an isolated red signal without a corresponding green for his own train.

Developments in multiple-aspect signalling (MAS)

Out on the line the basic three- and four-aspect colour light system has not changed in principle since its adoption in 1925 and with the widespread expansion of power signalling in the last 50 years is now used on nearly all main lines and many secondary routes. Additional aspects and altered practices have developed however, particularly allied to junctions. Although the meaning of the double yellow aspect into the 1930s effectively gave it a role as a junction distant signal, 'Attention run at medium speed, at a junction may indicate that points are set for a diverging route', that function was gradually eroded and after the Bourne End derailment in 1945 certainly that meaning disappeared from isolated colour light distants in otherwise semaphore areas. It was also becoming the practice in semaphore signalling, certainly at low speed junctions, not to provide splitting distants, the sole remaining distant signal being cleared only when the route ahead was set and cleared for the principal higher speed line.

So with multiple-aspect signalling it became the practice to display a single yellow on the signal preceding the junction home signal when the points were set for the low speed route and to hold the junction signal at red until the speed of the approaching train had been reduced, in theory, to the speed of the turnout. Only then would the junction signal clear to yellow, double yellow or green depending on the signals ahead, with the junction indicator lit. This was called approach control and it was adopted at nearly all low speed turnouts, low meaning 30mph or less from an otherwise higher speed main track. Approach control was fine in slowing trains down in theory, often the signals were over restrictive and were sited in some places well before the points to which they applied so

The use of colour light splitting distants originally developed from semaphore practice, where splitting distants were often employed for main line route junctions. Although the Great Western normally did not provide splitting distants if the diversion speed of the points was less than 40mph, at Northolt Junction on the Great Western–Great Central Joint Line, LNER regulations applied for the 25mph turnouts towards the Marylebone line from the Birmingham–Paddington route. Hence this array of distant signals at Northolt Junction West, reading from right to left, up main to Paddington, up main to Marylebone, up main to relief to Paddington, up main to relief to Marylebone (these last two applying over a main to relief crossover at Northolt Junction West), up relief to Paddington, up relief to Marylebone. In recent years the semaphore signals have gone, the track layout simplified and this route, carrying Chiltern Line turbo trains has been used for ATP trials (C. R. L. Coles)

On four-track sections of the 1960s West Coast Main Line electrification and resignalling with down/up, down/up tracks, signals were evenly spaced for fast and slow lines and many were suspended from these overhead gantries as here at Carpenders Park. (BR, LMR)

Siting of modern four-aspect signals on lines electrified on the overhead system has to allow for other structures including the overhead catenary masts, and on this curve the four-aspect signal has been bracketed out to be nearer the track. Notice the safety cage to prevent technicians from getting close to high voltage elements of the catenary. (BR, LMR)

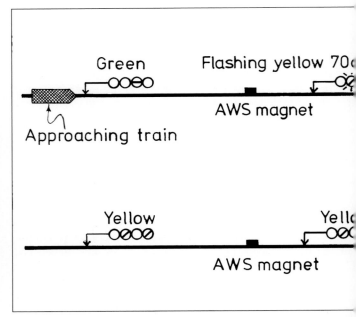

Fig. 30. *The aspect sequence as a train approaches a junction signalled with flashing yellow aspects.*

that drivers often accelerated again before reaching the points. Also drivers on regular trips through the same junctions became adept at anticipating the signal change from red and did not always slow to the required speed, getting caught out when the signal remained obstinately at red because of another train ahead or conflicting move, at best resulting in a signal passed at danger (SPAD) or at worst an accident. In more recent years the potential dangers of wrongly passing signals approach controlled from red have been recognised. Many have therefore been modified so that they now clear after the train has passed the previous signal at single yellow, at a point where the driver of an approaching train would have first sighted the junction signal at red and could see it change with the junction indicator illuminated. It is up to the driver to regulate his speed accordingly.

Although points suitable for higher speeds on the diversion have been used for many years from the 1940s or earlier at certain main line route junctions, the 50mph points at Wootton Bassett for example, (where the South Wales main line leaves the route via Bath to Bristol), increasing use since the 1960s of large radius points with 50, 60, or even 70mph on the diversion meant that approach control from red was totally unsuited for this type of junction. At these locations, originally approach release from yellow was provided by holding the signal beyond the junction at red. The driver would first encounter double yellow at the signal before the junction signal and sight the junction signal at single yellow with the junction indicator lit. The approach controls would then trigger the signal beyond the junction to step up to a proceed aspect assuming

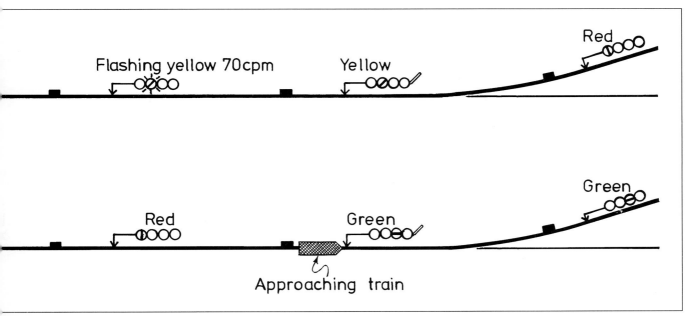

the line beyond was clear and the junction signal would step up in sequence. At junctions where the speed differential between the main and diversion track was less than 10mph there was no approach control and the junction signal could show green for either route on sight, with the junction indicator lit as necessary for the geographical left or right turn. The preceding signal gave no indication of which route was set and while from a speed point of view it did not affect safety, it caused no end of inconvenience if the wrong route was set. The train could not stop before taking the wrong route because the train was well past braking distance before the driver saw which route was shown on the junction signal.

Flashing aspects

In the mid-1970s, when the then new InterCity 125 trains were introduced, it was realised that with the superior brakes of the new trains a driver passing a double yellow thinking that he would have to stop at the second signal ahead, might approach a junction signal next ahead at single yellow with the junction indicator lit, travelling too fast for the turnout speed off the main line. Clearly a more positive form of junction distant signal was needed. It was decided to adopt flashing yellow aspects as an advanced warning of a route set for the diversion ahead. The first indication in four-aspect areas was a flashing double yellow, followed by a flashing single yellow at the next signal, and then at the junction signal itself by a steady yellow with the junction indicator lit, stepping up to a less restrictive aspect if conditions ahead allowed, once the driver was in a position to see the junction indicator or the whole signal. At first a complex set of speed bands was applied to both main and turnout speeds before flashing yellows could be used but in recent years the

speed conditions have been relaxed although normally the flashing yellows can only be used for one specified diversion ahead, usually the highest speed turnout. Where the junction signal applied to two or more turnouts the lower speed routes had the more restrictive approach controls applied.

Although splitting colour light distant indications have not been unknown over the last 50 years they have not been numerous. At Ely for example before the recent resignalling there was a triple colour light splitting distant. But in selected locations on high speed lines there has been a case for giving the driver a positive advanced indication of which route is set ahead and the splitting distant could well be used again. At Hayes on the main line out of Paddington, the new Airport Junction will have not only a splitting colour light distant, but in advance of that, a white light arrow pointing diagonally left when the points ahead are set for Heathrow Airport or vertically when set for the main line. The signalling here is also complicated with a high speed 70mph fast to slow crossover calling for flashing yellows. Could there be a case for a display of speed limit figures at signals preceding junctions? If cab signalling is adopted, like that through the Channel Tunnel, to be described later, then the indications on the driver's control desk show the permissible speed, so traditional route signalling may well have a speed element in it in future.

Junction confusion

With so many ways of telling a driver that the train is to be diverted off the principal main line at a junction ahead it is hardly surprising that today's junction signalling and the advance indications, if any, can lead to misunderstandings. At Colwich in September 1986, certainly the driver of a down Euston–Manchester

Piccadilly express became confused when the train was switched from the down fast line to the down slow on his right, as the first stage of a crossing move towards the line to Stoke-on-Trent. The junction here was unusual because the layout design provided a two-stage crossing from the down fast to the down Stoke line, first by switching a train from the down fast to down slow line and then 1,100 yards or so further on, by the down slow crossing the up fast to form the down Stoke line. It was done like this to allow a down Stoke line train to clear the down fast if a second train bound for the Crewe direction was not too far behind, and to give room for the down Stoke line train to be stopped on the down slow before the diamond crossing if a train was already signalled on the up fast from Crewe.

This was the situation on 19 September that year. The diversion from the down fast to down slow was preceded by flashing double and single yellows at the two signals before the junction signal itself which was showing a steady single yellow and the junction indicator. The next signal beyond the facing turnout was a normal four-aspect colour light 260 yards before

Not all lines with high voltage overhead electrification were completely resignalled with colour lights. At Wemyss Bay for the Glasgow South Clyde electrification in 1967 these semaphores were retained but with shortened arms to keep within the wire mesh protection and clearance limits from the overhead live wires. (Geoffrey Kichenside)

the diamond crossing, showing red for the Manchester train because an up Liverpool–Euston train had already been signalled on the up fast. The driver of the Manchester train became confused by the sequence of aspects and as he approached the signal protecting the diamond he thought it was approach controlled from red although of course no turnout was involved. Elsewhere, and if the line had been clear ahead at Colwich, the junction signal for the down fast to down slow points preceded by flashing yellows would have been approach controlled from yellow, so the seeds of approach control were already in his mind. But the signal protecting the diamond was not approach controlled then nor at any other time. It was at red firmly because another train had been signalled across the diamond in the opposite direction. The driver of the Manchester train realised too late that the signal was not going to clear, went past it braking hard and stopped with the front end of his electric locomotive just on the diamond crossing and with the up Liverpool train approaching at 100mph. The ensuing head-on collision resulted in a mound of eleven coaches derailed, overturned and piled one on another, but astonishingly not a single passenger was killed, the only fatality being the unfortunate driver of the Liverpool train. The accident was caused by an improper understanding of the signals by the Manchester driver which means he was not properly trained, and by the lack of rule book amendments for flashing aspects covering all the various applications. After the accident, the signalling sequence was altered so that flashing yellows were only used when the line was clear right through both halves of the junction.

As line speeds increased in the 1960s and 1970s so that 100mph was allowed on many sections of principal main lines, multiple-aspect signalling was spaced to give braking over two sections where four-aspect signalling was employed for locomotive hauled trains at 100mph. The new InterCity 125 diesel trains were designed to run at 125mph on parts of selected routes, namely the former GWR main line from Paddington and the East Coast Main Line from King's Cross. It might be thought that signal spacing would need to be altered but the superior braking of the IC 125s meant that they could stop in the same distance as a conventional train at 100mph and few signal alterations were needed. When the East Coast route was electrified in 1991 the new InterCity 225 locomotives were designed for 140mph running – 225 being the metric equivalent in kph. At 125mph they could stop as quickly as their diesel IC125 counterparts but at 140mph they needed a longer braking distance. Although they have not run in regular service at 140mph they have undertaken trials at that speed and to give that extra braking distance, a fifth aspect was used, flashing green, meaning line clear for at least three sections. A steady green indicated 'reduce to normal maximum line speed ready to act on more restrictive signal aspects ahead'. The aspect sequence to stop was thus flashing green, steady green, double yellow, single yellow, red. At a junction, flashing double yellow and flashing single yellow were in the sequence instead of steady double yellow, the steady single yellow being the junction signal itself. Certainly, what had been the simple four-aspect signalling code has been complicated by the need for the system to be all things to all men as a block signal with caution and stop indications, as a junction signal with advanced warnings, and as a speed signal without any definition of speed.

Shunting signals

Finally, the humble shunting signal deserves mention. Until the 1960s the Southern still used the disc signal in colour light areas for both ground shunting signals and as subsidiary signals under a main colour light head. The disc was electrically powered and rotated so that the horizontal red stripe across the white face was inclined up for clear. Then the Southern fell into line with the practice elsewhere of using position light shunting signals. These had three lights, red and white displayed horizontally for danger across the bottom of the signal and two white lights shown diagonally for proceed. The right hand white light was used for both danger and proceed indications. At locations where shunting moves could be made freely into a headshunt and where in mechanical signalling, a yellow disc would be used, a position light signal would have a yellow instead of a red light. Position light subsidiaries were similar but did not have a red light since the main red aspect above provided the stop indication. Position light type signals have also been used as 'limit of shunt' indications with double red horizontal lights.

Hot axlebox detectors

The control areas of some of the later panel boxes were so large that trains often ran long distances without being observed by signalmen and so automated detection systems were added to give warnings of a train defect, particularly hot axleboxes. The danger lay in the fact that a hot axlebox could break up and cause a derailment. Hot axlebox detectors were sited at the lineside at strategic locations and gave alarms in the controlling signalling centre identifying which axlebox was defective and giving the signalman a chance to stop the train and shunt it into a suitable siding or yard and remove the offending vehicle.

Track circuit problems

During the 1980s came the first signs of a revival of an old problem that track circuits could be vulnerable to false operation by the increasing use of lightweight diesel trains, combined with rail surface contamination from such things as leaf mulch from trees overhanging the line. Good track circuit operation relies on a clean rail surface and wheels, and enough weight for the wheels to make good electrical contact with the rails to shunt the track relay. In GWR days, diesel railcars could not be relied on to operate track circuits and the same problem showed itself with modern BR types. To overcome the difficulties BR trains were fitted with track circuit actuating equipment feeding a current from the train into the track to enhance the correct operation of the track equipment.

Another factor is electrical or electronic interference from electric train control and traction systems in which, under fault conditions, enough stray current might be passed from the train through the wheels to the rails and falsely energise the track relay. The latest electric multiple unit trains, including the 'Eurostars', with three-phase traction motors working from the third rail system, have had to be fitted with monitoring equipment to cut the traction supply if a sufficiently strong current returning to the rails likely to interfere with track circuits is detected. As we shall see in Chapters 15 and 16, other forms of train detection have already been used on some lines and further developments with radio detection are contemplated in the future.

Chapter 15

THE
METRO WAY

FOR NEARLY 80 years until the end of the 1970s there were only two railway systems in Britain which would fall within the category of what today many call a Metro service, the London Underground and the Glasgow Underground. The exact terminology which has developed over many years to describe a railway which primarily serves an urban area, or within a city, having closely spaced stations a few hundred yards apart, and with trains, normally electric multiple units, every few minutes and often operated by a local transport authority, comes from a variety of sources. Probably the longest established is 'metropolitan', meaning belonging to a metropolis and usually now abbreviated to metro. Others are, 'rapid transit', coined in North America, the 'elevated' from the inner city lines carried largely on viaducts like the one-time Liverpool Overhead Railway in Britain but again deriving from North America, the obvious 'underground' from London and Glasgow, and from Germany the 'S-Bahn' and France the 'Regional Express'. Neither of these latter two terms has yet found a base in Britain but they effectively define a longer distance outer suburban service running at higher speeds than their inner city counterparts and could well have a future British application. There are also various marketing or brand names, some based on the established terms, used locally hence the capital U of the Underground systems in London and Glasgow. Then there are trams. But this book is not about trams. Trams usually have little formal signalling and run on sight. How then do you describe Manchester's new Metrolink which certainly has street running but it also travels at higher speeds through the outer suburbs on former British Rail tracks and has lineside signals?

The truth is that today there is a very fuzzy distinction between the traditional heavyweight suburban railway, the underground, metro, rapid transit, light rapid transit and tram. In Britain now we have systems which overlap into more than one of these descriptions and in signalling, their needs are related. For simplicity we will use the term metro to embrace all the variations as a sort of middle ground.

The expansion of metro systems in the British Isles took place in the 1980s although planning had begun during the previous decade, but with much prevarication in funding arrangements between national and local government in some cases. First on the scene was the Tyne & Wear Metro serving Newcastle and surrounding areas, taking over former BR lines but with new underground sections and a new bridge across the River Tyne. It was opened in stages between 1980 and 1983. More or less concurrently came a system in Ireland, the Dublin Area Rapid Transit line (DART) opened in October 1984 which, in bringing main line trains into the highly automated signalling system of the DART suburban electric trains, took the Irish railways ahead of main line signalling in current use on British Rail. The Docklands Light Railway in London followed in 1987 and although it was linked with London Transport, its concept was totally unlike anything on the London Underground system. Then into the early 1990s Manchester's Metrolink trams came into service. Other tram/light rapid transit schemes followed, next being Sheffield, but this was entirely based on street running with on-sight operation, while systems for Croydon, the West Midlands and elsewhere are in hand.

The Glasgow Subway

The Glasgow Underground, originally known as the Subway, is unique in Britain because of its gauge, 4ft, and small 11ft diameter tunnels. It was originally cable worked with two car trains, both with grippers in which the driver applied them to the cable to start the train and released them to stop at a station. While the cars could run singly, when working as a pair only the front one gripped the cable and the cars had air brakes. The line was, and still is, a double-track circular route about six miles long with sharp curves and steep gradients of as much as 1 in 18 to pass under the River Clyde. The cars were free to clamp on and leave the cable which ran continuously at about 13mph so a signalling system was needed. The cars were lit electrically, picking up current from a pair of conductor wires on the side of the tunnel through wiper arms. Although this was not at first a factor in the signalling arrangements it was to be used so in later years.

Each station was equipped with a semaphore starting signal on the tunnel end wall worked from a lever at the station. The lever was electrically released when the train ahead had moved on from the next station and operated a treadle which placed a block indicator at 'line clear' at the first station and released the lever lock. Treadles were situated in a similar position at every station and served a dual function, placing the signal immediately behind the train to danger and releasing the lever of the one behind that. In 1935 the line was electrified on the third rail system and given new signalling with two-aspect colour lights, but because the line had steel sleepers conventional track circuiting was not possible. The cable cars were given traction motors and continued in service. While treadles were still used to place the signal immediately behind the train to danger the lighting conductors were used in the signalling controls. An isolated section was provided approximately 100 yards beyond each station, more at some locations and less at others, and when the wiper arms of the train entered the isolated section a relay was energised which cleared the starting signal at the previous station. Trip apparatus was added and small control panels provided at each station to control the signalling in an emergency.

This system lasted until 1977 when the entire railway was closed for rebuilding – the cars alone were already 70 years old – with new trains, slab track with the rails mounted on a solid concrete base, signalling, power supply, and depot connections, reopening in 1980. The colour light signals and trainstops were renewed, ac track circuits controlled the automatic sections, supplemented by treadles and infra-red train detection at stations. Full block overlaps, meaning a complete signal section, were used as the overlaps beyond a signal. A relay interlocking was provided for the areas with points linking the main tracks with each other and the depot, and the whole line was depicted on an indication panel with an entrance–exit control panel in a new central control room located at Broomloan. CCTV relayed pictures to a bank of control room VDUs showing the activities at stations. The new trains were equipped with automatic train operation (ATO) with track mounted transponders transmitting the relevant information to receivers on the trains. One-person operation became the rule with the drivers operating the door controls and pressing the start buttons for ATO.

Unfortunately, some of the equipment, particularly wiring, soon showed signs that it would not have a long life in the tunnel environment and by 1993 it was decided to renew the signalling again within the next few years. This would take advantage of the further advances made in technology with jointless audio frequency track circuits, wholly relay based automatic signalling and computer based controls and supervision. The depot interlocking and running line connections are also to be computer based using American equipment known as Vital Processor Interlocking and part of both tracks near the depot connections will be signalled for bi-directional working. The final level of equipment had not been agreed at the time of writing.

More automation on the London Underground

We have already described the early signalling on the London Underground in Chapter 8, and by the Second World War, a clearly distinctive pattern had emerged with two-aspect colour light signals accompanied by train stops at stop signals, full track circuiting, and gradually evolving centralised control. Many stop signals with sighting within the braking distance had no advance distant or repeater signals, especially in tunnels, although repeaters were usually provided at the approach to the outermost home signal before reaching a station. Where, because of limited sighting, it was necessary for a stop signal to have a caution aspect to repeat the next stop signal ahead the first stop signal remained as a two-aspect head and a repeater head showing yellow or green was mounted below it. This was either on the post on surface lines or on the tunnel wall on the underground sections. Sometimes on open sections the two signals were combined into a single four-lamp head but only showing three aspects, red (in the second lens down) danger stop, green (top) over yellow (bottom), caution next signal is at danger, and double green (top and third lenses) proceed, next stop signal clear. On open sections fog repeater signals are used just ahead of stop signals to which they apply with the lights switched on in the signal during fog.

As on the main line railways, London Transport adopted the white light junction indicator giving the route to be taken by the angle of the row of white lights. Like the Southern Railway, LT used the three-light indicator. On plain line, signalling worked automatically but with signalboxes controlling points and crossings. At automatic stop signals and controlled signals when working automatically, denoted by an illuminated letter A on the signalpost, stop and proceed working was and still is permitted in the event of a delay with a signal remaining at danger. If a driver is authorised to pass a signal at danger then the train has to draw slowly past the raised ground trip arm, the bogie mounted trip arm on the train is knocked back and applies the brakes automatically. After the driver has reset the trip arm by a resetting cord or lever he may then proceed at caution ready to stop short of any obstruction or a train ahead.

In the 1930s there was still a mixture of mechanical signalboxes and power operation and at the country end of the Metropolitan Line to Aylesbury, operation was no different from any other secondary line of the main line companies. Much of the central area Underground system was equipped with an air main, for LT made great use of electro-pneumatic operation of points and train stops. The characteristic 'whoosh' of air from the point machine can still be heard on many parts of the Underground network as points change. The Underground system was an early user of power operation with miniature lever frames. By the 1950s control desk operation was beginning to take over where the signalman was seated at a desk with banks of route switches in front of him and an illuminated diagram behind. But this was not route relay interlocking, for on LT this was done through interlocking machines situated in interlocking rooms, several of which might be controlled from one control desk. The interlocking machines had mechanical interlocking between what appeared to be normal miniature levers, but the levers were operated by air cylinders controlled through relays in the command circuits from the control desk. The levers were also subject to electric locks just as on a normal power

frame and when the lever movement was complete electric circuits were set up for the operation of point machines and signals. Interlocking machines have had a long life as part of LT signalling and today still provide vital interlocking functions at many locations, even though their control circuits may be initiated by push button, other automated equipment or computers.

By the late 1950s, LT was moving towards automation in the control of junctions and of controlled signals through what were called programme machines. These were like a piano roll carrying details of the day's train service for a particular set of points and related signals in printed form and with the information for each train punched out in a series of holes in binary form to represent train numbers, time, and route. Feelers made electrical contacts through the punched holes to initiate electric circuits through relays which were fed to the interlocking machines to set up a route. Some machines were sequence machines and others were time machines working together and taking information from track circuits and the train describer. At converging junctions the programmes could be arranged to work on a first come, first served principle, or in accordance with the timetable with the equipment able to store details for a train that was late and which arrived out of order.

As a train passed through the junction so the machine stepped forward for the next entry. Groups of machines were provided for each junction or part of a junction and were supervised from a control room. The supervisor could intervene and set routes manually if needed, say for an extra train, or could step the machines or arrange for the machine to step for a cancelled train. In normal working the machines provided automatic junction setting and replaced the hand pressing a button or pulling a lever. Naturally the

London Transport moved from the era of miniature levers to control desks during the 1950s where the signalman controlled the signalling from banks of route setting switches or buttons. This was the new signalling control room at Barking where London Transport shared the building with the BR signalling centre looking after the London, Tilbury & Southend line from the late 1950s in readiness for the LTS electrification. (London Transport)

Close-up of an LT programme machine in which feeler arms making contacts through 'piano roll' punched holes representing a train movement, initiate route setting at a junction. (London Transport)

equipment relied totally on track circuit operation to ensure that trains had passed given locations before route setting began for a following move. Ordinary push button control desks could also pre-select routes, and to ensure that the pre-selected route or a second programme machine route could not start to be set before it was safe to do so in the event of a normal track circuit relay momentarily 'bobbing', a novel form of short track circuit was used. In this, what was known as a delta track circuit of high frequency, 10kHz, was overlaid on the ordinary track circuit at the required proving point, and was arranged to be normally dead except when a train was in the vicinity of the bonds. Then, the wheels would complete the circuit and energise the relay, the circuit from which allowed route setting for the next move to start.

The extension of programme machine control during the following decade led to complete lines being totally controlled by programme machines, with supervision from one control centre which had an illuminated diagram of the entire route. The system was gradually extended to cover several of LT's routes but during the 1970s a further advance in technology brought computers into the control system with a pilot scheme of computer control replacing programme machines at Watford. Supervision was from the signalbox at Rickmansworth which had a coloured VDU screen to show track occupation, routes set and the indication of signals. By the mid-1980s, when a new control room covering the whole of the Jubilee Line from Stanmore

Total automation on LT in the 1960s meant control of junctions through programme machines and overall supervision of a complete line from a control room as here, covering the Victoria Line. The supervisor could intervene to over-ride a programme machine either by direct junction setting or by commands to the programme machine. (London Transport)

The first moves towards computers for signalling on London Transport came in the early 1970s with a trial at Rickmansworth signalbox to control Watford Metropolitan station instead of through the miniature levers of the conventional lever frame. The visual display unit (VDU) for Watford can be seen at the far end of the lever frame. (London Transport)

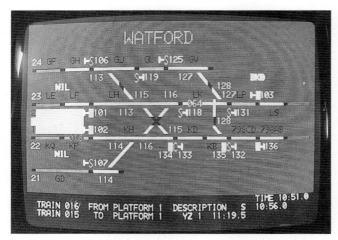

A close-up of the Watford station layout on the VDU in Rickmansworth signalbox showing the track layout. The VDU itself has coloured graphics and depicts train occupation, train number, signal aspects, and programmed movements. (London Transport)

Another stage of automation on London Transport was the development of automatic train operation during the 1960s. Although the driver, eventually known as the train operator, pressed a start button, onward movement to the next station stop including any slowings or stops for trains ahead was automated with the train picking up safety codes through the rails and commands from command spots to regulate speed. Early trials were carried out on an open air section of the District Line Hounslow branch, as seen here, then on the Central Line Hainault loop in readiness for regular service on the Victoria Line. (London Transport)

to Charing Cross, and part of the Metropolitan Line was commissioned at Baker Street, computers had taken over the function of programme machines or surviving signalboxes on those lines and provided the links between the control room and the interlocking machines which still controlled the final vital circuits to the point machines and signals themselves, and computers brought back the indications from the track and signalling to the control room. The computers also have their part in information collection and dissemination, for example to platform indicators for information to the public and for management functions.

By the early 1990s, the Central Line was being totally modernised with new trains, automated train operation, and new signalling including new pattern jointless track circuits and computer control of most functions, although with conventional relay interlockings (conventional that is in the BR sense since the interlocking machine had for so long been at the heart of LT signalling) on most of the lines and solid state interlocking on the final sections. The local lineside signalbox was almost a thing of the past on London Underground.

While automation of signalling controls was progressing in the 1960s LT was developing another area of automation, the control of trains. In readiness for the new Victoria Line being built during the 1960s, trials had taken place with automatically driven trains on short lengths of the District and Central Lines. They proved the principles and with modifications the Victoria Line was commissioned in 1958/9 with

Fig. 31. The track circuit safety codes and command spots for automatic train operation on LT's Victoria Line.

Station A	420	420
	420	420
	420	420
	420	420
	420	420

automatic train control (ATC) in a new guise meaning what it said, with two components, automatic train operation (ATO) covering the driving controls, and automatic train protection (ATP) covering the signalling and safety aspects. Put simply, ATO made the train go and slow down and stop when required at signals and at stations, but only provided that ATP allowed it to by confirming that the line was clear and that the train did not exceed the maximum permitted speed according to the commands. The trains were one-person operated and the driver, retitled the train operator, was at the front to control the train doors and to start the train by operating push buttons at stations. There was no guard.

The running rails not only carried the track circuits but they were coded track circuits giving as far as the train was concerned three pulsed codes, 420 impulses per minute, 270, 180, and a fourth state, no code. If a train's receiving coils did not pick up a code the train could not move, and if it was moving already and lost the code, the emergency brakes were applied. The 420 code allowed a train to run at maximum speed, the 270 code at 22mph, and the 180 code also at 22mph but without motoring. The driving commands were given by audio frequency transmission spots passed through short lengths of one rail and detected by the train. Apart from a command to slow down and stop at a signal given by a 20kHz spot and a station stop command of 15kHz further spots along the line gave the train speed command in accordance with the theoretical braking curve for that location to halt at the platform to within a yard or so of the target. The speed command spots were based on a 100Hz frequency scale representing 1mph. In the event of equipment failure the train operator could drive the train manually up to

a speed of 22mph provided the train was receiving a safety code, and a maximum of 10mph if the train was not receiving a safety code. For this purpose a scattering of lineside signals was provided on the Victoria Line, although not covering all the coded track circuit sections which would be open to trains working in automatic mode. Now, nearly 30 years later, a second London Underground line is going automatic with full ATC on the Central Line as part of its total modernisation. On lines operating under ATC, track and trains are no longer equipped with train stop trip apparatus since if a train over-runs a stopping point or exceeds a speed command which in theory it cannot do the emergency brake is applied automatically.

How tragic it was, that on 28 February 1975 the London Underground should have suffered its worst ever accident when a train on the short Finsbury Park–Moorgate branch of the Northern City Line failed to stop in Moorgate platform. It continued on with power applied and hit the tunnel end wall at speed, the impact crushing three cars and resulting in 42 deaths. For all its emphasis on signalling safety features no one on London Transport or at the Railway Inspectorate could possibly have thought that after a train had passed the last stop signal at clear with the ground trip arm lowered the driver would make no attempt to stop at the dead end, as trains had done day in, day out for over 70 years without a single previous failure. ATP would have prevented the accident but the line was in the process of being handed over to British Rail and ATP was not part of that plan. The result was greater use of trip arms along the final part of the track leading to the dead end here, and in other similar locations where train stops are used, with timing sections checking that train speed was within limits to

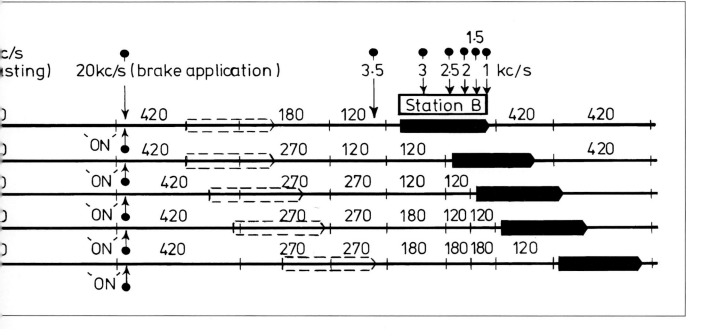

release the trip arms, often used by LT at the approach to stations to allow trains to close up. Another feature to come out of the Moorgate accident was a reversion to a practice used on one or two railways in earlier years, the Ealing & Shepherds Bush for example in 1920 with its three-position semaphores, the display of a yellow caution aspect on colour light signals rather than green on the last stop signal approaching a dead end terminus. This new recommendation applied to British Rail as well as London Underground.

No drivers on Docklands

Another line in London was fully automated right from the start, for the Docklands Light Railway when opened in 1987, was totally computer controlled. Compared with some schemes its approval, funding, and construction seemed to go ahead with indecent haste, doubtless with political considerations. As first envisaged the back-of-the-envelope ideas seemed to suggest a tramway style operation with some on sight running, even a roundabout at the delta junction at Poplar. But the version as built was one of the most highly automated railways in the world.

The Docklands trains were two-element lightweight articulated cars working from dc third rail track which was characterised by sharp curves and steep gradients even though much of it took over redundant BR tracks. The automatic train control comprised the elements we have seen before on London Transport, ATO and ATP but with an added ingredient ATS, automatic train supervision which provides the central control room with a complete overview of the whole railway through the computers with VDUs at workstations in the control room. What that means is that instead of a signalman pulling levers in an old style signalbox the signalling control centre has become an office with desks containing VDUs and computer keyboards and while the system is functioning normally in automatic mode the supervisor keeps an overseeing eye on what information is appearing on his screens. But when things go wrong he is there to take direct control if it is needed by changing instructions given through the computer keyboard.

Out on the line as built the Docklands Light Railway had fixed track circuit block sections normally station to station, but occasionally with two sections between stations. The track circuits were of the reed type operating between 366 and 384Hz and avoided any interference from the chopper control of the dc traction which inevitably had running rail return. Right from the early days of track circuits on electrified railways, precautions had to be taken to avoid false clearance of track circuits by stray traction currents, especially under fault conditions as we have already seen. Usually this was achieved by using ac track circuits for dc traction and vice versa. By the 1960s however, when new forms of traction control were beginning to appear

with thyristors, choppers and more recently the adoption of three-phase alternating current for motors produced by train-borne equipment which, even with filters and safety devices, did not rule out entirely the odd stray current which might affect safe track circuit operation, something more was wanted. Track circuit design has thus been developed to ensure as far as possible that they cannot be affected by both ac and dc traction, and with ATO and ATP they might need to have coded impulses from track to train. Part of the DLR runs parallel, a few yards away from the London, Tilbury & Southend line electrified at 25kV ac.

Additionally the Docklands line was equipped with a cable loop along the centre of the track and in the web of one of the rails. At intervals the loop cables were transposed in varying distances corresponding to speed limits so that the closer the transpositions the lower the speed. For ATP there were two vital signals, one through the cable loops telling the train equipment the maximum speed and the second through the rails giving clearance to proceed and without which the train could not move in automatic mode. Timing equipment on the trains measured the time taken between the cable loops and if the train passed a loop, usually spaced at one second intervals, faster than that the emergency brakes were applied. The ATP signals were picked up by induction through coils on the train. At stations was another control feature, the docking data link (DDL) which was another form of induction communication passing information from the train to the trackside for onward transmission to the control centre covering train number and destination, and from the trackside to the train. This told it which station it was at, its destination, the time allowed for the station stop and that it was time to close the doors, the details of how the train was to run to the next station (speed restrictions, how far, etc), and whether the doors were to be released on the left or the right. Finally it told the train in which direction it was to go.

Trains were in the charge not of a train operator but a train captain. His function was largely to keep an eye on things and to do ticket checking. At stations passengers opened the doors by push button after they were released automatically when a train stopped in the station, but they were closed by the train captain from any door position. Restarting of the train was automatic. Only if there was a fault did the train captain have to take over and drive. This could be up to full line speed if ATP codes were being received but only up to 20kph on instructions from the control centre if the ATP codes were lost. There were no lineside operating signals but stop boards were provided at the entrance to each block section for manual driving without ATP, also speed limit signs and fibre optic point indicators showing which way points were set by a white arrow on a blue background.

The control centre normally did not intervene except

when things went wrong but had facilities to get things back to normal automatically. For example, when trains were delayed the supervisor could instruct the computers to speed up the trains to give faster times between stations subject to the maximum instead of normal working where economy speeds were usually provided by trains switching off the motoring mode and coasting. The supervisor could change operation on an all trains basis or for an individual train and in the event of route setting faults the supervisor could take over and set up instructions manually to the solid state interlocking (SSI) which had been provided to control the interlockings. This was based on the BR type of SSI which was then just coming into service after trial periods.

All too soon after opening, it became apparent that the Docklands Light Railway in its original form, was not going to cope with the traffic. It would be easy in hindsight to say that the wrong type of railway was built and that it should have had greater capacity and been more like a heavyweight railway. But Docklands was what had been provided. By the early 1990s moves were afoot to increase capacity with reduced headways from the 7½ minutes of the original service. The old system was replaced by the Seltrac system already used for rapid transit services in North America and cable loops were still used but not as originally laid out, since in the new system, the loops crossed every 25 metres. The loops were used to transmit and receive information with trains and train detection was supplemented by inductive axle counters. The loops have three functions, the transmission of digital data between the control centre and trains, transmission of voice communication between the control centre and passengers or train operators, as they were now called, and they detect vehicle position. The Vehicle Control Centre (VCC) is the hub with a complex of computers controlling and monitoring all functions. The VCC issues instructions to trains on safe stopping points, maximum speeds, and other commands every second, while Vehicle On Board Controllers (VOBC), microprocessor units, act on validated commands from the VCC to move the train within the imposed limits. In return the VOBC tells the VCC where the train is and how fast it is going. Unlike the first system which had fixed block sections the Seltrac system employs moving block derived from the train's passage past the crossed cable loops, supplemented by fine tuning of position between cable crossovers by measuring devices on the train to give a stopping accuracy of just 200mm. As a train proceeds it has a safety envelope being continuously drawn behind it so that a following train can keep an even pace rather than the stop/start of a fixed block system, yet always with a safe margin between them. With these fully automated systems the signal engineering art has progressed from being one

of providing signals to a driver to one where the signalling equipment drives the trains.

Tyne & Wear Metro, a new generation

Not all the new systems of the 1980s were fully automated. The philosophy surrounding the Tyne & Wear Metro, the first of the new generation metro systems in the UK, opened in stages between 1980 and 1983, was that if you needed a person on board the train then he or she might as well drive and save the complexities of an automated system. Moreover the Tyne & Wear Metro was a long time a'comin, being in the planning, financing, and construction stages right through the 1970s. Since the Second World War a decade has been a long time in the development of new technology and what was current practice and what equipment was available in the 1970s was nothing like what had been proved and tested for the 1980s, certainly in the field of computer technology for a railway application. Certainly computers were available but in the 1970s were used normally for gathering and disseminating information. They were just being tried in the mid-1970s for controlling signalling but not to perform the vital interlocking functions. So to a large extent the Tyne & Wear was conventional with track circuit block, colour light signals and trains driven with a hand on the controller in the cab.

The Tyne & Wear Metro scheme took over several former BR lines between Newcastle and the coastal commuter towns, with in all 56 route kilometres, of

A basic signal on the Tyne & Wear Metro in which a road style traffic light sign was used as a distant marker board for a stop signal ahead. (Geoffrey Kichenside)

stations. Where the distance between stations is longer than normal a few locations have intermediate signals. Cost was an important factor on the T&W Metro and since all passenger trains stopped at all stations it was felt that in most locations there was no need for a working distant or repeater signal. Instead, Department of Transport standard road signs depicting a traffic light were installed at braking distance from a stop signal with an indication of distance, nominally 250 metres, marked below the traffic light sign. A few stop signals were preceded by colour light distant signals particularly between Benton and the Bankfoot branch originally intended for BR freight trains which needed to work on the same tracks and on the north side of the Gosforth triangle. The BR freights were limited in speed to 20mph with duplicate speed restriction signs provided on this section in metric and imperial as BR speedometers were in miles per hour. In London there was a similar problem on the Metropolitan Line after resignalling in the 1960s when BR freights had to use tracks north of Harrow with LT signalling and short braking distances, so additional disc distant signals

A Tyne & Wear two-aspect stop signal. The line has a number of level crossings without barriers but protected by steady yellow/flashing red lights for road traffic. Originally the railway approach had flashing white lights, one is seen here below the signal head, to prove the road signals were displayed and even though the signal was green trains were not permitted to move on to the crossing unless the white light was showing. Later, the white lights were removed and the signal would not clear to green unless the road signals were displayed. The Metro used the metric system from the start hence the 80kph speed limit board but originally it also had mph speed limit boards on the parts used by BR freight services. (Geoffrey Kichenside)

The Tyne & Wear philosophy was that if you needed a person at the front he might as well drive rather than the automation of the Victoria Line in London, but much else on the Metro was automated. Just under the front of the train is an inductive train stop for the signal applying in the opposite direction. (Geoffrey Kichenside)

which 43 were former BR routes. Right from the start T&W Metro went metric with speed limits in kilometres per hour and in other respects. New construction included 5km in tunnel and a massive bridge across the River Tyne to provide through running between North and South Tyneside routes. The Metro lines were electrified on the 1,500V dc overhead system and the trains were articulated twin units. The signalling system was primarily two-aspect largely with just stop signals at the departure end of further out were provided to give BR drivers the longer braking distances required.

The whole of the T&W Metro was supervised from one control centre at South Gosforth which was equipped with three control positions, one for operation and signalling, one for station supervision, and one for power control. The whole line was depicted on a signalling panel and while, for much of the time, trains operated with automatic signalling the operating supervisor could intervene and control junctions manually through a one-control switch route setting console. Trains controlled the junctions themselves through a device known as positive train identification (PTI). Before the start of each journey the driver set up a code through thumbwheels on his control panel to give details of destination, train working number and status. This information was put into a train-mounted transponder which at intervals was interrogated by track-mounted PTI loops particularly at the approach to interlocking areas where the information transmitted by the train was passed on to a control processor for initiating route setting through a relay interlocking. At converging junctions or for the single line sections – there are several on the T&W Metro – operation was normally on a first-come, first-served basis but if this resulted in out of course working which the controller did not want, if for example a train was a few minutes late, he could set the processor to operate on a second-come, first-served basis. At diverging junctions as at South Gosforth and in other situations, to prevent premature clearance of a signal which in turn might delay another train the junction signal would not clear until station work was complete and the driver pressed a 'train ready to start' button on his desk. To prevent trains passing signals at danger the line and trains were fitted with the German style Indusi inductive train stops at stop signals, and elsewhere for speed control. If a driver is instructed to pass a signal at danger, the inductive trip is activated which can be cancelled by a button on the driver's desk but a yellow light is then illuminated to remind him of a mandatory 30kph speed restriction until passing the next signal at clear.

A feature of parts of the Metro are level crossings, one or two over busy main roads. Open crossings monitored by the train drivers were provided with the usual steady yellow and flashing red lights for road users triggered when a train approached the crossing. Originally a flashing white light was provided at the signal immediately before the crossing and even though the signal might have been showing green trains were not permitted to go over the crossing until the flashing white light was displayed. After several collisions with road vehicles, due primarily to road drivers ignoring the flashing red lights, the timings of the warnings were changed but from a signalling point of view the flashing white light was discontinued. Controls were transferred

One of the positive train identification loops used for interrogating passing trains on the Tyne & Wear Metro. Details of the train are then recorded in the system as a train description. (Geoffrey Kichenside)

to the normal rail signals so that the signal immediately before the crossing was held at red for the train until the road flashing red lights were activated when the rail signal changed to green.

The control centre set the pattern for what has followed elsewhere with its overall control and with CCTV, VDU screens and radio communication with stations and trains. The station operator can see what is going on at stations and can make announcements to passengers, including deterrence of vandals, or for other security needs. The whole of the Tyne & Wear Metro set a new standard for urban lines, it did things differently in many ways from both BR and London Transport in adopting some practices from overseas. It introduced for example, audible on-train warnings before doors were closed instead of the shouted 'mind the doors' heard in London, but then T&W Metro platforms were unstaffed. Tickets were obtained from machines, and if machines ran short of tickets or change a warning flashed on the station controller's alarms in the control centre. But above all T&W Metro showed a slickness of operation unmatched at that time anywhere else in Britain.

A leap forward in Dublin

The Dublin Area Rapid Transit (DART) suburban electric train service introduced between Bray and Howth in 1984, which also used the 1,500V dc overhead system, did not include the level of automation in the accompanying resignalling to the extent that we have just seen on the Docklands Light Railway. It is noteworthy however, for not only did it include automatic train protection for the electric trains but in conjunction with BR four-aspect colour light practice, it introduced a continuous automatic warning system (CAWS) and cab signalling to other trains using the line, several stages above the basic BR AWS, standard then and today on BR lines.

The DART lines were resignalled with full track circuiting and multiple-aspect signalling using the BR three- and four-aspect system controlled from a central computer based control room linked to points and signals through several relay interlockings. Coded track circuits at $83^{1}/_{3}$Hz for train detection were employed to pass the ATP information to the trains by low frequency impulses detected by coils on the train. The impulses provided both full ATP for the electric trains and cab signalling and AWS for other trains, and the two types of information had to be carefully selected to provide the equivalent detail for drivers. There are more codes than on London Transport's similar system and more speed bands:

CODE	CAWS	ATP
Pulses/min	*Signal aspect*	*Speed kph*
420	Green	100
270	Double yellow	75
180	Green	50
120	Yellow	50
75	Green	30
50	Yellow	30
0	Red	0

The use of more than one code for the same signal aspect in the CAWS part of the system arose from the combination of yellow or green lineside signals but coinciding with speed restrictions. On the electric trains the route signalling seen out on the line was translated into speed indications in the cab. Trains received the cab indication of the next signal about 200 to 400 metres before reaching it, and approaching a red signal no code would be detected by electric trains and a full brake application would be made automatically. Once speed had dropped below 15kph the driver could press a running release button to release the brake and continue coasting with a '15' shown on his ATP display

and an audible bleep warning sounding. At other times when electric trains received a lower speed indication, provided the driver shut off power or started to brake, the ATP system would automatically take over braking until the required speed had been reached when the brakes would release. If the driver took no action the service brake application would continue until he did. In the case of other trains the driver was presented with cab indications of the four-aspect signalling. A change to a less restrictive aspect called for no acknowledgement but a change to a more restrictive aspect meant the driver had to press an acknowledgement button. Failure to do so triggered a full brake application, but the system was not proof against a non ATP fitted train passing a signal at danger once the driver had acknowledged an AWS warning. Nevertheless the CAWS system is being extended to other lines in Ireland as part of resignalling.

The control room had banks of VDUs displaying the track diagrams with routes set, position of trains and whether signals were at danger or clear. Normally the tracks were displayed in white but when a route was being set the section concerned changed to yellow and when the signals cleared the route was shown in green with the overlap alone in yellow. The presence of the train was shown by the appropriate track circuit displays changing to red. Supervisors did not usually need to intervene for junctions as these were set automatically from train numbers which incorporated a class of train letter, destination number and a unique two-figure train number which was rarely repeated during the day. Once keyed into the system the computer would initiate route setting ahead of the train. Converging junctions were worked on the first-come, first-served principle unless the control room supervisor intervened to set routes manually. This he did by using a qwerty keyboard with added buttons for specific functions.

Allied to the signalling was an extensive radio communications network principally between the control centre and trains which could be called uniquely using their train number. This was essential if a driver was to be instructed to pass a signal at danger. Although train drivers could not initiate a speech call they could send a signal to control denoting they wanted to make a call and the controller then called the train. An unusual facility was the ability to link radio calls between the control centre and trains to the national telephone service meaning that for example, a driver could call the maintenance depot to explain a fault, and later the depot could call the driver and tell him how to overcome it.

Out on the line the Dublin area signals were not quite like those on BR since the American suppliers, WABCo Westinghouse, did not have four-aspect signal heads. They thus supplied three-aspect signals with an extra single lens yellow signal mounted below the three-aspect head. Shunting signals were something like the BR position light type but in practice they were from American three-position semaphore repeaters normally showing a white and red light horizontally, a yellow and white light diagonally and green and white light vertically. By replacing the coloured filters except for the red and by using the 45 degree left white light with the top light of the vertical display for a right hand diagonal, the signal could give three clear indications by route, shunt to the left, shunt straight ahead, and shunt to the right.

Metrolink's special needs

Manchester's Metrolink system, opened in 1992, brought back the sight of trams running through city centre streets which, for nearly three decades had been absent in British towns and cities after the last systems closed down in the 1960s (with the notable exception of Blackpool's trams and the cable-worked Great Orme Tramway at Llandudno). There are trams and trams, and the new Metrolink vehicles were nothing like the traditional image of the British tram, for Manchester drew heavily on Continental practice for its new transport system. The cars themselves, like Tyne & Wear and Docklands, were twin bodied articulated units but unlike those two systems they ran on both segregated tracks, utilising former BR routes, and through the streets both on alignments for exclusive use of Metrolink and on some sections where they shared roadspace with other road users. The new cars were officially designated as LRVs – Light Rail Vehicles – and unlike the trams of old, modern technology provided a high level of automation although not to the extent of the Docklands Light Railway. On the former railway tracks used by Metrolink conventional railway signalling, much of it automatic, was provided, with continuous track circuiting. The two-aspect signals showed red or green and while some which could be seen from braking distance at the 50mph maximum permitted speed were not provided with repeaters, a few where sighting was limited had a yellow/green repeater located at the braking distance from the relevant stop signal. In a few instances it was possible for drivers to see a stop signal and the following repeater at the same time so there might have been dangers in reading through to the second signal. Repeaters were thus arranged to be unlit when the stop signal in the rear was showing red. Inductive train stops were provided to ensure that the LRVs would be stopped if they passed a signal at danger. While the central operations room could control the points and signals at the terminal stations, automatic route setting was provided to set points into the station and clear the appropriate signal and then to reset the points for the next outward move.

On the street sections operation was largely on sight but on some parts the view ahead was limited. Special street running signals were employed at road junctions and since there were points for Metrolink track junctions special point indicating signals were devised to indicate to the driver that the points were set and locked. The road junction signals which applied to the LRVs instead of the normal traffic lights had white light displays with five lamps giving position light indications, horizontal – danger stop, a cluster of lights in the centre – prepare to stop, diagonally to the left – proceed to the left, vertical – proceed straight ahead, and diagonally to the right – proceed to the right. The point indicators gave similar indications though with a seven-light display to indicate which way the points were set. If the points could not be detected as fully set or not set for the direction called for, a horizontal row of lights provided a stop indication. At the boundary between segregated and street running a hybrid signal was provided showing a red aspect for stop and a white light street running display for proceed. At that point the driver operated a changeover switch to alter the running mode of the LRV. The LRVs were fitted with a 'train ready to start' (TRTS) button which was used to initiate the clearance of the signal. At the opposite change from street to segregated running, again the LRV had to stop to change mode before the signal could be called to clear. The TRTS button was also pressed by the driver to trigger parts of the automatic route setting feature. Parts of the street sections were track circuited near points to provide route interlocking in the solid state interlocking equipment. Elsewhere on the street sections short high frequency track circuits up to the points together with a proximity coil buried in the road underneath the points provided locking through the points.

The LRVs were fitted with identification equipment known as the vehicle recognition system (VRS) set up from a keypad in the driver's cab with information transmitted from the LRV to lineside equipment as needed through an inductive loop buried in the road between the rails. The VRS on-board equipment formed the basis of calls from the LRV to set points automatically, to call for a traffic light phase to allow the LRV to proceed at road junctions and to transmit the TRTS indications. It could also transmit details of faults to the operations and maintenance centre through other parts of the system's computer network which looked after the signalled sections through the SSIs, the train describer, train reporting details and the telecommunications system.

Mail Rail, a pioneer automated railway

Finally in this chapter we take a brief glance at one of the first automated railways in the world and one which would confirm a view often heard in railway circles, that railways would run much better without passengers, for this particular line does not carry passengers in normal working, although it has been known to work the odd passenger special. This is the Post Office tube railway, today known as Mail Rail, between Paddington and Whitechapel underground across the heart of London. It was a narrow gauge line (2ft) and was built to speed mail carrying between the principal sorting offices and some of the main line stations. The trains ran without drivers and since there were no drivers there was no need to have signals, but the system had full signalling controls and instead of signal levers changing the signals they set the routes and applied or removed the traction current to the electrified third rail. Each station had its own signalbox, originally with mechanically locked lever slide frames. Coming at the same time as the Great Western's route setting installation at Newport in the latter 1920s it is interesting to compare the operation of a lever. Like its main line counterpart when pulled it was first checklocked while track circuits were proved to be clear, then at the next position the lever was checked while points were set and locked and finally, when the lever was fully pulled it operated a relay to feed traction current to the conductor rail of the selected route. Just two voltages were used, 440V dc for maximum speed, 35mph, and 150V dc for a lower speed of 7mph. If the train did not receive any voltage the brakes were applied automatically. Unusually, although the traction supply was dc, direct current track circuits were employed but using negative potential -25V to earth.

Renewals were made to the system in the 1960s and 1970s utilising relay interlockings but in 1993 the signalling equipment was renewed with a computer based system working from a central control room, although retaining the relay interlockings. Automatic junction setting could be used, based on the train service details held in the computer but the controller could intervene to set routes manually, or could change the train service patterns while retaining automatic junction setting. One of the features of the train control computer was the inclusion of interlocking tables in its memory so that while it did not carry out the vital interlocking functions itself it would only transmit orders to the relay interlockings to set routes that were actually free to be used. Although junction setting could be an automatic function, route setting for a train scheduled to leave a station would only be triggered when the staff had completed station work and operated a train ready to start button to trigger the computer.

In this chapter we have looked in some detail at the individual systems for the latest Metro and allied railways in the British Isles because of their individual requirements and different levels of automation. The differences in automation may not have arisen only from need and cost, and in the 1980s were undoubtedly influenced by what had been perfected and proved as being suitable for railway service. A decade was a long time in the world of technology. The descriptions of the various systems have been phrased in the past tense, not because they are no longer there but from the fact that history begins yesterday and we have described them as they were installed or in the case of Docklands, re-installed. Automation of metro railways is more advanced than on the main line systems but it is much easier when the train fleet is standardised to one type, everything except for passengers is the same for all trains, and speed profiles and train performance are identical. On a mixed traffic railway automation is much more difficult but in the following chapter we shall look at the various forms of automation that can be applied to the conventional heavyweight railway, and the even greater potential for railway communications and data links using space technology.

Chapter 16

DO WE
NEED DRIVERS?

FOR OVER 150 years railway signals have been provided to give train drivers an indication of the state of the line ahead and whether it is safe for the train to proceed. But as we near the end of the 20th century and on towards the 200th anniversary in 2003 of the first steam locomotive to run on rails, technology is already available which could eliminate the train driver. The signal engineer is no longer designing a signalling system to tell the driver what to do, he has become a transportation engineer designing a system which not only confirms that the line is clear and safe for a train to run on the correct route, but can transmit the commands to make the train go, speed up, slow down, and stop without a hand on the train touching the controls. This is not fantasy for we have already described the automated metro systems, the London Underground Victoria Line which has been operating for more than 25 years, and the London Docklands Light Railway for a decade, not forgetting the grandfather of all automated railways, Mail Rail. Originally the Post Office tube railway in London, it is now over 70 years old and without a driver in sight although it has a control system which comes nowhere near the sophistication of that of a modern automated passenger railway.

Metro lines, usually with identical train formations of uniform weight, standard braking performance, standard speed profiles, and each train doing the same thing as all the others, are one thing. Mixed traffic main line railways with stopping passenger trains, fast Inter-City services and freight trains of all shapes and sizes with varying speeds, weights and lengths, are quite another unless dedicated tracks can be provided. Thus, with the given technology it is fairly easy to automate a metro line. Whether there is a staff person on board the train to provide a presence to passengers who might be nervous of travelling in a robot (or to control their behaviour), or to supervise the equipment, open and shut the doors, press the start button to trigger the automated system, or to take over in an emergency, is purely academic and depends on what image the line management wishes to put over to passengers. So far,

the Railway Inspectorate, in its most recent guise as part of the Health & Safety Executive has not yet had to consider the implications of staffless trains since no railway organisation in Britain has yet had the courage to run trains without at least one staff member on board, whether he or she is called an operator, captain, conductor, or whatever. Automated people movers in the form of lifts have been used for many years and other more recent forms of guided travel, such as monorails at garden festivals or magnetically levitated 'Maglev' cars at airports have run without on-board staff however.

Eliminating signalling errors

For the main line railways we have yet to see total automation and just how much automation is desirable/feasible/affordable and above all justified, and what would be achieved by further automation? Over the last 130 or so years the actions of signalmen have gradually had automated assistance from locks to stop them pulling a signal lever if the points were not in the right position through interlocking, and the first developments in 1876 with the Sykes lock and block system which helped to ensure that trains passing through a block section locked and released signals and influenced the operation of the block system. Then track circuits from the 1890s which helped to prevent signalmen from forgetting a train, a further development a decade later with track circuits to control signals automatically, Welwyn control from 1936 which helped to prevent premature clearance of a block section until a train was proved to have passed through the section. This was followed by track circuit block and full track circuiting through interlocked areas which brought technology to a state whereby signalmen's safety errors in normal working were virtually eliminated in power signalling centres.

In information collection and dissemination much has been automated. In the last century, the single-needle telegraph was the means by which signalmen communicated with each other. Look back in these pages at the accident at Abbots Ripton, with the signalman desperately trying to get a response from the signalman at Huntingdon to signal to him on the telegraph that the Scotch express had been wrecked. Then came telephones, box to box, omnibus circuits, box to control, signalpost telephones. By the 1950s automatic train describers passed on the train detail from line to line and box to box automatically. A decade or so later computers were involved in train describers and much information could be pulled out of the system on train running, equipment performance, for management supervision, and for public information display. No longer should signalmen in modern centres need to telephone reports of train movement.

The ultimate in signalling automation

Computers also brought such new features as junction optimisation techniques in which details of service disruptions at say a multi-tracked major station could be fed into a computer which would produce solutions to keep delays to a minimum and make maximum use of the track layout. It did not always work like that though, but it was a start. With the new 1970s signalling on the Brighton line controlled from Three Bridges signalling centre came a small measure of automatic junction setting (ARS), at Keymer Junction,

The contrast between the interiors of mechanical signalboxes and even the power signalboxes of the 1960s could not be greater than the interior of an integrated electronic control centre of today. This is Liverpool Street which has all the ambience of a modern office. The track layout with train position, routes set, signal aspects, etc, is displayed on VDUs, with one monitor showing the entire overview and the others detailed portions of the layout. (BR)

where the Eastbourne and Hastings line left the route to Brighton, with information taken off the train describer. The principle was not new in itself since the Mersey Railway had installed automatic terminal working at Liverpool, operated through track circuits half a century earlier. Also, London Transport had been using automatic junction setting with programme machines from the 1950s. But it pointed the way signalling automation was going.

Enter SSIs and IECCs

The real boost to automation of the signalling function came with the development of micro-processor interlocking in the 1980s, at first with a trial in parallel with relay equipment at Henley-on-Thames and then in 1985, with the installation of the first solid state interlocking (SSI) at Leamington Spa. This was a development involving a combination of British Rail and signalling contractors Westinghouse Signals and GEC-General Signals. Since then SSIs have been introduced at a number of installations, both for new work and part replacement of or extension of relay installations in Britain, and not just on BR but has also seen use in overseas contracts.

Solid state is the interlocking equipment for the foreseeable future but by its very nature needs more careful design work and rigid testing procedures to ensure fail-safe integrity and reliability than relay equipment. That is not to say that relay interlocking does not need careful design and testing, but at its simplest, a technician can usually see whether a relay is energised or not which cannot be done with micro-processors. Computers in vital functions in railway signalling must have an integrity at least equal to older

technology and this is achieved either by running three computers side by side fed with the same inputs on the same program and if two out of three agree the output is valid, or by a two out of two arrangement. Allied to this are the data links and other equipment much of which is duplicated. By these methods a fault within the processor will show itself and will trigger a self diagnostic print out or alarm to the technician. A potentially dangerous fault in one computer will be detected by the others and they can shut the system down, putting signals to danger. Most of the equipment is in the form of modules so that if a fault occurs the technician will be told by the equipment which module needs replacement.

In Chapter 14 we looked at the advances in miniaturisation of relays so that relay rooms could be smaller. But SSI is almost postage stamp size by comparison, with the processors for one interlocking contained in a cabinet no more than 1ft 7in wide and which, depending on the track layout, can control around 40 signals and up to 40 sets of points. Unlike most relay systems, all the interlocking processors can be at the control centre with what are known as trackside data links to the modules at the site driving signals and points. These links can be a basic 10km in length or with repeater equipment up to 40km, and with a more sophisticated long line data link the control distance can be as long as you like in Britain.

Computers have been part of signalling control for some years. Panel processors for example have been part of the control between panel push buttons and relay equipment or remote control equipment and gradually, computers have become involved in reproducing track diagram information on VDUs supplementing the large panel indication diagrams. If a VDU can display all the information, what need is there for a large track diagram? The latest signalling centres have dispensed with these and signalmen now watch VDUs which can display an overview of the whole area or can close in on part of the layout with much more detailed information. Several colour monitors may be provided at each signalman's position, known as a workstation, one displaying the whole area and the others portions of it. Control is not by levers, or entrance–exit buttons, but by a computer qwerty keyboard, supplemented if needed by specific function buttons, and by a tracker ball. The modern computerised office has entered the world of signalling and in the latest signal control centres the signalman is seated at a desk surrounded by the new technology, in what are now called integrated electronic control centres (IECCs). As in offices in other businesses in which keyboards and VDU screens form the principal part of the work operation, the effects of looking intently at the screen have to be taken into account and signalmen at IECCs have to be given breaks between periods at the desk to avoid effects of repetitive strain.

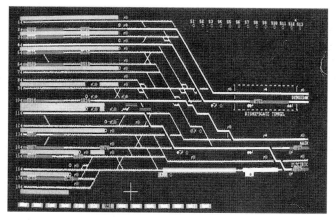

A close look at the overview at Liverpool Street, displayed on a monitor about the size of an average domestic television set, with the detail previously shown on the large track diagram panels in older power signalboxes. (BR)

It was never like that in mechanical signalling. The signalmen just had to put up with backache from pulling heavy levers and standing and walking along the lever frame for most of the shift, with little time to sit, in a busy mechanical box.

With the small area needed for the SSI cubicles and in the operating room for the signalmen's workstation, meaning that the building for an IECC can be considerably smaller than for an entrance–exit panel control centre and relay interlocking room, and the use of normal commercial computer hardware and common software with data configuration for each application, it is hardly surprising that the new breed of electronic signalling centres cost less than the electro-magnetic types of the previous three decades. From an operating point of view, since automatic junction setting is employed on a wide scale at IECCs, with route setting information derived from the timetable database and the train describer, for much of the time the signalman in an IECC is largely a supervisor. He only takes active control to override the equipment, mainly when he can see a situation developing that he would prefer to avoid. It means that an IECC needs fewer signalmen than an equivalent signalling centre with relay technology.

Reversible working

A feature which is becoming more widely used in today's signalling is reversible working so that trains can run in either direction on a double-track line. There are two forms – simple bi-directional running known as SIMBIDS, in which signals are primarily located for wrong direction running at crossovers between up and down tracks and allows single line working to be instituted for engineering work when one track is closed without the old formalities, other than to ensure that track staff are aware trains are working both ways on the remaining track, and full. For this full signalling

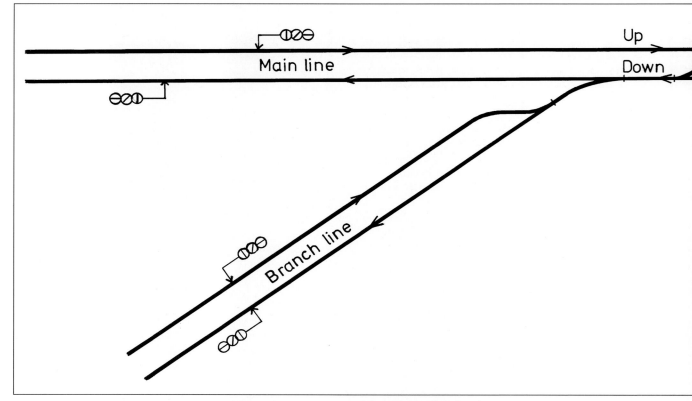

Fig. 32. *Turnouts at a single lead junction after rationalisation with colour light signalling. With a train signalled from the up branch to the up main there is no physical protection to prevent a train over-running signal 1 at danger from avoiding a collision as there would be in the layout in Fig. 17.*

is provided in both directions on both or all tracks allowing trains in the same direction to overtake, as in multiple track areas. It is also frequently used at principal stations.

Train radio

Another development in communication in the last two decades has been cab to signalbox radio, largely as a prerequisite of driver-only train operation. Its aim has been to give the signalman the facility of calling up specific trains to give instructions to the driver and for the driver to initiate a call to the signalman in place of using signalpost telephones. This saves the driver from having to leave his cab. The driver cannot simply start a conversation with the signalman but presses a button on his radio which indicates to the signalman that the specific train is calling and the signalman then calls up the train in question and a two-way conversation can then take place. The system operates through the train describer and the unit number of the train. Another form is cab to shore radio in which the driver can dial into the BR national telephone system and although this was to be introduced widely, progress has been slow but it is all part of the communication revolution.

Automation for the driver

So far in this chapter we have looked at automation in signalling control, so that in the latest control centres the signalman is largely keeping an overseeing eye on what is going on with the equipment programmed to set points and signals automatically. In the signalmen to driver control loop, that provides for full automation of the first part – the control of the block sections, the setting of the correct route, the display of the correct signals – in other words all the signalman's actions whether he presses the button or watches a computer doing it for him. With the exception of some metro lines such as Docklands, described in Chapter 15, the other part of the control loop, the correct interpretation of the signals by the driver and the correct handling of the train thereafter, in contrast has little automation, and what it has is based on a principle established 90 years ago with the basic Great Western automatic train control system of 1906. That is the extent of automation in regular daily service today on ex-British Rail lines now within the privatised Railtrack empire.

There is no doubt that GWR ATC, the Hudd magnetic development, and BR standard AWS, have all helped to prevent accidents arising from driver error. These three were warning types of control, originally operating only at distant signals although the BR type and, to a limited extent the GWR system, were later used in multiple-aspect colour light signalling areas but still giving only caution or clear indications. The caution warning covered all aspects except clear and

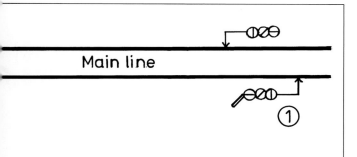

Main line

①

that has been its great weakness as a driver of a train following a section or two behind another train will be running on successive single or double yellow aspects and needing to cancel the warning at each one. The danger is unconscious cancellation as a red signal is approached, even if not following another train, resulting in a signal passed at danger and on occasions has led to accidents, Wembley in 1984, Battersea Park in 1985, and Purley in 1989. It does not provide an adequate reminder of an AWS acknowledgement of a platform starting signal at danger because the track magnet is usually sited as a train is running into a station, as we described in Chapter 13.

The accidents at Paisley in 1979, Bellgrove Junction in 1989, Newton in 1991 and Cowden in 1995, all provide testimony to the inadequacies of AWS when a driver does not respond to a red signal. Moreover, the collisions at Bellgrove Junction and Newton highlighted the potential danger in simplified track layouts as part of rationalisation and modernisation, since single sets of points and short lengths of single line with both ways working had replaced the old style double junction. The absurdity is that at many locations with what are called single lead junctions between otherwise double-track routes, the same number of points is required as a double junction using points rather than a diamond crossing, although space may be a factor. Also, Cowden showed the dangers of a signal passed at danger by a train leaving a passing loop on to a single line operated by track circuit block

without any form of token, resulting in a head-on-collision. We have already noted in Chapter 14 the accident at Colwich in 1986 where the driver knew he was acknowledging an AWS warning of a red signal but thought the signal was approach controlled and expected it to clear.

It is not only signals which can be over-run but approaching temporary or permanent speed restrictions

Fig. 33. *The display given to a driver in signal repeating AWS at the top in which the aspect of the signal approaching was displayed. At the bottom were the acknowledgement buttons and the signal passed display.*

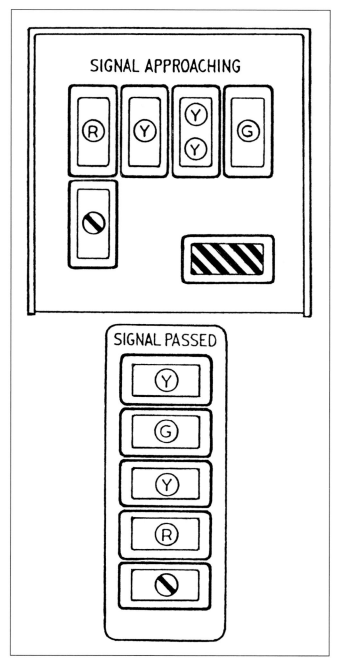

By the end of the 1960s British Rail was undertaking research into more sophisticated forms of train control using the SRAWS cab signal indications and acknowledgements with added information transmitted through wire loops on the track to trains for maximum permitted speed and speed restrictions ahead. At that time punched cards were fed into a computer reader at the start of a journey giving details of the train itself including braking performance. Overspeeding would result in an automatic brake application. (BRB)

Fig. 34. *The layout of signal repeating AWS which provided drivers with an intermittent cab signalling display.*

at too high a speed, or running into buffers at terminal stations. Although AWS was adopted for signals in the late 1950s it took the major derailment on the sharply curved East Coast Main Line at Morpeth in 1969 to bring AWS to permanent speed restrictions. However, this was with such complex criteria for their use that it took two more major accidents, at Paddington in 1983 and another at Morpeth in 1984, before official minds realised the rules needed simplification to be more widely embracing. Even so, temporary speed

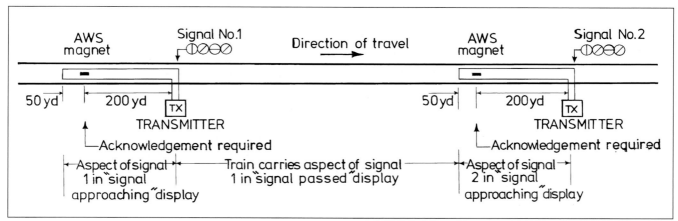

restrictions had not been included until the major derailment at Nuneaton in 1975 showed the disaster potential of a missed warning board and AWS was prescribed for these as well.

This was a period in which the Railway Inspectorate and those in high places on BR, did not seem to appreciate the need for automated assistance for drivers in the new world of higher speeds when a few seconds delay in braking, or a moment's hesitation while a driver rethought what signal aspect he had just seen, or where was the warning board that should be there, could be the precursor of disaster. As he had been since the dawn of railways, the driver was there to see and obey signals and any assistance with AWS was merely an aid and not a substitution for seeing the signal. Quite so, but why then almost total automation for signalmen but not drivers?

The first moves towards a more sophisticated form of AWS on BR came in the late 1960s. The initial steps comprised an enhanced AWS with a cab display showing the exact aspects that had been acknowledged. It was tried out on the Southern Region between Southampton and Bournemouth and was at first known as the 'Southern Region automatic warning system' (SRAWS) but this was soon changed to 'signal repeating AWS'. There were two cab signal displays, one showing the 'signal approaching' after the equipment had been triggered by an AWS permanent magnet placed at the usual 200 yards before the signal, with a high frequency inductive wire loop laid along the sleepers to the signal to transmit the appropriate frequency to show the exact aspect displayed by the signal. The driver had to acknowledge anything other than green by a button alongside the displayed aspect and if he pressed the wrong button it was treated as no acknowledgement and a cancellable brake application was made automatically. If a red signal was passed at danger a full brake application was made which the driver could not cancel, but there was no speed supervision in the basic system. That part came in other experiments in the Wilmslow area which included an on-train computer fed with punched card details of train weight and other characteristics and geographical

A close view of the wire loops on the track for BR research into more advanced train control in the 1960s. By transposing the loops at fixed intervals details of train location would automatically be transmitted to the train. These loops at the time were ungraciously known as the wiggly wire system. (BRB)

information fed from a continuous track loop. This gave details in the form of 'telegrams' of inducted information about the location of following signals, of speed restrictions, and gradients so that the on-board computer could calculate speed profiles and distance to run information. But with the technology then available in the 1970s the experiments did not progress to general adoption.

Automatic train protection (ATP)

During the following decade, railways in other countries were developing more advanced train control systems with speed supervision and automatic brake applications if trains were travelling too fast for speed limits or to stop at a red signal. During the 1980s the Railway Inspectorate was calling for some form of automatic control in recommendations after accidents arising from signals passed at danger. Rapid developments in micro-electronic technology were already providing considerable automation in metro systems which, as we have seen in other chapters on earlier developments, often pre-dated use on the main lines. In November 1988 BR adopted a policy of developing an automatic train protection (ATP) system which, endorsed by the public inquiry into the Clapham collision the following month (although that accident itself would not have been prevented by ATP), envisaged a working system being in use on principal routes within five years.

By the early 1970s transponders, fixed packages of information transmitted to a train by a signal bounced from the train, were being tried on BR in readiness for the higher speeds of the Advanced Passenger Train which in the event was later aborted. But transponders, one is seen here just in front of the locomotive, have progressed and are today used in some parts of the world including trials on BR for an intermittent form of automatic train protection. (BRB)

ATP is one part of a new definition of automatic train control (ATC) which is much more advanced than was ever possible or even thought of in the original GWR ATC. ATC today has two principal parts, ATP which covers the safe running of trains within speed limits and signal aspects, and ATO, automatic train operation which takes over the driving of the train from the train driver. Generally there are two forms of ATP, continuous, and intermittent and the intermittent form can have added fill-in controls. Inducted signals from the track are picked up by the train to provide the parameters within which the train operates, through coded track circuits in the rails, as in London Underground's Victoria and Central lines, and on Irish Rail's continuous AWS system, by wire loops laid along the track and crossed over at intervals, or by transponders, beacons, or balises to use the French term which is gradually encroaching into signalling English. Lineside signals themselves are an intermittent form since the driver sees a signal, and then does not see anything until he sees the next signal. Thus intermittent ATP is merely reflecting the existing lineside signalling.

Continuous ATP is a more sophisticated form since it can update the cab equipment to a change of state ahead as a signal out of sight of the driver changes from say a caution aspect to a clear aspect. But ATP has to be carefully balanced between the instruction of the last signal passed against the next signal ahead. It might be too restrictive if the last signal was at single yellow meaning stop at the next signal which is the instruction on the driver's control desk, yet he can see the next signal has changed to a proceed aspect. With continuous ATP the cab instruction would also change, but with intermittent ATP, cab indications can only change when passing over a loop or beacon and this is where a fill in loop or beacon can update information to respond to a signal change. In some ways this is like the NER's electrical train control system of the 1920s.

BR ATP proposed total speed supervision keeping a watching brief on maximum line speed, permanent speed restrictions, temporary speed restrictions, and the braking curve to stop at a danger signal. If by chance a train passed a signal at danger an automatic emergency brake application would be applied, which cannot be cancelled, to stop the train within the overlap of the signal. A train cannot start from a station against a signal at danger. The driver still drives the train but the maximum permitted speed is shown in his speedometer and on other indications and he must keep within the displayed speed, and reduce speed where a target speed ahead calls for a lower speed. Three miles an hour over and a warning sounds, six miles an hour over and the brakes are applied automatically to bring the speed within the limit.

ATP on BR was to be the control system of the future, probably of the intermittent type to keep costs within reasonable bounds but certainly without ATO. The finance to install the system would be made available said the Government. By 1991 two types were under trial, the Selcab type on the Chiltern lines out of Marylebone by GEC Alsthom Signalling and Standard Elektrik Lorenz, which has its origins in the LZB system used by several European railways, and the Belgian ACEC system installed on the Great Western main line between Paddington and Bristol and also used in Belgium and Holland. Apart from the basic speed supervision features there is communication between the train and loops or beacons to exchange data since the train has to know where it is in relation to gradients, speed limits, and signals ahead, and it must be given details on where the next beacon is and what detail to expect. Thus if vandals damaged or removed a loop the train would know because it would not receive the information at the distance it had been told to expect it.

A European standard train control system?

The imposition of ATP on to an existing signalling system and existing rolling stock is not thought to be the best way of doing it and if costs are to be kept down, ATP is without doubt, expensive. As this book goes to press the trial sections have not been increased and there is no sign of countrywide installation of ATP on BR. An added complication has arisen in that with the Channel Tunnel, BR or its privatised successors, now have trains which run directly to France and Belgium and the transport masters in the European Union have called for a Europe-wide form of ATC in its modern sense which will be capable of international operation. Recognising all the different forms of AWS or ATP systems already used in Europe the system would have to cope with transmission of existing codes from track equipment on whichever line the train is running and on-board processors would translate that information into the standard on-board equipment. With the London–Paris/Brussels 'Eurostar' trains having to cope with five types of warning or train protection system, with the potential for a sixth if BR ATP is adopted nationally, standardisation would make sense.

The European train control system (ETCS) in its standard form would use an on-train computer system known as Eurocab to provide the link between the commands and information transmitted from the track or lineside to the train controls. There would be track loops or beacons known as Eurobalise and Euroloop for intermittent or semi-continuous transmission to trains of information and instructions, and continuous lineside radio data links knows as Euroradio. As for its use there would be three levels of application. Level 1 would provide ATP and speed control in conjunction with existing lineside signalling

but the driver would still drive and if he acted within the overall speed limits and signal aspects, the equipment would not intervene. Level 2 is still an add-on to existing lineside signalling and relies on conventional train detection through track circuits or axle counters but would provide much more speed information with target speeds, distance to stop and could provide a measure of automatic control of train speed. Level 3 is the full package providing full ATC, adding automatic train operation, train reporting and other supervisory features. Lineside signals would not be needed and new forms of detection would allow the train to locate itself through the lineside beacons. Since the occupation of line space by the train within fixed track circuits would no longer be used, meaning that track circuits would not have a long-term future in train detection, and the fact that the position of a moving train could be determined within fine limits, the adoption of moving block becomes a possibility for lines with dense traffic. Following trains would be kept apart at a continuous braking distance plus a safety margin, rather than in a series of steps for each signal and track circuit section. In Britain, Railtrack, which now looks after track, signalling, and stations, is planning to resignal the West Coast Main Line from Euston to Glasgow with a Level 3 installation with all the data exchanges of commands and reports, sometime early in the 21st century although at this early stage in planning, possibly not with automatic train operation. With train detection and transmission of instructions to on-train processors and information from train to control centres being passed by induction between train mounted equipment and the track or by radio between the train and lineside equipment, rather than by the direct contact of wheels and track circuits through the rails, the system is known as transmission based signalling (TBS).

Future strategy

During 1997 Railtrack, now responsible for track and signalling on former BR lines, outlined its signalling strategy towards the year 2010. By then it seems likely that track circuit block with MAS would survive only on dc electric lines south of the Thames, also in an area bounded by Liverpool and Preston in the west, across the North of England conurbations to Hull in the east, and in the Forth-Clyde valley. Most trunk routes would have TBS, other secondary routes would have lineside signals controlled by axle counters, and RETB would be retained on existing remote single lines and extended to a handful not so far equipped.

Global positioning satellites (GPS)

Other forms of automation have also been developed although the differences lie in the way they are achieved more than what they do. Space technology can also be involved, for global positioning satellites (GPS) can be used to determine train position which, although it would hardly be suitable for signalling densely worked urban lines it finds an application on long distance lines in the USA for example where the Burlington Northern controls over 23,000 miles of route from one vast computerised control centre, the largest in the world. Experiments are in hand though in Britain, to use GPS for information technology. On lightly used lines automated add-ons can provide a form of ATP to radio electronic token block (RETB) described in Chapter 7. Track transponders can be added to tell the train where it is, which, linked to the on-board computer, as the train passes over and interrogates the transponder can determine whether the electronic token is valid for that location and if not, will stop the train. With a transponder the train radio link can confirm to the control centre where it is.

The price of safety

Computers and data links by wire, induction or radio, have revolutionised the possibilities of track to train communication. But they cost money and adding systems to existing locomotives and stock is fraught with difficulty, not least in some instances with the physical problems of finding space on a traction unit to put the new equipment, and in adding wiring runs where they will not be affected by existing equipment.

Some people within and outside the railway industry are now questioning the cost of automation and whether it is more a wish list of goodies or a practicable and above all economic programme to enhance safety. After all, what is ATP going to protect and how many lives will it save? In seven out of the last 20 years not a single passenger has been killed in a train accident on British Rail lines. In the other 13, a total of 100 gives an average of 7.7 fatalities a year, and that includes all train accidents whether caused by signalling or driver error, and anything else which ATP would not prevent. Nevertheless, there have been around 18 collisions involving passenger trains each year until the early 1990s and about 40 bufferstop collisions, all involving to a lesser or greater extent, damage to stock and injuries if not fatalities. Even with modern signalling, there have been about 800 cases a year where trains pass signals at danger. Some, it is true, result from wheel slide where wheels lock when braked because of slippery rails and erode braking distances, but the cost of ATP has to be balanced against that level of accidents, or potential accidents.

Meanwhile minor improvements to prevent signals from being passed at danger are in hand, particularly on starting from stations at locations identified as having a high risk potential with added warnings beyond the signal at danger showing a flashing 'STOP' indication if a train ventures beyond a red signal. Other measures are being undertaken including risk assessments to see whether signals need repositioning or junction layouts need alteration to lessen the accident potential of a signal passed at danger. Also, 'black box' data recorders on trains and in signalling centres, both of relay and solid state types, can show how the signalling was set and which route or routes were clear, and what information was picked up by a train from AWS or ATP indications and how the driver responded. Thus in the event of an accident the data recorders can confirm the situation leading to the crash and supplement evidence from eye witnesses always assuming that they are in working order and actually have tapes in them. In one recent accident it was found that the recorders did not have tapes and that nothing was available for analysis after the event.

Just as this book closed for press the newly privatised railway industry had shock waves sent through it when an InterCity 125 with a single driver on a Swansea–Paddington working in September 1997 collided at high speed with an empty aggregates train crossing its path at Southall, killing seven passengers and injuring many others. This was a line with newly installed multiple-aspect signalling, track circuit block, and control through an integrated electronic control centre at Slough. The line had conventional AWS and for the last few years had been subject to one of the two experimental ATP installations. While the results of the public enquiry had not been published in time for inclusion in this edition, enough was in the public domain to suggest that not merely was the ATP not in use because of reliability problems but because of a fault the train's AWS was isolated. This meant that the driver had no automated assistance whatever and was in no better position than his Great Western predecessors 90 years earlier before the introduction of GWR ATC in 1906 following the collision at Slough in 1900. If that is confirmed then the driver had to carry the entire weight of responsibility in seeing and acting on signals every 20-30 seconds at 125mph and was not permitted to make a mistake or misjudgement.

In the context of train operation in the 1990s that was an impossible situation and one which is akin to a signalman being allowed to give unrestricted clear signals with a total failure of interlocking, or an airline pilot taking a Jumbo Jet through intensively used airspace without the benefit of navigational aids.

The Southall collision, like that at Clapham nine years before, raised questions not just about the actions of one man but the whole system of automated aids for train drivers, the policies, the requirements of Health & Safety legislation and its interpretation, but above all the part played by politicians who controlled the purse strings in sowing the seeds of doubt about the cost effectiveness of ATP and just how much on-train automation can be justified. Southall, like the accidents at Armagh, Welwyn, Harrow and Clapham, should go down in signalling history as one leading to a leap forward in the progress of railway safety.

Chapter 17

THROUGH THE TUNNEL
AND ACROSS THE POND

THIS BOOK IS primarily a survey of railway signalling from the dawn of railways to the present time in Britain, but it is worth having a glance to see how others have done it. If we take a peep through the Channel Tunnel, figuratively speaking, we can see vastly different forms of signalling from those familiar on the British system at the other end. Indeed, if we look further afield, south west across France to Spain and Portugal, or south east to Switzerland and Italy, and east through Belgium and Holland to Germany and the other countries of Central Europe we find signalling systems in families where similar types but with detailed variations are, or have been, used in several countries.

The signalling systems in most Western European countries have gone through much the same sort of evolution as those in Britain with the development of mechanical signalling in the last century, the adoption of the block system although often applied differently and with varying levels of equipment, the use of interlocking although even today a few secondary and branch lines still rely on hand-worked points, and in some cases little formal signalling, and the introduction of block locking. On some secondary or branch lines there was, and on a few still is, no formal block system and trains run under timetable and train order conditions. On single lines at least this means following the timetable for crossing moves at passing stations unless otherwise instructed by written order if trains are running late. On some, the telephone is used to operate a verbal block system but it has its dangers if the staff operating the system are not disciplined to the precise form of words which are laid down. Sloppy use of the telephone led to one of Germany's worst train disasters since the Second World War in 1975 at Warngau in Bavaria when two traffic supervisors using telephone block each thought he had offered a train to the supervisor at the opposite end of the single line section and had it accepted. Both sent their trains away and the two diesel-hauled trains met head-on and 38 passengers and the two drivers were killed in the collision. The single line token systems used in Britain

were virtually unknown on railways of mainland Europe but formal block signalling equipment for both double and single lines was often of the lock and block pattern. Although track circuiting is used, axle counters are also widely employed, particularly if tracks have steel sleepers. Operating methods in Europe may not have been so tightly regulated as in Britain but some signalling developments have been at the forefront of technology. AWS was adopted more widely and earlier than in Britain and more recently, ATP has been used on some railways for the last two decades. Some single lines, on the Rhaetian Railway in Switzerland for example, have had automatic passing facilities at crossing stations where the trains signal themselves past a train in the opposite direction, for the last two decades. On other railways the control of the block system is conducted in the station office while the points, particularly for shunting, are worked from a signalbox out on the line. Sometimes all the functions are worked from one location. Point indicators alongside the turnouts show drivers which way they are set.

From the turn of the century power operation was beginning to be employed and later, colour light signals began to take over from the mechanical forms. The original colour light aspects though were usually based on the night-time indications of the mechanical signals rather than on a new code as in Britain. With higher speeds as locomotives became more powerful and larger radius points allowed higher turnout speeds, new signal aspects were introduced in some countries expanding the existing codes, though without any mechanical equivalent. This often led to multi-light displays particularly where distant indications were combined with stop signals. Some locations in what were Eastern bloc countries have complex speed signalling aspects.

Basically the operating needs of signalling are exactly the same as in Britain. The driver needs to know if the line is clear for his train and whether he can proceed at maximum line speed, whether the signals ahead are at danger and he needs to slow down ready to stop, and at junctions and stations some indication of which way the train is to go or at what speed it can run to take diversions at points safely. It is in the detailed methods of telling drivers the state of the line and whether it is safe to proceed which differs from country to country but some may use part or all of another.

Station track layouts often seem to be distinctive to a particular country. In Switzerland many country town stations on through routes not only have double-track main lines in the centre but loops on each side which, with headshunts at one or both ends, provide goods facilities right in the station area, and there is not the dislike of facing points as in Britain. Often at Swiss stations, the station tracks are signalled for both ways running with facing and trailing crossovers at both ends of the station. It is much the same in Austria and Germany. Some railways in Europe have left hand running on double lines, notably France, Belgium, Switzerland, and Italy. Other countries mainly have right hand running, but history often plays a part as in Eastern France, for a time until the First World War part of Germany, where right hand running is the rule. Today many double lines are fully reversible.

On single lines at passing stations there is no set rule and non-stopping trains are usually routed by the track least restricted by speed limits through points. Usually, the first train to arrive if two trains are to cross, will take the more restricted track often nearest to the station building, so that passengers without the benefit of bridges or underpasses do not have to cross the other passing track as the second train arrives or passes. At many European country stations the low platforms and lack of segregated access to platforms have meant that station and train staff have to watch passengers boarding or alighting very carefully to ensure that they do not stray across tracks in use. On many lines though, standards are much the same as in Britain.

Contrasting signal meanings

As for the signals themselves, the standard light colours of red for danger – stop, yellow for caution, and green for clear are used, sometimes almost exactly as is done on BR in three-aspect colour light signalling, although occasionally the lights are not in the same vertical order. Quite often combinations of signal lights have either subtle or major variations of meaning from one country to another. Until recently drivers rarely crossed frontiers except possibly to the first major station near the border so that different meanings were not a great problem. But now, with the advent of through high speed trains running or proposed between France, Belgium, Holland, and Germany, as well as the London–Paris/Brussels 'Eurostars', for the first time drivers, and many more traction units, are routinely working across national borders. Thus drivers can encounter the same light combinations in signals in the various countries not merely with different meanings

but sometimes with contrary meanings which must, from a psychological view, increase the risk of driver error if ATP is not added to conventional signalling. Just three examples will show the potential dangers – double yellow in Britain is a preliminary caution signal, in France it is a junction signal, in Switzerland it means there is reduced braking distance to a stop signal. Flashing green in France is the preliminary caution following a steady green, in Britain flashing green is the full clear on the East Coast route for 140mph trains and steady green means reduce to normal line speed. However, the most dangerous misinterpretation would be for a French 'Eurostar' driver, well used to the stop and proceed rules for a single red aspect (semaphore) in France, forgetting that a single red aspect in Britain is an absolute stop signal.

Signalling terminology

Signalling terminology is different in Europe than in Britain. In Britain we talk about entry to a block section, that is leaving a station. In Europe an entry signal means entry to a station which in Britain would be called a home signal. The exit signal or leaving signal is what in Britain would be known as a starting signal, but a block signal is a block signal in any terminology. Usually at a station the exit signal or in Britain the starting signal (or sometimes the advanced starting signal) is the block signal covering movements into a block section. In Europe the tracks for each direction are usually denoted by numbers, odd numbered tracks one way and even numbered tracks the other. Also, signals are said to be 'closed' when at danger and 'open' when they are at clear. Mechanical signalling, including points, is commonly worked by the double-wire system and the levers normally standing almost upright in the lever frame are pulled forward and down to clear a signal or change points.

French signalling

Briefly looking at mechanical signalling around Europe, the French used primarily boards in the form of squares, triangles, discs, or diamonds (in reality a square board tilted through 45 degrees), and semaphores. The semaphore was principally used on plain line and at night showed a single red light. In certain circumstances a semaphore could be passed at danger with the train proceeding cautiously (with 'prudence' in the French rule book) running on sight. Country stations had little more than a semaphore signal in the middle of the station for each direction, which with a distant signal were the only signals provided. They usually had a miniature semaphore arm lower down the mast which was actually the block indicator for the next section ahead for the information of the person in charge of the signalling. Other than the semaphore which had positive danger (or caution) indications when horizontal, and clear when lowered,

French mechanical signals with the 'carré' absolute stop signal square chequerboard panel on the left, a 'ralentissement' junction distant at the top and an 'avertissement' distant signal on the right. The layout of a French mechanically signalled junction is shown in Fig. 41. (Geoffrey Kichenside)

French colour light signal displaying the 'carré' absolute stop double red aspect. In the foreground are the crocodile automatic warning system ramps. (Alan Williams)

French colour light signal showing the single red semaphore stop aspect, meaning 'stop and proceed at caution'. (Alan Williams)

the mechanical panel signals rotated on a vertical axis to be edge on for clear. In contrast the red and white square chequerboard was the stop signal known as the carré and when at danger was an absolute stop signal showing two red lights at night. It was used at junctions and other controlled areas where permissive working was forbidden and the double red colour light today has the same absolute stop meaning. The yellow diamond board is a distant signal repeating the next stop signal ahead, while the red disc, 'disque rouge', a sort of distant signal, is rather akin to the indeterminate distant signals in Britain in the 1860s meaning, when face on and showing a red and a yellow light, 'pass me but stop before the first points ahead' probably by a marker post. Junction diversion through points are denoted by a vertical triangular board known as the ralentissement, showing horizontal double yellow lights, at braking distance from the points and an inverted triangular board known as the rappel de ralentissement showing vertical double yellow lights at the junction signal. When the points are set for the diversion the ralentissement and the rappel would be face on but the carré at the junction would be edge on. Speed limit figures for the turnout usually supplement triangular boards.

A mixture in Spain

Spain had a curious mixture of three-position upper

quadrant semaphores with route signalling and multi-arm displays, and some of the French type boards including the red disc, an inverted yellow triangle showing green over yellow for preliminary caution and the yellow diamond showing vertical double yellow for caution, the normal distant signal. Some stations were equipped only with the red disc and yellow distant on the same post. If both signals were face on the train had to stop before the first points but if the red disc was edge on and the distant face on the train could enter the station. In the station itself onward movement was by hand or flag signals, a clear signal being a furled red flag held vertically above the head by the stationmaster or person in charge. Hand signals in Spain were almost the same as in Britain until 1936, with both arms raised above the head for danger and one arm horizontal for clear.

Italian signalling

Italy was about the only European country with a signalling system that would be recognised by those familiar with British practice. Mechanical signals were lower quadrant semaphore arms painted red with a white vertical stripe for stop signals and yellow with the vee notch cut from the left hand end for distants just as in Britain, with multiple arms at junctions. The arms had an uncanny resemblance to GWR types. A major difference was on signals with stop and distant arms where the distant was mounted behind the stop arm and invisible when both were at danger. With the stop arm clear the distant could be seen at caution behind it or lowered at a different angle for clear. Early Italian colour light signals showed the same night-time indications of just red, or yellow, or green and were either of the multi-lens type with red at the top, or of

the searchlight pattern, and at junctions had separate heads for each route. Later, an expanded colour-light code including flashing aspects provided speed indications.

German signalling

German mechanical signalling used semaphore stop signals with the arms to the right of the mast and usually with a circular end to the arm, and disc distants horizontally pivoted to lie flat edge on when clear. Junction signals had two semaphore arms one above the other, the top arm alone used for the straight route and both arms when the points were set for the diversion. They were upper quadrants, horizontal for danger and inclined up at 45 degrees when clear but the second arm was vertical when not wanted for showing the diversion. The top arm showed red when at danger and green when clear, and when the second arm was in the 45 degree position for the diversion it showed yellow to give a green over yellow display. German pattern signalling was also used in Austria and Switzerland though with detailed variations. Colour light signals were based on the night-time mechanical indications, but the green over yellow for diversion at points eventually came to refer to those with a 40kph restriction. In Switzerland, the colour light code was expanded to give double green for 60kph points and triple green for 90kph points. Distant indications became complex with horizontal double yellow for caution, diagonal double green for clear on the straight route and other combinations of yellow and green for the various speed restrictions ahead for point

Fig. 36. *Layout of German mechanical signals at a local station with an added loop and an element of reversible working.*

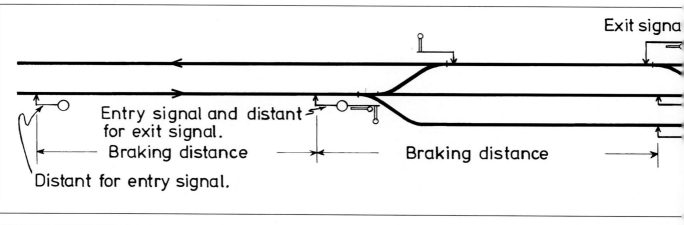

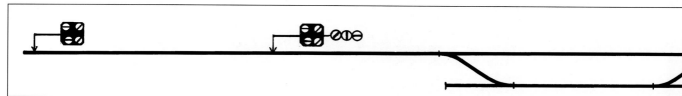

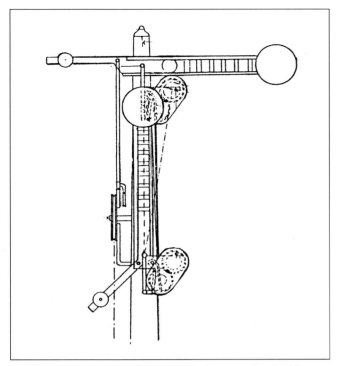

Fig. 35. *German semaphore signal showing the double arm arrangement of a junction signal.*

German semaphores showing the line clear for a movement from a lower speed track to the main line. (Alan Williams)

German colour light signal showing double red side by side indicating that all movements including shunting must stop. (Alan Williams)

diversions. On German pattern signalling, the first distant signal approaching a station usually applied only to the entry (home) signal. Normally braking distance existed between the entry and exit signals and an inner distant repeating the exit signal was mounted under the entry signal. In Swiss colour light practice this often meant a combination of five lights at the entry signal, two on the entry signal itself and three on

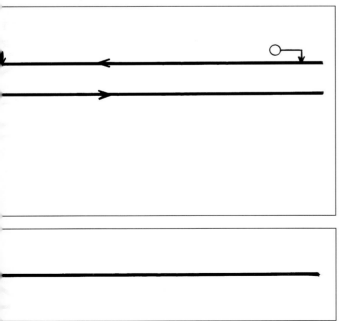

Fig. 37. *An example of Swiss practice at some stations in which the exit signal from the station is beyond the points and would show single green for a movement from the straight route and green over yellow (or green over green if higher speed points are used) for a movement from the loop.*

Austrian signalling is largely based on the German pattern but the distant signals seen lower down the post are rectangular with the caution double yellow side by side rather than diagonally as in Germany. (Alan Williams)

the distant below if a train was routed in and out of a loop with higher speed points. More recently the Swiss have introduced simple red, yellow, green aspects along with speed indications in figures.

North America

Glancing further afield briefly, in North America semaphore signalling was fairly standard by the turn of the century, originally lower quadrant, and later upper quadrant with three-position arms. Colour lights began to replace semaphores with indications on a like for like basis with combinations of arms or searchlight heads to give up to three lights at a time, plus a marker light in some cases, with complex combinations for different speed ranges now or ahead in interlocking areas or for block signalling on plain line. Operational methods ranged from basic timetable and train order working with a three-position semaphore at a passing station meaning danger stop when horizontal, raised at 45 degrees meaning slow for orders, which the despatcher passed up to the driver clipped to the top of a pole, and vertical, proceed in accordance with instructions. Stations were linked by the telegraph system. At the other extreme is Centralised Traffic Control (CTC) where a central office can control signals and points at distant stations through remote

International signalling at Sarreguemines in the early 1970s with German semaphores providing entry to the station from the east and French 'avertissement' diamond distant boards below giving warning of the next French signals ahead. Luxembourg used this combination on its railways but the German style junction semaphore showed double yellow lights at night when clear for a diversion. (Roger Siviter)

control links, to the present computerised automated systems on some lines as we saw in the last chapter. At some remote passing loops, usually called sidings in American terminology, train crews themselves operated points to let their train in and out of the loop to let another train pass.

British practice abroad

Looking around the world, British pattern semaphore signals were used in a number of countries where British engineers built the railways as in South America, Eastern and Southern Africa, India and today's Pakistan, parts of South East Asia and Australia and New Zealand. American influences later crept in as in the three-position semaphores on some Australian lines and speed signal colour lights in New Zealand. Today, British style colour light signals with junction indicators can be found in Queensland and in parts of South East Asia and the supply of signalling equipment is now very much an international operation. Token systems were used on many railways built under British influence, although CTC has been adopted by some railways. RETB, as developed by British Railways, is in use on a number of lines overseas.

TVM 430 through the
Channel Tunnel and on towards Paris

Returning to that link through the Channel Tunnel, the signalling there deserves a more detailed mention for it has brought a highly automated system right to the doors of the British railway network.

Signalling in the Channel Tunnel is entirely novel to British experience, because there are no external fixed running signals of any sort, the entire system depending on a cab signalling system which is a variation of the TVM 430 system developed for the SNCF TGV Nord line. This is itself a more sophisticated version of the TVM 300 system used on the earlier TGV Sud-Est and Atlantique lines. The tunnel system is essentially a 'four aspect' speed-band signalling system with marker boards, or 'repères', to indicate sections, each of which are about 500m long, although the actual length depends on gradients.

The cab equipment on the Eurotunnel 'Le Shuttle' locomotives, Class 373 'Eurostar' power cars and the Class 92 locomotives all include displays giving the 'target' speed at which the driver should drive his train through the next section. Running under 'clear' signals – green in British signalling practice – the display in a 'Le Shuttle' or Class 373 shows '160' (160kph) in black on a green background. On a Class 92 locomotive, because the maximum speed varies according to load, it simply shows green. If the train then begins to approach a 'signal' at danger some way ahead, the first indication that the driver would receive would be that this steady display would give way to a flashing '160' display, indicating that a more restrictive indication will

British style signalling abroad with a colour light signal on Queensland Railways in Australia on the line west from Brisbane. British type AWS magnets are also used but with transponders (BELOW) to provide intermittent automatic train protection. (Alan Williams)

TGV 'repère' marker board on the TGV Sud Est line to the south at Macon Loché. With a junction ahead, if the cab signal remains at danger it is of the 'non franchissable' type, 'Nf', having the same absolute stop meaning as a 'carré'. (Alan Williams)

be displayed at the next section, and that he or she should slow down. At the next section the cab indication would change to a steady '080' (80kph) on 'Eurostar' in black on a white background as the train passes the 'repère' marker board. To give sufficient braking distance, 'Eurostars' run through a second section during which a steady '080' is displayed before encountering a flashing '080' at the marker board at the beginning of the third section, warning the driver that he will receive a more restrictive indication at the next marker board and should slow down further. On 'Le Shuttles', the three sections are marked with flashing indications of '130', '115' and '080'. If the more restrictive indication ahead is in fact 'stop' then the indication will be '000' in black on a red background, warning the driver that he must stop at the marker board at the end of that section. Should a driver attempt to drive his train above the target speed – to 'overspeed' in signalling jargon – an emergency brake application is initiated, and although the brake can be released once the speed has fallen back within the permitted range, by the time the brakes have released and power is reapplied, in practice the train is at or approaching a stand. Nevertheless, despite this 'overspeed' control, unlike in conventional BR

signalling practice, a full additional section is provided between the rear of a train and the one following it, allowing in effect a minimum of 500m overlap in case a driver misjudges his braking, or 'overspeeds'. Should he for any reason encroach upon this additional section, his indicator changes from '000' to a solid red. This is also displayed if, because of failure, a driver is instructed to proceed beyond a 'stop' indication. In these circumstances, he must drive on sight, prepared to stop short of any obstruction, at a maximum speed of 30kph.

Although these are the only running target speeds, 'Le Shuttle' locomotives and 'Eurostar' trains have two others – '100' and '060'. The '100' is for use when running through any part of the tunnel where the ventilation cross shafts have been closed for engineering work, in which case the line speed is restricted to 100kph to minimise problems of air pressure and turbulence, while the '060' display is used on the approach to a diversion from one running tunnel to the other through the 60kph scissors crossovers installed at two locations within the tunnel. This display is preceded by the flashing '080' display, and is also used, if necessary, to give warning of temporary speed restrictions.

The cab displays on a Class 92 work in a similar way, and give a similar sequence of progressively declining target speeds, but the actual speeds are different: 'line speed' on the Class 92 is 140kph for passenger and some freight trains, but can also be 120, 100 or even possibly 80kph for freight trains, so the driver needs to select his target speed regime before setting out. Running under clear signals, his display will show three steady green lights; approaching a reduction in speed, this will change to a row of flashing green lights, and then the next target speed will be '060', which is maintained for one further section, and then becomes a flashing '060' before the steady '000'. The sequence for all three types of trains is shown in Fig. 39.

Audio frequency track circuits are used with 26 codes, 19 of which are available for operational messages. There is an identifier code on each track circuit so that the train can locate and report its position in the tunnel, as well as interpret coded information on gradients and other features to enable on-board equipment on the train to monitor performance. Although not strictly part of the 'signalling', if the driver's vigilance device is released, an alarm code alerts the supervisor in the control centre, who can then speak to the driver. On-board train equipment monitors the track-borne codes continuously, and if all codes are lost, an emergency brake application is initiated. In the unlikely event of a total failure, the equipment allows the driver to proceed at very restricted speed, driving on sight but under instruction from the control centre. For this reason,

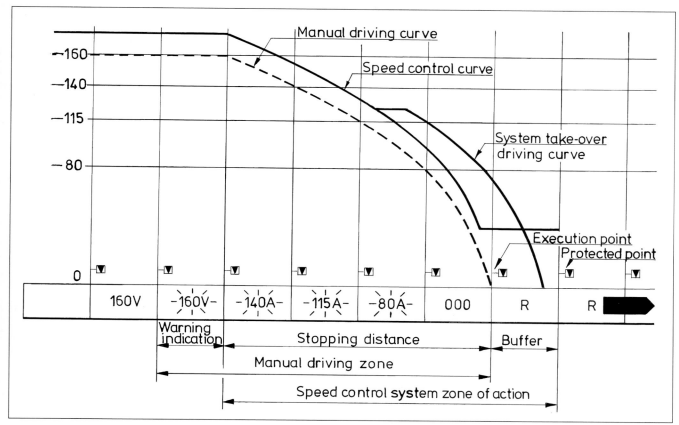

although no fixed visual signals are provided other than the 'repère' marker boards to indicate each section, there are French-style point indicators at the two sets of scissors crossovers within the tunnel. Both running lines in the tunnel are fully equipped for bi-

Fig. 38. *The Eurotunnel speed curve in relation to the cab signalling displays for 'Le Shuttle' in the Channel Tunnel.*

Fig. 39. *The cab signalling displays for 'Le Shuttle', 'Eurostar' and a Class 92 hauled train for a stop in relation to the 'repère' marker boards through the Channel Tunnel.*

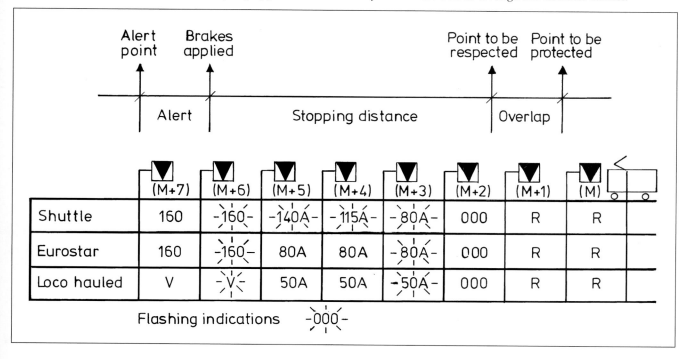

directional running and in the case of emergency, provided the line is clear behind it, a train can be driven 'wrong line' out of the tunnel.

The Eurotunnel Control Centre for the entire tunnel is normally at Cheriton, at the English end, but the control system has been duplicated on the French side at Fréthun and can be brought into use in case of emergency. SNCF standard relay interlocking equipment is used throughout, and French-style physical signals are used where necessary throughout Eurotunnel complexes on both sides of the Channel.

Three types of train use the tunnel – the Eurotunnel 'Le Shuttle' vehicle-carrying trains, the Class 373 'Eurostar' high speed passenger trains from London to Paris and Brussels, and Class 92 locomotive-hauled freight trains. Of these, the Eurotunnel 'Le Shuttle' trains are equipped only with the tunnel signalling equipment, as their dedicated turnaround loops at each end of the tunnel are also similarly equipped. The Class 92 is fitted with tunnel signalling equipment in addition to its standard BR AWS (and incorporates provision for the fitting of any new BR Automatic Train Protection equipment) and is thus able to work through to the Fréthun terminal in France. To enable the Class 92 locomotives to move around in the Fréthun complex beyond the limits of the Channel Tunnel signalling, without having to be fitted with French equipment, certain signals in the Fréthun area have been equipped with conventional BR AWS magnets but located at, rather than on the approach to, each signal, reflecting SNCF practice with 'crocodile' ramps, of which more later.

By far the most complex signalling system is that aboard the Class 373 'Eurostar' London–Paris–Brussels units, which have to interface with BR AWS, tunnel cab signalling, the very similar LGV Nord system, the conventional SNCF and SNCB 'crocodile' ramps, the French KVB system used on conventional high speed lines, and the Belgian TBL system – and still allow for the subsequent fitting of BR ATP! Worse still, transition from one system to the other, including proving that the new system is working, has to be achieved at full line speed – and, in the case of the transition from BR AWS to tunnel signalling for trains entering the tunnel at the English end, while also raising two pantographs and then retracting third rail shoe gear.

As far as the signalling is concerned, as the Class 373 units and Class 92 locomotives traverse the section approaching the Tunnel entrance, the on-train equipment for the tunnel signalling has to be 'armed', because it needs to be proven working before the train actually enters the tunnel. On the Class 373 units, the

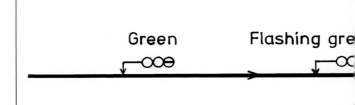

Fig. 40. *French five-aspect colour light sequence on conventional high speed lines up to 220kph.*

equipment is first triggered by a track-mounted TVM loop, and then a KVB beacon of the type used for cab signalling on the conventional SNCF high speed lines (for which the Class 373 is fitted). It then checks that it is correctly set, as happens on TGV units entering French high speed lines. On the Class 92, which work only to Fréthun, and are not therefore fitted with KVB equipment, the lineside automatic power control APC magnets, normally used to switch current off, then back on again before and after neutral sections in the overhead in ac areas, also initiate a check of the on-train Tunnel signalling equipment. In both cases, if the equipment does not automatically 'arm' in response to passage over the track-side equipment within about six seconds, the train is automatically brought to a stand by a full service application of the brakes. If the driver cannot then arm the equipment manually the train is forbidden to continue its journey, and will be required to remain on BR or SNCF tracks until the malfunction

Fig. 41. *French mechanical signals approaching a junction. If the line is clear for the straight route all boards would be edge-on to an approaching train.*

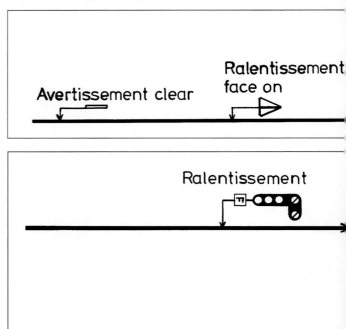

Fig. 42. *French colour light signals approaching a junction. If the turnout speed is 60kph or more both signals will flash. The main signal aspect on the junction is out unless the following signal is at danger.*

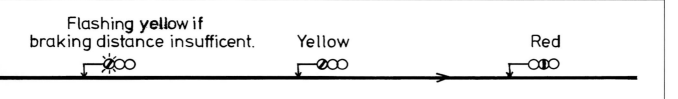

Flashing **yellow** if braking distance insufficent.   Yellow   Red

is cured. The Tunnel Safety Authority demands extreme reliability in all aspects of tunnel signalling and the very act of a train coming to a stand in or on the immediate approaches to the tunnel is regarded as a 'potential hazard'. Once it has been armed, the on-board train equipment needs to be updated as it passes the subsequent conventional running signals on the approaches to the tunnel, so these approach tracks are equipped with tunnel signalling, giving a cab display corresponding to whatever aspect the conventional British signalling is showing. Likewise, coming out of the English portal of the tunnel, the on-train equipment needs to be 'disarmed' by the same process before it enters conventional BR signalling territory – otherwise, the loss of the tunnel audio track circuit signals would very rapidly bring the train to a stand! At the 'handover' point, the on-train equipment proves the BR AWS is working before it switches itself off. An add-on to the signalling for freight trains approaching the French end of the tunnel is an out-of-gauge detector to check that wagons are within the British height and width limits.

In France, the specially-built high speed lines for 'Trains à Grande Vitesse', or TGV, are equipped with the same TVM cab signalling system as is used in the Channel Tunnel, and lineside signals are not provided.

However, because of the higher maximum speed, there are more speed bands; maximum speed on the original Sud Est line is 270kph, but on the later Atlantique and Nord lines, the maximum is 300kph. If the line is clear and the train is authorised to run at the maximum line speed, the cab indication would show VL ('voie libre', or line clear). This would then change to '260' at the next 'repère', indicating that the driver should slow to 260kph, and then to '220', '160', and '80' at the next three markers, before '000', which instructs the driver to stop at the next marker. Other special target speeds can be displayed if necessary, for example on the approach to junctions, or where lower temporary or permanent speed limits apply. One great advantage of cab signalling over normal lineside signalling is that if the line ahead clears, the target speed can be increased immediately, and the driver does not have to wait until he passes the next 'signal' for this new information.

All French high speed lines are controlled from the equivalent of a power box and are fully reversible with the controllers having direct radio links with individual drivers. TGVs, however, also run over older lines which they share with lower speed passenger and freight trains, and these lines have conventional lineside signals. The basic colour-light signal is a three-aspect automatic signal, perhaps confusingly, called a

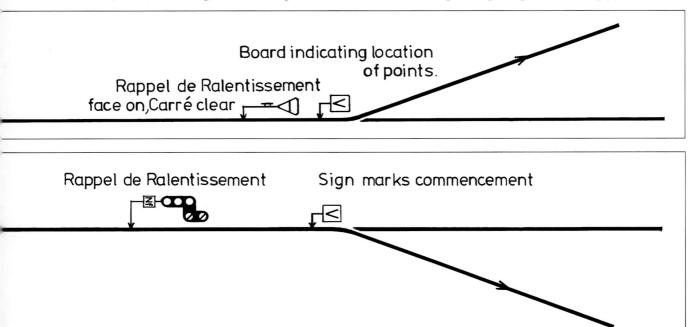

Board indicating location of points.

Rappel de Ralentissement face on, Carré clear

Rappel de Ralentissement   Sign marks commencement

semaphore, showing red for danger in the centre, yellow for caution at the bottom, and green for all clear at the top. A semaphore signal carries a plate with a large letter 'F' (for 'franchissable') meaning that it can be passed at danger. Under these circumstances, a driver understands that the line ahead may be occupied, and that he should stop and then drive on sight at low speed prepared to stop short of any obstruction. This is known as 'Marche à vue'. Such 'semaphore' signals are normally placed at braking distance apart, but where for traffic or other reasons the spacing does not give sufficient braking distance, a flashing yellow is used on the previous signal, in effect giving a fourth aspect, similar to a double yellow in British practice. This flashing yellow, known as 'preavertissement', instructs drivers of passenger trains to reduce speed to 90kph, and freight trains to 50kph until they either pass the next signal showing a steady yellow, in which case they must brake further and expect to find the next signal at danger, or until they pass the next signal showing green, in which case speed can be increased again.

On conventional lines, where TGVs run at up to 220kph, even this greater braking distance is insufficient, and a flashing green signal, known as 'preannonce', instructs the driver to reduce speed to 160kph by the next signal, which will be showing a flashing yellow. The aspect sequence on such lines is therefore green – line clear; flashing green reduce – speed to 160kph; flashing yellow – reduce speed to 90kph; yellow – expect to stop at the next signal, which will be at red. This is shown in Fig. 40.

Of course, a signal that can be passed at danger is of no use in protecting junctions or complicated track layouts at stations. In such cases, controlled signals, known as 'carré' are used, and show two red aspects, normally one above the other. These signals carry plates showing the letters 'Nf' meaning 'non franchissable', and must not normally be passed at danger. Stop and stay stopped is the message. However, such signals also carry a small, subsidiary signal which can show a white light but is normally unlit. When a signalman wants to set a route for a second train to enter an occupied section – what in Britain would be a 'calling on' manoeuvre – this white light, known as an 'oeilleton' comes on, the top red aspect goes out – and the signal changes its meaning and becomes 'franchissable', allowing the driver to proceed under the 'marche à vue' rules mentioned earlier. Track circuits normally run from signal to signal, and there are no overlaps to allow for any errors in braking.

As it is speed signalling rather than route signalling,

French signals do not usually indicate a specific route at simple junctions, but warn drivers to slow down ready for a divergence. For this, a 'ralentissement' (decelerate) signal of two horizontal yellow lights is used on the signal preceding that controlling the junction, while the junction signal itself carries a 'rappel de ralentissement' (reminder to decelerate) signal of two vertical yellow lights. This would be the aspect sequence leading to a slow-speed, 30kph divergence. If the line speed through the divergence is 60kph, both signals flash. In both cases, the other signal aspects are extinguished.

At junctions where the divergence is more than 60kph, the signal protecting the junction carries a theatre-type speed indication, called a 'tableau indication de vitesse', or TIV, which is illuminated at the appropriate speed when the diverging route is set, but it is extinguished when the main higher speed route is set. Such indicators also have advance warning indicators, showing the speed limit on a diamond-shaped plate with small, alternately flashing white lights above and below it to attract attention. These are placed at the braking distance from the actual turnout, rather than to the protecting signal.

Although junction signals as such are not used, where there are a number of possible routes, as often when approaching a main station or terminus, the controlling signal carries a horizontal indicator which can show a series of white lights above the main signal. One light is illuminated when the most left hand of the available routes is set, two lights when the next route to the right is set, and so on.

Shunting movements are normally controlled by 'carré violet' signals, which are 'non franchissable' and normally show a violet light for danger and a single white light for proceed. However, a flashing red main aspect on a running signal is sometimes used instead to authorise a coupling move, and in certain circumstances, on lines with heavy gradients, to authorise trains to pass the signal at danger without stopping and to proceed on a 'marche a vue' basis, subject to a maximum speed of 15kph. A flashing white signal on a running signal specifically authorises a driver to draw ahead of the signal before setting back into a siding.

French Railways have an automatic warning system on their conventional lines, but it is an electro-mechanical system, rather like the Great Western Railway type in Britain described earlier, and takes the form of a horizontal zig-zag strip known as a 'crocodile', placed longitudinally between the running rails, and with which equipment mounted on the train makes mechanical contact.

Chapter 18

THE QUEST FOR THE UNATTAINABLE – ABSOLUTE SAFETY

FROM THE DAWN of railways a safety culture has gradually developed, imperceptibly at first, once the first railway accidents had shown up weaknesses. The pioneer railwaymen were on a very long learning curve because there had been nothing like railways before the 19th century, and man had never before travelled faster than the speed of the horse. Even on the very first day of the opening of the Liverpool & Manchester Railway, when MP William Huskisson became the first fatality in a movement accident on a steam passenger railway, it sent warning signals that people on the line and trains did not mix. With the introduction of the regulatory body, the Railway Inspectorate in 1840, the officers of that organisation began pressing for improvements to make railway operation safer, often against railway management, some of whom seemed to be more concerned with the welfare of shareholders than the safety of passengers. But right through the history of railways, even today, safety improvements have had to be set against the benefits in reducing accidents and in saving lives on the one hand and economic justification on the other. Although there have been and still are rare lapses, there is no doubt that railways are a safe form of transport.

It is a sobering thought that since the first records were kept from 1840 until 1994, just over 3,000 passengers have been killed in train accidents in Britain (and Ireland until 1921) – we repeat, a total of 3,000 or so in 154 years – compared with totals of people killed on the roads ranging from about 3,500 to nearly 8,000 every single *year* from the 1920s in Britain alone. True, the road figure includes all users, pedestrians, cyclists, vehicle drivers and passengers, while the railway figures are only for trains involved in accidents and do not include passengers falling under or from trains – that is movement accidents, (or passengers who fall down stairs or become a casualty in some other way on railway premises not involving a train), but the comparison is valid. The railway, with its regulated and ordered operation, though, should be safer than roads which have only traffic lights, general speed limits, and the highway code and no form of space control between vehicles.

All the improvements in signalling over the years – interlocking, the block system, the block system add-ons such as lock and block, line clear release, Welwyn control, track circuits, and multiple-aspect signalling – have all made a substantial contribution to safer working. ATC/AWS, call it what you will, has also helped but in the signalling/driver control loop there is still a gap, the totally automated prevention of driver error. Can that final push to ATP to eliminate driver errors be justified? Many years see not a single fatality to passengers in train accidents but in the average year around 800 cases are reported of trains passing signals at danger, fortunately with few resulting in accidents, but Purley in 1989, Cowden in 1994 and Watford in 1996 proved that accidents can still happen. Chapter 16 showed that about 60 passenger trains each year are involved in collisions with other trains or buffers at terminal stations, largely low speed accidents usually without fatalities but often with injuries.

The technology we have described can provide a totally automated railway which, in normal operation, can eliminate human error but at a cost. In Germany some local freight trains are remotely controlled without drivers for example. Yet in the safety conscious 1990s where, after an accident, popular opinion led by the media seems to want vengeance for those responsible, risk assessment and a safety case culture has been developed which in Britain is being applied to the interworking of the developing privatised railway system. Yet assessment of risks, which in simple terms is thinking of all the things which might cause an accident from what happens if the smallest bolt fails, to stray electric currents defeating signalling controls, apart from the more direct causes of derailment through ineffective maintenance of track or stock or collisions arising from human error or technical failure and then, proving by calculation or discussion that they will not, had it been employed years ago might have prevented certain accidents.

The quest for cost cutting in which track simplification accompanied resignalling was a case in point because some of the new track layouts relied for their total safety on strict observance of signals. But surely that is what railway signalling is all about – obedience to signals is the driver's first duty. So it might be, but from the earliest days of railways to the present time train drivers have only been human and occasionally a moment's inattention or misjudgment has resulted in a signal passed at danger and possibly an accident. In the past the philosophy has always been to have another trick up your sleeve so that if a train does pass a danger signal in some track configurations it will be diverted away from confrontation with another train. Simple track layouts like single lead junctions have removed that flexibility. In contrast modern signalling following laid down principles is often more restrictive than old style mechanical signalling. At junctions years back the splitting distant signals told the driver quite clearly where he was going and it was up to him to regulate his speed accordingly. In recent years standard colour light practice has decreed that you do not tell the driver where he is going until the last minute at a signal approach controlled from red in an endeavour to ensure that the speed has been brought down to the diversion speed at the points. There are merits in both systems but ATP would give the driver a positive target speed and supervise his handling of the train and ATO would drive the train at the right speed anyway.

Whatever new equipment is provided for full automation, safety, in the final event, lies with the people who design the equipment, the people who install it, and the people who use it. You can have all the checks you like on a computer program for controlling an interlocking, and as many testers as you can organise to prove that the person who put the wire in the terminal has put it in the right place, but when a driver calls up by radio and tells the supervisor in the integrated electronic control centre 100 miles away that he has been stopped at a red signal for several minutes, or that he has lost the code on his cab signalling display, as soon as the signalling supervisor tells him 'we've got a problem on that one' and to go forward past the signal at danger, or despite a stop indication on his control desk, all the automation in the world is now at the mercy of the human factor. The collisions at Charing Cross on London Transport's District Line in 1938, and at Farnley Junction in 1977 showed that technicians can be fallible, while the double collision at Clapham Junction in 1988 highlighted not one man's error when working under pressure but threw into the public domain the whole organisation of signal engineering on BR, its installation and testing methods.

While risk assessment and safety cases have swung the safety pendulum too far the other way, at least safety is being talked about as part of the other assessments covering operating need and financial justification of new signalling schemes. In the past the operators said what they wanted, the permanent way department said whether they could provide the track layout and how much it would cost, and the signal engineers said what signals would be needed and what their costs would be. But nobody consulted the drivers or the signalmen. Nobody thought of 'what ifs' in the case of a signal over-run at danger. Drivers were presented with the weekly notice showing the altered signalling and were expected to obey the signals.

We started this book with drivers and very few signals. As railways reach their 200th birthday in the 21st century there will probably still be drivers or train supervisors but a declining number of visible signals. There will be considerable automation which will either prevent driver's errors or drive trains automatically, set routes automatically, and all sorts of controls and checks, but we will not have absolute safety. There will always be that one chance which, in the wrong combination of circumstances will bring disaster, but it will be rare.

ANATOMY OF A SIGNAL – 1, SEMAPHORE

BY THE TIME of the 1889 Regulation of Railways Act the two-position lower quadrant semaphore signal was rapidly becoming standardised, with the semaphore arm horizontal meaning danger and with it inclined down usually at 45 degrees, less on some lines and more on others, with the Great Western arms lowered at 60 degrees, meaning clear. These signals were worked by single wires, as distinct from the double-wire system used extensively on the European mainland. They were pulled from the controlling signalbox, and were usually fitted with counterbalance weights near the foot of the post to ensure the arm returned to 'danger' when the signalbox lever was replaced to that position in the frame, to take up friction and the weight of the wire, or if a wire broke. Some early signals had separate coloured glass spectacles part way up the post to give the night-time indications but the practice of mounting a spectacle plate carrying the red and blue/green glasses at the right hand end of the semaphore arm, arranged to move in front of an oil lamp set on the right hand side of the signal post quickly became standard. The 'green' glass was often a bluish green since the yellow flame of the oil lamp shining through a blue glass appeared as green. From the outset, stop signal arms were painted red on the front face with a white vertical stripe near the left hand end. On the back the arm was white with a black stripe.

Arms were 4–5ft long, originally made of wood and later of metal with corrugated steel arms or pressed steel arms with a small right angle edge, to stiffen the arm. Actual sizes and even shape varied slightly between suppliers and from railway to railway. In more recent times the usual Great Western and Western Region lower quadrant steel arms have generally been 4ft long and 1ft deep to which must be added the length of the spectacle casting which overlapped the arm. The spectacle casting was heavy so that it counterbalanced the lower quadrant arm to pull it up to the danger position if any fittings on the signal post, such as the down rod connections, broke which were beyond the influence of the balance weight near the

foot of the post. Including the spectacle casting the overall length of the signal arm was about 5ft 2in.

Normal upper quadrant arms, first introduced on the main line railways from the mid-1920s following the recommendation by the Institution of Railway Signal Engineers to abandon the three-position upper quadrant type of signal tried out during the previous ten years, are about the same overall length but the parts of the assembly vary. The arm itself, in recent years, has been nearly 3ft 6in long by $10^{3}/_{8}$in deep but the much lighter spectacle pressing, with the side by side glasses, is longer than the lower quadrant pattern to make a total length also of 5ft 2in.

Posts were of varying heights to suit individual locations and sighting. Originally they were of timber, often tapered, but metal had also appeared before the end of the 19th century with light lattice construction. In more recent times concrete posts were tried and the Southern Railway and its Regional successor, ever anxious not to waste anything that could be re-used, made signal posts from old bull head rail. Elsewhere, even on the Great Western for much of the last 60 years, tubular steel posts have been used for renewals and new work. A fairly typical straight post carrying just one or two arms would have a tube $6^{3}/_{4}$in diameter for the bottom half narrowing to $5^{1}/_{2}$in for the top half and capped with a finial. These are usually fairly plain round caps for upper quadrants, but decorative ball and spike patterns were used on Great Western lower quadrants. More complicated bracket or gantry signals needed heavier construction with larger diameter posts. Steel ladders usually ran up the back of the post to a small landing with a single protecting rail at about waist level to allow the signal lineman access to the signal arm for maintenance and to get at the oil lamp to refill it with paraffin. Long burning oil lamps lasting several days between fillings took away much of the drudgery of daily filling of the old signals, some of which had oil lamps raised and lowered by a wire pulley from their housings to ground level for servicing.

Distant signals, to begin with also had red arms, but with a vee shaped notch cut in the left hand end and a

A montage of mechanical signalling practice. TOP LEFT A three-doll bracket of Midland Railway lower quadrant arms, the most important route being the right hand one ahead with the highest signals and the two diversions to the left being of lesser importance. Included on the middle doll is a fixed distant so that drivers would always need to keep speed low approaching the next signal. On the right hand doll is a calling on signal displaying the letter C whether or not the signal was clear. LEFT This upper quadrant signal is a standard LMS/LMR pattern on a tubular post. The white diamond sign tells the driver that this section of line has a track circuit and if detained, he need not immediately carry out Rule 55. ABOVE A dwarf semaphore as used by the LNWR, pre-dating the disc type. (BR, LMR and Geoffrey Kichenside)

matching vee-shaped or vertical stripe. At night they displayed the same red or green lights as stop signals. In February 1925, taking its cue from the yellow caution light used in the then to be abandoned three-position upper quadrants, the Ministry of Transport decreed that distant signal arms on all railways should follow the example of the Metropolitan and District railways some years earlier, and be painted yellow with a black vee shaped band and display a yellow light at night for the newly defined caution horizontal position.

Where sighting of signals from a cab was difficult, perhaps because of a bridge or platform awning, co-acting arms on the same post were sometimes used, one high up so that it could be seen from afar against the sky, the other much lower down and usually at driver's eye level to be visible at close range. In such cases both arms would be worked from the same lever and wire and fittings on the post and would work together. Alternatively, from the 1920s banner repeater signals would be used. These were usually sited between 50 and 200 yards on the approach to the signal they repeated and took the form of a rectangular black arm (with vee notch at the left hand end if repeating a distant signal) pivoted in the middle and usually mounted in a circular frame with a white background and lit from behind at night to show the black arm silhouetted against the bright background. The arm was horizontal at danger or caution and inclined down or up at 45 degrees for clear, depending on whether the signal they repeated was a lower or upper quadrant. There is a modern type using fibre optics. There were also red banner signals which were stop signals in their own right and not repeaters, sometimes used in connection with Sykes lock and block working rather than full size semaphore arms.

Signals protecting junctions almost always had a separate arm for each route carried on its own post or doll on a bracket or gantry. Usually the arm for the most important or highest speed route was the tallest. Occasionally, at low speed junctions just one arm with a mechanical route indicator displaying a letter or figure was used. If separate distant signals were provided for each route at a junction ahead they were known as splitting distants and where signalboxes were close together the distant signals were displayed below the stop signals of the previous signalbox. If that box had only one route ahead then sometimes the one stop signal would have two, even three, splitting distants

below it, one on the same post and the others on separate posts. On some railways splitting distant signals were rarely provided, only one arm being worked for the principal route ahead and being left at caution when the route ahead was set for the low speed turnout. In a few locations because of siting restrictions junction stop signals would be mounted one on top of another on the same post, the topmost arm applying to the most left hand route, the next arm down to the next route to the right and so on.

Signals for certain low speed movements originally were normal arms with added indications on the arm. A signal with a ring towards the left hand end was sometimes used for moves into a goods yard, or on a goods line parallel to a main line or, in the case of the LNWR, for slow passenger lines when adjacent to main lines. In the upper quadrant form only the Southern used the ringed arm for moves into a goods yard.

Signals controlling a 'calling on' move, normally towards a station, was embellished with a letter C, those for a shunt ahead move usually away from a station or yard with a letter S and those when the warning arrangement applied to the next signalbox a letter W. More recently these types of signal have been provided by miniature arms just 1ft 9in long plus spectacle plate and $6^1/_4$in deep painted with horizontal red/white/red stripes and usually revealing the letter C, S, or W behind the arm when in the clear position. Shunting signals originally took the form of discs rotating in a vertical plane with red and green faces, or tiny semaphore arms. For about the last 60 years white discs with a red stripe across and centre pivoted to display the stripe horizontal for danger or inclined at 45 degrees down or up when at clear have become fairly standard. At the exit of some sidings or yards a disc with a yellow stripe allows unrestricted movement past it at danger provided the points are set to a headshunt and not out on to the main line.

Appendix 2

ANATOMY OF A SIGNAL – 2, COLOUR LIGHT

COLOUR LIGHT SIGNALS being a product from the 1920s onwards were not subject to primitive pioneering like their mechanical predecessors. Yet, although there have been major elements of standardisation, there have also been variations of detail even in the last 30 years since the major resignalling schemes of the 1960s when different suppliers had embellishments which made different makes distinctive, the shape of the back plates for example, or the shape and size of hoods keeping sky reflections away from the lenses.

The first colour light signals on the Southern and LMS had separate heads for junction signals and the white light position light junction indicator only came into being during the 1930s, at first on the LNER. Even then there were variations since the LNER and LMS used a five-light indicator while the Southern and London Transport used a three-light version. The original four-aspect signals, from top to bottom, displayed green, yellow, red, yellow, whereas colour light practice normally decreed that the red light should be at the bottom. This was both to bring the red light more-or-less at driver's eye level and to ensure that there was no hood close below it on which an obstruction such as snow could build up and obscure the light. While the resignalling schemes from the 1930s placed the red light at the bottom of four-aspect signals with yellow, green, yellow in the lights rising above it, the original pattern including the multi-headed junction signals lasted on parts of the Southern's Eastern section until renewal or complete resignalling in the 1960s or even later.

In some places on the LNER and LMS, and also on the Great Western, the searchlight signal was used rather than multi-lens units. In searchlight signals there was only one lamp and the colour variations were given by a small colour filter unit with up to three colours, red, yellow, green in a spectacle swinging across in front of the lamp under electro-magnetic control. The red filter was in the neutral position so that if current to the control units was lost the spectacle would revert by gravity to its mid or normal position with the red filter in the line of light. A second lens, either out or showing yellow when lit, was needed to show the double yellow aspect. Although the searchlight type was specified for several resignalling schemes the multi-lens signal always seemed to be the preferred type and by the end of the 1980s the searchlight type was no longer to be used for new work.

The multi-lens type consisted of a signal head formed by a rectangular box structure about 9in wide containing the lamp housings accessible from the back by a locked door, light proof partitions, reflectors to enhance the light and lenses to beam the light towards an oncoming train through the colour lenses, and some of the control equipment. The front lenses concentrating the beam of light were $8^1/_4$in diameter clear to view and spaced at about $9^3/_4$in centres. For about 20 years colour light signals had a small side lamp alongside each main lens so that if a multiple unit train with its cab right at the front had drawn up close to the signal out of eye view of the main beam the driver could see the aspect displayed by the small repeater lamp. Because of their small cast hoods these side repeater lamps acquired the nickname of pigs ears. From the 1960s the glass of the main lenses had a prism portion in which light from the main beam was diverted sideways towards a train standing right up to the signal and so the pigs ears were no longer needed. The signal heads were attached to a bottom bracket incorporating a circular casting which fitted snugly over a $5^1/_2$in diameter steel tubular post to which bolts were tightened to secure the head. As the signal head was usually mounted on top of the post it needed no finial for weather protection, unless the signal head was bracketed out from the front or side of the post for sighting purposes.

If a signal was fitted with a position light junction indicator it was usually mounted above the main head, with the appropriate inclinations of lights, depending on how many route possibilities lay beyond the signal. Just one route diversion off the principal line meant one indicator with the lights at 45 degrees inclined upwards to left or right depending on the direction of the

LEFT *The typical Southern Railway four-aspect colour light signal of the mid-1930s showing the main head bracketed forward from the post. Above it is the three-light junction indicator used by the SR rather than the five-light pattern of the LMS and LNER, and later standardised by BR. The 'pigs ears' containing the small side lights for trains standing close to the signal can be clearly seen. RIGHT A three-aspect multi-lens colour light signal at Rugby surrounded by the protective wire mesh to allow servicing by the technician without risk of him getting in range of high voltage overhead wires. Above the signal is a theatre type route indicator, below the main signal is a position light subsidiary for shunting moves and to its left a bank of route indicating displays illuminated as required for the shunting signal. (Alan Williams, BR, LMR)*

turnout. The white lights were lunar lights, that is with a tinge of blue in the clear glass, $4\frac{1}{4}$in in diameter and spaced $7\frac{1}{2}$in centres apart. There were exceptions to the rule that the principal line did not have a junction indication but just the main aspect. Perhaps due to quirks of geometry in track layouts the principal route might have had a speed restriction, such as through points, and as a reminder a junction indicator might be provided, possibly with some form of approach control. At some low speed junctions, as for example on entering or leaving a principal station, theatre type route indicators are used displaying letters or figures to show which route is set. The display is made up by a grid of small white lights selectively lit to form the letter or figure.

Subsidiary signals for slow speed running or shunting moves for almost the last 60 years have been in the form of small position light signals with three lights $3\frac{1}{2}$in in diameter. They are in the form of a triangle with a red light in the bottom left and a white

light in the bottom right position. Above the red light and slightly inclined away is a second white light. With the red light and bottom right white light displayed the signal is at danger. With the red light out and the two white lights displayed diagonally the signal is clear. If used as an independent shunting signal all three lights are employed but if this type of signal is mounted underneath a normal main colour light signal the red light of the shunting signal is blanked off since the red aspect of the main signal acts as the stop indication. Only the two diagonal white lights are used to authorise a slow speed shunting move past the signal or effectively as a calling on signal, allowing a second train to enter an occupied section as at a principal station, for coupling two trains or admitting a second train to an already occupied platform for connections to other trains.

Other displays on colour light signals include at main stations, a right away indicator operated by platform staff in which a white letter R is shown on a blue background as the driver's authorisation to go, which can only be displayed if the signal is showing a proceed aspect. Other small letter displays serve as route indications when the shunting or subsidiary signal is clear.

Originally, simple steel ladders with a small platform were positioned up the back of the signal post so that the technician could work on the inside of the signal head to replace lamps or for fault finding. On lines electrified on the 25kV ac overhead catenary system something more was required and the top part of ladders as well as the working platforms, are surrounded by wire mesh protection to make absolutely sure that technicians cannot lean out into the danger area adjacent to high voltage cables where flashovers can occur.

SIGNALLING TERMINOLOGY

Absolute block
The normal form of operation on passenger lines in which not more than one train is permitted at one time on one line in a block section, or in a signal section in track circuit block.

Acceptance of a train
In block signalling the act of a signalman in giving permission to the signalbox in the rear to send a train forward into the block section towards him.

Annunciator
A buzzer or other audible device which sounds to alert a signalman to a position of a train, as for example a train approaching a home signal at danger triggered by occupation of the berth track circuit or operation of a treadle.

Approach control
A colour light junction signal held at red or yellow, depending on the speed of the turnout, even though the line is clear ahead to ensure that the driver reduces speed to that required for the diversion to the lower speed route through facing points ahead, before it clears.

Approach release
Part of the approach control circuits for a junction signal in which the signal is stepped up to a less restrictive aspect if the line is clear when the approaching train occupies a specific track circuit, possibly also triggering a timing device.

Approach locking
The extra locking of facing points ahead of an approaching train running under proceed signals, achieved by track circuit occupation. In mechanical signalling this is achieved over a short distance through the points by a mechanical lock bar linked to the facing point lock.

Aspect
The colour shown by a colour light signal.

Auto button
A button on an entrance–exit panel alongside the entry button for a controlled signal route, usually for a junction which, when pressed, sets the junction signal to work as an automatic signal when set for the principal route.

Automatic half barrier level crossing (AHB)
A level crossing with half barriers across the road, operation of which is triggered automatically by an approaching train occupying track circuits and operating treadles installed to provide a prescribed timing sequence.

Automatic open crossing (AOCL)
A level crossing without barriers but with road warning and stop lights triggered by an approaching train and with rail repeater signals to advise the train driver that the road lights are in operation, which he must see before proceeding.

Automatic route setting
A feature of recent signalling installations and particularly IECCs in which the computer can set routes automatically when programmed to pre-set priorities, and fed with real time information from the train describer about train identity and location.

Automatic signal
A signal controlling entry to a section of line either isolated or in a track circuit block area, which is controlled automatically by track circuit occupation or in a few locations, by axle counters.

Automatic train control (ATC)
The original name for (usually) audible cab indications at distant signals with automatic brake application if a caution warning was not acknowledged, and best known in the electro-mechanical form used by the Great Western Railway from 1906. Now known as the automatic warning system. ATC is now the generic term applied in a modern context covering

a complete automated package including ATP and ATO.

Automatic train operation (ATO)
The automatic driving of a train from lineside commands. Already in use on some metro systems and with trials in certain main line applications in other countries.

Automatic train protection (ATP)
An automated supervisory system to ensure that drivers do not exceed pre-announced speed limits or pass signals at danger. Operated through track to train inductive links and on-board train equipment.

Automatic warning system (AWS)
The present name for the audible cab indications at a distant signal or colour light signals, originally called automatic train control. The track to train communication is by magnetic induction.

Axle counters
Track-mounted apparatus which counts the axles of a passing train at that particular location. With one axle counter at the entry to a signal section and another at the end they can be used for automatic signalling instead of track circuits, especially in damp or wet areas where track circuits are difficult to maintain. The counters are linked and have to agree the total number of axles to clear a section.

Back board
A term used by engine crews for a distant signal.

Banner signal
A signal displayed as a small rectangular semaphore arm within a circular case against a white opaque glass background, lit from behind. A red banner was a running signal in its own right. A black arm is a repeater of a signal ahead. Recent versions are formed from fibre optic displays.

Be ready
A term sometimes used by older signalmen referring to offering or accepting a train on the block instruments. The term dates back to the last century and the type of operation with open block.

Berth track circuit
A track circuit in the rear of (approaching) a signal.

Bi-directional running
A line fully signalled for trains to operate in either direction, on double or multi-track routes. A simpler form is also used, see SIMBIDS.

Block bell
The bell used for sending bell signals by coded rings between adjacent signalboxes.

Block controls
The addition of links from track circuits or treadles, signal indications and signal levers to block indicator circuits to prevent 'line clear' from being shown unless certain criteria have been met, and to ensure that 'train on line' is displayed when it should be. The circuits are designed to prevent signalmen's errors in block working.

Block instruments
The bells, tapper, and block indicators used for sending messages between (usually) mechanical signalboxes about train movement in and out of block sections.

Block section
The section of line from the most advanced starting signal of one signalbox to the outermost home signal of the box in advance.

Block signalling
The form of signalling based on block sections. It can be absolute or permissive, (which see).

Block shelf
The shelf, usually above the levers in a mechanical signalbox, on which the block instruments are placed, also signal, lamp, and point repeaters, plungers and other operating devices used by the signalman.

Block switch
An electrical switch which, when operated, links the block instruments on each side of a middle signalbox that can be closed or 'switched out'.

Blocking back
A shunting move requiring the occupation of the line outside the home signal or within the clearing point and requiring permission to be sought from the signalbox in the rear.

Bobby
A term meaning a signalman and dating back to the earliest days of railways when policemen looked after train operation. The Metropolitan Police under Sir Robert Peel had not long been formed and were known as 'Bobby's men' and the term passed into railway use. Still found rarely today.

Braking distance
The distance needed to stop the fastest train on a route which must be related to gradients and to signal spacing from caution to stop signals.

Calling-on signal
A subsidiary signal to allow a train to enter an occupied section at low speed. Used when two parts of a train have to be coupled.

Calling a route

Setting up a route for a train movement in panel signalboxes, or IECCs.

Caution signal

A distant signal in the 'on' or 'caution' position or a colour light signal displaying a yellow aspect.

Clearing a signal

The signalman's action in changing a signal from 'danger' or 'caution' to 'clear'.

Clear signal

A semaphore signal in the 'off' position or a colour light signal showing green.

Clearing point

The distance beyond the outermost home signal which must be kept clear in addition to the block section when a train is accepted from the signalbox in the rear. The distance is usually $1/4$ mile. Today, in colour light practice it is called the overlap and the distance is usually less. (See Overlap)

Closed block

The normal situation in absolute block working in which the line is not cleared for a train to enter a block section until it needs to be.

Closed circuit television (CCTV)

Cameras and display units for remote monitoring or supervision, as for example at remotely controlled level crossings.

Co-acting signal

Usually a semaphore signal with two arms coupled together on the same post or bracket for sighting purposes, the top arm often visible at a distance above a bridge or platform roof in front of the signal and a lower arm nearer driver's eye level for close sighting. More rarely, it is two colour light signals, one behind the other and working together.

Colour light area

An area where the entire layout or a complete route is equipped with colour light signals, and usually full track circuiting.

Colour light signal

A signal which gives indications by coloured lights only.

Commencement or C board

The board erected at the start of a temporary speed restriction. Until the 1970s it displayed a letter C but today shows the speed in figures.

Console

The part of a power signalbox in which the control buttons and switches are placed. Some consoles have the controls on an almost horizontal display and a vertical panel at the back for the track diagram indications while others have these features combined. Also known as a panel.

Controlled signal

A signal worked by a signalman from a lever, switch, button or tracker ball.

Danger signal

A semaphore stop signal in the 'on' or 'danger' position or a colour light signal showing a red aspect.

Delayed yellow

A colour light signal in which the change from red to yellow is delayed to slow the speed of a train because there is not the normal clear overlap beyond the next signal ahead. In effect a delayed yellow serves almost the same purpose as a warning signal in semaphore areas but is used more widely.

Detection

A device to prove that facing points are fully home in their correct position and locked before the relevant signal will clear.

Detonators

Small biscuit-sized audible signalling devices clipped on the railhead which explode when depressed by the leading wheels of a passing train.

Distant signal

A warning signal which advises the driver whether he should prepare to stop at the next signal ahead or whether he can continue at speed.

Double yellow aspect

The preliminary caution in four-aspect colour light signalling advising the driver that he must be prepared to find the next signal at single yellow.

Drooping

A lower quadrant semaphore signal arm slightly inclined down and not in the proper horizontal danger position yet not displaying a good clear 'off' at the correct angle. Such signals must be treated as danger signals.

Electric token block

Signalling used on single lines in which tokens in various forms – large staff, miniature staff, tablet, key token – are contained in electrically interlocked token instruments in the signalboxes at each end of a single line section in such a way that only one token can be drawn out at one time. This physical token is the driver's authority to be on the single line.

Electronic token
An electronic form of token used in Radio Electronic Token Block (RETB) in which specific data relating to a specific train is transmitted by radio from the computer controlled signalling centre to a micro-processor on the train giving a visual display as the driver's authority to enter the single line.

Emergency indicator
A sign with chevrons and high powered strobe lights to draw the driver's attention to a temporary speed restriction not previously advised by printed notice.

Emergency replacement button
A button on a signalling control panel that allows an automatic signal to be placed at danger in an emergency.

Entrance–exit control panels (NX)
The method of route setting by turning switches or pressing buttons on the track diagram in a panel signalbox, one at the signal controlling the entrance to a route and the second on the destination track at the end of a route or at the next signal.

Examination of line
Prescribed regulations for using a locomotive, and in some circumstances a train, to run slowly through a section to examine the line to check for damage, obstruction, animals on the line, etc.

Facing points
Points which lead to diverging tracks.

Facing point lock
A lock engaging bars connected to the switch blades of facing points to ensure that they are fully set and held in that position and, linked to a locking bar or track circuit, cannot be changed under an approaching train. Modern types hold the switch by a clamplock.

Fail safe
A principle by which signalling equipment and circuits are designed so that in the event of a fault the signals for the relevant section of line will be placed or maintained at danger automatically.

Fixed signal
A permanent signal, as distinct from a handsignal, in a fixed location on a post or other structure and identified by its type, location, and by reference to milepost distances.

Fixed distant signal
A distant signal with the arm fixed permanently at caution and often with only a yellow spectacle, where low speeds were normally required at a stop signal ahead. Rarely also in colour light form as single yellow.

Fixed stop signal
A seemingly impossible signal but one that was occasionally used where a running line, possibly a branch, continued to a main line connection through a goods yard or sidings. Onward movement was by a shunting or subsidiary signal and did not allow the passage of loaded passenger trains.

Flashing yellow aspects
A form of caution signal with double flashing yellows (in four-aspect areas) followed by single flashing yellow giving advice that the next signal ahead is at a junction and that the route is set for a lower speed diversion off a high speed main line. It is one form of a junction distant in colour light areas.

Fouling bar
A mechanical bar or treadle to detect the presence of a vehicle and designed to operate indicators or locks in the signalbox or act on facing point locks.

Fouling point
The point where vehicles on converging tracks will touch each other.

Four-aspect area
Lines where all the colour light signals display four aspects.

Four foot
The generic term for the distance between the two running rails of a track actually set at 4ft $8\frac{1}{2}$in or today at 1,435mm.

Gate box
A signalbox controlling a level crossing with barriers or gates and the immediate protecting signal but not the block system. Might be released from a main signalbox.

Giving on
Giving 'train entering section' as a train passes into a block section.

Giving out
Giving 'train out of section' when a train leaves a block section and passes beyond the clearing point.

Global positioning satellite (GPS)
The use of space technology with satellite communication to determine train position.

Goods line
A line which is signalled to lesser standards than those

of a passenger line. Permissive working for example may be authorised.

Green aspect

The least restrictive aspect in colour light signalling meaning that the line is clear for the maximum permitted speed at least to the next signal which may be expected to be showing a proceed aspect. Flashing green aspects on the East Coast Main Line allow speeds over 125mph.

Ground frame

An open stage or hut with a switch panel or small frame of mechanical levers controlling little used points and possibly relevant signals locally, but which can only be used when released by the signalbox controlling through running moves or by special track circuits or by key.

Half cock

An upper quadrant signal with the arm inclined slightly upwards not fully in the horizontal danger position and not inclined upwards sufficiently to be a clear off signal. It must be treated as a danger signal.

Handsignal

A signal given by the hands and arms alone to a prescribed code, or by flag, or at night by a handlamp with white or coloured indications.

Handsignalman

A person standing by the lineside authorised to give handsignals to approaching trains, usually by flag or lamp and in prescribed circumstances, as for example a signal failure or during engineering work.

Home signal

In mechanical signalling the first stop signal approaching a signalbox in the normal direction of running. In some locations there might be two or even three home signals called outer, intermediate and inner homes, or home 1, 2, and 3.

Hot axlebox detector

Lineside equipment for detecting an overheated axlebox which sends a warning to the supervising signalbox and can pinpoint the location of the axlebox.

Hudd automatic warning system

The pioneer automatic warning system to give audible cab signals at distant signals using magnetic indication as distinct from the electro-mechanical GWR ATC system. The Hudd system was installed on the Fenchurch Street–Southend–Shoeburyness line.

Illuminated diagram

A panel in a signalbox containing a diagram of the track it controls, including the location of signals and with the routes set and train location shown by different colour lights.

In advance

Everything in front of a person looking forwards along a line in the normal direction of travel is 'in advance'.

In rear

Everything behind that same person looking forwards along a line in the normal direction of travel is 'in rear'.

Integrated electronic control centre (IECC)

The latest type of computerised signalling control centre. Signalmen operate at work stations seated at a desk in an office environment, with computer keyboards and tracker balls for route setting, visual display units showing the track diagram with overviews and close-ups, signals, routes set, and train location, and through the processors with a timetable database and train describer information automatic junction setting is employed. The controls are linked to solid state interlockings.

Interlinking

The proving of a distant signal arm at 'caution' and its related home signal arm at 'danger' before a signalman can place the rear section block indicator for that line to 'line clear'. This feature is part of modern block controls, especially in Welwyn control.

Intermediate block section

One or more additional block sections between two signalboxes, usually controlled from the signalbox in the rear with individual distant and home signals, often of the colour light type. Track circuits are installed between the controlling signalbox and the clearing point of the most advanced intermediate block home signal.

Junction indicator

A row of five (three on London Underground) lunar white lights to right or left displayed (usually) above the main signal head at colour light junction signals to show which way the junction is set. With no lights displayed the route is set for the main, highest speed track although there are local exceptions depending on track geometry.

King lever

A lever which, when operated, unlocks other levers often as a group, at a ground frame for example. If a ground frame is released from a main signalbox it will be the king lever which is released as the key to the rest of the levers.

Lamp proving

The detection circuit in colour light practice proving a

signal lamp is lit before the signal in rear can show a proceed aspect. All red lamps have double-filament bulbs to reduce total lamp failure with a warning given to the controlling signalbox when the first filament fails. If both filaments fail the signal in the rear is held at red.

Lever collar
In mechanical signalling a cast iron or steel collar which fits over the lever handle and stops the catch handle from being pulled as a reminder to the signalman not to pull the lever for example because of an obstruction. In panel boxes a small device like a large thimble serves the same purpose when placed over a route setting button.

Line clear
The indication shown on a block indicator after permission has been given for a train to enter a block section but before it actually does so.

Line names
Tracks are usually designated by direction, and if there are more than two to a route, by use and sometimes by destination. The basic division is by direction, up (normally towards London except on cross-country routes), down, and in multiple track areas fast/slow, main/goods, main/relief, through/local, etc.

Line clear release
A lock placed on the most advanced starting signal (section signal) so that the lever can only be pulled and then usually for one pull only if 'line clear' is displayed on the relevant block indicator.

Main aspect
The red, yellow, and green aspects in a colour light signal.

Manually controlled barriers
A level crossing with barriers controlled directly from an adjoining, or with CCTV a remote, signalbox.

Mechanical interlocking
Interlocking in a mechanical signalbox achieved by sliding bars moved by levers with wedges engaging slots in other bars to lock other levers, or with wedges pushed away from slots to release other levers.

Mechanical signalbox
A signalbox in which levers primarily work signals and points by mechanical linkage through wires and rods.

Miniature warning lights
At user-worked level crossing gates miniature red and green lights advise road users whether it is safe to open the gates and cross the line.

Moorgate control
At dead end stations the last signal shows no more than a caution aspect for trains to enter the platform. On London Underground lines extra train stops and speed supervision are provided to prevent over-runs into platform end stop blocks which might be in a tunnel. So called following the Moorgate collision in 1975.

Multiple-aspect signalling (MAS)
Colour light signals able to display three or four aspects as part of a prescribed sequence working in conjunction with the signals ahead, often automatically through track circuits. Synonymous with track circuit block.

Nearside
The left hand side of a train in the direction of travel.

Normal
1 The normal position of signal and points levers in the lever frame lying away from the signalman and with the signal at danger and points usually set for the principal straight route. Facing point locks in some signalboxes particularly on the Great Western, had the levers in the reverse position when the points were locked so the levers could be quickly identified.
2 The position of the block indicator needle when no train has been accepted and with no train in a block section.

No-signalman token
Single line electric token operation in which drivers operate the token machines themselves at passing loops. There is no offering or acceptance procedure and a token can only be obtained if no other token for the section is already out. The operation is under the remote supervision of a signalman at, for example, a branch junction or main centre.

Occupation level crossing
A level crossing on a private road or track usually giving access between fields of a farm or linking a farm or building to a road.

Occupied
The presence of a train on a section of line, sometimes shown on a signalbox indicator displaying the word 'occupied', or in the form of (usually) red lights on the relevant portion of a track diagram.

Off
A proceed aspect in a colour light signal or a semaphore signal arm inclined at 45 degrees up or down to the clear position (but 60 degrees on Great Western lower quadrant signals).

Off side
The right hand side of a train in the direction of travel.

On

The red or danger aspect of a colour light signal or a semaphore stop or distant signal arm in the horizontal position. The terms 'on' and 'off' derive from the pioneer days of railways when policemen were said to turn on a danger signal, that is to turn a board signal to be face on to a train.

One Control Switch (OCS)

The route setting method in relay interlocking in which a complete route from signal to signal was set by turning a single switch on a console.

One train operation (OTO)

A method of operating a single line with one train only. Normally suitable only for relatively short dead end branches. The train might be issued with a token or staff but on some branches security of the single line is assured by the interlocking at the junction which prevents a second train from entering the branch until the first has returned and left the single line.

Open block

The original form of absolute block working in which the block section was always regarded as being clear for a train to enter whether or not one was due unless there was a train already in the section. After the Abbots Ripton collision in 1876, closed block with the offering and acceptance procedure was adopted. In modern track circuit block, automatic signals work on the open block system with signals clearing to green when the line is clear whether or not a train is due.

Out of correspondence

Points not correctly set and not as called for by the controls.

Overlap

A section of line beyond a colour light signal normally on main lines not more than 200 yards in length which must be clear before the next signal in rear can show a proceed aspect.

Overlap track circuit

A track circuit in advance of a colour light signal corresponding to the overlap distance. Sometimes, to simplify circuitry and equipment, a berth track circuit extending for a signal section and overlap track circuit are combined as one so that the track circuit runs from the overlap of one signal to the overlap point of the next signal ahead.

Panel

The term usually embracing the controls, indications and track diagram in a power signalbox with one control switch or entrance–exit systems.

Panel box

A power signalbox or signalling control centre with control from buttons or switches on a panel, as distinct from miniature levers.

Passenger line

A line used by passenger trains and signalled to required standards on absolute block principles.

Pegging up

The act of placing the block indicator to 'line clear' or 'train on line' by turning the operating handle, switch, plunger or button. The term dates from the last century when the block indicator handle had to be held to right or left by a peg inserted into a hole

Permanent speed restriction

A speed restriction imposed permanently because of curves, alignment, or limitations of engineering structures.

Permissive block

The form of signalling which allows more than one train to be in a block section or signal section at one time. Some goods lines are worked by this method, and more rarely, passenger lines under more stringent rules at some large stations to allow two trains to stand together at a platform for connections or for coupling.

Pilotman

A person appointed to accompany trains over a single line when the token or other regular form of security is not available or during special single line working on an otherwise double line when one line is not in use. A pilotman is not required on lines equipped with full reversible signalling or SIMBIDS.

Policeman

The person controlling train movement at stations and junctions in the pioneering days of railways from the 1830s until the 1850s/60s when the signalmen's duties were separated from general security.

Position light signal

A small signal with two diagonal white lights indicating 'clear' for shunting, or low speed moves into an occupied section. Placed under a main colour light signal there is no 'danger' aspect, the red aspect of the main signal applying. As a separate ground signal it shows 'danger' by a horizontal red and white light.

Power signalbox

A signalbox in which points and signals are controlled by power (usually electric), rather than mechanical links, through miniature levers, switches, or push buttons. In panel boxes with switch or button control interlocking is usually by relays. Power signalboxes often control large areas with several hundred miles of track and are often referred to as signalling centres.

Print out

A printed list of train times passing specific locations and other incidents and events, usually taken from the train describer through the controlling computer and its printer in a power signalling centre or from several centres. It is the modern equivalent of the train register book. Can also be used for fault finding.

Preliminary caution

The double yellow aspect of a four-aspect colour light signal.

Proceed aspect

Any main aspect other than red in colour light signalling.

Protection

Action taken to stop trains in an emergency following a train failure or accident or obstruction on the line by using detonators, emergency hand signals, track circuit clips, and by placing fixed signals at danger, also by radio instruction.

Pulling off

The act of pulling signal levers (and points levers that precede them if necessary) in a mechanical signalbox to the clear position for a train movement, the equivalent of route setting in a power signalbox.

Radio electronic token block (RETB)

A signalling system used on single lines using radio data links between the control centre computer and an on-train processor to ensure the security of the single line sections by a unique electronic token displayed in the driver's cab.

Red aspect

The danger, stop, aspect displayed by a colour light signal.

Relay

The electro-magnetic apparatus within a case, energised by an electric circuit being switched on (or de-energised by being switched off) for example by a track circuit being occupied or cleared, or by other relays, so that movement of a hinged arm will make or break other electrical circuits. The relay is the basis of relay interlocking achieved purely by changes in the state of electrical circuits.

Relay interlocking

Interlocking between signals, other signals, and points, and fed with circuits from track circuits and control panels providing an all-electric means of ensuring that signals and points cannot conflict and signals can only show a proceed aspect if points are correctly set and the line is clear.

Release

An electric or electronic (and originally mechanical) lock on ground or shunting frames or gate box levers or switches, controlled from a main signalbox.

Reminder appliance

Various devices in mechanical signalling used to remind signalmen of trains or vehicles on a line unprotected by track circuits. They included such things as 'vehicle on line' switches or lever collars.

Remote interlocking

A room or equipment cabinet containing interlocking not within a signalbox or control centre but linked to the signalbox controls either by direct wire or by an electronic means of remote control or, in modern computer control systems, by data links.

Reverse

Points lying in their secondary position or levers in a signalbox when pulled forward to clear the signals.

Rotary block

A type of block instrument used by the Midland Railway providing block controls and a form of lock and block to reduce signalmen's errors in block signalling.

Route

In modern signalling the section of line, usually from one signal to the next, including points and crossings. Also an overall line from city to city or one end of the country to the other.

Route lever

A signalbox lever which, when pulled, set a complete route. It was the predecessor of route setting switches and buttons.

Rule 55

Probably the most famous and important rule in the rulebook. It required a member of the train crew, if a train was detained on a running line by a signal at danger, to go to the signalbox to remind the signalman of the position of the train, sign the train register book and to ensure that safety reminder appliances were used. Telephones or call plungers were sometimes provided but today track circuits have largely replaced the need to go to the signalbox (which might be 50 or more miles away). Today the rule is known as K3.

Running line

A principal through line as distinct from sidings.

Running movement
A normal through train movement on a running line signalled by the normal running signals.

Running signal
The main aspects in colour light signals, or semaphore distant or stop signals, as distinct from shunting or subsidiary signals.

Satellite interlocking
Another term for a remote interlocking.

Section signal
In block working the most advanced starting signal controlling entry to a block section.

Semaphore signal
A fixed signal with the indications given by the angle of a rectangular arm during daylight and by coloured filters in the end of the arm known as the spectacle lit from behind, usually by an oil lamp but sometimes by an electric lamp, at night. Normally worked mechanically but could be power-worked by electricity or pneumatically.

Semi-automatic signal
A colour light signal capable of working automatically by track circuit occupation but also sometimes controlled from a signalbox, ground frame or gate box.

Sequential locking
Interlocking between signal levers to ensure that they were pulled to clear in the correct order. Before the lever for one stop signal could be pulled, the lever for the stop signal in advance within in the same lever frame had to be at danger. This type of locking was usually allied to line clear release on the most advanced starting signal. It was part of the system of block controls and proved that the levers had been restored to danger behind the previous train.

Setting back
A shunting or low speed movement backing, for example into a siding.

Setting a route
The act of turning the control switch or pressing the route setting entrance–exit buttons in a panel signalbox to set up a route from signal to signal. In an IECC a route can be set by using a tracker ball. Before the entry signal will clear, the relay interlocking proves the route is free for use, no conflicting routes have been set, and that points are in the correct position.

Shunt ahead signal
A subsidiary signal authorising a shunting move past a main signal.

Shunting frame
This is similar to a ground frame but can be a former signalbox with an elevated lever frame to control local points and signals for shunting off a main line and within a goods yard, but without any responsibility for signalling though running moves. The levers would be released from a power signalbox.

Sighting distance
The distance at which a driver can first see a signal ahead.

Signal post replacement switch
A key-operated switch on the post of an automatic colour light signal which allows the signal to be set at red in an emergency or for engineering work.

Signalpost telephone
A telephone provided on a signalpost or nearby to allow a driver to speak to the signalman in the controlling signalbox. It is gradually being made redundant by cab to signalbox radio developments.

Signalling centre
A super power signalbox controlling extensive areas with perhaps over 100 route miles and several hundred track miles – often a complete line.

Signal repeater
1 In a signalbox, a signal repeater shows the indication of a signal arm or light by a needle indicator, a light repeater, off/on indicators or, in earlier power installations, by a display of the actual colour light aspects. Recent practice for multiple-aspect signals is to show only if a signal is at danger, or showing a proceed aspect with no differentiation between caution and clear.
2 On the line it is a special signal, usually a banner repeater, situated up to 200 yards in the rear of the signal to which it applies. A repeater may be needed because a bridge, platform canopy or line curvature makes sighting of the main signal difficult.

Signing the book
In the days before widespread use of track circuits, a fireman would be told by his driver to go and 'sign the book' if a train was detained at a signal, in other words carry out Rule 55.

SIMBIDS
SIMplified BI-Directional Signalling. Modern form of reversible working on double or multi-track routes. It is simplified by comparison with full reversible working in that it is normally only used for emergencies or engineering work and generally signals for the wrong direction moves are only provided at the crossovers concerned and do not have AWS.

Six foot
The generic term for the distance between adjacent tracks on double or multi-track routes although in practice the distance is sometimes more than 6ft.

Slip coach working
One of the few instances when two separate parts of a train could be on the move together in close proximity when the rear coach or coaches were slipped or uncoupled from the back of a non-stopping train as it approached a station, provided the signals were clear. The practice lasted on the Great Western Railway and BR Western Region until 1960, long after it finished on other railways.

Slotting
An arrangement of balance weights on a signal post where two signalboxes control signals on the same post to ensure that the arms will only clear when both signalmen have pulled the appropriate levers. Also, can be carried out electrically through relay interlocking where two power signalboxes or signalbox and gatebox control the same signal.

Solid State Interlocking (SSI)
Computerised software forming the interlocking between signals, other signals, and points, with data fed from track circuits and control panels.

SPAD
Signal Passed At Danger. Potentially the worst mistake a driver can make. Without ATP control a train is solely in the hands of a driver. Risk assessments are now identifying locations most at risk from a SPAD and additional warnings such as flashing red signals are being provided, coming into operation if a train runs past a normal red signal.

Spectacle
The coloured glasses in a semaphore signal arm with a lamp behind to give the night-time indications.

Splitting distants
Two, and rarely three or more, distant signals mounted side by side to give a driver an indication of the way a train is routed at a junction ahead.

Staff or token
A physical token given to a driver as his authority to be on a single line section.

Staff and ticket operation
One of the methods of ensuring the security on a single line. There was only one staff and for a group of trains passing through the section in the same direction, each driver was shown the staff and given a printed ticket with handwritten details of the train

time or number. The last train of a group carried the staff.

Starting signal
A stop signal in advance of the controlling signalbox, and sometimes is the section signal. There might be two or more starting signals called the starter, intermediate starter and advanced starter.

Station limits
The section of line from the outermost home signal controlled by one signalbox to the most advanced starting signal controlled by the same box.

Station working
The special instructions applying to working at certain major stations which can include the use of permissive working or calling on signals to allow more than one passenger train to be in the same block or signal section through the platform at the same time, although under very stringent conditions, for coupling or making connections.

Stop board
A board requiring trains to stop with instructions to the train crew to carry out an operating procedure (operate level crossing barriers, obtain token, etc) before proceeding. Found on lightly used lines without full signalling.

Stop signal
A signal capable of showing a 'danger, stop' indication or aspect.

Stop and proceed
A system of operation usually on metro lines, but not entirely unknown on main lines where, under prescribed conditions, a train detained at an automatic signal at danger can proceed past the signal slowly ready to stop on sight of an obstruction or a train ahead.

Subsidiary signal
A signal below a main signal for shunting moves or low speed running moves.

Switched out
The closing of a signalbox, and through a closing switch, the linking of the block instrument circuits to the signalboxes on each side to each other, bypassing the closed box.

Sykes lock and block
A type of block working devised in the mid-1870s in which train-operated treadles completed electric circuits to the signalbox to lock or release block indicators and signal levers. An early form of block control.

Temporary speed restriction
A speed restriction applied on a temporary basis, usually because of engineering work involving the track, its foundations, or civil engineering structures.

Termination or T board
The end of a temporary speed restriction marked by a board displaying a letter T.

Tokenless block
A form of single line operation relying on special block instruments and isolated track circuits at each end of the section to prove trains have entered and left the single line. Some single lines are worked by track circuit block with full track circuiting and without tokens.

Track circuit (TC)
A train detection system originally developed in the 1870s in the USA using an electric circuit through electrically insulated rails from a power source (battery or derived from mains electricity) at one end to a relay at the other which is switched automatically when a train is present and the wheels short circuit the path of the current. The track circuit has been at the heart of modern signalling for much of the present century.

Track circuit block (TCB)
A route with continuous track circuiting providing signal sections from one signal to the next, equivalent to block sections in mechanical signalling, with multiple-aspect colour light signals many of which on plain line operate automatically. In the past this was also used with electrically or pneumatically powered semaphore signals in a few installations.

Track circuit clip
A safety device which is part of the protection equipment carried on trains which, when clipped to the top of the running rails, short circuits the track circuit and will place the signal in rear to red.

Tracker ball
The computer device which a signalman uses in an IECC to set routes manually.

Trailing points
Points which bring converging tracks together.

Train describer
Apparatus used in signalboxes to indicate the identity and destination of a train. Old style describers had a needle pointer on a clock face to a printed destination, the magazine type had lights against a vertical list, and the modern type have the four character code usually indicating train location on the track diagram.

Train description
A four-character code of figure, letter, and two figures given to a train in the working timetable as a unique identity or as a class and route, and displayed on train describers in signalboxes.

Train on line
The position of the block indicator when a train is in the relevant block section.

Train-operated route release
An automatic feature on route setting panels in which trains clearing track circuits through junctions automatically free part of the original route for another move before the first train has cleared the whole route from signal to signal.

Train ready to start
A plunger or key switch provided for platform supervisors at stations to advise the signalman that station work is complete and the train is ready to start.

Train register book
A book used in signalboxes for the signalman (or in former times a booking lad) to record the times of block instrument messages regarding train movement between signalboxes, also anything else affecting the running of trains, Rule 55 for example.

Transmission based signalling (TBS)
A form of signalling proposed for the future and already in use in one form or another on a few railways in other countries. It uses the transmission of data messages between lineside or track equipment and the train by induction or radio, including train detection, so that track circuits are unnecessary.

Transponder
Equipment usually fixed in the four foot which transmits data to a passing train when interrogated by the train-borne equipment.

Treadle
In former times a mechanical device fixed to the rails, but today it is electronic apparatus, which detects the passing of a train. It is not continuous and can only indicate that a train has passed that particular spot. Today they are used, for example, to trigger automatic level crossing warnings.

Visual display unit (VDU)
A television or computer screen for displaying information which may be a list of train times or graphics showing a track layout with real time details of signal aspects, train location, and routes set. In IECCs VDUs are used instead of the large track diagrams of earlier power signalboxes.

Warning arrangement

A special dispensation in absolute block working known as Regulation 5, for a signalman to accept a train from the box in the rear with the line clear to the home signal only and not to the 1/4-mile clearing point. It could only be used in specified circumstances and trains had to be warned at the signalbox in the rear.

Warning board

The rectangular yellow board and speed figures placed at braking distance from a temporary speed restriction ahead.

Warning indicator

An inverted triangle with yellow border and speed figures, and on high speed lines in certain locations, accompanied by an AWS permanent magnet, at braking distance from a permanent speed restriction ahead.

Warning signal

A semaphore signal bearing a letter W on the arm or revealed when clear to indicate to a driver that the train has been accepted under the warning arrangement at the next signalbox ahead. Where a warning signal is not provided a green handsignal held steadily as a train approaches the signalbox has the same meaning.

Welwyn control

Track circuits, sequential locking and line clear release controls added to block indicator circuits to prevent a second train from being signalled until the first has been proved to have cleared the block section. So called following the recommendations after the Welwyn collision in 1935.

Whistle signals

Audible signals to a prescribed code given by a signalman, guard or shunter, blowing into a pea whistle to start a train, or during shunting, to indicate the next move, or to stop. Also, whistle signals by a locomotive as a warning of approach, on starting or to indicate clear of points etc, and while running by code whistles approaching junctions to confirm route wanted, etc.

Wire adjusters

Mechanical linkage in a signalbox for adjusting the tension of signal wire in hot and cold weather.

Work station

The signalman's position in an IECC at a desk with computer keyboard, tracker ball, and VDU, for train signalling.

Wrong direction

A train movement in the opposite direction to the normal direction of running. The term does not mean that the move is incorrect.

Wrong line order

A printed order with handwritten train details authorising a movement in the wrong direction in the event of train failure or accident to provide rescue and retrieval. There were four types of order, A, B, C and D, on different coloured paper to cover different circumstances. Now obsolete because of the large control areas of modern signalling and other methods are now used for authorising wrong direction moves.

Wrong side failure

A fault in signalling equipment which, for some reason, does not correctly place the relevant signals at danger and is potentially dangerous.

Yellow aspect

The caution aspect in a colour light signal.

Appendix 4

SELECTED BRITISH BLOCK BELL CODES FOR TRAIN SIGNALLING

Great Western Railway 1937

* Call Attention signal	1
* Emergency 'Call Attention' signal (to precede emergency bell signals only).	**A number of beats in rapid succession**

'Is line clear?' – for:

Express passenger train, express streamline rail car, break-down van train going to clear the line, or light engine going to assist disabled train or empty coaching stock train timed at express passenger speed ('A' headlamps)	4
Ordinary passenger train, 'mixed' train, or break down van train not going to clear the line ('B')	3–1
Branch passenger train? ('B' headlamps)	1–3
Rail motor-car, auto-train or streamline rail car	3–1–3
Parcels, newspapers, fish, meat, fruit, milk, horse, cattle or perishable train composed entirely of vacuum-fitted stock with the vacuum pipe connected to the engine ('C')	5
Express freight, livestock, perishable, or ballast train partly vacuum fitted with not less than one third vacuum braked vehicles connected by vacuum pipe to engine ('C' headlamps)	4–4
Express freight or ballast train conveying a stipulated number of vacuum-braked vehicles connected by vacuum pipe to engine and authorised to run at a maximum speed of 35mph ('D' headlamps)	2–2–3
Empty coaching stock train not specially authorised to carry 'A' headlamps	2–2–1
Express freight, fish, meat, fruit, or cattle train or ballast train or breakdown crane not proceeding to an accident ('E' headlamps)	3–2
Through fast freight train conveying through load ('F' headlamps)	1–4
Light engine, or light engines coupled together, or engine and brake van	2–3

Freight, mineral or ballast train, or train of empties carrying through load to destination ('H' headlamps)	3–4–1
Through freight, mineral, or ballast train stopping at intermediate stations ('J' headlamps)	4–1
Ordinary freight, mineral or ballast train stopping at local stations ('K' headlamps)	3
Pilot trip ('K' headlamps)	3–1–2
Train conveying out-of-gauge or exceptional load	2–6–2
Branch freight train	1–2
Ballast train, freight train or inspection train requiring to stop in section	1–2–2
Trolley requiring to go into or pass through tunnel	2–1–2
* Train approaching	1–2–1
* Train entering section	2
* Section clear but station or junction blocked	3–5–5
* Line clear to clearing point only	2–2–2
* Engine assisting in rear of train	2–2
* Train out of section, or obstruction removed	2–1
Engine arrived	2–1–3
Train drawn back clear of section	3–2–3
+ Obstruction danger	6
+ Train an unusually long time in section	6–2
Blocking back *Inside* home signal	2–4
Outside home signal	3–3
Blocking back outside home signal for train already in section	1–2–3
+ Stop and examine train	7
Cancelling 'Is line clear?' or 'Train entering section' signal	3–5,
+ Train passed without tail lamp	**9 to box in advance**
	4–5 to box in rear
+ Train divided	5–5
Shunt train for following train to pass	1–5–5
+ Train or vehicles running away on wrong line	2–5–5
+ Train or vehicles running away on right line	4–5–5
Opening of signal box	5–5–5
Closing of signal box	7–5–5
Testing block instruments, bells and gongs	16

Time	8–5–5
Lampman or fog signalman required	9–5–5
Testing controlled or slotted signals	5–5–5–5
Take slot off, train waiting	3–4

The ordinary 'Call Attention' signal (1 beat) must precede all signals except those marked thus *.

The emergency call attention bell signal must precede the signals marked thus +.

Bell codes on the LMS and LNER were broadly similar but there were variations in the way freight trains were classified. Rail motors and electric trains were also distinctly identified. They did not have an emergency call attention code.

LMS bell code variations

Rail motor, motor train or electric train	3–1–2
Parcels, newspaper, fish, meat, fruit, milk, horse or perishable train composed of coaching stock	1–1–3
Fitted freight, fish, or cattle train with the continuous brake in use on not less than one third of the vehicles	5
Express freight or cattle train with the continuous brake in use on less than one third of the vehicles but in use on at least four vehicles connected to the engine	2–2–3
Express freight or cattle train not fitted with the continuous brake or in use on less than four vehicles	3–2
Through freight or ballast train running not less than 15 miles without stopping	1–4
Through mineral or empty wagon train	4–1

LNER bell code variations (1930s)

No. 1 express milk, fish, meat, fruit, horse, cattle or goods train	1–3–1
No. 2 express fish, meat, fruit, horse, cattle, or perishable train composed of coaching stock	5
Class A fish, meat, or fruit train composed of goods stock, express cattle, or express goods train	3–2
Class B cattle or express goods train	1–4
Through goods or ballast train	4–1

Southern Railway 1938

Call attention signal	1
'Is line clear?'–for:	
Passenger train or breakdown van train not going to clear the line	
Main Line	3–1
Branch	1–3
Breakdown van train going to clear the line, or light engine going to assist disabled train	
Main Line	2–2
Branch	4–4

Fish, meat, fruit, horse, cattle, milk or perishable train composed of coaching stock	
Main Line	4–2–2
Branch	2–2–4
Empty train	
Main Line	2–2–1
Branch	1–2–2
Goods or through ballast train or engines and brakes	
Main Line	3–2
Branch	2–3
Light engine or light engines coupled together	
Main Line	4–1
Branch	1–4
Ballast train requiring to stop in section or goods train working at intermediate sidings?	5
Trolley requiring to pass through tunnel?	2–2–2
Power-worked inspection car or mechanically or power-worked trolley	
Through	1–2–1
Required to stop in section	1–3–1
Train entering section	
Main line	2
Branch	4
Section clear but station or junction blocked	3–5–5
Bank engine in rear of train	1–4–1
Train out of section or obstruction removed	2–1
Engine arrived	2–1–3
Train drawn back clear of section	3–2–3
Train an unusually long time in section	6–2
Obstruction danger	6
Blocking back	
Inside home signal	2–4
Outside home signal	3–3
Stop and examine train	7
Cancelling 'Is line clear?' or 'Train entering section' signal	3–5
Last train signalled incorrectly described	5–3
Train passed without tail lamp	
To box in advance	9
To box in rear	4–5
Train divided	5–5
Shunt train for following train to pass	1–5–5
Vehicles running away on wrong line	2–5–5
Vehicles running away on right line	4–5–5
Opening of signal box	5–5–5
Closing of signal box	7–5–5
Testing block indicators and bells	16
Is line clear for shunt movement on down line	4–2
Is line clear for shunt movement on up line	4–3
Shunt movement entering section	2
Shunt movement out of section	2–1
Release slot for shunting	2–1–2
Replace slot – shunting completed	3
Cancelling 'Is line clear for shunt movement?' or 'Shunt movement entering section' signal	3–5–1
May shunt movement be made on wrong line	1–2

Shunting between signal boxes wrong line shunt movement clear of section at box in rear   2–3–2

Wrong line shunt movement clear of section at box in advance   2–1

British Rail 1970

1 Call attention	1

'Is line clear?'–for:

Class

1 Express passenger train, postal train, newspaper train, or breakdown van train or snow plough going to clear the line, or light locomotive going to assist disabled train	4
Officers' Special train not requiring to stop in section	
Electric express passenger train (not applicable on Southern Region)	4–2
2 Ordinary passenger train, mixed train, or breakdown van train or snow plough NOT going to clear the line	3–1
Electric ordinary passenger train (not applicable on Southern Region)	3–1–2
3 Express parcels train composed of vehicles permitted to run at 90mph or over	1–3–1
4 Freightliner train	3–2–5
Parcels train, Company or express freight train composed of vehicles permitted to run at 75mph or over	3–1–1
5 Empty coaching stock train (not specially authorised to carry Class 1 headcode)	2–2–1
Electric empty coaching stock train (not applicable on Southern Region)	2–2–1–2
6 (a) Fully-fitted Company or block train, parcels train or milk train	5
(b) Ordinary fully-fitted express freight train	4–1
7 Express freight train, not fully-fitted, but with brake force not less than that shown in Section E of the Working Manual for Rail Staff	1–2–2
8 Freight train, not fully-fitted, but with brake force not less than that shown in Section E of the Working Manual for Rail Staff	3–2
9 Unfitted freight train (where authorised)	1–4
Freight train, Officers' Special train or Engineer's train requiring to stop in section	2–2–3
0 Light locomotive, light locomotives coupled or locomotive with brake tender(s)	2–3
Locomotive with not more than two brake vans	1–1–3
– Trolley requiring to go into or pass through tunnel	2–1–2
Train entering section	2
Train which can pass an out-of-gauge or exceptional load similarly signalled on the opposite or an adjoining line	2–6–1
Train which cannot be allowed to pass an out-of-gauge load of any description on the opposite or an adjoining line between specified points	2–6–2
Train which requires the opposite or an adjoining line to be blocked between specified points	2–6–3
Opposite line, or an adjoining line used in the same or opposite direction, to be blocked for passage of train conveying out-of-gauge load	1–2–6
Out-of-gauge load requiring to pass in wrong direction	1–6–2
Train approaching (where authorised)	1–2–1
Cancelling	3–5
Last train signalled incorrectly described	5–3
Warning Acceptance	3–5–5
Line now clear in accordance with Regulation 4 for train to approach	3–3–5
Train out of section, or Obstruction Removed	2–1
Blocking back inside home signal	2–4
Blocking back outside home signal	3–3
Train or vehicles at a stand	3–3–4
Locomotive assisting in rear of train	2–2
Locomotive with one or two brake vans assisting in rear of train	2–3–1
Locomotive arrived	2–1–3
Train drawn back clear of section	3–2–3
Obstruction Danger	6
Train an unusually long time in section	6–2
Stop and examine train	7
Train passed without tail lamp	
to box in advance	9
to box in rear	4–5
Train divided	5–5
Shunt train for following train to pass	1–5–5
Train or vehicles running away in wrong direction	2–5–5
Train or vehicles running away in right direction	4–5–5
Opening of signal box	5–5–5
Closing of signal box	7–5–5
Closing of signal box where section signal is locked by the block	5–5–7
Testing block indicators and bells	16
Shunting into forward section	3–3–2
Shunt withdrawn	8
Working in wrong direction	2–3–3
Train clear of section	5–2
Train withdrawn	2–5
Distant signal defective	8–2
Home signal defective	2–8

The variations between the bell codes of the four Group companies reflects to a certain degree their operating practices. The Southern did not distinguish between express and ordinary passenger trains but was more concerned with the route of the train and whether it was continuing on the main line or was being turned off on to a branch. In the context of bell codes a branch train was not necessarily a short local train heading for a remote country branch. Branch codes were often used for route purposes on main lines. The 'Cornish Riviera Express' was a branch train for signalling purposes as it approached Reading heading west since the Berks & Hants line was regarded as the 'branch' by comparison with the main line to Bristol. Similarly, down South Wales express passenger trains were signalled as branch trains from Swindon to Wootton Bassett, the junction box, which then reverted to normal bell codes as the trains were belled forward. In many complex areas special bell codes were devised for route purposes or to denote stopping or non-stopping trains. Just a selection are shown below.

Approaching Willesden Junction (main line)

Passenger train not calling at Willesden	4–4–4

At Acton Wells Junction (near Willesden)

Up passenger train for Willesden	4
Up passenger train for Midland lines	3–1
Down freight for Acton WR	1–2
Down freight for SR via Old Kew	4–1–2
Down freight for Battersea via New Kew	4–1–4

At Exeter

GW express passenger train not booked to call at Exeter	3–3–3

(this bell signal would revert to the normal 4 bell code from the box beyond the station but in the down direction Exeter West would then use special codes on to Newton Abbot)

Express passenger train not booked to call at Newton Abbot and to take the Plymouth line	3–3–3
Express passenger train not booked to call at Newton Abbot and to take the Torquay line	3–3–1
Southern Railway passenger trains between Cowley Bridge Junction and Exeter West	5–1

In some instances 'special train entering section' or 'special train approaching' codes were used as route indications.

On the LMS 'train entering section' was not acknowledged on the bell but by placing the block indicator at 'train on line'.

The 'train out of section' bell signal was acknowledged by one beat on the bell. Unlike the other companies, LMS regulations prescribed the use of 'call attention' for both these bell signals. Other companies did not use 'call attention' before giving 'train entering section' and did not always use 'call attention' before 'train out of section', although the bell signals had to be acknowledged by repetition.

Over the years there were alterations to the bell codes and those shown applied in the year concerned. Many were long lasting and the majority, except for freight trains which today are classified differently since all have continuous brakes, survive where bell codes are still used in mechanically signalled areas.

Great Northern Railway 1876 Open block
Bell signals

Call attention	1
Be ready	2
Line blocked	5
Stop and examine train	6

Dial signals on block indicator

Passenger train on line	**2 beats of needle to left**
Goods or cattle train on line	**3 beats**
Mineral or ballast train on line or light engine	**4 beats**
Line blocked	**5 beats**

Until the Abbots Ripton collision on 21 January 1876, the block section was clear unless there was actually a train in section. Thus trains were not offered and accepted forward but merely advised. The procedure was as follows. When a train entered the section in the rear at Ayton the signalman at Beeford sent the two-bell signal, 'Be ready' to the signalbox ahead at Seaside which was acknowledged. As the train passed Beeford the signalman called attention on the bell to Seaside and after acknowledgement, gave prescribed beats on the needle to the left to describe the class of train and that it was entering the section. The signalman at Seaside acknowledged with the same number of beats and then pegged the indicator at train on line. When the train passed Seaside signalbox and the last vehicle had passed the signal post the signalman called attention on the bell to Beeford and after acknowledgement gave the prescribed beats on the indicator needle to the right (using the same code beats as to the left when the train entered the section) and following acknowledgement, pegged the indicator needle at 'line clear', ready for the next train whether or not it was due.

SIGNAL BOX LEVER COLOURS

Lever colour	Function
Red	Stop signals, shunting signals
Yellow	Distant signals
Black	Points
Blue	Facing point locks; clearance bars; bolt lock
Brown	Level crossing bolt lock; gate stops and wickets, bridge locks, turntable locks
Green	Gongs; electrical ground frame release; direction lever; mechanical indicators for barrow crossings, 'King' levers
Black & White (4in Chevrons)	Detonator placers (Pointing up for up lines down for down lines)
Blue & Black	Facing point lock and points worked from one lever
Blue & Brown	Electrical ground frame release; direction levers
Brown (white stripes)	'King' levers
Red (three narrow white stripes)	'King' levers
Red & Yellow	Stop and distant signals worked from one lever (eg intermediate block signals)
Red & Black	Relief line stop signals (WR only)
Yellow & Black	Relief line distant signals (WR only)
Red (with 3in white stripe)	Stop signal electrically released from another box (eg 'Line Clear' Release)
Yellow (with 3in white stripe)	Distant signal electrically released from another box (eg 'indicator' working with electric release on lever)
Red & Brown	Direction or acceptance lever
White	Spare

These are the colours used generally since the Second World War and still in current use in so far as they still apply in mechanically signalled areas. The basic red, black and blue levers colours go back to the last century for the same functions, although blue was applied to a wider range of locks and bolts including level crossings and wicket gates. The essential change was that when distant signal arms were painted red, distant signal levers were generally painted green. If a lever works two items of equipment, for example stop and distant intermediate block signals, it carries both colours, the top colour representing the apparatus moving first.

Usually the main rectangular shaft of the lever was painted in the distinctive colour according to function while the bottom few inches and the catch block were black. The round handle at the top of the lever and the catch handle were left unpainted. Because the lever and catch handle were of steel they could easily rust, particularly because of perspiration from signalmen's hands, and for that reason most signalmen had a soft duster or cloth in the hands when operating levers. Since the Second World War some mechanical levers had plastic surrounds to the handle to overcome this.

Entrance–Exit panel button colours

Button colour	Function
Red	Main signal
Yellow	Subsidiary or shunt signal
Green	Signal slot
Light blue	Auto button
Black	Overlap selection

INDEX